Lecture Notes in Computer Science　　13134

More information about this subseries at https://link.springer.com/bookseries/7409

Francesca de Rosa · Iza Marfisi Schottman ·
Jannicke Baalsrud Hauge · Francesco Bellotti ·
Pierpaolo Dondio · Margarida Romero (Eds.)

Games and Learning Alliance

10th International Conference, GALA 2021
La Spezia, Italy, December 1–2, 2021
Proceedings

 Springer

Editors
Francesca de Rosa ⓘ
NATO STO
La Spezia, Italy

Jannicke Baalsrud Hauge ⓘ
HPU
Royal Institute of Technology
Södertälje, Stockholms Län, Sweden

Pierpaolo Dondio ⓘ
Dublin Institute of Technology
Dublin, Ireland

Iza Marfisi Schottman ⓘ
Le Mans University
Le Mans Cedex 9, France

Francesco Bellotti ⓘ
University of Genoa
Genoa, Italy

Margarida Romero ⓘ
Université Côte d'Azur
Nice, France

ISSN 0302-9743 ISSN 1611-3349 (electronic)
Lecture Notes in Computer Science
ISBN 978-3-030-92181-1 ISBN 978-3-030-92182-8 (eBook)
https://doi.org/10.1007/978-3-030-92182-8

LNCS Sublibrary: SL3 – Information Systems and Applications, incl. Internet/Web, and HCI

Preface

This volume includes contributions from the Game and Learning Alliance (GALA) conference, which is dedicated to the science and application of serious games. The tenth edition of the GALA conference was originally set to be held in La Spezia, Italy. However, due to the COVID-19 pandemic, the conference took place in a virtual format during December 1–2, 2021. This edition was organized by the Serious Games Society (SGS) and the NATO Science and Technology Organisation – Centre for Maritime Research and Experimentation (CMRE). The rich two-day event provided an international forum to discuss the advancement to the theories, technologies, and knowledge that support the development and deployment of serious games. The conference attracted academic researchers and practitioners from around the world, including most European nations, United States of America and Canada. Each paper was reviewed by three Program Committee members and those accepted, covering different aspects of serious games theories and applications, were grouped into four paper sessions and a poster session. The sections hereafter outline the work presented in the paper sessions, which focused on serious games design, technology used for serious games, serious game usage, serious games applications, and literacy improvement through serious games. The first section includes design guidelines related to co-design, to cooperative serious games, to the use of metaphors for explaining complex mechanics, and the use of role-playing game models and interactions. The technology section covers various aspects ranging from the use of functional near-infrared spectroscopy for measuring brain activity during gameplay, models for automatic motorway simulation, gender difference in virtual reality user experience, and learning outcome prediction through Bayesian networks. The usage section includes studies looking at the use of applications to support teachers in setting up games, at teachers' acceptance of games in higher education, and the use of virtual reality for debriefing. Moreover, it includes contributions on the use of data analytics and learning analytics within serious games. Finally, the last two sections summarize serious games applications in several different fields, such as historical and political events, chemistry, anti-phishing, and increased literacy. Specifically, the papers focus on increasing engagement in a mandatory postmodern novella through serious games, learning to read and assess graphs through serious games, and support to non-programmers to create games based on fairy tales. We were delighted to have two prominent keynote speakers, Effie Lai-Chong Law and Wayne D. Gray, who enlightened the audience on recent advancements in the evaluation of gameplay experience and the use of games as experimental paradigms respectively. The conference featured a workshop, organized by European Project Games for Nature, and a game competition. Moreover, a panel discussion on crisis management, emergency response, and pandemic games took place. As in previous years, selected best papers presented at the GALA conference will to be published in a dedicated special issue of the International Journal of Serious Games, the scientific journal managed by the Serious Games Society, which is an important reference point for keeping informed on the latest research on serious games. We thank the authors for submitting many interesting papers and the international Program Committee for reviewing them. Finally, we gratefully acknowledge the SGS and CMRE for organizing the conference.

October 2021

Francesca de Rosa
Iza Marfisi Schottman
Jannicke Baalsrud Hauge
Margarida Romero
Pierpaolo Dondio

Organization

General Chair

Francesca de Rosa NATO STO Centre for Maritime Research and Experimentation, Belgium

Program Chairs

Iza Marfisi Schottman Le Mans University, France
Jannicke Baalsrud Hauge BIBA, Germany/KTH, Sweden
Margarida Romero Université de Nice Sophia Antipolis, France
Pierpaolo Dondio Technological University Dublin, Ireland

Tutorials and Keynotes Chair

Manuel Gentile National Research Council, Italy

Competition Chair

Sandro Carniel NATO STO Centre for Maritime Research and Experimentation, Belgium

Publication Chair

Riccardo Berta University of Genoa, Italia

Communication and Promotion Chair

Elena Camossi NATO STO Centre for Maritime Research and Experimentation, Belgium

Administrative and Financial Chair

Francesco Bellotti University of Genoa, Italia

Local Arrangements Chair

Elena Camossi NATO STO Centre for Maritime Research and Experimentation, Belgium

Program Committee

Mario Allegra	National Research Council ITD, Italy
Julian Alvarez	University of Lille, France
Angeliki Antoniou	University of Peloponnese, Greece
Aida Azadegan	The Open University, UK
Jannicke Baalsrud Hauge	BIBA, Germany/KTH, Sweden
Per Backlund	University of Skövde, Sweden
Francesco Bellotti	University of Genoa, Italy
Riccardo Berta	University of Genoa, Italy
Rafael Bidarra	Delft University of Technology, The Netherlands
Lucas Blair	Little Bird Games, USA
Luca Botturi	Università della Svizzera italiana, Switzerland
Tharrenos Bratitsis	University of Western Macedonia, Greece
Wayne Buck	NATO Allied Command Transformation, USA
Elena Camossi	NATO STO Centre for Maritime Research and Experimentation, Belgium
Sandro Carniel	NATO STO Centre for Maritime Research and Experimentation, Belgium
Maira B. Carvalho	Tilburg University, The Netherlands
Chiara Catalano	National Research Council, IMATI, Italy
Giuseppe Città	National Research Council, ITD, Italy
Valentina Dal Grande	National Research Council, Italy
Alessandro De Gloria	University of Genoa, Italy
Teresa de La Hera Conde-Pumpido	Erasmus University Rotterdam, The Netherlands
Francesca de Rosa	NATO STO Centre for Maritime Research and Experimentation, Belgium
Murray Dixon	Defence Research and Development Canada, Canada
Pierpaolo Dondio	Technological University Dublin, Ireland
Nour El Mawas	University of Lille, France
Luis Miguel Encarnacao	Regions Bank, USA
Georgios Fesakis	University of Aegean, Greece
Jan Dirk Fijnheer	Utrecht University, The Netherlands
Laura Freina	National Research Council, Italy
Samir Garbaya	Art et Metiers ParisTech, France
Manuel Gentile	National Research Council, Italy
Dimitris Grammenos	FORTH-ICS, Greece
Ludovic Hamon	Le Mans Université, France
Dirk Ifenthaler	University of Mannheim, Germany
Carolina A. Islas Sedano	University of Canterbury, UK
Anne-Laure Jousselme	NATO STO Centre for Maritime Research and Experimentation, Belgium

Kostas Karpouzis	National Technical University of Athens, Greece
Vlasios Kasapakis	University of the Aegean, Greece
Michael Kickmeier-Rust	Graz University of Technology, Austria
Ralf Klamma	RWTH Aachen University, Germany
Georgios Kritikos	University of the Aegean, Greece
Jean-Marc Labat	Sorbonne University, France
Pierre Laforcade	Le Mans Université, France
George Lepouras	University of the Peloponnese, Greece
Sandy Louchart	Glasgow School of Art, UK
Heide Lukosch	University of Canterbury, UK
Katerina Mania	Technical University of Crete, Greece
Iza Marfisi-Schottman	Le Mans Université, France
Ivan Martinez-Ortiz	Universidad Complutense de Madrid, Spain
Adam Mayes	Uppsala University, Sweden
Michela Mortara	National Research Council, IMATI, Italy
Mathieu Muratet	Sorbonne University, France
Thierry Nabeth	P-Val Conseil, France
Rob Nadolski	Open University of The Netherlands-Welten Institute, The Netherlands
Manuel Ninaus	Leibniz-Institut fuer Wissensmedien, Germany
Lahcen Oubahssi	Le Mans Université, France
Lucia Pannese	Imaginary, Italy
Sobah Abbas Petersen	Norwegian University of Science and Technology, Norway
Petros Petridis	University of Thessaly, Greece
Yurgos Politis	Technological University Dublin, Ireland
Cathy Pons Lelardeux	Champollion National University Institute, France
Maria Popescu	Carol I National Defence University, Romania
Marius Preda	Institut Mines-Télécom, France
Ion Roceanu	Carol I National Defence University, Romania
Margarida Romero	Université de Nice Sophia Antipolis, France
Pedro A. Santos	Universidade de Lisboa, Portugal
Bettina Schneider	Fachhochschule Nordwestschweiz, Switzerland
Avo Schönbohm	Berlin School of Economics and Law, Germany
Heinrich Söbke	Bauhaus-Universität Weimar, Germany
Ioana Andreea Stefan	Advanced Technology Systems, Romania
Matthias Teine	University of Paderborn, Germany
Alessandra Tesei	NATO STO Centre for Maritime Research and Experimentation, Belgium
Maria Tsourma	Centre for Research and Technology Hellas, ITI, Greece
Erik van Der Spek	Eindhoven University of Technology, The Netherlands
Herre van Oostendorp	Utrecht University, The Netherlands

Contents

Serious Games Applications

A Playful Learning Exercise: Kashmir Crisis

Charlie Murray[1], Hans-Wolfgang Loidl[1]([⊠]), and Brian Train[2]

[1] Heriot-Watt University, Edinburgh, Scotland
{cm149,H.W.Loidl}@hw.ac.uk
[2] Victoria, Canada

Abstract. This paper summarises the development and evaluation of a digital board game on the "Kashmir Crisis" in 2019. It is based on a card-driven board-game design of one of the authors, with the concept of "games as journalism" as one underlying design principle. As such, this is a serious game with the aim of providing information on the context of recent political events in Kashmir. In this paper we focus on the design, implementation, and evaluation of a multi-platform, digital instance of this game. The evaluation results of using the game show significantly increased engagement and slightly better learning effectiveness, compared to a control group using standard learning techniques.

Keywords: Serious games · Playful learning · Game design

1 Introduction

Playful learning is a powerful approach for engaging learners in the learning process, to convey information, to critically evaluate facts and to engage in discussions. In this sense, serious games, i.e. games with a concrete learning objective, can be seen as a form of "journalism". The work summarised in this paper focuses on our notion as "games as journalism" [12] in building on a board-game design that explicitly focuses on modelling a concrete diplomatic and military situation. Specifically, we develop a digital implementation for this board game and evaluate its effectiveness as a learning tool.

The concrete board-game is "Kashmir Crisis" [13]. It is a card-driven game with context based in the 2019 border conflict in the Kashmir region between India and Pakistan. Its main themes are the simulation of the various elements that make up modern conflict, including military and political components. The game's basis in real-world events makes it suitable for evaluating wargames as learning tools, allowing learning about the conflict using the game to be compared to more traditional learning methods.

In order to evaluate this effectiveness, two user groups are tested on their learning about the conflict: one group uses traditional learning tools in the form

B. Train—Independent Game Designer.

F. de Rosa et al. (Eds.): GALA 2021, LNCS 13134, pp. 3–13, 2021.
https://doi.org/10.1007/978-3-030-92182-8_1

of reading, while the second group learns exclusively using the game. Both groups then answer the same questionnaire, which includes both a subjective self-report and a quantitative learning test, in order to directly compare the results of each group. These two groups are separate, in order to prevent knowledge crossover between learning methods.

2   Background

Serious Games: Serious games are characterised as being "used for purposes other than mere entertainment" [11], or "games whose first purpose was not mere entertainment" [1]. Benjamin Sawyer, the founder of 'The Serious Game Initiative' in 2002, classified the field as "[...] developers, researchers and industrial people, who are looking at ways to use video games and video game technologies outside entertainment" [1].

A literature survey about the effectiveness of serious games in [2] showed a largely positive or neutral impact on learning effectiveness. The survey, "Educational Games – Are They Worth The Effort?" [2], made a meta-analysis of several studies into the effectiveness of serious games in education, focusing on empirical studies made from 2002 to 2012, in the frame of the EduGameLab in formal school contexts. The studies showed "a fair amount of evidence that serious games have a positive effect on learning" [2], with 29 of the studies showing positive results and 7 showing neutral results. On the other hand, only 2 showed negative results, with the final 2 giving unclear results.

Conflict Simulation: One of the key areas studied through serious games is conflict simulation: studying the nature of conflict and its ramifications. This includes the modelling of conflicts to study strengths and weaknesses, as well as gaining insight into the motives and key dynamics in various types of conflict, typically with the goal of conflict resolution in mind.

PAXSims [5] is an online blog focused on the use of games for learning about conflict and peace-building. It discusses many of the topics surrounding conflict simulation and serious games, with the aim of promoting humanitarian and peace development. Another prominent resource on the topic is Philip Sabin's Simulating War [10], a book which discusses the uses of simulating conflict, as well as outlining the various ways in which this knowledge can be used.

Within the area of conflict simulation there are a number of more specific related topics, including war studies, peace studies and wargaming. War and peace studies are more academic topics, focusing on understanding the complexities of war and its prevention respectively, rather than the strategy and logistics of a conflict itself. These topics are often studied in the context of history, with the Handbook of War Studies II [7] describing a connection with political science and international relations.

Wargaming is less academically focused than war and peace studies, having two main connotations: an entertainment hobby consisting of simulating either historical or fictional battles, as well as an official training tool for the military to improve combat strategy and tactics, for example the UK MOD Defence Wargaming Handbook [14]. The book, "Zones of Control" [6] discusses both of these definitions and their histories, and Peter Perla's "The Art of Wargaming" [8] also discusses wargaming as a whole, including its history, connotations and its usefulness as part of military training.

As an official training tool, wargaming is a similar, more specific area within conflict simulation, focusing on the gaming aspect of conflict simulation, with the same aim of training and learning. As stated in Peter Perla's "Why Wargaming Works", wargaming has been a longstanding "tool used for military training, education and research" [9], with varied success based on the specific circumstances. Many of wargaming's benefits come from its ability to integrate learning experiences with a narrative: wargames are most effective when linked with real-world context, allowing players to make connections more easily [9]. As opposed to other forms of media, the interactive element of wargames make players engage "in ways more similar to acting in the real world" [9], namely with greater emotional and intellectual engagement, improving the learning benefit.

3 Design of the Board-Game "Kashmir Crisis"

3.1 Motivation and Background

The word *"news-game"* is a fairly recent invention, first used in 2003 by the video game designer and academic researcher Gonzalo Frasca, then much more widely used when Ian Bogost, Simon Ferrari and Bobby Schweizer published "Newsgames: Journalism at Play" in 2011 [3]. Bogost wrote about how videogames, produced by journalists and distributed through the Internet, could fulfil the basic objectives of journalism: to inform, educate, criticise and persuade.

While the success of video-games in this role was limited, analogue games that perform the same function constitute a substantial body of work that not only predates video-games themselves, it continues today. Analogue newsgames offer concerned and motivated individual citizens a platform to interpret the world around them, and to share that interpretation. *Kashmir Crisis* is a rather simple demonstration of this, born of the fortunate meeting of a wargame designer (Brian Train) and an experienced photo-journalist (Nathaniel Brunt), after the former's presentation about "Games as Journalism", given at the annual Connections-UK conference on professional wargaming [12].

3.2 Game Design and Mechanics

The original game design looked abstractly at the 30 year insurgency in Kashmir, but soon it became clear that a focus on events subsequent to the February 2019 suicide bomber attack at Pulwama would make for a more engaging topic. The analogue result, Kashmir Crisis, is a simple card-based game for two players that takes about 15 min to play, using a deck of ordinary playing cards and a short set of rules (see [13] for rules).

The main concept and mechanic of the game involves players choosing cards representing resources and playing them on different "fronts" during play (see the game board in Fig. 1). This abstractly shows the scale of effort a country is investing in obtaining a favourable result in that sphere of activity. For example, the *Diplomatic Front* concerns a country's efforts to get international support and assistance for its viewpoint or to condemn its adversary's, or to pursue legal and economic threats and harassment against the enemy. *"Information"* relates to message dominance and ability to control the narrative on the conflict. Finally, the *"Military Front"* is a more straightforward application of covert and overt military forces and assistance to pursue insurgent/counter-insurgent warfare, or to prepare for large-scale conventional conflict. This three-front game design concept has been used in another attempt at an analogue news-game, Ukrainian Crisis—designed during the very weekend in March 2014 that the inhabitants of the Crimea voted in a referendum, and a Russian overt invasion seemed likely.

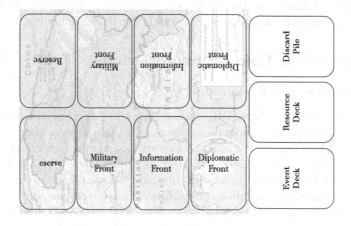

Fig. 1. Kashmir crisis analogue game board [13]

Resource cards (standard playing cards) are dealt to players based on their colour (red to one side and black to the other) and the card number dictates its point value in winning a front. Eight cards are dealt each turn, so the number of cards each player receives each turn is not necessarily equal.

The core game loop is made up of a number of turns, each with a number of stages within them:

1. Event Card Draw and Resolution
2. Resource Card Draw
3. Play of Resource Cards
4. Scoring.

Turns are continually played until the joker is drawn. At this point, the deck is reshuffled and play begins again, where a second joker ends the game. Each player has a victory point tracker and if, by the end of the game, one player has a significant enough lead over the other (11 or more), that player wins.

The event card drawn each turn denotes the primary front and any special effects on the turn. This, therefore, affects *scoring*: if the total value of cards played to both players' fronts this turn is 40 or more, the players' scores on the primary front are compared, and the winning player gains victory points equal to the difference. The other 2 fronts are then resolved: the loser's cards are permanently removed from the game and they lose 1 victory point. If the total card values don't reach 40, the primary front is resolved the same way.

A full description of the game rules can be found at the game's webpage [13].

4 A Digital Version of "Kashmir Crisis"

Overview: A primary aspect of this project was the multi-platform focus for the implementation, which therefore factored into the choice of development environment and framework/engine. This major decision came down to two main choices: using a pre-made (board) game platform to create a game implementation on (e.g. Vassal Engine or Tabletop Simulator), or create the implementation from scratch using a game engine or framework (e.g. Unity). As the game was intended to be released on Android, a multi-platform or Android-based development environment was needed, leading to the decision to use **LibGDX**.

LibGDX is a Java-based, Apache 2 licensed open source game development framework designed with cross-platform development in mind: it supports all major platforms in mobile, desktop and web environments. It is relatively lightweight, having no core engine, instead providing flexible libraries suited to the development of small-scale projects such as this. A practical advantage of using Java and developing for Android is the good support and ample documentation for these technologies.

Interface: As shown in Fig. 2 below, the game interface has a number of key components mirroring those found in the original board game:

– Score counter (top)
– 8 card fronts, in which each player can play their cards (centre)
– 3 decks which cards are either drawn from or discarded to (centre right)
– The game log, which shows a history of game events and moves (right)
– Player hand, which is used to play cards to the board (bottom).

There are two main types of cards in Kashmir crisis, which have been abstracted from the original game.

The resource (number) card is played by players to fronts, with the number denoting the strength of the card. The event (text) card shows and explains the event for the current turn, including its effects and any flavour text.

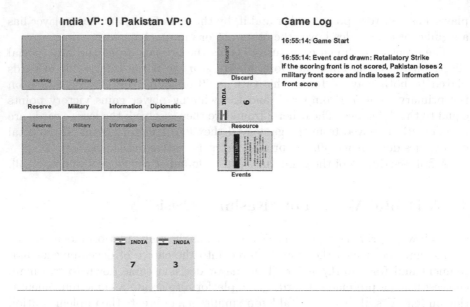

Fig. 2. Main (digital) game interface

Design of the AI: The game contains a simple AI opponent for players to play against, based on a minimax-style heuristic search. Instead of generating a search tree and best choice move simultaneously, these functions are split into two parts: first the full move tree is generated, with each state holding its heuristic score, and then all of the terminal states are searched through to find the best set of moves to reach that end state. The AI has the general overall structure:

1. A tree of possible moves from the current board state is generated, during each child state generation, its heuristic score is calculated.
2. The terminal states from this tree are selected.
3. The terminal state with the highest heuristic score from this list is selected.
4. The AI plays its cards so as to reach this end state.

The *heuristic calculation* (scoring) can be tuned by biasing the variables used to calculate it. These are:

– The difference in number of cards in each of the scoring fronts.
– The difference in number of cards in reserve.
– The player scores at the end of the previous turn.

5   Evaluation

The goal of the user evaluation was to compare the learning effectiveness and experience in using a digital game as opposed to more traditional methods.

Experimental Setup: The experiment was designed so participants would answer the same set of questions having either played the game (game-testing group) or having read a couple of articles about the 2019 border conflict (control group). After studying respective materials for a short time, participants would answer the learning experiences and knowledge test. This provided a direct comparison of learning effectiveness between groups, without knowledge crossover between groups. Additionally, the game-testing group answered questionnaires about the usability of the game specifically, including a standard SUS questionnaire.

In total 10 participants were recruited, where participants for the game group were chosen for higher technical capability. Participants were a selection of adults with a wide range of ages, including both students and non-students. 6 of these participants learned using the game and 4 learned using traditional methods, with 7 of these participants giving feedback on the usability of the game.

5.1 Usability

For the game testing group, the usability evaluation was composed of 2 parts: a qualitative survey of participants' perceived usability of the game, as well as a standard SUS survey, to provide a standardised, reliable quantitative metric of perceived usability [4]. The majority of the surveys about the game's usability were done in a likert-format, with available responses including: very poor, poor, average, good and very good.

Game Feedback: All of the participants testing the game used the desktop PC version of the game. Results from the experiences portion of the survey in Fig. 3a showed a generally weak positive response to the functionality and usability of the game, with more negative responses for the visual aspects of the game and the understanding of the game's mechanics. This reflects the fairly basic nature of the graphical assets provided by LibGDX, compared to larger game engines, and limited familiarity of the testers with modern, card-driven games. The response to the AI component of the game was universally perceived as 'good', which indicates that the AI is a plausible opponent in this game.

The second part of this survey asked participants background questions about their enjoyment of each category of game that Kashmir Crisis falls under. Responses to this in Fig. 3b showed that participants generally enjoyed games in the surrounding genres, with a more neutral response to digital card games and this game in particular. Most likely the testers are more familiar with designed-for-digital games, as opposed to digital versions of existing (card-driven) games.

The final sections of the survey asked for an overall score and any further comments on the game. The average score given was 6/10, and the comments made were focused on UI elements, such as the game buttons and event log.

SUS Results: The SUS results for usability in Fig. 4 were found to be generally positive and in line with the responses to the game feedback survey. Responses

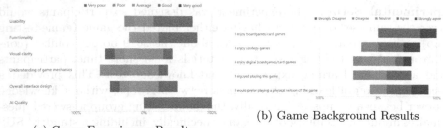

(a) Game Experiences Results

(b) Game Background Results

Fig. 3. Game group results

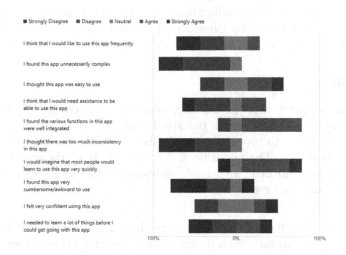

Fig. 4. SUS results

indicated that the game wasn't too complex or difficult to use, but would require more knowledge to effectively use than was given, with a low confidence in the first use of the game. Although this is expected with a strategy game, this could have been alleviated with a more in-depth tutorial system.

The SUS responses were converted to scores as per [4], giving an average SUS score of 66.1 and a standard deviation of 17.8. Translating this into a grade, based on a graph of over 3,500 SUS survey results [4], this resulted in a D (high marginal).

5.2   Learning Effectiveness

The learning evaluation survey asked a number of self-evaluation questions related to the participants' learning experiences, as well as performing a short knowledge recall test. Two groups were used: a control group which learned by reading given material and a game group which used the implemented game to learn with. Both groups performed the same evaluation, providing the ability to directly compare the two group in terms of learning effectiveness.

The self evaluation section was performed in a likert scale format, where strong disagreement was codified as a 1, up to strong agreement which was codified as a 5. Some key areas within this evaluation were:

- In questions asking participants to self-evaluate the *effectiveness of their learning* method, the traditional group gave an average response of 3.69/5, while the game group gave a slightly higher average of 3.83/5. Both results represent a weak positive response.
- In questions asking participants about the *enjoyment and engagement of the learning* method, the traditional group participants gave an average of 2/5 (negative), while those in the game group reported an average of 3.58/5 (weak positive).
- Both groups reported little prior knowledge of the 2019 event, with only the game group having an average score above 1 (with 1.67/5).
- Both groups reported a neutral *ease of learning*, with the game group's average response being slightly higher, 3.25/5 as opposed to 3/5 from the traditional group.

The final part of this survey was the *knowledge test*, in which 8 questions related to the event were asked. The answers to these questions could be found in both the game's content, as well as the provided articles for the traditional learning group. Participants from both groups scored the same average value, 56.25%, indicating that neither method is meaningfully better than the other for knowledge recall. This value was calculated for each user group by first finding the percentage of correct answers for all participants on each individual question. These percentages were then averaged across all of the questions to find the average number of correct answers for the user group.

6   Conclusions

We have presented the development and evaluation of a digital, card-driven board-game, modelling the conflict in Kashmir between India and Pakistan. The design of the board-game follows the principle of "games as journalism" with the key objectives to inform, educate, criticise and persuade. Our evaluation of the game, through user surveys, underlines the effectiveness of the game in these aspects: testers using the game rated the engagement in the learning process as significantly higher compared to a control group (3.58/5 vs 2/5); in terms of direct learning effectiveness the games group rated the outcome slightly higher than the control group (3.83/5 vs 3.69/5). This indicates that, in this context, the playful learning approach improves the process of learning, but only marginally improves the knowledge transfer. However, the knowledge recall part of the evaluation didn't show a concrete benefit of the games-based approach over the traditional approach of learning.

From a technical point of view, advantages of the digital game are: accessibility (it is online available on several platforms, without the need for physical components or physical presence), linkage with ample background information through the internet, and interaction with an AI to explore the game in the user's own time. The use of an open-source platform-independent library for games development (LibGDX), rather than a closed game engine, added flexibility, but also programmer effort, in the development of the digital game.

Due to the narrow focus of the evaluation, our results don't provide a conclusive answer to the comparison of traditional and game-based learning methods, however it does provide a useful case study when combined with similar work.

Future improvements could be made on the technical level (AI improvements, 2-player mode) or on the usage of the game in a learning context. While this is just one short term case study of playful learning, with a limited users group, our long term plan is to embed playful learning components, like this game, into an educational course on conflict studies or history. In this way, segments of traditional learning can be evaluated and compared with segments of playful learning on the same target audience. We are working with colleagues in a history department to realise this vision and to provide longer term insights.

Acknowledgements. The research presented in this paper was supported by the EPSRC project "Serious Coding: a Game Approach to Security for the new Code-Citizens" (EP/T017511/1).

References

1. Alvarez, J., et al.: An introduction to serious game definitions and concepts. Serious Games Simul. Risks Manage. **11**(1), 11–15 (2011)
2. Backlund, P., Hendrix, M.: Educational games – are they worth the effort? A literature survey of the effectiveness of serious games. In: International Conference on Games and Virtual Worlds for Serious Applications (VS-GAMES), pp. 1–8. IEEE (2013)
3. Bogost, I., Ferrari, S.: Journalism at Play. MIT Press, Cambridge (2010)
4. Brooke, J.: SUS: a retrospective. J. Usability Stud. **8**(2), 29–40 (2013)
5. Brynen, R.: About PAXsims. https://paxsims.wordpress.com/about/
6. Harrigan, P., Kirschenbaum, M.G., Dunnigan, J.F., Peterson, J., Curry, J.: Zones of Control: Perspectives on Wargaming. MIT Press, Cambridge (2016)
7. Midlarsky, M.I.: Handbook of War Studies II. University of Michigan Press, Ann Arbor (2000)
8. Perla, P., Curry, J.: The Art of Wargaming: A Guide for Professionals and Hobbyists. lulu.com (2012)
9. Perla, P., McGrady, E.: Why wargaming works. Naval War College Rev. **64**(3), 111–130 (2011)
10. Sabin, P.: Simulating War: Studying Conflict through Simulation Games. Bloomsbury Academic, London (2014)

11. Susi, T., Johannesson, M., Backlund, P.: Serious games: an overview. University of Skövde, Sweden, Technical report (2007)
12. Train, B.: Games as Journalism. https://www.professionalwargaming.co.uk/2018-Journalism-Train.pdf
13. Train, B.: New Game: Kashmir Crisis. https://brtrain.wordpress.com/2019/08/29/new-game-kashmir-crisis/
14. UK Ministry of Defence: Defence Wargaming Handbook. https://www.gov.uk/government/publications/defence-wargaming-handbook

Micro-games for Quick Learning of Declarative Knowledge: Preliminary Application and Usability Testing

Sasha Blue Godfrey$^{(\boxtimes)}$ (iD), Pilar Caamaño Sobrino, and Alberto Tremori

Modelling and Simulation, NATO STO Centre for Maritime Research and Experimentation, La Spezia, Italy

{sasha.godfrey,pilar.caamano,alberto.tremori}@cmre.nato.int

Abstract. Serious games and gamified applications are increasingly used in a wide variety of contexts including education, corporate and military training, and healthcare to teach or train students and personnel in an engaging manner. Puzzle-based micro-games may be an advantageous method for quickly learning declarative knowledge, i.e. knowledge pertaining to facts and definitions. In military exercises and wargames, there is a need to quickly absorb declarative knowledge pertaining to a hypothetical scenario before beginning the exercise. In this work, an application of the micro-game concept within a military context, the Organizational Chart Puzzle (OCP) for learning a Command and Control (C2) structure, and results of usability testing are presented. The OCP was well-liked and easily learned by usability testing participants. Additionally, participants were asked to recreate the C2 structure from memory after playing the OCP and showed high knowledge transfer from the game to the paper test, suggesting this concept may be a viable path for quick learning of declarative knowledge.

Keywords: Serious games · Military training · Usability testing

1 Introduction

There is a long and continuing tradition of using games for learning and training in military environments. According to Smith [1], games have been used for thousands of years in education, training, analysis of strategy, and mission planning. Historically, these games have been in-person, team affairs that necessarily relied on physical materials and models, given the technology available. With the advent of computers, more advanced methods and tools were incorporated, providing increased realism and complexity [1]. Two decades ago, as computers became more and more ubiquitous, and the Internet rapidly gained in popularity, the military, along with many educational institutions, faced the dilemma of how best to exploit this new technology for training [2]. We are now squarely in the digital age: interactive digital media and games have become popular and easily accessible and are increasingly being used for military applications and research in the military sector. For example, the US Army debuted "America's Army," a realistic training and recruitment game in 2002 [3] that has been updated over the years and is

© Springer Nature Switzerland AG 2021
F. de Rosa et al. (Eds.): GALA 2021, LNCS 13134, pp. 14–22, 2021.
https://doi.org/10.1007/978-3-030-92182-8_2

still available today as "America's Army: Proving Grounds" [4]. As another example, Webster [5] compared an immersive VR game for teaching corrosion prevention to military personnel with lecture-based learning.

To better understand the appeal of games for learning, both in military and other contexts, it is helpful to consider learning and knowledge itself. The concept of knowledge is typically broken down into different categories based on the type of information stored, where it is stored, how it is recalled and used, and other factors. Two of the most well-known are declarative and procedural knowledge. Declarative knowledge, also called factual or semantic knowledge, relates to facts and definitions and requires learning by memorization. It is an essential foundation for procedural learning, or the knowledge of how to perform a skill or task, but can be tedious for the learner. Games are an engaging form of interactive media, imbuing them with great potential as a learning tool and giving rise to serious games, games used for purposes other than pure entertainment, and gamification, using game elements in a non-game context [6]. As such, game-based approaches have been implemented in myriad fields including traditional education, medicine, and corporate training and have been shown to be effective learning tools [7].

Looking specifically at declarative knowledge acquisition, the rewarding nature of games promotes this kind of learning [8], and the literature is rich with innovative examples, e.g. [5, 9]. This work presents an application of a micro-game for the acquisition of declarative knowledge in a military context. In the military environment, wargaming and exercises are by nature quite dynamic. They are focused on learning procedure and learning to develop strategies in response to hypothetical events. To enable this process, participants must quickly familiarize themselves with the hypothetical scenario; they need to acquire declarative knowledge about the situation, organization, and other details. In this work, the development and preliminary usability testing of a puzzle micro-game for the purpose of learning an organizational chart is explained as an example application of this paradigm.

2 Methodology

In reviewing game features for engagement and learning, Abdul Jabbar and Felicia [6] note the importance of providing players with challenges to increase motivation. They also recognize the genre of puzzle-based games as having simple mechanics that are engaging and generally easy to learn. Many games have extensive story components, making them more involved and tending toward longer game-play. Conversely, puzzle games can be easily designed for short game-play, making them ideal for brief, targeted lessons. As mentioned above, this work presents the concept of creating micro-games for learning declarative knowledge and applies it to learning an organizational chart for a military exercise. In these exercises, the training audience has to familiarize themselves with one or more command structures. These structures are typically designed for the purpose of the exercise with the goal of understanding and training interoperability and information flow between entities. Rather than engage in typical study or memorization of a paper chart, this micro-game engages the student in learning through exploration, action, and play.

2.1 Puzzle Micro-game Design

Command structures, including the Command and Control (C2) structure used in this application, are typically represented as organizational charts, showing various entities or individuals and the hierarchy that guides their relationship. As such, many organizational charts are not absolute, but rather abstract in the sense that only the relationships between elements are important. Each individual element's position can be freely changed, so long as these relationships are maintained. Since these relationships are the key information presented in such a chart, they were chosen as the basis for grading and feedback of the Organizational Chart Puzzle (OCP) micro-game.

The OCP was designed in the Unity3D game engine with three distinct levels of difficulty. Figure 1 shows the "Easy" puzzle level on the left. (Note: entity names in the figure have been changed to make the relationships between the entities more intuitive to the reader.) All three levels had the same basic structure: a menu of draggable puzzle components, an empty organizational chart, time and error feedback, and a pop-up relationship legend. The content of the chart was based on a paper chart provided as study material in a previous military exercise. The original paper chart included color-coding of entities by type, rather than hierarchy. Although it was considered that the colors could suggest relationships, sometimes incorrectly (see Fig. 2 for filled-in example), the color-coding was maintained in all three levels of the OCP to maintain fidelity with typical study materials.

The "Easy" level was intended to familiarize users with the entities and their relationships. As such, the relationships are already filled in on the chart connecting blank entity blocks. A pop-up relationship legend was available at the bottom of the screen and showed the type of relationship associated with each color and style connection. The user plays by dragging entities into the empty block and receiving feedback. Feedback was provided in four ways. First, in the bottom left of the screen and always visible, the user sees the number of total and current errors, displayed as Total (Current), along with a countdown timer. Second, when an error is committed, a pop-up window briefly designates the two elements in conflict and why, for example "Entity X cannot be in a relationship of Type Z with Entity Y," see Fig. 1, bottom. In order to continue playing, this feedback window must be closed. Third, errors in the organizational chart are shown by changing the relationship connection between them to red. Finally, upon completion, the user sees cumulative feedback indicating time left on the countdown and the total number of errors committed. To aid in better understanding and memorizing these relationships, the "Medium" level requires all entities and some of the relationships to be filled in, while the "Hard" level requires all of the entities and relationships to be filled in. The structure or layout (of the empty blocks and relationships) is the same in all three levels.

As part of the research and development of the OCP, an editing environment (Puzzle Editor) to design new games was developed. In this environment, a 2D interface can be used to easily add new organizational charts. This is performed by dragging and dropping chart elements and setting the parameters of the new element, such as name, color, and other visual characteristics as well as its relationship to other elements, as seen in Fig. 2. To aid this creation, three base charts were included, with varying types of entities and connections: a headquarters structure, a C2 structure, and a generic hierarchical

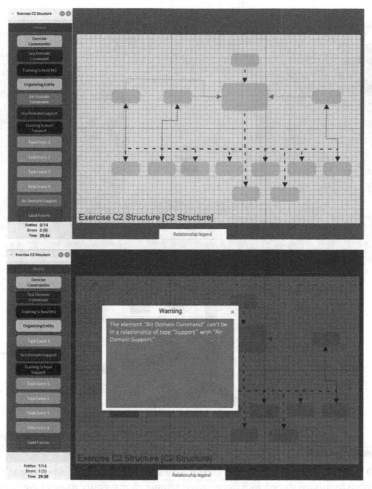

Fig. 1. OCP: easy level (top) and example feedback (bottom); entity names have been changed.

structure. The Puzzle Editor also includes a 3D interface that allows developing and managing multiple organizational charts with the possibility of adding inter-diagram connections, moving between them in an intuitive way. An example of the view within this interface is shown in Fig. 2 with three sample charts; entity names have been blurred for security reasons.

2.2 Puzzle Evaluation and Testing Protocol

Five male participants were recruited from a convenience sample of Centre for Maritime Research and Experimentation (CMRE) employees; demographics available in Table 1. At this stage of development, it is advisable to perform usability testing with a small but relevant sample of end-users [10]. Restrictions due to the COVID-19 pandemic made recruiting external participants a challenge, and the chosen population was

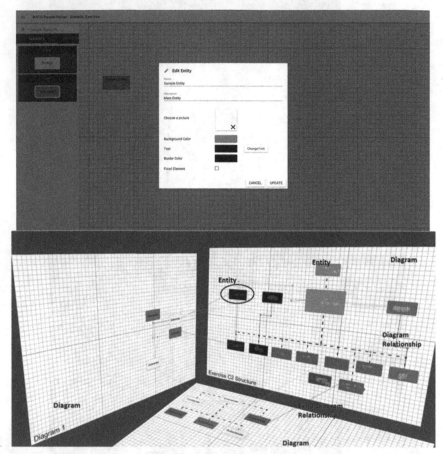

Fig. 2. 2D puzzle editor interface (top); shown with entity parameter window open. 3D puzzle editor interface (bottom); shown with three linked sample charts; entity names have been blurred.

deemed appropriate as their familiarity with NATO entities would likely aid them in understanding and learning the organizational chart. It was thus hypothesized that the CMRE population would bear a close resemblance to the target population. Demographic information collected included participant age and years working in a military environment as a civilian and/or in the military. The puzzle evaluation consisted of three parts: playing the puzzle, testing the participant's knowledge of the organizational chart, and finally responding to two short surveys regarding learning and puzzle usability. While playing the puzzle, the screen was recorded and play was observed by the experimenter to assess the quality of the user's experience (UX) with the user interface (UI).

Participants played all three levels of the puzzle: easy, medium, and hard. They had up to 30 min to complete each level and could take breaks between levels if desired. Before playing, participants were instructed to drag elements from the left menu into the blank chart. The decision was made while the first participant was using the easy puzzle to also point out the pop-up relationship legend that can be opened by the player. It was evident from the first participant that this information could easily be overlooked, so for consistency, all participants were informed of this ability shortly after beginning free-play with the puzzle.

After completing all levels, participants were again offered a break before beginning the test. Participants were provided with a list of entities and types of connections (without any of the color-coding seen in the puzzle) and a blank sheet of paper on which to draw the organizational chart. Participants were not given a time limit to complete the test.

After completing the test, participants were given the System Usability Scale (SUS) [11] to evaluate the puzzle game. As the first question asks if they would like to use the system frequently, they were asked to consider the questions under the premise that they needed to learn similar information to what was taught in the puzzle (i.e. other organizational charts). Finally, they were asked four questions related to play time and in-game feedback with responses given on a 5-point Likert scale.

Table 1. Participant demographics.

Participant	Years working in military environment: Civilian (Military)	Age
P1	15 (0)	38
P2	4 (0)	30
P3	1.5 (0)	30
P4	5 (0)	33
P5	9 (0)	47

3   OCP Usability Testing Results

Results of the usability testing of the OCP are presented in Fig. 3 and Table 2 below. As our sample size is small, individual results are presented as well as minimal aggregate results for ease of understanding. All participants were able to complete the three levels of the puzzle game in the allotted time without encountering fatal system errors. As can be seen in Fig. 3, participants required the most time to complete the Easy (first) level of the puzzle and committed the most errors; the errors committed in the "Easy" level are plotted on an independent axis to allow the reader to better see the errors committed in the other three test conditions. There was a dramatic reduction in both measures in completing the Medium and Hard puzzles. For 3 out of 5 participants, time to completion on the paper test was lower than the Easy puzzle level but higher than the other two levels; two participants took longer to complete the paper test than any of the puzzle levels. Three out of 5 participants had no errors on the paper test; the other two participants had 3 and 13 errors.

Participants were asked about their experience with the puzzle game through the SUS and a short (4-question) survey specifically about learning. While SUS scores can

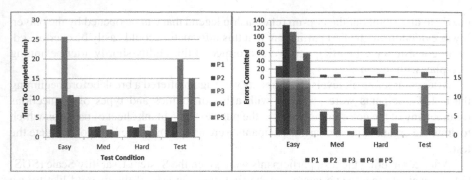

Fig. 3. Quantitative OCP Results: time to completion (left) and errors committed (right) shown by test condition (puzzle level or paper test) and participant. NB: The "Easy" level errors committed are shown on a separate axis from the other test conditions to improve readability of the data.

range from 0 to 100, they cannot be interpreted as percentages. Four out of 5 participants graded the system between 80 and 90, scoring a "B," or "excellent" rating, compared to historical data [12]. The remaining participant scored the system as "good" or a "C." The learning survey asked participants to provide their agreement (on a 5-point Likert scale) to the following 4 statements: The play time was sufficient to learn the organizational diagram; Additional time and/or rounds of play would be helpful; The feedback provided by the puzzle is sufficient to understand your mistakes; and Additional feedback would be helpful. Unlike the SUS, responses to these four questions lacked uniformity, with the exception of the first question (4 out of 5 agreed or strongly agreed that play time was sufficient). Finally, from observations of the UX, some elements of the UI were found to be sub-optimal, such as, it was seen that users may fail to notice the interactivity of the pop-up relationship legend, as mentioned in Sect. 2; for arrows that were close together, some users struggled to place the relationship connection on their chosen arrow, leading to occasional errors; and a bug was identified that allowed the menu of draggable items to move.

Table 2. Qualitative OCP results: 4-question learning survey and SUS scores

Participant	Sufficient time	More time	Sufficient feedback	More feedback	SUS score
P1	Strongly agree	Strongly agree	Disagree	Strongly agree	70
P2	Strongly disagree	Strongly disagree	Agree	Neutral	87.5
P3	Strongly agree	Agree	Agree	Agree	85
P4	Agree	Neutral	Disagree	Agree	85
P5	Agree	Agree	Strongly agree	Disagree	82.5

4 Discussion and Conclusions

In this work, the authors suggest that micro-games, specifically puzzle-type micro-games, could be useful for the quick uptake of declarative knowledge. The authors then present a specific application of this concept, the Organizational Chart Puzzle, for learning a C2 organizational chart within the context of a military exercise. Following the breakdown of serious game usability testing developed in Olsen et al. [10], an Alpha 2 usability test with a small and semi-relevant sample population (n = 5) has been presented. (As mentioned in Sect. 2, due to COVID-19, it was difficult to recruit participants directly from the target population and a proxy population was used.) The results of this test were quite promising. Qualitatively, participants quickly understood how to interact with the game and generally enjoyed playing it. Three participants felt that the playtime was sufficient to learn the chart but that more rounds of play would be helpful, potentially suggesting that more playtime could help cement certain concepts. Conversely, P2 disagreed with both of these statements; in free comments, he suggested the OCP could be complemented by explanatory text or links following puzzle completion to better explain the individual entities and their relationships. Additionally, from observing game-play and from participant comments, several minor aspects that could be improved in terms of the user interface and game feedback have been identified.

Considering the quantitative results, time to completion and errors across puzzle levels suggest that players quickly memorized the structure of the organizational chart. Furthermore, the results of the test on paper show generally high transfer of information from the OCP. Unlike in the game, participants could not rely on visuospatial cues (like color and block position) to aid in their completion of the organizational chart. Nonetheless, three participants completed the paper test with no errors and another had only three errors. (The remaining participant had 13 errors; this participant commented as testing began that he felt lost without the color-coding. It may be worth exploring adding this aspect to the levels in the game, phasing out color as players advance through the levels.) Taken together, these results support the use of a simple puzzle micro-game for quick learning of declarative knowledge.

At this stage of development, testing immediately following training was performed to provide a knowledge transfer baseline. In the domain of military exercises, much of the declarative knowledge needed for the exercise does not need to be retained long term, as it pertains to hypothetical scenarios. In future beta-testing of the OCP, short- and medium-term retention to determine its efficacy as a learning tool will be examined.

References

1. Smith, R.: The long history of gaming in military training. Simul. Gaming **41**(1), 6–19 (2010)
2. Macedonia, M.: Games, simulation, and the military education dilemma. In: Internet and the University: 2001 Forum, Educause (2002)
3. Britannica, T.: America's Army. Encyclopaedia Britannica, 8 August 2011. https://www.britannica.com/topic/Americas-Army. Accessed 25 June 2021
4. America's Army: US Army. https://www.americasarmy.com/. Accessed 25 June 2021
5. Webster, R.: Declarative knowledge acquisition in immersive virtual learning environments. Interact. Learn. Environ. **24**(6), 1319–1333 (2015)

6. Abdul Jabbar, A.I.: Gameplay engagement and learning in game-based learning: A systematic review. Rev. Educ. Res. **85**(4), 740–779 (2015)
7. Freitas, S.D.: Are games effective learning tools? A review of educational games. J. Educ. Technol. Soc. **21**(2), 74–84 (2018)
8. Howard-Jones, P.A., Jay, T.: Reward, learning and games. Curr. Opin. Behav. Sci. **10**, 65–72 (2016)
9. Shabaneh, Y., Farrah, M.: The effect of games on vocabulary retention. Indonesian J. Learn. Instr. **2**(01), 79–90 (2019)
10. Olsen, T., Procci, K., Bowers, C.: Serious games usability testing: How to ensure proper usability, playability, and effectiveness. In: Marcus, Aaron (ed.) DUXU 2011. LNCS, vol. 6770, pp. 625–634. Springer, Heidelberg (2011). https://doi.org/10.1007/978-3-642-21708-1_70
11. Brooke, J.: Sus: a "quick and dirty" usability. Usability Eval. Indus. **11**, 189 (1996)
12. Brooke, J.: SUS: a retrospective. J. Usability Stud. **8**(2), 29–40 (2013)

Design and Development of a VR Serious Game for Chemical Laboratory Safety

Philippe Chan[1](✉) (iD), Tom Van Gerven[2] (iD), Jean-Luc Dubois[3] (iD),
and Kristel Bernaerts[2] (iD)

[1] Centre de Recherche Rhône-Alpes (CRRA), Arkema France, Rue Henri Moissan,
69310 Pierre-Bénite, France
philippe.chan@arkema.com
[2] Department of Chemical Engineering, KU Leuven, Celestijnenlaan 200F (box 2424),
3001 Leuven, Belgium
{tom.vangerven,kristel.bernaerts}@kuleuven.be
[3] Corporate R&D, Arkema France, 420 Rue d'Estienne d'Orves, 92705 Colombes, France
jean-luc.dubois@arkema.com

Abstract. Virtual reality (VR) technologies are becoming more and more popular, not only as a gaming console, but also as a viable training tool. Especially for health and safety training programmes, VR can be very useful to train people in dangerous environments and situations without imposing real danger on them or others. Chemical laboratories are environments where risks of severe injury or even fatality are always present. For this, we developed a VR serious game, called VR LaboSafe Game, as a tool for laboratory safety training. However, designing a VR serious game is a challenging task. There are many factors to consider for an optimal game design. In this study, we discuss important design considerations and we present the game design of VR LaboSafe Game. Preliminary tests of an early version of the game show usability issues and minor discomforting symptoms for some participants. Nevertheless, participants do agree that VR LaboSafe Game is useful for learning laboratory safety; is more active and responsive in their learning process and makes safety training more engaging.

Keywords: Virtual reality · Laboratory safety · Serious games · Game design

1 Introduction

Training interventions on the topic of Health, Safety and Environment (HSE) are of major importance for any workplace where hazardous chemicals are involved. This holds especially true for chemical laboratories in academia and industry. Insufficient safety training could lead to a lack of safety awareness and at-risk behaviour, which then increases the risk of causing accidents in chemical laboratories [1].

Current safety training interventions are commonly provided using traditional teaching methods, such as classroom lectures, videos and printed safety manuals. However, they are considered as low engaging teaching methods as the trainee is required to

© Springer Nature Switzerland AG 2021
F. de Rosa et al. (Eds.): GALA 2021, LNCS 13134, pp. 23–33, 2021.
https://doi.org/10.1007/978-3-030-92182-8_3

passively listen to the instructor [2]. As such, low engagement can lead to boredom and diminished attention to the learning content, thus making the training less effective [3]. Researchers and HSE experts agree that there is a need for learner-centred safety training programmes utilising more engaging learning methods and incorporating competency-based skills development [2].

Since the last decades, simulation technologies such as, immersive virtual reality (VR) and digital games, have been creating great opportunities to improve safety training methods. With these technologies, the trainee can be trained in a realistic representation of the workplace environment, performing realistic tasks with a high degree of interaction [4]. This makes it possible to improve decision-making skills on important safety issues, where mistakes can be made without real-life hazardous consequences. Also, games are widely known for effectively sustaining the engagement and entertainment of the player within the virtual environment [5]. The activity of learning-by-doing and learning from mistakes can make the learning experience more engaging and more memorable.

In this paper, we present the design and development of a serious game using VR technology as a training tool for chemical laboratory safety, called VR LaboSafe Game. At first we describe theoretical design principles that are necessary in order to design an effective VR serious game. Then we discuss the game design of VR LaboSafe Game and the tools used for development. Our ultimate goal is to investigate the learning effectiveness and motivation of this game. However, to ensure optimal conditions for final evaluations, we analysed whether the game has good usability and does not induce severe simulator sickness. This study may be considered useful by other researchers and designers who are also interested in designing and developing VR serious games for health and safety training.

2 Theoretical Design Foundation

Although VR and games are promising novel tools for educational purposes, there are some complications in designing effective learning experiences for such technologies. For example, immersive VR Head-Mounted Display (HMD) devices are known to cause users to feel nauseous while being immersed; this is often called simulator sickness [6]. Moreover, it has been proven that implementing VR experiences can inhibit effective learning by overloading the cognitive processing with overwhelming information [7]. While games can sustain engagement and active involvement of the trainee, researchers have mentioned that implementing game elements does not automatically make the training motivating [8]. It is a more complex interplay between cognitive capabilities and psychological factors of the learner. In general, designing such complex training systems is not easy and requires many factors to be considered in order to maximise its effectiveness. In this section, we discuss several well-researched design principles that can overcome these challenges and examples are given how these are implemented in the VR LaboSafe Game's design.

2.1 Cognitive Instructional Design

According to the cognitive theory of multimedia learning, three types of cognitive processing occur while learning [9]: essential, generative and extraneous cognitive processing. Instructional support should be designed in a way that supports the cognitive processing system so that cognitive load of the learner is efficiently managed in serious games using virtual reality.

Manage Essential Processing. Essential cognitive processing refers to cognitive processing in the working memory that is needed to mentally select the visual and verbal information from the learning content. Providing pre-training sessions about key concepts of the learning content and familiarisation of the technological medium prior to the learning experience can manage the intrinsic cognitive load of the learner [9]. Another method is by dividing tasks to learn a complex skill or knowledge into smaller sections and sequencing it from simple to difficult according to the expertise growth of the learner [9]. In the VR LaboSafe game, a VR tutorial is provided before starting the game levels. These game levels are sequenced to correspond to a specific subskill.

Reduce Extraneous Processing. Extraneous cognitive processing refers to cognitive processing that does not support the learning objective. In the case of VR environments and games, excessive extraneous processing is highly probable because high amounts of distracting details are displayed to the learner [7]. Some techniques are: highlighting elements, that are relevant to the learning material, with attention-drawing cues [9] and eliminating redundant information that is not necessary for achieving the learning objectives [9]. In the VR LaboSafe game, important information is indicated with a prominent colour or a distinct shape. On the other hand, information that is not needed yet in the early game levels is made invisible.

Foster Generative Processing. Generative cognitive processing refers to cognitive processing aimed at comprehension by organizing and integrating the content into knowledge. Several techniques have been researched that provide guidance to the learner to enhance deep learning of the learning content, such as scaffolding the learning content by providing instructional support for novice learners in the beginning, but fades away as the learner gains more skill and expertise [9]. Another technique is by bringing a sufficiently high variability in learning tasks throughout the whole training experience [9]. In the VR LaboSafe game, we designed the game levels such that hints are provided when the player is struggling. For more experienced players, these hints are not immediately shown, but can be requested when needed. To implement variability, each game level has different objectives with randomised content appearing at random locations in the virtual environment.

2.2 Motivational Game Design

Although the novelty and increased sense of presence of VR technology can be inherently motivating, the interactivity of the player with the virtual environment is also very important for sustained engagement [4]. To achieve this high level of engagement, the serious game design should support the motivational needs of the player. Game elements that are based on the self-determination theory (SDT) of Ryan and Deci (2002) can sustain the intrinsic motivation of the player by supporting the psychological needs of autonomy, competence and relatedness.

Autonomy. The ability to feel in control of one's behaviour and goals is one of the elements of SDT. A flexible game design that allows players to make their own choices creates a more meaningful and motivating experience [10]. Moreover, allowing players to explore and have a sense of control over the environment, sparks their interest and curiosity of the virtual space [11]. In the VR LaboSafe game, safe or dangerous situations can appear depending on the players' decisions. They can choose how to interact with objects and can freely move in the virtual environment.

Competence. Another element of SDT is the feeling of confidence over one's mastery to overcome new challenging tasks effectively. Providing a challenge scaffolding that tailors the level of difficulty to be not too easy nor too hard for the players, can boost their confidence in their abilities [12]. This also means that such game design allows a graceful failure of these challenges making it a part of the learning experience to enhance the players' ability to overcome them the next time [13]. In the VR LaboSafe game, this is related to the scaffolding structure of the game levels as mentioned before. When the players fail, they receive feedback on what they did wrong and how to do better next time.

Relatedness. The third psychological need involved in the SDT is the feeling of being socially connected with others. Although not all games can afford multiple players, this satisfaction feeling can also be achieved by meaningful interactions with non-player characters (NPCS) in the game [14]. Especially with VR technology, a realistic social presence can be simulated. In the VR LaboSafe game, a virtual character follows the player as a guiding companion. Moreover, there are virtual co-workers whom the player will need to keep safe.

2.3 Virtual Reality Considerations

VR HMDs allow users to be visually closed off from the real-world surroundings, enhancing the sense of presence in a virtual environment. However, users might become disoriented and develop symptoms of feeling nauseous when visual actions inside the device do not match with the actual physical movement of the human body [15]. Research has been done to search for solutions to prevent or minimise this simulator sickness. Improving the immersion of the user by using adequate hardware and interactive design considerations seems to reduce these symptoms [6].

Immersion. While there are different definitions of immersion in literature, one of the definitions is the technical capability of a system where the user perceives a virtual environment through natural sensorimotor contingencies [16]. This means that VR HMDS with more advanced technological features can provide a high level of immersion and reduce symptoms of simulator sickness. Some technological characteristics that can affect simulator sickness are: visual performance, spatial audio and motion tracking quality [6]. The VR LaboSafe game uses the Oculus Quest 2, which provides high-quality performance and comfort by allowing free movement untethered to a computer.

Interactivity. The term interactivity refers to the interaction between the user and the virtual environment, allowing the user to influence the environment in real-time [17]. VR technology is able to bring a high level of interactivity with natural and intuitive user interactions. This improves the immersion and reduces simulator sickness [18]. Moreover, allowing users to freely move in the virtual environment by means of teleportation also prevents symptoms of nausea [19]. In the VR LaboSafe game, players are able to intuitively interact with virtual objects, such as grabbing, throwing, pinching, etc. Moreover, they can teleport to different locations in the virtual environment.

3   VR LaboSafe Game Design

We developed VR LaboSafe Game, which is a serious game that utilises immersive virtual reality to train the safety awareness and safety behaviour in chemical laboratories. The genre of the game is a single player simulation game with a problem solving characteristic. A realistically accurate laboratory environment is simulated with task-based activities that are related to laboratory activities in real-life (see Fig. 1). In general, the game is divided in several modes and levels with three specific objectives: risk spotting, risk minimisation and performing safe experimental procedures. The goal is to complete these objectives as safe as possible without causing accidents and losing health points. In this section, we reveal more information on the learning objectives, level design and development of the VR LaboSafe Game.

3.1   Health and Safety Learning Objectives

The main learning objective of the game is to improve the player's decision-making skills in context of laboratory safety by practicing safety awareness and safety behaviour. The target audience of the game can be anyone who frequently works in a chemical laboratory, including students, researchers and lab technicians. These learning objectives are derived from the RAMP principles of laboratory safety skills [20] and the dynamic human decision-making model of Endsley [21]. Safety awareness is the constant consciousness of the state of safety in the surrounding environment and consists of the subskills hazard identification and risk assessment. Safety behaviour, in this case, refers to the practical application of safety measures in the workplace. After completing the VR LaboSafe Game, the player is able to recognise hazards that are present in the chemical laboratory, assess the risks and apply safety measures to minimise risks in the chemical laboratory, and demonstrate safe procedural skills of laboratory procedures.

3.2   Level Design

The VR LaboSafe Game has three different game modes: tutorial, training and evaluation mode.

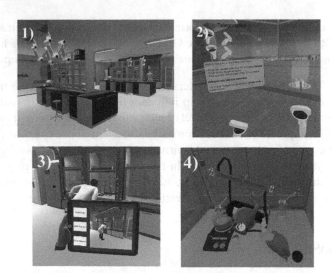

Fig. 1. In-game screenshots of VR LaboSafe Game: 1) the virtual laboratory environment; 2) tutorial of teleportation; 3) risk spotting mission; and 4) safe experimental procedure mission.

Tutorial Mode. This mode has the purpose to get the player familiarised with the controls and interactions of the game (See Fig. 1). Especially for beginners who are new to VR, tutorial sessions are recommended prior to using the game to its full extent [4]. In this way, the player could be able to handle the controls more easily during the learning experience, thus reducing cognitive load, which leads to performing the tasks more effectively [22]. The tutorial, that we developed, includes instructions for interacting with graphical user interfaces (GUI) in the 3D Environment, teleporting in the environment, grabbing objects, using a virtual tablet touch UI, taking pictures, and displaying safety data sheet (SDS) documents of chemicals. For each instruction we incorporated small minigame tasks related to the VR interaction. With these minigames, the player can practice and improve their skills of interacting and handling in VR.

Training Mode. This mode has the purpose to train the player's skills of laboratory safety in an interactive and engaging way. There are three distinct game levels with different tasks: 1) Risk Spotting; 2) Risk Minimisation; and 3) Safe Experiment. In the first game level the player needs to search and find a certain number of risks that appear in the virtual laboratory (see Fig. 1). The player takes a picture of this risk and answers questions related to its hazards and consequences. This game level is completed when all risks are found. The second game level is an extension of the first game level in a way that the player not only needs to spot risks in the lab but also needs to correctly eliminate or minimise these risks. In the third game level, the player needs to complete a chemical experimental procedure with the necessary safety measures (see Fig. 1). Unsafe and dangerous decisions of the player can result in an accident with a reduction of health points.

Evaluation Mode. The evaluation mode is where the safety awareness skills and safety behaviour of the player are taken to the test. The different objectives, that are also found in the training levels, are combined into one game level where the choices of the player can influence the scenario of the level. For example, the player needs to spot safety risks in the beginning of the level before performing an experimental procedure. When crucial safety risks are not recognised and eliminated, these risks can cause an accident during the chemical experiment procedure. The in-game assessment of the player's decisions and actions can evaluate the player's competence in laboratory safety.

3.3 Development

For the development of the VR LaboSafe Game, we selected inexpensive and easy-to-use development software and VR hardware.

Software. We used the Unity3D game engine to develop the VR LaboSafe game. Unity3D is a widely used game engine that is based on C# programming language and has a free licensing option. It offers a lot of advanced options to develop the game with high quality, while also offering an abundance of support. With Unity's XR Interaction Toolkit, ready-to-use solutions are provided to implement VR interactions easily. In addition, we used the free-to-use 3D modelling software Blender in order to make 3D models for the game. Other 3D models are bought or downloaded for free online.

Hardware. We selected the Oculus Quest 2 as VR HMD for this game due to its affordance to move freely while providing high performances. This device does not require a cable connection to a computer, allows six degrees of freedom (6DOF) Tracking and provides a resolution of 1832×1920 per eye. This device's comfort and high-quality performance can reduce the symptoms of simulator sickness.

4 Evaluation

In order to eventually perform evaluations on the learning effectiveness and motivation of using the VR LaboSafe Game, we must ensure that its usability should be optimal and the severity of simulator sickness should be minimal. Therefore, we have conducted preliminary tests with an early version of the VR LaboSafe Game in order to examine the usability, simulator sickness and feedback from laboratory technicians. The tested version contained only the first game level of Risk Spotting and tutorial levels with textual step-by-step instructions without a pedagogical agent.

4.1 Participants and Methodology

We recruited 10 participants (5 female, 5 male, age 20–30) who were assigned as interns or students at a research centre of the chemical company Arkema in France. Only 3 participants said they had prior experience with a VR HMD. During the testing sessions, they played an early version of the VR LaboSafe Game for a duration of approximately 40 min continuously with no one dropping out before the end. Because of the COVID-19 sanitary measures, the participants wore a face mask and the VR HMD, the Oculus

Quest 2, was disinfected before each use. In order to analyse the usability and simulator sickness, we used the questionnaires System Usability Scale (SUS) [23] and Simulator Sickness Questionnaire (SSQ) [24] after playing the game. Additional questions were added on the usefulness of the game, their perceived learning and intention to use. Although most of the participants were French, they stated that they had no issues playing the game and replying to questionnaires in English.

4.2 Results and Discussion

Results of the SUS and SSQ scores are presented per participant in Fig. 2. The SUS questionnaire contains 10-items on a 1 (strongly disagree) to 5 (strongly agree) Likert scale. The calculated SUS score can range from 0 to 100, wherein values of above 68 are desirable in order to present a good usability [23]. The SSQ contains 16-items on a 0 (none) to 4 (severe) Likert scale [24]. The calculated SSQ scores are rather not a quantitative measure, but can be used to compare simulator sickness between users or other comparisons. The SUS scores measured in these tests vary widely from 40.00 to 72.50 with an overall mean score of 58.25 among the 10 participants. The best scoring item states that VR LaboSafe Game is 'well integrated', whereas the worst scoring item states that the participants 'would need the support of a technical person'. In terms of simulator sickness, 5 participants scored an SSQ score below 20 and only reported zero to two symptoms, while the other 5 participants scored higher SSQ scores. The most frequently reported (6/10) symptoms are 'eye strain' and 'blurred vision', but also 'general discomfort' and 'difficulty focusing' (5/10).

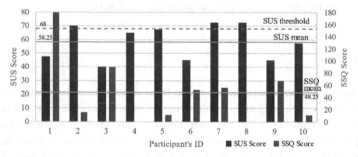

Fig. 2. System Usability Scale (SUS) (blue) and Simulator Sickness Questionnaire (SSQ) (red) scores per participant (Color figure online)

The varying SUS scores show that the usability of VR LaboSafe Game should be improved in a way that supports the users better. Indeed, we have observed some participants having issues with controlling the VR interactions more confidently, especially for people using VR for the first time. This could be caused by the abundance of visual and textual instructions in another language resulting in a high impact on the cognitive load of the user. Thus, improved versions of the VR LaboSafe Game should replace most textual information with spoken instructions via a pedagogical agent and add more comprehensible animations demonstrating the VR controls [9].

Despite no one dropping out and symptoms of simulator sickness were not apparent from our observations, some participants have experienced mild symptoms of visual discomfort according to the SSQ results. This could be explained by the relatively long duration of 40 min continuous VR experience. Prolonged duration of visual exposure to a digital screen can cause ocular sickness symptoms, such as eye strain and headaches [25]. Therefore, it is important for the future use of VR LaboSafe Game to allow frequent breaks of a few minutes, especially for first-time VR users in order to minimise discomforting symptoms.

Nevertheless, participants still agree that VR LaboSafe Game is useful for learning laboratory safety; is more active and responsive in their learning process; makes safety training more engaging; and that they would like to participate in other training programmes using VR LaboSafe Game.

5 Conclusion

We designed and developed a serious game using VR technology as a training tool for chemical laboratory safety, called VR LaboSafe Game. This VR serious game could improve training programmes for chemical lab safety in order to make them more engaging and to deliver realistic dangerous experiences without real danger. The game design contains an elaborate level design in order to prepare laboratory technicians to be aware of risks in the lab and make decisions to deal with these risks in a safe manner. Because designing such serious game is not an easy task, we also presented design principles on how to implement elements to efficiently manage the cognitive load of learners, to intrinsically motivate them and how to minimise the severity of simulator sickness due to the use of VR. Although the sample size is rather small, the evaluation of an early version of VR LaboSafe Game shows a first indication that there are usability issues and minor symptomatic discomfort for some participants. Improvements of the VR LaboSafe Game should be focused on reducing textual information and allowing short breaks while playing. Despite these issues, participants still agree on the usefulness, active learning and the intention to play the VR LaboSafe Game more frequently.

For the future work of this research, we will investigate the added value of motivation and the learning effectiveness by using VR LaboSafe Game as a tool for chemical laboratory safety training. Moreover, we will examine this added value on populations with different age and experience, including laboratory employees in the chemical industry and students in academia.

Acknowledgements. This project has received funding from the European Union's EU Framework Programme for Research and Innovation Horizon 2020 under Grant Agreement 812716. This publication reflects only the authors' view exempting the community from any liability. Project website: https://charming-etn.eu/.

References

1. Gopalaswami, N., Han, Z.: Analysis of laboratory incident database. J. Loss. Prev. Process Ind. **64**, 104027 (2020). https://doi.org/10.1016/j.jlp.2019.104027
2. Burke, M.J., et al.: Relative effectiveness of worker safety and health training methods. Am. J. Public Health. **96**, 315–324 (2006). https://doi.org/10.2105/AJPH.2004.059840
3. Fivizzani, K.P.: The evolution of chemical safety training. J. Chem. Health Saf. **12**, 11–15 (2005). https://doi.org/10.1016/j.chs.2005.08.005
4. Checa, D., Bustillo, A.: A review of immersive virtual reality serious games to enhance learning and training. Multimed. Tools App. **79**(9–10), 5501–5527 (2019). https://doi.org/10.1007/s11042-019-08348-9
5. Garris, R., Ahlers, R., Driskell, J.E.: Games, motivation, and learning: a research and practice model. Simul. Gaming. **33**, 441–467 (2002). https://doi.org/10.1177/1046878102238607
6. Kourtesis, P., et al.: Technological competence is a pre-condition for effective implementation of virtual reality head mounted displays in human neuroscience: a technological review and meta-analysis. Front. Hum. Neurosci. **13**, 1 (2019). https://doi.org/10.3389/fnhum.2019.00342
7. Makransky, G., et al.: Adding immersive virtual reality to a science lab simulation causes more presence but less learning. Learn. Instr. **60**, 225–236 (2019). https://doi.org/10.1016/j.learninstruc.2017.12.007
8. Hu, Y., et al.: Game-based learning has good chemistry with chemistry education: A three-level meta-analysis. J. Res. Sci. Teach. (2021). Submitted for publication
9. Mayer, R.: The Cambridge Handbook of Multimedia Learning. Cambridge University Press, Cambridge (2014). https://doi.org/10.1017/CBO9781139547369
10. Nicholson, S.: A recipe for meaningful gamification. In: Reiners, T., Wood, L.C. (eds.) Gamification in Education and Business, pp. 1–20. Springer, Cham (2015). https://doi.org/10.1007/978-3-319-10208-5_1
11. Minocha, S., Tudor, A.-D., Tilling, S.: Affordances of Mobile Virtual Reality and their Role in Learning and Teaching. In: Proc. BCS HCI. {BCS} Learning & Development (2017). https://doi.org/10.14236/ewic/hci2017.44
12. Csikszentmihalyi, M., et al.: Flow: The Psychology of Optimal Experience. Harper & Row, New York (1990)
13. Anderson, C.G., et al.: Failing up: How failure in a game environment promotes learning through discourse. Think. Skills Creat. **30**, 135–144 (2018). https://doi.org/10.1016/j.tsc.2018.03.002
14. Ryan, R.M., Rigby, C.S.: Motivational foundations of game-based learning. In: Mayer, J.L.P.R.E., Homer, B.D. (eds.) Handbook of Game-Based Learning. pp. 153–177. The MIT Press, Cambridge (2020)
15. Davis, S., Nesbitt, K., Nalivaiko, E.: Comparing the onset of cybersickness using the Oculus Rift and two virtual roller coasters. In: Proceedings of IE, p. 30 (2015)
16. Slater, M., et al.: A framework for immersive virtual environments (FIVE): speculations on the role of presence in virtual environments. Presence (CAMB) **6**, 603–616 (1997). https://doi.org/10.1162/pres.1997.6.6.603
17. Steuer, J.: Defining virtual reality: dimensions determining telepresence. J. Commun. **42**, 73–93 (1992). https://doi.org/10.1111/j.1460-2466.1992.tb00812.x
18. Stanney, K.M., Hash, P.: Locus of user-initiated control in virtual environments: influences on cybersickness. Presence (CAMB) **7**, 447–459 (1998). https://doi.org/10.1162/105474698565848
19. Cherni, H., Métayer, N., Souliman, N.: Literature review of locomotion techniques in virtual reality. IJVR **20**, 1–20 (2020). https://doi.org/10.20870/ijvr.2020.20.1.3183

20. Hill, R.H., Nelson, D.A.: Strengthening safety education of chemistry undergraduates. Chem. Health Saf. **12**, 19–23 (2005). https://doi.org/10.1016/j.chs.2005.07.012
21. Endsley, M.R.: Toward a theory of situation awareness in dynamic systems. Hum. Factors **37**, 32–64 (1995). https://doi.org/10.1518/001872095779049543
22. Kalyuga, S., Plass, J.L.: Evaluating and managing cognitive load in games. In: Ferdig, R.E. (ed.) Handbook of Research on Effective Electronic Gaming in Education, pp. 719–737. IGI Global, Hershey (2009). https://doi.org/10.4018/978-1-59904-808-6.ch041
23. Brooke, J.: SUS: a quick and dirty usability scale. Usability Eval. Ind. **189**, 1–7 (1995)
24. Kennedy, R.S., et al.: Simulator sickness questionnaire: an enhanced method for quantifying simulator sickness. Int. J. Aviat. Psychol. **3**, 203–220 (1993). https://doi.org/10.1207/s15327 108ijap0303_3
25. Hirzle, T., Cordts, M., Rukzio, E., Gugenheimer, J., Bulling, A.: A critical assessment of the use of SSQ as a measure of general discomfort in VR head-mounted displays. In: Proceedings of CHI Association for Computing Machinery, New York, NY, USA (2021). https://doi.org/10.1145/3411764.3445361

Exploring Different Game Mechanics
for Anti-phishing Learning Games

Rene Roepke[1]([⊠])(iD), Vincent Drury[2](iD), Ulrike Meyer[2], and Ulrik Schroeder[1](iD)

[1] Learning Technologies Research Group, RWTH Aachen University,
Aachen, Germany
{roepke,schroeder}@cs.rwth-aachen.de
[2] IT-Security Research Group, RWTH Aachen University, Aachen, Germany
{drury,meyer}@itsec.rwth-aachen.de

Abstract. Existing anti-phishing learning games rely on the same simple game mechanics that do not allow for detailed assessment of the players' acquired knowledge and skills. They focus mostly on factual and conceptual knowledge to remember or understand. To extend the research field, this paper presents two new games: The first game implements an extended classification mechanic to better assess the player's decision process, while the second game implements a different game mechanic, which requires players to combine given URL parts to construct their own phishing URLs. Both games aim to address higher-order cognitive processes as well as procedural knowledge. The games' functionality and user experience were evaluated by a group of 40 CS students, resulting in general improvements of the games.

Keywords: Learning games · Game design · Learning goals · Phishing

1 Introduction

When using the Internet and IT systems, end-users are immediately exposed to various threats, one of which is phishing, a deception-based threat in which impersonation is used to obtain information from a target [8]. Although technical countermeasures exist, they fail to completely stop the threat [2]. As a complementary approach, user education can support end-users in acquiring relevant knowledge and skills to recognize and mitigate phishing. Here, game-based anti-phishing education is an approach which earned a lot of interest over the last decade. However, recent reviews [6,11] indicate limited success and distinct commonalities among developed games: a focus on factual and conceptual knowledge as well as limited use of game mechanics. This indicates a potential for the development of new, different anti-phishing learning games. This paper addresses this potential by presenting two new games which on the one hand extend the use of game mechanics to provide better assessment and feedback and on the other hand explore different game mechanics to foster higher-order cognitive processes.

© Springer Nature Switzerland AG 2021
F. de Rosa et al. (Eds.): GALA 2021, LNCS 13134, pp. 34–43, 2021.
https://doi.org/10.1007/978-3-030-92182-8_4

2   Review of Existing Games

Over the last decade, various learning games for security education have been developed. Alongside these developments, different researchers reviewed existing games to analyze the achievements and challenges within the research domain [1, 4–6, 10–13]. In these reviews, researchers identified the need for more extensive research [1] and to further explore interactive, immersive simulations for practical, hands-on training [4, 10, 13]. Existing user studies in game-based security education show positive effects but they are criticized for small sample sizes and non-discussed effect sizes [5]. Lastly, although many games are found in literature, the availability of learning games for end-users is limited [12].

While in existing reviews, authors analyzed and compared games for the wide field of security education, less review work exists focusing solely on anti-phishing learning games. In [11], the authors identified the need for a more in-depth review of anti-phishing learning games and hence, they created and reviewed a data set on available publications on games. They analyzed publications using Bloom's Revised Taxonomy (BRT) [7] and found that the majority of games convey factual or conceptual knowledge and skills. Further cognitive processes along the BRT as well as procedural knowledge are mostly neglected by existing games. Lastly, the review of covered learning content in available games showed that the focus often lies on phishing URLs and emails. More complex or advanced contemporary phishing techniques are usually not covered by existing games. The review also revealed that most games rely on a singular game mechanic: a binary decision where players have to decide whether a given URL or email is malicious or benign. This type of assessment is very limited, since it does not convey how and why players decide. The mechanic also forces players to make a decision even if they are unsure and lastly, feedback is limited since the decision does not reflect possible misconceptions. Only one game provides an additional game mechanic where players have to select different components of given URLs to show that they can parse URLs [3].

All in all, the limited use of game mechanics results in limited assessment possibilities. Although existing games might cover necessary learning content on phishing URLs, gameplay does not support the assessment of players' abilities. While focusing on factual and conceptual knowledge to remember and understand, existing games also miss the opportunity to target further cognitive processes and convey procedural knowledge. Conclusively, we identify the potential for new learning games exploring different game mechanics and providing more in-depth assessment. Also, new games should provide gameplay supporting procedural knowledge acquisition and address higher-order cognitive processes.

3   Designing New Game Prototypes

Since existing games are limited in their use of different game mechanics and mostly focus on factual and conceptual knowledge, we want to explore different game mechanics and cognitive processes of BRT. For the development of new game prototypes we set the following design goals:

1. Extend the binary decision game mechanic of classifying phishing URLs to provide better assessment and feedback
2. Address higher-order cognitive processes of applying, analyzing, evaluating and creating by using different game mechanics

In order to fulfill these design goals we decided to implement two novel learning games. For the first game, we decided to extend the decision mechanic and provide multiple options as well as an option to discard. This way, we can potentially assess more accurately, how players decide and when they are unable to decide. Feedback is provided for correct and incorrect classifications. The second game replaces the currently favored game mechanic of classifying by introducing a puzzle or combining game mechanic. Here, players have to create a solution to a given task by combining URL pieces and feedback is given based on a set of automated checks. We decided to implement two independent games since we want to compare both games in later user studies.

3.1 Learning Content

The main requirement for the learning content of our games was to provide knowledge and skills that are robust against adversarial influence and simple to understand, while retaining general applicability. To this end, we decided to focus on URLs, as they uniquely identify a website, thus providing robustness, and are also applicable in a wide range of potential attack scenarios: they can always be used to analyze a potential phishing website, regardless of how the website was delivered to the user, and knowledge about URLs can be used in several other scenarios, e.g. when analyzing email headers to determine the sender. The two games therefore aim to teach the basics of URLs and, in particular, how to identify the Registrable Domain (RD) of a URL, as it is the discerning factor to decide between legitimate and phishing URLs.

In order to support a better understanding of how to identify potential phishing URLs, the games include a number of techniques attackers use to construct phishing URLs. These techniques are based on attacks that were found in the wild and described in related work (see e.g. [9]), and also capture the structure of URLs as taught in the games, thus creating a foundation what to look out for in phishing attacks while strengthening the players' understanding of URLs. Attackers typically construct phishing URLs that make the user believe that they lead to a specific benign target domain. We refer to this target domain as the "original domain". The manipulation techniques included in the games are:

- **Subdomain**: Including (parts of) the original domain in the subdomain
- **Path**: Using a random domain and (parts of) the original domain in the path
- **IP address**: Using an IP address as host and (parts of) the original domain in the path
- **RD**: Modifying (e.g., adding to) the RD of the original domain
- **Random**: URL is completely random; no connection to the original domain
- **Top Level Domain (TLD)**: Using the original domain, except for changing the TLD

Both games require example URLs, which we based on the login websites of a set of existing services that are popular in our country of origin (based on the Alexa[1] and Tranco[2] lists).

In all, the games aim to impart the knowledge and skills that are necessary to detect phishing attacks. To successfully protect against a real attack, the user also requires the awareness to apply the conveyed knowledge and skills, which requires a behavioral change in their daily activities. Even if the proposed games might facilitate such a behavioral change, it is not the main goal or focus of our current prototypes and might be studied in more detail in the future.

3.2 Learning Goals

Based on the learning content described above, we defined learning goals for both games using BRT [7]. We structured these learning goals alongside the six different cognitive processes of the taxonomy and followed a fixed prefix sentence: "After playing the learning game, players should be able to..." (see Table 1). Regarding the knowledge dimension of BRT, covered learning content ranges from terminology, concepts and principles to subject-specific techniques and methods, i.e. URL parsing and manipulation. Hence, the learning goals cover factual, conceptual but also procedural knowledge. Solely, meta-cognitive knowledge is not explicitly imparted, i.e. knowledge and awareness of one's own cognition [7].

4   Implementation

Following our design goals, we implemented two learning game prototypes with the aforementioned learning content and learning goals. The first game is called "All sorts of Phish"[3] and it follows an analytical approach similar to existing games where players have to analyze a given URL. Instead of only deciding whether it is malicious or benign, players have to sort it based on the applied manipulation technique (addressing our first design goal). The second game is called "A Phisher's Bag of Tricks"[4]. Addressing the second design goal, this game requires players to apply manipulation techniques to create their own phishing URLs while keeping the URL structure intact. In the following we refer to the first game as *analysis game*, and the second game as *creation game*.

The structure of both games follows an alternating tutorial-level scheme where players are first introduced to a specific learning content delivered in a tutorial and then continue to practice and acquire desired skills by completing one or more levels. To navigate through the tutorials and levels, a tutor character is introduced in the beginning of each game.

---

[1] https://www.alexa.com/topsites/countries, accessed 2021-06-25.
[2] https://tranco-list.eu/, accessed 2021-06-25.
[3] https://gitlab.com/learntech-rwth/erbse/analysis-game, accessed 07-09-2021.
[4] https://gitlab.com/learntech-rwth/erbse/creation-game, accessed 07-09-2021.

Table 1. Learning goals including the mapping to both games (marked with x if a learning goal applies to the analysis game (A) or creation game (C))

After playing the learning game, players should be able to ...	A	C
Remember ... know the structure of URLs by recalling its components.	x	x
... name the manipulation techniques for URLs by listing the manipulation techniques for individual components.	x	x
... know the manipulation techniques for URLs by describing the manipulation of the components.	x	x
Understand ... understand the structure of URLs by explaining the purpose of the components.	x	x
... understand the manipulation of the structure of URLs by explaining manipulation techniques for the components.	x	x
Apply ... determine the individual components of a URL by performing URL parsing.	x	x
... compose valid URLs by combining the (necessary) components in the correct order.		x
... compose valid URLs by creating the (necessary) components in the correct order.		x
... change the structure of a URL by modifying components.		x
... manipulate the structure of a URL by modifying (necessary) components based on specific rules.		x
Analyze ... analyze the structure of a URL by identifying the components.	x	x
... detect manipulations in the structure of a URL by identifying manipulated components.	x	
... recognize the manipulation technique applied to a URL by identifying/recognizing the manipulated component.	x	
Evaluate ... assess the correctness of the structure of a URL by checking the components.	x	
... assess the manipulation of the structure of a URL by checking the components and identifying manipulated components.	x	
... distinguish benign URLs from manipulated URLs by comparing both URLs in terms of applied manipulation(s).	x	
Create ... create correct URLs by creating and combining the (necessary) components.		x
... create manipulated URLs by manipulating and combining (necessary) components based on rules and the URL structure		x

4.1 Tutorial Structure

Both games introduce new concepts in interactive, stepwise tutorial sections. The knowledge is impaired by the respective tutor character, that guides players through the game by explaining the game mechanics and teaching the required knowledge to progress through the following levels. Players can follow the tutorials in a self-paced manner and can go back to previous steps if needed. In the current game prototypes, the tutorials do not diverge into digital storytelling beyond the introduction of the tutor characters. This way, tutorials are kept short so players would not get discouraged by lengthy explanations. The tutorials of both games include interactive elements, where players hover over a given URL and discover hidden information regarding different components of the URL.

Within four tutorials, the analysis game covers the URL structure and key concepts like RD and IP addresses as well as manipulation techniques for RD, subdomains and paths. In the creation game, in contrast, the learning content is distributed using five tutorials. In the current implementation, the tutorial content is similar but not equal: IP and random URLs are only included in the analysis game, since they offer an easy starting point there but do not add meaningful manipulations to the creation game. Similarly TLDs are an easy, first manipulation technique in the creation game, but are often very complicated to classify without knowledge of the original URL.

4.2   Level Structure and Feedback

In both games, levels follow a tutorial section and are used to reinforce and test the concepts and knowledge that were introduced in the tutorials.

Analysis Game: A level in the analysis game (see Fig. 1) requires players to analyze given URLs and sort them into different buckets representing different manipulation techniques via drag-and-drop actions. URLs are hidden behind moving coins which flip and reveal the URL when players click on them. The player can choose between a bucket for benign URLs and up to five buckets for different phishing URLs: IP, random, subdomain, RD, path. Lastly, there is an additional bucket ("no-idea") if players are not sure how to sort a given URL. This way, players are not forced to make a decision and can discard URLs. The number of buckets for phishing URLs is increased with each completed tutorial, and they correspond to the different manipulation techniques explained above. The benign and "no-idea" buckets are present from the beginning and remain throughout the game. Each level lasts a fixed amount of time (default: 90 s) and to complete the level successfully, players have to pass a preset score while not making too many mistakes. When dropping a coin into a bucket, players receive instant feedback in the form of a colored aura over the bucket (green: correct; yellow: correct tendency, i.e. a URL classified as phishing but

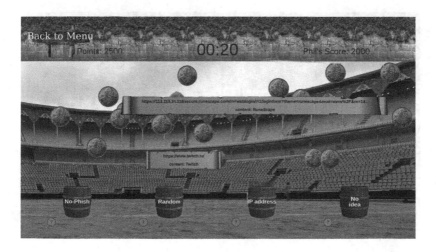

Fig. 1. Level of the analysis game.

not the correct manipulation technique; red: incorrect; black: discarded) and the increase/decrease of their score (plus points for correct decisions (400 points) or correct tendency (200 points), no points for incorrect decisions or discarded URLs). After the time is up, the game checks whether players achieved a higher score than a preset value (to challenge players to classify as many URLs as possible; default: 2000 points), and that they did not make too many mistakes and achieved a high classification accuracy (to prevent random guessing; default: at least 75% accuracy must be achieved). Players complete a level successfully if both conditions are met. If they do not meet either one of the conditions, they have to repeat the level. Next, feedback is presented for different types of mistakes in an evaluation screen (if URLs were incorrectly classified as benign, or if URLs were classified as phishing but not the correct type).

Creation Game: In the creation game, the levels require players to solve a set of tasks called *presets* by creating their own URLs. For each preset, players are given a task description and a set of URL parts (e.g., "https", ".com"). The task is displayed at the top of the screen, and is focused on the manipulation techniques that were introduced in the previous tutorial. To solve the task, players have to combine URL parts by moving them into the initially empty URL bar in the center of the screen. Within the URL bar, all URL parts can be sorted to complete a valid URL structure. The first level only establishes vocabulary and the basic structure of URLs, while the tasks in following levels are always based on an original benign service and domain name (e.g., Amazon - amazon.com). Based on this, players are asked to apply manipulation techniques to create their own phishing URLs. For example, players might be asked to create a phishing URL that includes the target name (e.g., "Amazon") in a subdomain, with a given RD that must not be changed (see Fig. 2). To complete the task, players have to combine and later even create their own URL parts, that can be arranged

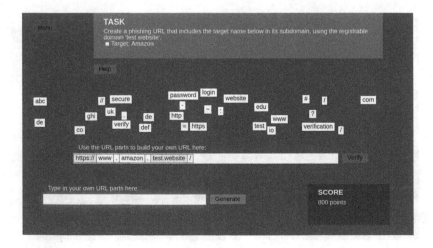

Fig. 2. Level of the creation game.

by dragging them into a URL drop area, which shows the current solution URL. Creating new URL parts is possible via a keyboard input area, that can be activated to allow players to create arbitrary input.

Possible task solutions can be checked by clicking on the corresponding button labeled "Verify". When a solution is submitted, the game runs a number of checks on the created URL and provides feedback on which parts of the task were performed correctly and what has to be changed in case of a failed check. Players get points for passing different types of checks, indicating which tasks are more complicated and opening up the possibility to include non-mandatory challenges, that give additional points but do not have to be completed to advance in the game. As opposed to the analysis game, tasks in the creation game do not have to be completed in a fixed amount of time (default setting), however, depending on the context the game is played in, a timer can be activated.

4.3 Development

Both game prototypes are implemented using the MTLG framework[5]. It is a game development framework based on the HTML5 Canvas element and native JavaScript. The framework utilizes CreateJS[6], a suite of modular libraries to enable rich interactive content via HTML5. Originally developed to support game development on multi-touch tabletop displays, MTLG is a modular and versatile game development framework for any browser-capable device. Both games are deployed using a webserver and when accessed, immediately downloaded to the player's webbrowser.

For future evaluation and to support learning analytics, both games support event logging to capture all player actions and results achieved in the games. Log data is transmitted asynchronously to an external log server for further processing and analysis. For identification of players, human-readable and unique player IDs are generated by the log server. This way, we are able to match game sessions to external evaluation instruments (e.g., questionnaires). Currently, logging is done using a game-specific data format, however, recent support of Experience API[7] (xAPI) for the MTLG framework allows us to switch and provide xAPI data stored in a Learning Record Store. Since logging and player IDs are only needed for evaluation purposes in future user studies, they can be deactivated for production environments without evaluation.

5 Preliminary Evaluation

In a one-hour session, 40 CS students ($N_{\text{Creation}} = 22$, $N_{\text{Analysis}} = 18$) played the games and answered a short survey about the functionality and user experience. The survey consisted of questions about positive and negative aspects of the games, bugs that were encountered during gameplay, and possible improvements.

---

[5] https://mtlg-framework.gitlab.io/, accessed 07-09-2021.
[6] https://createjs.com/, accessed 23-06-2021.
[7] https://xapi.com/, accessed 23-06-2021.

The importance of the topic and how it was motivated, engaging aspects and the feedback after playing a level were received as positive aspects of the games. One student described the experience of playing the creation game as a fun and engaging way to learn about phishing, while another student highlighted how the combination mechanic invited tinkering with the URL manipulations.

Students also identified several bugs, including a game-breaking problem in the creation game that only appeared in a small number of cases due to the random selection of URLs in the task descriptions, and problems on slower devices that made it complicated to open coins to reveal URLs in the analysis game. They criticized the explanation texts, which were received as too long and boring by the students, as well as missing context and the lack of advanced URL manipulation techniques. This was also reflected in the suggested improvements, where some students proposed interactive elements in our tutorials, which we implemented in updated versions of the games. Other proposed improvements include a competitive multiplayer mode and even more variety in game mechanics.

In addition to reported bugs and problems while playing the games, some students also noted, that they did not know all of the services that were presented in the analysis game. Due to possible difficulties in classifying URLs of unknown services, they asked for a list of legitimate domains that they could compare the given URLs to. This indicates potential problems in classifying URLs of services users are not familiar with. We plan to analyze this more closely by taking a look at log data, to find out if unknown services are actually classified with less accuracy, and if this might also have an effect on the overall learning outcome.

6   Conclusion and Future Work

In this paper, we presented two new learning games developed to extend the current research domain. While existing games are characterized by a lack of game mechanics covering more than factual and conceptual knowledge and higher-order cognitive processes, the presented games follow a more elaborate analytical approach as well as a constructive approach utilizing an alternative game mechanic in this context. Learning goals were carefully identified and applied in the games implemented using a browser-based framework to provide good accessibility. Since the games are currently limited to the topic of phishing URLs, the effects on general phishing awareness are limited. Hence, we suggest using additional educational resources to achieve well-rounded user education.

While a preliminary user evaluation identified improvement potential, a proper evaluation of the games' effectiveness and comparison to existing approaches is still needed. We plan to evaluate both game prototypes using an extensive pre-/post-test design and retention tests to evaluate potential long-term effects. Furthermore, we want to explore personalization to analyze the effects of unknown services. Event logging capabilities also support in-depth game analytics to understand how learning occurs within the games.

Acknowledgements. This research was supported by the research training group "Human Centered Systems Security" sponsored by the state of North Rhine-Westphalia, Germany.

References

1. Alotaibi, F., Furnell, S., Stengel, I., Papadaki, M.: A review of using gaming technology for cyber-security awareness. Inf. Secur. Res. **6**(2), 660–666 (2016). https://doi.org/10.20533/ijisr.2042.4639.2016.0076
2. Anti-Phishing Working Group: Phishing activity trends report, 4th quarter 2020. Report, Anti-Phishing Working Group (2021)
3. Canova, G., Volkamer, M., Bergmann, C., Borza, R.: NoPhish: an anti-phishing education app. In: Mauw, S., Jensen, C.D. (eds.) STM 2014. LNCS, vol. 8743, pp. 188–192. Springer, Cham (2014). https://doi.org/10.1007/978-3-319-11851-2_14
4. Compte, A.L., Elizondo, D., Watson, T.: A renewed approach to serious games for cyber security. In: International Conference on Cyber Conflict: Architectures in Cyberspace, Tallinn, pp. 203–216. IEEE (2015). https://doi.org/10.1109/CYCON.2015.7158478
5. Hendrix, M., Al-Sherbaz, A., Bloom, V.: Game based cyber security training: are serious games suitable for cyber security training? Serious Games **3**(1), 53–61 (2016). https://doi.org/10.17083/ijsg.v3i1.107
6. Köhler, K., Röpke, R., Wolf, M.R.: Through a mirror darkly – on the obscurity of teaching goals in game-based learning in IT security. In: Simulation & Gaming Through Times and Across Disciplines, pp. 324–335. Akademia Leona Kozminskiego, Warsaw (2019)
7. Krathwohl, D.R.: A revision of Bloom's taxonomy: an overview. Theory Pract. **41**(4), 212–218 (2002). https://doi.org/10.1207/s15430421tip4104_2
8. Lastdrager, E.E.H.: Achieving a consensual definition of phishing based on a systematic review of the literature. Crime Sci. **3**(1), 1–10 (2014). https://doi.org/10.1186/s40163-014-0009-y
9. Oest, A., Safei, Y., Doupé, A., Ahn, G.J., Wardman, B., Warner, G.: Inside a phisher's mind: understanding the anti-phishing ecosystem through phishing kit analysis. In: APWG Symposium on Electronic Crime Research (eCrime), pp. 1–12 (2018). https://doi.org/10.1109/ECRIME.2018.8376206
10. Pastor, V., Díaz, G., Castro, M.: State-of-the-art simulation systems for information security education, training and awareness. In: IEEE EDUCON Conference, Madrid, pp. 1907–1916. IEEE (2010). https://doi.org/10.1109/EDUCON.2010.5492435
11. Roepke, R., Koehler, K., Drury, V., Schroeder, U., Wolf, M.R., Meyer, U.: A pond full of phishing games - analysis of learning games for anti-phishing education. In: Hatzivasilis, G., Ioannidis, S. (eds.) MSTEC 2020. LNCS, vol. 12512, pp. 41–60. Springer, Cham (2020). https://doi.org/10.1007/978-3-030-62433-0_3
12. Roepke, R., Schroeder, U.: The problem with teaching defence against the dark arts: a review of game-based learning applications and serious games for cyber security education. In: International Conference on Computer Supported Education, vol. 2, pp. 58–66. SciTePress, Heraklion (2019). https://doi.org/10.5220/0007706100580066
13. Tioh, J.N., Mina, M., Jacobson, D.W.: Cyber security training a survey of serious games in cyber security. In: IEEE Frontiers in Education Conference (FIE), Indianapolis, pp. 1–5. IEEE (2017). https://doi.org/10.1109/FIE.2017.8190712

Phishing Academy: Evaluation of a Digital Educational Game on URLs and Phishing

Sven Schoebel[✉], Rene Roepke, and Ulrik Schroeder

Learning Technologies Research Group, RWTH Aachen, Aachen, Germany
{schoebel,roepke,schroeder}@cs.rwth-aachen.de

Abstract. Due to a lack of learning opportunities, untrained access to the Internet is a potential danger for children and teenagers. This paper presents a comprehensive evaluation of a digital educational game that teaches children and teenagers between the ages of ten and thirteen in-depth knowledge and skills about the structure of a URL and how to recognize and mitigate phishing. Playing the educational game led to a significant increase of the participants' phishing detection rate. Furthermore, a comparison of different phishing types revealed on which phishing types future work should focus due to lower detection rates. Phishing Academy is a browser-based educational game, which is available in German and English and can also be played via touch gestures.

Keywords: Digital educational game · Phishing · URL · IT-security · School

1 Introduction

The increasingly high availability of digital devices gives children and teenagers largely unfiltered access to the Internet. Therefore, children and teenagers are exposed to the dangers and risks of digital communication. Since they first have to develop a routine for handling private and confidential information when starting to use digital media and the Internet, children and teenagers are particularly at risk and need to be made aware risks like data and identity theft. Phishing continues to be a widespread threat in the field of cybercrime [1]. Teaching people how to recognize phishing presents a complementary approach to technical countermeasures which fail to completely stop the threat. Educational material is given mainly through information texts or videos [2]. However, these sources of information are only of limited interest for teaching children and teenagers between the ages of ten and thirteen about phishing, as they only enable static knowledge transfer. Alternatively, educational games can provide a suitable learning environment for the target group. So far, existing educational games were mostly developed without a focus on children and teenagers and subsequently evaluated only with adults [3–5]. Therefore, it is necessary to evaluate games with respect to their effectiveness and age appropriateness with children and teenagers. This paper presents a comprehensive evaluation of the educational game *Phishing Academy* which was intentionally developed for children and teenagers (ages ten to thirteen) [6, 7].

© Springer Nature Switzerland AG 2021
F. de Rosa et al. (Eds.): GALA 2021, LNCS 13134, pp. 44–53, 2021.
https://doi.org/10.1007/978-3-030-92182-8_5

2 Related Work

Roepke et al. [8] investigated the availability and content of anti-phishing educational games in 2020. Of the thirteen available games, only one was designed for use within a school context for teenagers and children. The other games are targeting either adult end users, college students and corporate employees [8].

Existing user studies on anti-phishing games show an increase in the detection rate of phishing URLs after playing, however, some types of phishing URLs have higher detection rates than others [3–5]. Canova et al. [4] state that the detection rate of phishing URLs decreases over time and a content repetition is needed on a regular basis. The correct identification of benign URLs increases after playing [4] and test persons also reported increased confidence in their answers. While these results have been reported in studies with adults, so far, there have been no evaluations of anti-phishing games with children and teenagers. This indicates a need for the development and evaluation of educational games with the before mentioned target group.

3 Phishing Academy

Phishing Academy is a digital educational game designed to teach students the structure of a website URL and how to detect phishing based on website URLs (further on referred to as URLs). As a foundation, digital storytelling is used, which introduces the detective character *Detective Dot* as a mentor in the fictional city of *Tech City*. The players are already "employed" as detectives in *Tech City* themselves and are supposed to complete further training to become phishing detectives. Within Phishing Academy, players complete a thematic introduction and a training center consisting of six levels. Each level consists of three steps: *knowledge motivation, knowledge transfer* and *knowledge verification*. The next level can only be played once the knowledge verification step of the previous level has been successfully completed. While the first two levels address the construction of a URL, the other four levels cover possible types of URL-based phishing attacks. To ensure that a scheme of the three steps per level does not become tedious, five different interaction features were implemented. For example, searching for hidden information on different parts of a URL through a magnifying glass. Other interactions are given through drag and drop of URL-parts or an emulated browser interface for displaying screenshots of websites in different tabs together with a benign or phishing URL. For the game's evaluation, an identification process as well as tracking of the performed in-game actions using *Experience API* (xAPI) was implemented. For further details on the educational game Phishing Academy, we refer to [9].

4 Evaluation

Since no user studies on anti-phishing educational games have been conducted with children and teenagers so far, a user study with Phishing Academy was conducted to compare the results with previous studies, which had exclusively older participants.

4.1 Research Design

In analogy to existing studies with other target groups, the user study was implemented as a within-subject design consisting of pretest, posttest, and retest[1]. Since a realistic scenario for Phishing Academy is the use in school lessons, the user study was tailored to a realistic school context. To minimize potential space and equipment constraints, only computer science courses between grades 6 to 9 were recruited. Considering students in grade 9 allowed for a larger sample size and test use of the game beyond its immediate target group.

4.2 Materials

For the user study, we developed an introductory presentation, three tests (pre-, post- and retest) and two questionnaires. The introductory presentation was used to clarify the terms "URL", "address bar" and "phishing". Furthermore, various examples of phishing were used to motivate everyday relevance. Pre-, post- and retest were integrated into the game to avoid switching between multiple applications. In all three tests, students were asked to judge URLs as to whether they lead to a phishing website or not. For each URL the original target was displayed to ensure that it was possible to make a classification based on the own knowledge, even for providers or brands that students were not familiar with. Subsequently, the students were each asked to indicate how confident they were regarding their own answer (from $1 =$ "very unconfident" to $5 =$ "very confident"). The pretest contained 24 URLs (base set), of which 12 were benign URLs and 12 were phishing URLs based on six predetermined categories. Each phishing category was covered by two URLs each. In the posttest and retest, the base set was expanded by six benign URLs and six phishing URLs each (one per category), leaving 36 URLs to be assessed in the posttest and 48 URLs[2] in the retest.

The first questionnaire included questions about the gaming experience, age and text appropriateness. The second questionnaire included questions about remembered content and about one's own behavior since playing Phishing Academy.

4.3 Procedure

The user study in each course consisted of two evaluation appointments at least four weeks apart. Due to pandemic-related restrictions and possible school closures during the study execution, the process was designed in such a way that a remote or hybrid execution of the evaluation appointments was also possible. The first appointment consisted of the following seven phases: (1) welcome, (2) thematic introduction, (3) pretest, (4) playing Phishing Academy, (5) posttest, (6) filling out the first questionnaire and (7) farewell. The introductory presentation was used for the thematic introduction. The second appointment consisted of five phases: (1) welcome, (2) retest explanations, (3) retest, (4) fill out second questionnaire, (5) farewell and thanks.

---

[1] Short for *Retention Test* to determine long-term effects after a specified period.

[2] All 48 URLs as well as the synthesis and categorization of the URLs can be found in [9].

4.4 Participants

Six courses participated in the user study. From the game data, 112 students were identified, distributed among one ninth-grade course, two eighth-grade courses, and three sixth-grade courses. In two sixth-grade courses both evaluation appointments were conducted remotely via a video conferencing software; in the other courses, the first evaluation appointment was conducted face-to-face and the second was conducted remotely. For the analysis of the gaming experience, 85 data sets could be used (grade 6: 30, grade 8: 37, grade 9: 18). For the examinations of the students' performance in pretest, posttest and retest, 55 of the 85 previously used data sets could still be used (stage 6: 12, stage 8: 28, stage 9: 15). All other data sets were incomplete[3].

Hypotheses
Before evaluating the data, we derived a set of hypotheses based on previous studies to be investigated regarding the recruited courses. The hypotheses relate to the students' performance in comparison to previous research results as well as the qualitative evaluation of the game.

- **H1**: Students perform better on average on the posttest and no worse on the retest.
- **H2**: Students identify more phishing URLs in the post- and retest than in the pretest.
- **H3**: Students reject on average more than half of the benign URLs in the pretest.
- **H4**: Students reject on average fewer benign URLs in the post- and retest than in the pretest.
- **H5**: Students report higher median confidence in their own response in the post- and retest than in the pretest.
- **H6**: URLs of different phishing types have different detection rates.
- **H7**: Grade 6 students rate the game overall, entertainment value, and age appropriateness better than grade 8 and 9 students.
- **H8**: Grade 8 and 9 students rate the amount as well as difficulty of the texts in the educational game as more appropriate than grade 6 students.

5 Results

Based on our hypotheses, we analyzed the collected data and applied various statistical tests with significance level of $\alpha = .05$. If no ordinal scaled data or a significant rejection of the normal distribution assumption was available for test groups with less than 30 records, parametric test procedures (t-tests) were used, otherwise nonparametric (Wilcoxon signed rank test). The following scores represent absolute values. The standard deviation (SD) is given as the measure of dispersion. For the statistical comparisons of students' performance, only the 24 URLs of the base set have been used below. A response was considered correct if a phishing URL was identified as phishing and a benign URL was identified as benign.

Regarding hypothesis **H1**, overall students performed better in the posttest ($M = 15.87$, $SD = 3.24$) and retest ($M = 16.40$, $SD = 3.45$) than in the pretest ($M = 14.55$,

---

[3] For a detailed breakdown and reasons for incompleteness consider [9].

48   S. Schoebel et al.

$SD = 2.55$). A one-tailed paired t-test regarding better performance in the posttest (pre < post) was significant ($t(54) = -3.28$, $p < .001$) with small effect (Cohen's $d = 0.44$) and with no deviation from normality (Shapiro-Wilk: $p = .135$). Another one-tailed paired t-test regarding better performance in the retest (post < re) without deviation from normality (Shapiro-Wilk: $p = .277$), however, was not significant ($t(54) = -1.43$, $p < .079$). Thus, **H1** can be partially accepted (see Fig. 1).

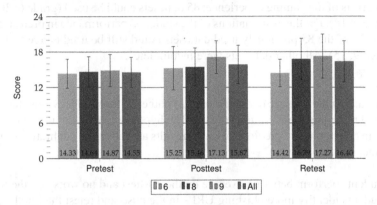

Fig. 1. Score on the base set for each test and grade. Error bars: SD.

For the analysis of hypotheses **H2**, **H3** and **H4**, the results were subdivided (see Fig. 2). Students identified more phishing URLs in the posttest ($M = 9.85$, $SD = 1.66$) and retest ($M = 8.65$, $SD = 2.05$) than in the pretest ($M = 8.15$, $SD = 1.99$). A one-tailed paired t-test (Shapiro-Wilk: $p = .058$) for the posttest compared to the pretest (pre < post) was significant ($t(54) = -6.07$, $p < .001$) with large effect (Cohen's $d = 0.82$). For the comparison between pretest and retest (pre < re), the normal distribution assumption was rejected (Shapiro-Wilk: $p = .045$) and therefore a Wilcoxon signed-rank test was performed, which was not significant ($W = 477.00$, $p = .126$). Hence, **H2** can only be partially accepted.

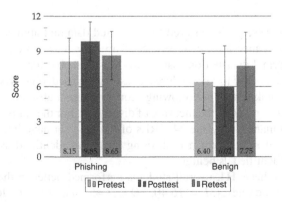

Fig. 2. Scores on the base set for phishing and benign URLs across all grades. Error Bars: SD.

H3 is not accepted due to the average score in the pretest ($M = 6.40$, $SD = 2.41$) (see Fig. 2). In the posttest, the score initially decreased ($M = 6.02$, $SD = 3.44$) and increased sharply for the retest ($M = 7.75$, $SD = 2.87$). Therefore, **H4** can only be accepted for the retest. The high standard deviations for benign URLs compared to phishing URLs are striking, suggesting a more heterogeneous performance field for benign URLs.

For **H5**, the median was determined for each student across the indicated confidence for the base set URLs (see Fig. 3). In all three tests, the value 4.0 or "rather confident" combines in median the highest number of students (Pre: 30, Post: 28, Re: 27). From the pretest to the posttest, a shift towards higher confidence was visible. Thus, from pretest to posttest, 17 times a higher confidence, 33 times a constant confidence, and 4 times a lower median confidence was indicated. From post- to retest, 7 students indicated a higher confidence, 36 indicated a consistent confidence, and 12 indicated a lower confidence. Comparing pre- and retest, a shift toward higher confidence is evident. Overall, 14 times a higher confidence, 34 times a constant confidence, and 7 times a lower confidence was indicated. Conclusively, **H5** is accepted.

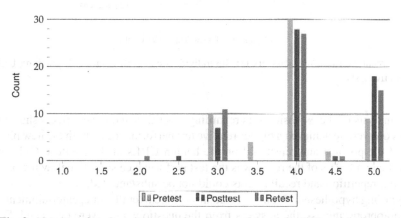

Fig. 3. Number of students in terms of median confidence for URLs of the base set.

Regarding hypothesis **H6**, the phishing URLs of the base set and the associated extension sets were evaluated together, so that 12 phishing URLs were included in the results in the pretest, 18 in the posttest, and 24 in the retest. Differences were found between the categories[4]. In the pretest, the percentage of correct answers in the first, second and sixth categories were significantly lower than in the other categories (see Fig. 4). In the posttest, the percentage increased in all categories, but also decreased again in the retest, except for the third and fifth categories. Noticeably, the use of a trustworthy

---

[4] The following phishing URLs have been used in the base set. [...] mark shortened parts. Subdomain: https://spotify.securelogin.com/de/login?account?m=2&i=1[...]. Word appendix: https://accounts.nintendo-login.com/mygames. IP address: https://173.31.166.156/de/login. Path: https://secure-store.com/www.apple.com/de/shop/account/[...]. Similar characters/combinations: https://yovtvbe.com/account/?userid=jlgkiSOIjXTbYnZAeL?m=2&i=2. Typos/Swaps: https://account.mircosoft.com/common/oauth2/authorize?client_id=4345[...].

word appendix (e.g. "-login") initially recorded a strong increase in correct answers from pre- to posttest, but also a strong decrease from post- to retest. Furthermore, students performed worse in the sixth category (typos and letter swapping) in the retest than in the pretest. **H6** is accepted based on these results.

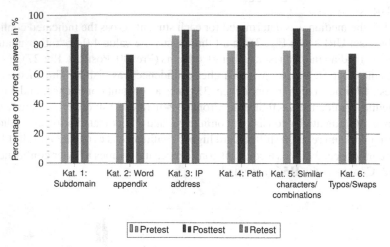

Fig. 4. Percentage of correct answers for the individual categories across all phishing ULRs of the respective tests.

An analysis of the extension sets regarding repetition and recall effects showed that students on average achieved a higher relative test performance on both the new phishing URLs of the posttest and retest and on the benign URLs of the posttest. Only on the six new benign URLs of the retest was the test performance slightly below the base set. Therefore, repetition and recall effects could not be substantiated.

Regarding hypothesis **H7**, on the evaluation of the overall game, entertainment value and age appropriateness, the answers from the questionnaires were evaluated. For the overall evaluation and entertainment value, school grades were used as evaluation measure. Grade 6 students rated the educational game overall with an average of 1.83, grade 8 students with 1.97, and grade 9 students with 1.50. Students rated the entertainment value similarly with 2.30 (grade 6), 2.43 (grade 8), and 2.33 (grade 9). Age appropriateness was surveyed through an open-ended question. Responses resulted in three categories "Yes", "Okay/Partial" and "No". In grade 6 27 (90%) responses were classified as "Yes", 2 (7%) were classified as "Okay/Partial", and 1 (3%) as "No". In grade 8 24 (65%) responses were classified as "Yes", 5 (14%) were classified as "Okay/Partial", and 6 (22%) "No". Of the grade 9 responses, 9 (50%) responses were classified as "Yes", 5 (28%) were classified as "Okay/Partial", and 4 (22%) "No". Based on the results, **H7** is accepted for age appropriateness only, since grade 9 students rated the educational game better overall than grade 6 students, and for entertainment value, the average scores showed only 0.13 as maximum difference.

The evaluation of the amount of text and the text difficulty with regard to hypothesis **H8** was conducted as a closed-ended question. A total of 38 (45%) students felt that the amount of text was too much (grade 6: 18 resp. 60%, grade 8: 14 resp. 38%, grade 9: 6

resp. 33%). Forty-seven (55%) of the students rated the amount of text as adequate (grade 6: 12 resp. 40%, grade 8: 23 resp. 62%, grade 9: 12 resp. 67%). The response option "Too little" was not given once. A similar trend for text difficulty. Thus, 50 (59%) of the students rated the texts as mostly easy (grade 6: 14 resp. 47%, grade 8: 23 resp. 62%, grade 9: 13 resp. 72%). Neither too easy nor too difficult was perceived by 30 (35%) students (grade 6: 12 resp. 40%, grade 8: 14 resp. 38%, grade 9: 4 resp. 22%). Finally, 5 (6%) students rated the text as mostly difficult (grade 6: 4 resp. 13%, grade 8: 0 resp. 0%, grade 9: 1 resp. 6%). **H8** is therefore accepted.

6 Discussion

Based on the statistical analysis of the collected data, the previously formulated hypotheses were examined. Overall, hypotheses **H5**, **H6** and **H8** were accepted. Hypotheses **H1**, **H2**, **H4** and **H7** were only partially accepted and hypothesis **H3** was rejected.

The presented results should first be discussed with regard to the participants of the study. Ninth grade performance and responses indicate that Phishing Academy can be used in grades with students above the actual targeted age group of ten to thirteen. For students in eighth grade and above, it also showed trouble-free use in a school context. In relation to the sixth grade, only a few data sets had to be sorted out here. For the sixth grade, further research is needed to determine what reasons led to an incomplete data set. It should be noted that the hybrid study execution required fewer grade six students to be screened out, suggesting less problematic use in face-to-face sessions for younger students. Playing remotely does appear to be problematic with sixth grade students. It is unclear to what extent the problems would also have looked like in grade 8 and 9 during a similar remote-only study execution. Besides that, the data described for grade 6 suggest an increase in performance.

Next, we discuss performance development in the context of the study and with reference to related work. Previous findings on performance development by Canova et al. [4] and Kunz et al. [5] could be confirmed for the phishing URLs. Thus, after playing the educational game, phishing URL detection increased (**H2**) and different categories showed different detection rates (**H6**). The observation that performance decreases after a fixed period could also be demonstrated for phishing URLs (**H2**). For benign URLs, the observed results contradict previous research. Several reasons for the decrease of the average score in the posttest are conceivable (**H3/H4**). First, individual information about the phishing types may have been misleading and led to overgeneralization. For example, three benign URLs with a subdomain other than "www" decreased from pretest to posttest. At the same time the recognition rate of another benign URL with an alternative subdomain increased. Furthermore, the benign URLs of the base set contained six URLs with a lower character count ($M = 39.17$) and six with a higher character count ($M = 79.67$). The length of the benign URLs per se does not appear to play a predominant role in the performance drop. Even though, it should be noted, that longer URLs tend to have a significantly lower average recognition rate in both, pre- and posttest. Since other studies have not yet looked at this aspect, further research is needed to determine why longer benign URLs are more often classified as phishing. Furthermore, it cannot be resolved as to why there was an increase in the score on benign URLs in the retest. Eventually students memorized at least single URLs after the first evaluation appointment due to a higher engagement with URLs and the use of everyday providers for the synthesis of the URLs.

In addition to the performance development, the results of Canova et al. [4] on confidence in one's own answer (H5) could be confirmed. It should be emphasized that the average score in the retest continues to increase, but the confidence initially decreases again. Concrete reasons for this cannot be identified on the basis of previous studies. This would require a case-by-case analysis of the students. One possible factor here could be the time that has passed between posttest and retest. Thus, the correctness of answers remained unconsciously at a mostly constant level, but the knowledge was less present than in the posttest, which led to a decreasing indication of confidence.

With reference to the defined target group in the development of Phishing Academy, it should be noted that an age-appropriate educational game was developed, and that the implementation appeals to the target group (**H7**). Furthermore, it is positive to note that Phishing Academy only suffers slight to moderate losses in terms of age appropriateness for students who are just below or above the age limit of the target group. In terms of entertainment value, a weighed and realistic assessment seems to have been made by the students. Since it is an educational game, the entertainment potential was correspondingly lower compared to other game genres (e.g., action games), which is also reflected in the grading. The answers to the amount of text and the text difficulty represent an expected result (**H8**). Since students in grade 6 predominantly assess the amount of text as too much and the text difficulty in some cases as too high, this is an area that should be addressed in the future. In higher grades, on the other hand, students are generally used to longer texts, which is visibly reflected in the evaluation.

Finally, several limitations of the user study need to be discussed. During the face-to-face appointments, students could be observed throughout, and no further research or collaboration among students regarding the tests was observed. In contrast, no monitoring was possible during the remote appointments. Accordingly, students were instructed not to use any further sources, but the use of aids or further research cannot be ruled out. Furthermore, the addressing of the topic of phishing was known to the students after the thematic introduction, which could have led to an increased attention to individual URLs that did not correspond to the real situation. This could also have led to increased rejection of benign URLs due to greater skepticism and caution.

7   Conclusion and Outlook

The evaluation suggests that Phishing Academy is an effective anti-phishing educational game for children and teenagers between the ages of ten and thirteen and even beyond. In a study conducted in the school context, the detection of phishing URLs was significantly increased. The grading of the educational game overall as well as the entertainment value indicate an acceptance of the game by targeted children and teenagers. Using the game in face-to-face classes is preferable for younger students, while for older children and teenagers the use in hybrid learning contexts appears unproblematic. The results indicate that sensitization to threats such as phishing is possible as soon as children and teenagers start using digital devices. In order for the knowledge about phishing to remain present, regular repetitions are necessary.

The focus of previous evaluations has been on student performance data. Besides that, since all interactions within the educational game are stored, further evaluations of concrete game progress and game situations are possible in the future. This offers the possibility for further analyses e.g. regarding a comparison of the performance and the individual processing of the training center. Furthermore, it can be specifically investigated whether individual game elements lead to problems. Initial studies on playing time suggest that the predicted playing time of the training center is realistic for the age group. With regard to a repeating use of the educational game, further concepts have to be developed. For example, at the beginning of a replay, there could be a test with personalized URLs, and based on the results, there would be a replay of the phishing types that were recognized worse in the test. For students without a need for repetition, advanced content on phishing should be provided. For the results that cannot be fully resolved (shorter vs. longer benign URLs, increased rejection of benign URLs, increase in judgment performance for the benign URLs in the retest), we suggest to explore qualitative evaluation approaches. This would allow a more comprehensive examination of the decision-making process of individual students.

References

1. Anti-Phishing Working Group: Phishing Activity Trends Report 3rd Quarter (2020). https://docs.apwg.org/reports/apwg_trends_report_q3_2020.pdf. Accessed 27 June 2021
2. Federal Trade Commission: How To Recognize and Avoid Phishing Scams. https://www.consumer.ftc.gov/articles/how-recognize-and-avoid-phishing-scams. Accessed 01 July 2021
3. Sheng, S., et al.: Anti-phishing Phil: the design and evaluation of a game that teaches people not to fall for Phish. In: Proceedings of the 3rd Symposium on Usable Privacy and Security, SOUPS 2007, pp. 88–99, Pittsburgh (2007)
4. Canova, G., et al.: NoPhish app evaluation: lab and retention study. In: Proceedings 2015 Workshop on Usable Security, Internet Society, San Diego (2015)
5. Kunz, A., et al.: NoPhish: evaluation of a web application that teaches people being aware of phishing attacks. In: Mayr, H., Pinzger, M. (eds.) INFORMATIK 2016, LNI, pp. 1–13. Gesellschaft für Informatik, Klagenfurt (2016)
6. Roepke, R., et al.: Mit der Lupe unterwegs. In Pinkwart, N., Konert, J., (eds.): Die 17. Fachtagung Bildungstechnologien, LNI, pp. 315–316. Gesellschaft für Informatik, Bonn (2019)
7. Schöbel, S.: Phishing Academy: Entwicklung und Umsetzung eines digitalen Lernspiels zu Website-URLs und Phishing. Bachelor-Thesis, Aachen (2019)
8. Roepke, R., Koehler, K., Drury, V., Schroeder, U., Wolf, M.R., Meyer, U.: A pond full of phishing games - analysis of learning games for anti-phishing education. In: Hatzivasilis, G., Ioannidis, S. (eds.) MSTEC 2020. LNCS, vol. 12512, pp. 41–60. Springer, Cham (2020). https://doi.org/10.1007/978-3-030-62433-0_3
9. Schöbel, S.: Erweiterung und Evaluation des digitalen Lernspiels Phishing Academy. Master-Thesis, Aachen (2021)

Serious Games to Improve Literacy

Can a Serious Game Be Designed to Increase Engagement in a Mandatory Postmodern Novella at Danish Gymnasiums?

Mads Strømberg Petersen, Gustav Søgaard Jakobsen, Daniel Bredgaard Hendriksen, Niklas Lee Skjold Hansen, and Thomas Bjørner$^{(\boxtimes)}$ (iD)

Department of Architecture, Design and Media Technology, Aalborg University, Copenhagen, Denmark
tbj@create.aau.dk

Abstract. For this study, we designed a serious game to engage Danish gymnasium students when reading the novella *A Love Story*, written by the prize-winning Danish author Naja Marie Aidt. The novella is mandatory reading in postmodernism. The study included 41 students from two Danish gymnasiums, who were divided into three classes. Two classes were included in the experimental study, which employed the serious game as part of reading the novella. One class served as the control group and engaged only in an analog reading of the novella. The evaluation criteria, which were assessed through a questionnaire, were based on items from the reading engagement index, the user engagement scale, and the narrative engagement scale. Furthermore, the evaluation consisted of in-depth interviews with teachers and students. The findings revealed a positive effect on students' engagement in the experimental group and the possibility for future work in the field of serious games implemented in high school curricula. The serious game developed for this study balanced challenge and skills appropriately, but it could be improved in terms of the story world and controls.

Keywords: Reading engagement · Serious games · Storytelling · Game design

1 Introduction

This study was aimed at supplementing a mandatory analogue reading of a novella in two Danish gymnasium (i.e., upper secondary) classes with a digital serious game. The novella was *A Love Story*, written by the Danish poet and writer Naja Marie Aidt, who won the Nordic Council's 2008 literature prize. *A Love Story* is taken from Aidt's novella collection *The Watermark*, published in 1993. Aidt's published work is part of the curriculum in Danish literature, as outlined in the learning objectives regarding mandatory readings in the style of postmodernism.

There is an international concern about reading engagement among young adults [1]. In Denmark, only 8.4% of Danish 15 year old students have a high level of reading, and 16% of Danish teens, aged 15, are reading at a very low level [1]. Furthermore, male students struggle more with reading engagement compared to female students [1, 2].

© Springer Nature Switzerland AG 2021
F. de Rosa et al. (Eds.): GALA 2021, LNCS 13134, pp. 57–67, 2021.
https://doi.org/10.1007/978-3-030-92182-8_6

This lack of reading engagement may partly explain why male students in particular lag behind compared to female students in Danish gymnasiums, a fact that poses challenges for male students in terms of later educational opportunities and access to the labor market [2]. In Danish gymnasiums, the average grade difference is 0.5 points (based on 7-point grading scale) in favor of female students [3]. However, in the subject Danish, female students' grades are 1.4 points higher on average [3].

Over the past few decades, young adults have changed their habits, reading less fiction, but spending more time reading online than before [4–6]. In Denmark, 20% of young adults do not read fiction [7], which is equivalent to other international reporting [1, 8]. On average, across OECD countries, 37% of young adults (students) report that they do not read for enjoyment at all [1]. Reading has always been encouraged through complex and diverse practices [5–9]. However, there is a huge concern that young adults do not read well enough to cope with the increasing literacy demands of an information society [5–9]. Reading fiction among young adults appears to be positively associated with higher performance on reading assessments [1]. Reading is a skill with many graduations of proficiency, and comes with lots of complexity, and it is not an easy task for young adults to read the mandatory literature in the Gymnasium. The research question for this study was: Can a serious game be designed to increase reading engagement in Naja Marie Aidt's novella *A Love Story* as part of the mandatory reading in Danish literature at Danish gymnasiums.

2 Previous Research

Reading engagement is multidimensional and used from various perspectives in various fields; it is also complex, with many variables, including e.g. behavioral and cognitive dimensions, the frequency of reading, emotional engagement, genre preferences, gender preferences, and the storytelling [10–14]. One way to motivate reading engagement is to include a text-based story in a serious game via digital storytelling [10, 11, 16, 19]. This opens an interactive story world, including both text and game, with the potential to engage a user in the digital storytelling experience and make them focus on the story itself instead of the text or gameplay alone. Digital storytelling is well covered and discussed within serious gaming [23–27]. However, digital storytelling is much more than telling a story in a digital format. In a serious game, it is mainly about making stories engaging and interactive, with meaningful skills and knowledge for the users.

Storytelling and reading engagement, both in serious games and in other media (analogue included), requires the reader to be motivated [15]. This involves, e.g., important elements within the text's content, comprehending the text, gaining new knowledge, and social interactions with used knowledge and/or lessons learned from the text [15]. Furthermore, to design a motivating reading experience in a serious game, scholars have already emphasized aspects of intrinsic motivation, such as curiosity, a desire for challenge, and involvement [15, 16]. However, the success of a serious game for reading engagement depends on players' motivation to start playing the game and spend their time, effort, and energy. Hence, players' intention to interact with the game for specific learning (reading) objectives is crucial [16]. It is assumed that the experiences of intrinsic motivation, flow, and engagement are crucial in this process [16–19]. In spite that O'Brien and Toms [20] define engagement as an ongoing process with quality of user experience, and provide an evaluation framework [22], it is still highly complex to define and integrate engagement in serious games. The challenge is that engagement, also in the context of serious games, is a complex subject, as it encompasses various related concepts related to the user experience, including e.g. immersion, presence, flow, transportation, and absorption [12, 17, 20–22]. Most often the engagement in serious gaming is a means to provide some kind of learning [18], and elements of game attention, perceived usability, aesthetic appeal, and worthwhile playing [10, 11, 20–22].

3   Methods

3.1   Participants and Ethical Issues

The participants were from two Danish gymnasiums in three separate classes, two from ZBC Vordingborg and one class from Ørestad Gymnasium. ZBC Vordingborg is a technical gymnasium located in the Danish region of Zealand, south from Copenhagen. The ZBC Gymnasium has a focus on technical skills and science subjects. One class from the ZBC Gymnasium functioned as a control group for the evaluation, provided with the same reading text and evaluation criteria, but without playing the game (only analogue novella read). The control group consisted of a class with 11 students (7 male and 4 female), and had math as their major. The other class (experimental group) from ZBC had game design as their major and consisted of 10 students (9 males and 1 female). Ørestad Gymnasium is located in Copenhagen, Denmark, and has a special profile focusing on media, communications and culture. The class from Ørestad Gymnasium consisted of 21 students (11 male and 10 female), and had science as their major.

All participants gave informed consent and were informed that they could withdraw from the study at any time and their participation did not influence their grade. In addition, all participants were provided with anonymized ID numbers, and all data were labeled with these IDs. We applied special considerations when recruiting teenagers (ages 17–19), in accordance with Danish data law, the international code of conduct and ethical approval from the gymnasium.

3.2   Procedure

An important focus of this study was to involve the teachers from both Ørestad Gymnasium and ZBC Vordingborg who taught the students about *A Love Story*. This was done by following a participatory design approach [30] in which the end-users included both teachers and students; also within a substantial work of pilot testing. The pilot testing was made with five students outside the experimental- and control group. The teachers served as gatekeepers who facilitated and controlled the reading process in areas such as the curriculum's aims, focus, knowledge, skills, and analysis. Therefore, the teachers were involved as co-designers very early in the process.

This study used a mixed method approach consisting of both a questionnaire and interviews. The questionnaire started with items regarding gender and experience of gaming. Participants were then asked three questions from the Reading Engagement Index [9], followed by items from the User Engagement Scale - short form [22], and lastly items from the narrative engagement scale [31]. The interviews follow a semi structured interview guide; and six students and two teachers were interviewed. One class from the ZBC Gymnasium and the class from Ørestad Gymnasium follow the experimental procedure as outlined in Fig. 1.

Fig. 1. The procedure for the experimental group. Combined analogue read and serious game.

The control group included in this study was from a class at the ZBC Vordingborg gymnasium, following the procedure as outlined in Fig. 2.

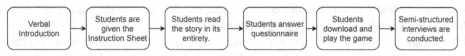

Fig. 2. The procedure for the control group. Analogue reading only.

3.3 Data Analysis

A total engagement score was calculated based on items and procedures from the narrative engagement [31] and the user engagement [22]. The interviews were analyzed by traditional coding [28] following four steps: organizing, recognizing, coding, and interpretation. The interviews were transcribed verbatim to be organized and prepared for data analysis. Researchers then coded and labelled the data in categories/subcategories, followed by content analysis and interpretation [28].

4 Design and Implementation

The serious game was designed in Unity using C# for Windows, Mac and Linux. The novella *A Love Story* is about the protagonist Louisa, who lives alone in a very messy apartment. Louisa has schizophrenia with symptoms including hallucinations (hearing voices), delusions, and disorganized thinking. It is a first person simulation game, as the player should experience the narrative from the protagonist's point of view and be engaged in the story in the 3D environment. The story and the game are as follows: 1. Introduction (analogue text book read): The reader is introduced to Louisa, her life and her messy apartment. Louisa goes shopping. 2. Door chains, bathroom, and apartment (Game start): Louisa locks the door with five chains after the shopping and goes into a clawfoot tub with very hot water. 3. Her Ex-boyfriend, income support, and fruit flies: Louisa recalls her time as a squatter with her ex-boyfriend (named Ole). Louisa gets a letter with her income support from municipal social security. She can hear the fruit flies talking. 4. Louisa recalls when a bumblebee entered the apartment and terrified her so that she had to hide in the bathroom. Since then, she has not let in fresh air (End of the game). 5. End (analogue text): The neighbor is asking about bug problems in the entire building. The next day the police and social authorities use force for having Louisa hospitalized (implicitly told).

In order to improve the engagement we reproduced the plot of the novel (story Sects. 2, 3 and 4) in an interactive and empathizing way. The design was developed by following the game principle for player enjoyment in games, suggested by Sweetser and Wyeth [29].

Players need to complete five tasks, in a specific order, in order to progress and finalize the story and the game. The first task (lock the door with five chains) is at the very start of the game (Fig. 3, left). The graphical user interface is designed with a "quest log" in the upper right corner of the screen, containing information about the specific task the player needs to complete, and how many out of the five tasks the player has completed (Fig. 3, left). The visual representation of the WASD controls is also shown in the graphical user interface (GUI) when the player starts the game (Fig. 3, left). The readings in the game were implemented through interactive and digital storytelling elements - for example as letters dropped through the letter slot or included as a diary (Fig. 3, right).

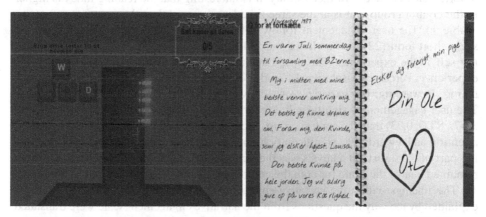

Fig. 3. The beginning of the game (left) with tasks, and the in-game text reading (right).

It was not an easy task to design and tell the story of Louisa and her schizophrenia, including the symptoms such as hallunications and voices. Therefore, we designed the game by mixing scenes between the clean and the messy (Fig. 4) to illustrate the schizophrenic perspective.

Fig. 4. Mixed perspectives of clean and messy to illustrate the schizophrenia perspective.

5   Findings

The quantitative findings reveals that the experimental groups had a significantly higher user engagement score than the control group (Table 1). Interestingly, there was a lower score than expected, for the experimental group in the narrative engagement. The items for the reading index (Table 1) included the following questions: I read often, I get easily distracted while reading, and I am good at reading. In spite that these self-reported answers needs further validity, it is interesting that the reading index is higher in the control group, but is at the same time less engaged than the experimental group (Table 1). The user engagement followed the validated items from user engagement scale short form [22], and included the following questions: Focused Attention: I lost my self in the experience. The time I spent just slipped away. I was absorbed in the experience. Perceived Usability: I found it confusing to play the game. The game was taxing. Rewarding: My experience was rewarding. I felt interested in this experience. The user engagement is significantly higher (Table 1) in the experimental group (Mean 3.47., STD: 0,93) than the control group (Mean 2.96/ STD: 0.67). Especially the focused attention and rewarding is significantly higher for the experimental groups. An interesting part of the statistical analysis was the items within the narrative engagement, which remained almost the same for both the control group and the experimental group (Table 1). The findings within the narrative engagement remains a bit unclear, but might be explained by the way the questions from the narrative engagement scale were translated into Danish. Possible explanations could also be within common desires to know how the story is going to unfold [17] (digital or not), with common curiosity, suspense, excitement, and involvement in the story and character [15, 23]. It is a well-told novella with some embedded emotions (both positive and negative) for Louisa and her schizophrenia. The included masturbation descriptions in the analogue story might also have an impact for the narrative engagement, especially taken the participants' ages into account.

Interviews revealed that most participants were very satisfied with the game. Most of the positive comments concerned reading engagement, but they also positively addressed the story world, and the match between challenge and skills (Table 2). No participants

Table 1. Findings based on questionnaire items. Con = control group (n = 11). Exp = Experimental group (n = 31).

	Con mean	Con STD	Exp mean	Exp STD	Mean Diff	STD Diff
Reading index	3.27	1.23	2.78	1.11	0.49	0.12
Narrative engagement	3.45	0.67	3.37	1.10	0.08	0.43
User engagement	2.96	0.67	3.47	0.93	0.51	0.26
Focused attention	2.91		3.55		0.64	
Perceived usability	3.18		3.50		0.32	
Rewarding	2.78		3.37		0.59	

Table 2. Accumulated number of coded interview statements with positive and negative aspects of the game. Based on six student interviews.

	Positive	Negative
Challenge/Skills	20: It was absorbing. The quests were good, and should not be more difficult. I like it is simple. The quests match the format	6: It could have been much more difficult. It was too easy to complete the quests. More complicated quests
Reading engagement	30: I liked the letters. I can actually recall what I read. More reading like this. It made me understand the story much better. Great supplement to the book read. Would like to continue the reading. Would for sure recommend this game as supplement to in-class readings. It makes the reading much more exciting	3: I could not really bear reading it. The reading was not paying much attention before the end of the game. Did not feel like reading the text in the game
The story world	10. Awesome. Pretty and fun. Realistic and creative. I was positively surprised. I got a shock with the bee, well done	6: Larger play area. A bit too scary for me. The in-game story should be longer. The bee was a bit strange
Controls	4: No problems of controls, it was perfect. Very straightforward and well known. I had control	7: The mouse was too sensitive. Shift and space did not respond as expected

expressed hindrance in progressing in the game, and only a few (especially the more experienced gamers) felt that the in-game quests should be more challenging. All participants expressed their excitement about the game experience, and several stated that it exceeded their expectations. Many participants expressed that they paid more attention to the details of the story when experiencing it through the game rather than the analog text reading. The most frequent critical comments concerned the controls; these included minor bugs and complaints that the mouse was too sensitive. The content analysis and interview examples are from the four categories extracted below in Table 2. It is interesting that, within the story world, some participants found the game too scary, but also realistic and creative.

6 Discussion and Conclusion

In this study, we implemented the novella *A Love Story* in Danish classes at a Danish gymnasium using a transmedia storytelling approach by supplementing the analog text reading with readings and storytelling delivered via a serious game. The results revealed a significantly higher user engagement (Mean 3.47., STD: 0,93) for the students in the experimental groups, reading parts of the novella by playing the game, than the control group not playing the game as part of the reading (Mean 2.96/STD: 0.67). Further, in the interviews, all participants stated that they could see the potential benefits of supplementing analog text reading with a serious game to improve reading engagement. However, some participants suggested that the reading elements, rather than the completion of specific quests, should receive more attention in the game. Both this study and previous research [10–12, 19] identified positive effects of serious games used to supplement and improve reading engagement, but this approach also faces some barriers. The main barrier is uncertainty regarding how to develop a successful serious game that engages students and fulfills specific learning objectives in a curriculum. These objectives need to be very clear from the beginning during the research design and game design processes. It is vital to know what the game is intended to achieve and specifically how it can supplement the text reading. It is also crucial to involve the teachers in the design process. Although we followed the methods of the participatory design approach [30], it was difficult to include the teachers at the applied level of improved matching between the text and game. The problem could be that we, as game researchers and designers, did not explain the foundation, framework, opportunities, and game design limitations clearly enough.

The story in the game was well told, and the learning outcome was achieved through increased engagement. However, future work is needed to create significant evidence of and insight into regarding students' reading engagement via transmedia storytelling. First, researchers need to include a much larger number of students from classes across various gymnasiums during the data collection process. Second, they need to collect additional identifying details about the readers, including their reading confidence levels. Third, there is a need for longitudinal studies that include well-defined data obtained through repeated measurements over time. Fourth, there is also a need for improved study designs that include comparable experimental and control groups. One of the strengths of this experimental study was its included experimental and control groups. However, in practice, it was difficult to match classes in terms of level and curriculum progression. In this study, the control group consisted of a class of math majors, which could constitute a potential bias in our research design, as the students from the experimental groups were game design and media communication majors. However, narrative engagement was similar between the experimental and control groups, and the reading index was higher in the control group. In the literature [18, 19, 32, 33], there are various examples of how to evaluate serious games. However, when performing evaluations in very specific contexts with real users, it can be difficult to conduct a perfect research evaluation. Logistics, time constraints, gatekeepers, legislation, lack of a proper posttest, technical issues, and resources can be barriers that prevent perfect evaluations. In addition, randomization is often impractical for evaluating serious game in a fieldwork context. It could also be unethical to randomize students in the same class, with some playing the game, and some not; this should also be avoided because of the potential learning effects.

There is no agreed taxonomy for reading engagement, and the inclusion of serious games is still both diverse in its outcomes and understudied as a transmedia subject for inclusion in gymnasiums. Future studies should be focused on designing various game options to accommodate diverse students and reader types.

References

1. OECD: PISA 2018 Results Volume III: What School Life Means for Students' Lives, PISA, OECD Publishing, Paris (2019). https://doi.org/10.1787/acd78851-en
2. Hamilton, P.L., Jones, L.: Illuminating the 'boy problem' from children's and teachers' perspectives: a pilot study. Education **44**(3), 241–254 (2016)
3. Statistics Denmark: Karaktergennemsnittet stiger for alle grupper af studenter [grade differences for all groups of students. https://www.dst.dk/da/. Accessed 21 May 2021
4. Baron, N.S.: Words Onscreen: The Fate of Reading in an Online World. Oxford University Press, Oxford (2015)
5. Ross, R.S., McKechnie, L., Rothbauer, P.M.: Reading Still Matters: What The Research Reveals About Reading, Libraries, and Community. Libraries Unlimited, Santa Barbara (2018)
6. Twenge, J.M., Martin, G.N., Spitzberg, B.H.: Trends in US Adolescents' media use, 1976–2016: the rise of digital media, the decline of TV, and the (near) demise of print. Psychol. Pop. Media Cult. **8**(4), 329–345 (2019)
7. Book and literature panel Annual Report: Bogen og litteraturens vilkår 2018 [The book and litteratur 2018]. SLKS, Agency for Culture and Palaces (2018)
8. Holloway, S.M., Gouthro, P.A.: Using a multiliteracies approach to foster critical and creative pedagogies for adult learners. J. Adult Contin. Educ. **26**(2), 203–220 (2020)
9. Wigfield, A., et al.: Role of reading engagement in mediating effects of reading comprehension instruction on reading outcomes. Psychol. Sch. **45**(5), 432–445 (2008)
10. Pasalic, A., Andersen, N.H., Carlsen, C.S., Karlsson, E.Å., Berthold, M., Bjørner, T.: How to increase boys' engagement in reading mandatory poems in the gymnasium: homer's "The Odyssey" as transmedia storytelling with the cyclopeia narrative as a computer game. In: Guidi, B., Ricci, L., Calafate, C., Gaggi, O., Marquez-Barja, J. (eds.) GOODTECHS 2017. LNICSSITE, vol. 233, pp. 216–225. Springer, Cham (2018). https://doi.org/10.1007/978-3-319-76111-4_22
11. Lauritsen, T.K., Ali, D.K., Jensen, N.F., Alamillo, I.U., Bjørner, T.: How to engage young adults in reading H. C. Andersen's fairy tale the little mermaid, through a serious game. In: Marfisi-Schottman, I., Bellotti, F., Hamon, L., Klemke, R. (eds.) GALA 2020. LNCS, vol. 12517, pp. 294–303. Springer, Cham (2020). https://doi.org/10.1007/978-3-030-63464-3_28
12. Rueda, R., O'Neil, H.F., Son, E.: The role of motivation, affect, and engagement in simulation/game environments: a proposed model. In: Using Games and Simulations for Teaching and Assessment, pp. 230–253. Routledge (2016)

13. Barber, A.T., et al.: Direct and indirect effects of executive functions, reading engagement, and higher order strategic processes in the reading comprehension of dual language learners and English monolinguals. Contemp. Educ. Psychol. **61**, 101848 (2020)
14. Brozo, W.G., Shiel, G., Topping, K.: Engagement in reading: lessons learned from three PISA countries. J. Adoles. Adult Liter. **51**(4), 304–315 (2007)
15. Guthrie, J.T., Wigfield, A., You, W.: Instructional contexts for engagement and achievement in reading. In: Christenson, S.L., Reschly, A.L., Wylie, C. (eds.) Handbook of Research on Student Engagement, pp. 601–634. Springer US, Boston, MA (2012). https://doi.org/10.1007/978-1-4614-2018-7_29
16. De Jans, S., Hudders, L., Herrewijn, L., Van Geit, K., Cauberghe, V.: Serious games going beyond the Call of Duty: Impact of an advertising literacy mini-game platform on adolescents' motivational outcomes through user experiences and learning outcomes. Cyberpsychol. J. Psychosoc. Res. Cybersp. **13**(2), 3 (2019). https://doi.org/10.5817/CP2019-2-3
17. Schønau-Fog, H., Bjørner, T.: "Sure, I would like to continue" a method for mapping the experience of engagement in video games. Bull. Sci. Technol. Soc. **32**(5), 405–412 (2012)
18. Wouters, P., Nimwegen, C., Oostendorp, H., der Spek, E.D.: A meta-analysis of the cognitive and motivational effects of serious games. J. Educ. Psychol. **105**, 249–265 (2013)
19. Jabbar, A.I., Felicia, P.: Gameplay engagement and learning in game-based learning: a systematic review. Rev. Educ. Res. **85**(4), 740–779 (2015)
20. O'Brien, H.L., Toms, E.G.: What is user engagement? A conceptual framework for defining user engagement with technology. J. Am. Soc. Inf. Sci. Technol. **59**(6), 938–955 (2008)
21. Csikszentmihalyi, M.: Finding Flow: The Psychology of Engagement with Everyday Life. Basic Books, New York (1997)
22. O'Brien, H.L., Cairns, P., Hall, M.: A practical approach to measuring user engagement with the refined user engagement scale (UES) and new UES short form. Int. J. Hum. Comput. Stud. **112**, 28–39 (2018)
23. Miller, C.H.: Digital Storytelling: A Creator's Guide to Interactive Entertainment, 4th edn. CRC Press, Boca Raton (2019)
24. De Vecchi, N., Kenny, A., Dickson-Swift, V., Kidd, S.: How digital storytelling is used in mental health: a scoping review. Int. J. Mental Health Nursing **25**(3), 183–193 (2016)
25. Vivitsou, M.: Digital storytelling in teaching and research. In: Tatnall, A., Multisilta, J. (eds.) Encyclopedia of Education and Information Technologies, pp. 1–15. Springer, Heidelberg (2018). https://doi.org/10.13140/RG.2.2.12404.86407
26. Yu, Z.: A meta-analysis of use of serious games in education over a decade. Int. J. Comput. Games Technol. **2019**, 1–8 (2019). https://doi.org/10.1155/2019/4797032
27. Báldy, I.D., Hansen, N., Bjørner, T.: An engaging serious game aiming at awareness of therapy skills associated with social anxiety disorder. Mob. Netw. App. **2021**, 1–12 (2021). https://doi.org/10.1007/s11036-021-01743-3
28. Bjørner, T.: Data analysis and findings. In: Bjørner, T. (ed.) Qualitative Methods for Consumer Research: The Value of the Qualitative Approach in Theory and Practice. Hans Reitzel: Copenhagen (2015). https://hansreitzel.dk/products/qualitative-methods-for-consumer-research-bog-36789-9788741258539
29. Sweetser, P., Wyeth, P.: GameFlow: a model for evaluating player enjoyment in games. Comput. Entertainment **3**(3), 14–27 (2005)
30. Halskov, K., Hansen, N.B.: The diversity of participatory design research practice at PDC 2002–2012. Int. J. Hum. Comput. Stud. **74**, 81–92 (2015)
31. Busselle, R., Bilandzic, H.: Measuring narrative engagement. Media Psychol. **12**(4), 321–347 (2009)

32. Boyle, E.A., et al.: An update to the systematic literature review of empirical evidence of the impacts and outcomes of computer games and serious games. Comput. Educ. **94**, 178–192 (2016)
33. Pérez-Colado, I.J., Pérez-Colado, V.M., Martínez-Ortiz, I., Freire, M., Fernández-Manjón, B.: A scalable architecture for one-stop evaluation of serious games. In: Marfisi-Schottman, I., Bellotti, F., Hamon, L., Klemke, R. (eds.) GALA 2020. LNCS, vol. 12517, pp. 69–78. Springer, Cham (2020). https://doi.org/10.1007/978-3-030-63464-3_7

Der Blonde Eckbert - A Serious Game Interpretation of the Eponymous Romantic Fairy Tale

Kevin Körner(✉) and Anna Katharina Turba

Digital Humanities, University of Tübingen, 72074 Tübingen, Germany
kevin.koerner@uni-tuebingen.de,
anna-katharina.turba@student.uni-tuebingen.de
https://uni-tuebingen.de/en/106265

Abstract. Literature-based sciences deal with plenty of great stories. As a combination of traditional knowledge transfer methods in the humanities and newer technologies associated with the digital humanities, serious games can be a great way to motivate a younger audience to deal with such heritage assets. In this paper we present our contribution to this: A serious game interpretation of Ludwig Tiecks *Der blonde Eckbert* (English: Fair-Headed Eckbert.). After a summary of the story and its literary relevance we introduce our concept of the game based around audiovisual storytelling with a runner game and provide an overview about included didactic elements. We discuss our strategy on how to keep players intrinsic motivation high to achieve a longer playtime and thereby better knowledge consolidation. Finally, we present several generalized code components which arose during development. These components - such as an audiovisual cutscene and an endless runner template - provide the opportunity to develop similar serious games without requiring coding skills.

Keywords: Serious games · Digital humanities · Digital literary

1 Introduction

A common task of the humanities is the preparation of cultural heritage and heritage assets in such way that their intellectual value is preserved for future generations. The so called *digital humanities* emerged by the digital transformation in the humanist research professions, providing new approaches for archiving, researching, publication and teaching. In this process digital storytelling emerged as mediation format in the literary studies, often enhanced by audio and visual elements[1]. These provide especially text-based professions with the possibility to create modern interpretations of historically relevant literature which convey their stories on different cognitive layers. Moreover, to satisfy a

---

[1] We'll use therefor the phrase *audiovisual novel* in the following.

© Springer Nature Switzerland AG 2021
F. de Rosa et al. (Eds.): GALA 2021, LNCS 13134, pp. 68–77, 2021.
https://doi.org/10.1007/978-3-030-92182-8_7

younger audience, audiovisual novels can be enhanced to serious games by adding gamified interactive elements.

In this area we implemented a serious game called *Der blonde Eckbert*[2] based on the same titled romantic tale written by Ludwig Tieck [1][3]. Our implementation tells the underlying historic text enhanced as audiovisual novel. Its gaming part is realized as runner game that is connected to important story parts. For didactic purposes, the application conveys literary interpretations of the fairy tale on different levels. Furthermore, after finishing the story once an achievement system retains players long-term motivation.

Fortunately, implementing *Der blonde Eckbert* resulted in several reusable components that can be used for similar projects in future; e.g. an audiovisual novel component, a runner game template and a modular achievement system. All components were built in the Godot engine[4] and have been published open source[5] under MIT Licence.

In this paper, we present the main ideas of our interpretation of *Der blonde Eckbert*. Initially, we present research that inspired our serious game concept, give a short overview of the story and discuss its relevance from literary perspective. Subsequently we present our serious game approach by giving an introduction in our storytelling, gameplay and the didactic elements. Based on this we discuss concepts that were added providing knowledge consolidation. Finally, we describe reusable technical components and provide a further outlook.

2   Related Work

Our serious game concept was inspired by the assumptions which we present in the following section.

According to Jones [2], (serious) games research was excluded in the humanities for several decades. Besides his assumption, it is *"because they [games] possess a stigma as mass entertainments"*, he presents possible topics that are of interest for humanistic research and how the humanities might gain of (serious) games. As he states: *"Because games [...] combine computing with modes of cultural expression associated with the humanities – storytelling, design, aesthetics, social communication – they would seem to be of obvious interest to the digital humanities."* Hergenrader [3] also presents connections between games and the humanities, and additionally proposes the use of (serious) games as persuasive and educational tools. Thinking further about his statement *"A digitally literate person is one who can thoughtfully use text, image, sound and interactive elements [...] to create a purposeful experience for a specific audience."*, then (serious) games are the next logical step in imparting knowledge in the humanities.

---

[2] English: Fair-Headed Eckbert.

[3] The game can be accessed at https://uni-tuebingen.de/en/213265, last access 30. 06.2021.

[4] https://godotengine.org/, last access 30.06.2021.

[5] The repository is accessible under https://gitlab.com/kkoerner/dh-templates.

Mortara et al. [4] also share this assessment and provide an overview on serious games made for teaching cultural heritage. The authors present serious games developed in the digital humanities, their educational objectives, and provide an analysis of relations between game genres, application contexts[6], technological solutions and finally learning effectiveness. They conclude two main factors as key for serious game effectiveness: "an appealing and meaningful environment and a suited and intuitive interaction paradigm."

Manero et al. [5] present their narration-based game concept for *La Dama Boba*[7], a game aiming to motivate students toward classic theater. In their publication the authors present their concept, a quantitative study, and conclude their discussion stating "*the performance of the game is directly related to whether the game genre is included or not among the player's gaming preferences.*"

3 Background Story

Ludwig Tieck's *Der blonde Eckbert*, first published in 1797, is a groundbreaking work for early German Romanticism. It is labeled as a "Kunstmärchen", an artificial fairy tale, that combines elements of a novella and a traditional fairy tale. As such, it centers on the knight Eckbert and his wife Bertha. The protagonists are stalked by a miraculous old woman, which finally drives Eckbert insane. Rabenstein discusses in [6], how Tieck mixes up the literary genres to separate fairy tale and realistic elements, only to combine them again. As a result, the further the recipients read, the more it becomes uncertain, what is real and what is fiction. This uncertainty led to a variety of interpretations - some in a fantastic-layered others in a more realistic-psychological reading. However, no approach is free of contradictions.

This goes to show, that *Der blonde Eckbert* is not interested in a singular, correct interpretation, but a variety of different, equally important readings existing simultaneously. As Rabenstein mentions, Tieck creates this multitudinousness using the poetics of the miraculous, which allows him to switch between elements that create and dismantle fiction. That way *Der blonde Eckbert* addresses uncertainty, subjectivity, confusion and the unease, that the story triggers within the recipients, as well as the deconstruction of the belief in a singular, correct interpretation. According to Rabenstein the entanglement in both content and design in Tieck's arabesque hence result in a literary-creative chaos. Thus, due to the narrative unreliability, Eckberts madness virtually crosses over to the recipient.

4 Our Serious Game Approach

4.1 Storytelling

For the game we subdivided the origin text of *Der blonde Eckbert* into five main chapters as illustrated in Fig. 1. Each chapter ends with the current protagonist

---

[6] Where is the application used; e.g. as part of an exhibition, within an curriculum.

[7] Eng.: The Foolish Lady.

fleeing, what we use as crossover to a runner game level. Furthermore, the story can be divided into a part where Bertha explains her story, a part where Eckberts story is told and a finale in which everything previously believable is questioned.

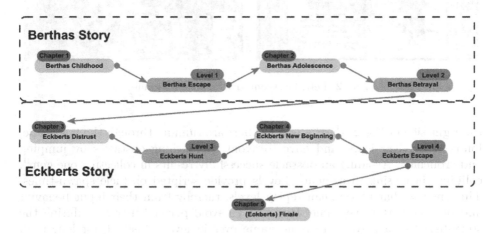

Fig. 1. Storyline of *Der Blonde Eckbert*

Each chapter is narrated in an individual audiovisual novel (see an example in left side of Fig. 2) we call *cutscene*. A cutscene presents a minor modified version of the origin text placed on an aquarelle painting, which visualizes the current story. Moreover, background music accompanies the current mood; e.g. a melancholic sound for sad parts and a more hectic melody during an escape. One of our main goals of the cutscenes has been to slow down its speed so the player has time to experience all textual, audio and visual aspects connected to the story. Therefore, the text becomes visible character by character. A fading system for texts and paintings, as well as a sound that emulates rustling paper, emphasize turning book pages.

4.2 The Runner Game

The runner game is inspired by the Google Chrome T-Rex-Runner [7][8]. The main story includes four individually scripted levels whose scenery depends on the previous chapter. Moreover, an endless-runner gets available to the players after finishing the last chapter. To keep the game elements in style with the novel parts, all elements are also (animated) aquarelle paintings.

Gameplay. The main theme for the runner game is the protagonists fleeing corresponding to the ending of each chapter. An exemplary scenery is shown on

---

[8] You can access the game by using the Google Chrome Browser, entering "chrome://dino" in the browsers adress bar.

 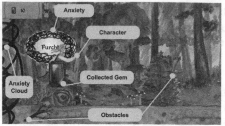

Fig. 2. Left: Cutscene, Right: Runner game

the right side of Fig. 2. Bertha and Eckbert are running through the landscape, followed by their fears, and have to avoid approaching obstacles by jumping and crouching. Avoiding an obstacle successfully results in collecting one gem[9], colliding in loosing three gems. Levels provide scripted obstacle spawn-times. This ensures that players can replay levels, thereby train their input behavior and become better over time. However, to avoid player frustration during the story-based gameplay, there is no game over in levels. Instead, for long-term motivation, we chose to show a small statistics page at the end of each level, that illustrates how well the player performed.

Scenery. The fleeing character runs in front of a parallax background presenting the player spatial depth. Depending on the story, the backgrounds layers may fade. This way players get the feeling of changing locations; e.g. level one is starting in a forest, passing through hills and ending in the mountains.

Obstacles appear on the right side of the screen and move toward the player. For simplicity we focused on four main obstacles: Stones, branches, buzzards and crows. The former two must be passed jumping, the latter ones need to be passed crouching.

For didactic purposes the scenery contains the so called *anxiety cloud* (see right side of Fig. 2). It follows the player frequently nearer or further away. Inside the cloud so called *anxieties* are spawned and rise from the ground above the player and move to the right side of the screen. Their use is described in the upcoming section.

4.3   Didactic Elements

The main goal of the game is to get the players into the story of *Der blonde Eckbert* and provide layers of interpretation. Obviously the cutscenes are the base element of the knowledge transfer since they present the story to the players. To connect cutscenes and levels each level provides a short introduction. This summarizes the main reasons which led to the escape wish of the protagonist in the previous cutscene.

---

[9] These gems are an important story element.

The *anxiety cloud* is used for illustrating important narrative elements such as the characters main fears and indicators for narrative unreliability that showed up in the story. Its movement - sometimes the cloud is nearer and sometimes it is further away from the character - visualizes that these elements are always there but not all the time omnipresent. These *anxieties* always rise above the characters and move ahead of them - symbolizing they'll be upcoming again in the future.

During the progressing story another main theme - Eckberts rising madness - slowly becomes discernible. We hide this motif from players at the beginning using the customized cutscene and level selection menu shown in Fig. 3. The first six buttons are illustrated as an icon showing a main component of the connected cutscene or level. The last three ones are hidden at first. Once the player finishes the third level, the menu is extended by a maelstrom representing Eckberts mental state. After the player finishes the final cutscene, the maelstrom is also extended by an illustration showing Eckbert walking right into it. Moreover, during the *cutscenes* some illustrations subliminally indicate Eckberts mental state: The miraculous old woman's face is blurred at all times and appropriate text sections feature overlapping background images which give the feeling that something is uncertain. This shall present players with the main question of the story: Was it real or was it all just Eckberts madness?

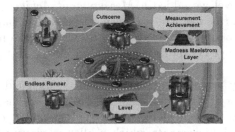

Fig. 3. Level selection

4.4 Long-Term Motivation

Playing through the main story takes around 30 min. Since we want to keep players interested in playing a longer time for knowledge consolidation we implemented two additional game components: An achievement system containing 24 individual achievements and an endless runner extension[10].

The endless runner uses the same gameplay and scenery as the runner game presented in Sect. 4.2. However there is a major modification: The first time the randomly chosen character collides with an obstacle it counts as game over. Also instead of scripted obstacle spawning, it features a randomized one containing

---

[10] External testers required approx. 2 h to unlock all achievements.

increasing difficulty with passing time by faster obstacles and more obstacle spawns. Consolidation of knowledge is achieved in that all anxieties of the levels are added randomly to the anxiety cloud each run. This way, the story elements found to be important are brought back to the players mind.

IDs	Challenge
1 - 4	Level completion
5 - 7	Gem collection
8 - 10	Obstacle avoiding
11 - 13	Playtime
14 - 16	Endless runner enduring
17 + 18	Completionist-based
19 + 20	Story-based
21 - 24	Miscellaneous

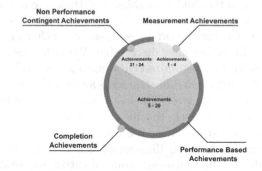

Fig. 4. Left: Challenges, Right: Challenge classification using Blairs system [8]

We implemented 24 achievements to challenge players. They were classified using the classification system of Lucas Blair [8] as illustrated on the right side of Fig. 4. For each level we added a *Measurement Achievement* (achievements 1–4): Since levels can't be lost, the achievement challenges players to collide with as few obstacles as possible during their run. As feedback on their performance players receive an image containing one, two, or three (best performance) gems (see Fig. 3).

The other twenty achievements (5–24) can be assigned to the *Completion Achievements* category. Their challenge descriptions are listed at the left side of Fig. 4. Going even more in detail using Blairs system, challenges 5–20 are *Performance Based Achievements* which challenge players to perform well in the game. Their challenges range from experiencing the story, collecting gems towards surviving an amount of time in the endless runner. Finally, challenges 21–24 can be classified as *Non-Performance Contingent Achievements*. Their challenges are mainly funny yet not difficult at all. They range from clicking on a link, forced obstacle-collision up to a cross-reference to a well-known video game. All *Completion Achievements* provide a positive feedback phrasing as well as a comic-like illustration to increase player self-efficacy; e.g. receiving the achievement *Olympian* for enduring 120 s in the endless runner without collision.

Based on the difficulty recommendations Blair postulated also in [8], we subdivided our *Completion Achievements* into three degrees of difficulty as illustrated in Fig. 5. Achievements located in the *Entry-Level Tasks* layer are easily unlocked during the initial playthrough. Their goal is to satisfy even inexperienced players by unlocking achievements and generate intrinsic motivation to unlock other achievements. Achievements located in the *Keep Going Tasks* layer need more effort to be unlocked: Players require the approx. timely effort of a second playthrough to unlock these. However, players might also use the endless runner to fulfill the required tasks. Achievements located in the *Challenging Tasks* layer require the most effort. They're designed a way that players require approx. two playthroughs and several rounds of the endless runner to receive their reward. To ensure that players understand their task to unlock achievements in the *Increasing Challenge Tasks* area, they are designed in such way that they build on one another. E.g. there are three achievements for collecting gems: *Merchant* for collecting 200 gems, *Lord* for collecting 350 gems and *King* for collecting 500 gems. All *Non-Performance Contingent Achievements* placed in the *Non Challenging Tasks* layer can be achieved anytime to let players explore the game additionally to the story.

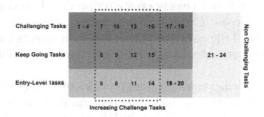

Fig. 5. Achievement challenge layers

5   Reusability and Adaptability

We implemented *Der blonde Eckbert* using the Godot-Engine (See Footnote 4) in version 3.2 and gdscript as programming language. Based on the approach presented in Sect. 4, we developed the core components of the game as Godot *scenes*. Since the discussion of the whole architecture would go beyond the scope of this paper, in the following we only present the main benefit - from an artist's or developer's perspective - of our implementation.

All implemented code has been published under MIT Licence on (See Footnote 5). Somebody planning a new game may reuse the following components, configuring all required information in the Godot inspector without requiring coding skills.

Storytelling is the main technique for knowledge transfer within our project. Out *Cutscene* implementation is designed in a way required texts, their screen positions, background images and audio files can be configured. Furthermore, it includes a typewriter effect, image fading and sound fading to achieve smooth story transition. Thus, artists can - with little technical effort - create audiovisual novels.

For scenery purposes we implemented Godot scenes for a *moving background*, a *fading background*, and a *parallax background*. These serve as reusable backgrounds for 2D games such as platformers. The first one is used as an infinite looping image. Artists may configure its speed, direction and reset point to achieve a seamless infinite background. The *fading background* provides two *moving background* layers of which only one is active at the same time. Moreover, artists can configure a set of background images, including their display duration, speed, direction, and positioning data. This way, over time multiple moving backgrounds will be shown and faded into another. Lastly, the *parallax background* provides multiple individually configurable *fading background* instances in one scene. Artists can thereby design multiple background layers, configure these in a way that the 'nearest' is the fastest, whereas the 'farthest' is the slowest, resulting in a parallax effect.

Our implementation of the endless runner is also reusable. For example, it contains implementations for the playable character, scripted and randomized obstacle spawn, an intro component, and asynchronous own-threaded scene loading. This allows developers to easily create scripted and randomized 2D runner games such as the *Google Chrome T-Rex Runner*. However, to provide more adaptability we created the entire code that way components interact mainly via Godot signaling to ensure interchangeability and used extendable state machines wherever possible.

The implemented achievement system provides twelve achievements that runner games can use immediately, including configurable challenges for playtime, dodging, object-collection and time-survival. However, since other projects might require individual achievements, we designed the architecture in a modular way: New achievements can be implemented in their own Godot scenes and then be hooked into the main achievement scene. This allows projects to use the achievement system, although coding is required to implement new achievements.

6   Future Outlook

We used the initial edition of *Der blonde Eckbert* for our texts, that's been written in German language. Therefore, the game is also in German language for now. Currently we are preparing the translation made by Thomas Carlyle (see [9]) as an English text base. Once this process is finished we're going to implement an internationalization component for the game providing an English version as well.

The acceptance and teaching success has not been thoroughly tested yet. During the project we discussed it with several researchers working in text-based sciences, used individual game testers and received quick-response feedback on what was good and bad. However, to get more reliable results we plan on creating an exemplary curriculum based around the game and for that a quantitative evaluation. Its main goals will be to identify user acceptance and how well the didactic elements perform in practice.

7   Conclusion

Our project *Der blonde Eckbert* is a great example for showing how the digital humanities can use serious games for creating modern interpretations of historically relevant literature. Players experience the eponymous literary heritage asset written by Ludwig Tieck in multiple cognitive layers instead of only reading a 19th century text. The included didactic elements convey the base aspects of the story which are used by the multiple existing layers of interpretation. Also the presented long-term motivation approach increases the players intrinsic motivation to deal with the story and thereby results in knowledge consolidation. Furthermore, using a dedicated curriculum build around our game, we assume this intrinsic motivation can be transferred on the discourse with additional existing literature and interpretations.

We contribute several reusable components licensed under MIT license to the community targeting especially researchers and artists that are not familiar with programming. These can be used as a base for creating new serious games and audiovisual novels and thereby extend the amount of available educational games in the (digital) humanities.

References

1. Thiek, L.: Der blonde Eckbert, Catalogue of the German National Library. http://d-nb.info/gnd/4132902-8. Accessed 30 June 2021
2. Jones, S.E.: New media and modeling: games and the digital humanities. In: Schreibman, S., Siemens, R., Unsworth, J. (eds.) A New Companion to Digital Humanities (2015). https://doi.org/10.1002/9781118680605.ch6
3. Hergenrader, T.: The place of videogames in the digital humanities. On Horiz. 24(1), 29–33. https://doi.org/10.1108/OTH-08-2015-0050
4. Mortara, M., Catalano, C.E., Bellotti, F., Fiucci, G., Houry-Panchetti, M., Petridis, P.: Learning cultural heritage by serious games. J. Cult. Herit. 15(3), 318–325 (2014). https://doi.org/10.1016/j.culher.2013.04.004. ISSN: 1296-2074
5. Manero, B., Torrente, J., Serrano, Á., Fernández-Manjón, B.: Are serious games working as expected? In: Chen, G., Kumar, V., Kinshuk, Huang, R., Kong, S.C. (eds.) Emerging Issues in Smart Learning. LNET, pp. 89–96. Springer, Heidelberg (2015). https://doi.org/10.1007/978-3-662-44188-6_12
6. Rabenstein, S.: Ludwig Tiecks Der blonde Eckbert: Eine individualpsychologisch-analytische Deutung des "Wahnsinnsmärchens". In: Zeitschrift für freie psychoanalytische Forschung und Individualpsychologie (2016). https://doi.org/10.15136/2016.3.2.58-80
7. Interview with Chrome Dino Developers: As the Chrome dino runs, we caught up with the Googlers who built it. Google Chrome Official Blog. https://www.blog.google/products/chrome/chrome-dino/. Accessed 15 June 2021
8. Blair, L.: The cake is not a lie: how to design effective achievements. In: GamaSutra - The Art Business of Making Games. https://www.gamasutra.com/view/feature/6360/the_cake_is_not_a_lie_how_to_.php?print=1. Accessed 30 June 2021
9. Carlyle, T.: The fair-headed Eckbert. In: German Romance in Two Volumes - Volume I: Musaeus, De La Motte Fouque, Tieck. Boston Dana Estes Company. https://archive.org/details/germanromance01carl. Accessed 30 June 2021

Using a Multi-step Research Approach to Inform the Development of a Graph Literacy Game

Kristian Kiili[1]([⊠]) [iD], Antero Lindstedt[1] [iD], Manuel Ninaus[2] [iD], and Tua Nylén[3] [iD]

[1] Faculty of Education and Culture, Tampere University, Tampere, Finland
`{kristian.kiili,antero.lindstedt}@tuni.fi`
[2] Department of Psychology, University of Innsbruck, Innsbruck, Austria
`Manuel.Ninaus@uibk.ac.at`
[3] Department of Geosciences and Geography, University of Helsinki, Helsinki, Finland
`tua.nylen@helsinki.fi`

Abstract. Critical reading - the ability to critically evaluate information - has become a crucial skill in our modern information society and the rise of fake news. Games might be able to help to address this rather new field of education. Therefore, we first conducted a literature analysis on the use of games that aim at supporting critical reading and media literacy. We found that most of the used games improved participants' critical reading skills, were mostly targeted at adults, and the games focused on written information and fake news, but omitted graph literacy. Next, we ran an empirical study to investigate adolescents' competencies in critically reading and interpreting graphs. In a storified setting, adolescents acted as fact checkers and were supposed to interpret graphs and identify misleading graphs. Our results revealed that adolescents struggled in both the identification of misleading graphs as well as the interpretation of graphs. Consequently, based on our literature review and empirical results, we developed a game to support graph reading. The design of the game is presented.

Keywords: Game-based learning · Graph literacy · Misleading graphs · Critical reading

1 Introduction

One of the main challenges of our times is the wide spread of misinformation and disinformation on the Internet [1]. The exposure to false information, in conjunction with poor critical reading skills, may endanger citizens' possibilities to form evidence-informed decisions on important issues. Recently, we have witnessed an example of the global spread of COVID-19-related misinformation that can have important consequences for how a disease ultimately affects the population [2]. Take a moment to imagine how the information flow around the pandemic might appear to young readers. The statements of experts, laypersons, and eminent leaders may provide conflicting information. Further, the conflicting information is shared in different social media channels. Who should I trust? What should I believe? What do the graphs illustrating the spread of the disease

© Springer Nature Switzerland AG 2021
F. de Rosa et al. (Eds.): GALA 2021, LNCS 13134, pp. 78–88, 2021.
https://doi.org/10.1007/978-3-030-92182-8_8

and the death curves around the globe mean? The central question here is whether our education system has prepared all students with sufficient critical reading skills to help them analyze, evaluate, and interpret the conflicting and misleading information they encounter. Previous research suggests that this is probably not the case [3–5], and there are worrying signs of the polarization of critical reading skills [3, 6]. Thus, there is a need to produce learning materials that support the development of critical reading skills, particularly among those individuals who struggle most.

This paper focuses on graph literacy. Graph literacy refers to the ability to read and understand graphs [7]. Graphs are used to display numerical data in graphical format and they present information in a two-dimensional space. Successful graph reading requires three competences, or going through three steps, which have been defined as 1) reading the data, 2) reading between the data and 3) reading beyond the data [8]. In short, the step of reading the data refers to the ability to extract data by visually inspecting the elements drawn in the graph, the step of reading between the data refers to the ability to infer the mathematical relationship between the variables of the graph, and the step of reading beyond the data refers to the ability to make a numerical forecast based on the graph's underlying trend [8].

Ciccione and Dehaene [8] have pointed out that although graphs have become ubiquitous in our life, the scientific investigation of graph reading is in its early phase. Thus, it is not surprising that studies that focus on critical reading of misleading graphs are rare. The concept of a misleading graph, refers to a graph that is based on valid data, but the appearance of the graph has been manipulated to distort the message of the graph. Emerging research in this field has shown that individuals with low graph literacy tend to neglect information in the axes labels and scales of graphs, and tend to rely more on spatial-to-conceptual mappings grounded in their real-world experience [9]. For example, individuals may assume that higher bars mean higher values also in graphs where the y-scale is reversed. Thus, spatial features that conflict with general conventions can be used to mislead graph readers. This is a common trend for example in social media. Unfortunately, graph literacy research has almost solely focused on reading well-formed graphs and very little is known about adolescents' abilities to evaluate and interpret misleading graphs.

We start bridging this gap and begin to characterize, in some detail, the perception of misleading graphs among adolescents, and we will utilize this knowledge to develop a game that aims to support critical reading of graphs. In order to be able to design a graph reading game for adolescents we first conducted a literature review to explore to what extent games have been used to support critical reading skills, particularly critical reading of graphs. Second, we conducted an experimental study to evaluate students' abilities to both identify and interpret misleading graphs. These research activities provided us a starting point to design the Chart Trace game. Before describing the details of Chart Trace, we report the results of the literature review and the graph reading study.

2 Previous Research on Critical Reading Games

With our literature review we aimed at identifying the current state-of-the-art of learning games to support critical reading, with the following search query on Scopus (scopus.com): **TITLE-ABS-KEY** [("epistemic games" OR "mobile games" OR gamification

OR gamified OR "game-based" OR "game based" OR "serious game" OR "learning game" OR "educational game" OR "video game" OR "board game" OR dgbl OR gbl OR "educational video game" OR "educational video game" OR "video game" OR "educational simulation" OR "learning simulation") *AND* ("fake news" OR "disinformation" OR "misinformation" OR "trustworthiness" OR "credibility" OR "misleading" OR "news literacy" OR "media literacy" OR "news literacies" OR "media literacies" OR "media education")] and searched for original research articles that were published in English. The search returned altogether 234 papers from which we identified only 10 papers (see Table 1) that fit our inclusion criteria. Our criteria were 1) that the game described by the paper was targeted for training critical reading and 2) that the paper provided empirical results.

Table 1. Summary of reviewed papers

Ref.	Approach	Game	Digital	Sample	Result
[12]	Learn to identify fake news by generating fake news	FakeYou	Yes	Adults	N/A
[13]	Finding logical fallacies in arguments; foster critical thinking	Global digital citizens (gamified)	Yes	Adults	+
[14]	Learn to identify fake news (information verification skills)	MAthE the game	Yes	Adults	+
[15]	Development of news literacy games; learning by participatory game design	Fakeopoly; the lying geese	No	Children	+
[16]	Learn to identify fake news by generating fake news	Bad News	Yes	Adults	+
[17]	Learn to identify fake news (information verification skills)	UNISON	No	Adults	+
[18]	Learn to identify fake news by generating fake news (Bad News); identify fake news (Fakefinder)	Bad news; fakefinder	Yes	Adults	+ -
[19]	Learn to identify fake news by generating fake news	Fake news game	Yes	Adults	+
[20]	Learn to identify fake news	Bad news	Yes	Adults	+ -
[21]	Learn to identify fake news	Trustme!	Yes	Adults	+

Most of the 10 papers had been published within the last three years. This already shows two things: (i) there is a recent increasing research interest into this rather young field of research due to its increasing relevance in our information society [cf. 10] and (ii) compared to other - more traditional - learning domains (e.g. STEM) the use of games is still rare [cf. 11] within this field of study. The latter, however, might be a result of the former: given the general efficacy of game-based learning, it seems likely that more critical reading games will be developed in the future.

Most of the games identified through the literature search emulated fake news and/or social media posts (90% of papers). Most games approached critical reading by either letting participants analyse blog posts, social media posts, or other online material (i.e. players acted as fake news detectors; 50%) or spread them or generate new ones (participants acted as fake news spreaders/generators; 40%). Further, the majority of studies reported positive outcomes related to critical reading skills after playing the game (70%). For instance, [16] showed that participants who had been practicing by playing Bad News (participants had the role of a fake news producer) rated real fake news significantly less reliable than a control group of participants who had been playing Tetris instead. All games primarily utilized written information, which was sometimes accompanied by photographs or images. None of the games or studies specifically addressed graphs or graph reading. Moreover, with the exception of one study [15], only adults participated in the respective studies. Therefore, we could not identify any clear guidelines on how to map graph reading onto game mechanics and how to take the characteristics of our target group into account in a graph reading game.

3 Graph Reading Study

3.1 Method

Participants
Thirty-six students from 3 classes participated in the study. The participants were 7th-9th graders (mean age = 14.6 years, SD = 0.96 years; 15 boys, 16 girls, 5 did not report their gender). The permission to conduct the study was received from the school principal and the teachers. Caretakers of the students were informed about the study. Students who did not provide consent to use their data as well as students without caretakers permission were excluded from the analyses.

Materials and Procedure
Two different types of graph literacy tasks were constructed: tasks of evaluating the misleadingness of graphs and tasks of interpreting information in the graphs. Half of the used graphs were line graphs and half were bar graphs. Each graph contained eight data points, a title, and the corresponding labels for both axes. All graphs presented quantitative information of phenomena familiar from the geography school subject (e.g. population growth, annual rainfall). In order to decrease the influence of geographical topic knowledge on the outcome, certain labels and titles were masked (e.g. title: countries and areas were replaced with general terms such as "one area" or "one country"; data labels: countries and areas were replaced with alphabets starting from A.).

Evaluation Tasks: 32 evaluation tasks were included in the study. Half of the graphs were well-formed and half contained spatial conflicts designed to mislead the readers.

Four types of spatial conflicts were used: 1) the y-axis did not start from zero, 2) the range of the y-axis was too large, 3) the x-axis was reversed and 4) the x-axis was uneven (for example the years shown on the x-axis did not increase or decrease linearly). Figure 1 shows an example of a misleading bar graph in which the y-axis does not start from zero. In evaluation tasks, participants were asked to respond to the following statement on a 6-point response scale (1 completely disagree – 6 completely agree): "The graph is misleading". In order to simulate fast reading behavior on the Internet, students had only 20 s to respond to each task.

Interpretation Tasks: All four graphs included in the interpretation part were designed to mislead students. The interpretation tasks measured students' ability to read between the data: students had to find relationships in the data represented by the graphs including spatial conflicts. For example, they had to examine differences in bar heights and the trends illustrated by line graphs (Fig. 2). Interpretations were measured using a multiple-choice item for each graph. The choices included (i) the correct choice; (ii) an incorrect choice aligned with the spatial manipulation (i.e. designed to be an obvious choice if the reader does not pay attention to y- or x-axis scales and labels); and (iii) two other incorrect choices. Students could score one point for each task. Interpretation tasks did not have a time limit.

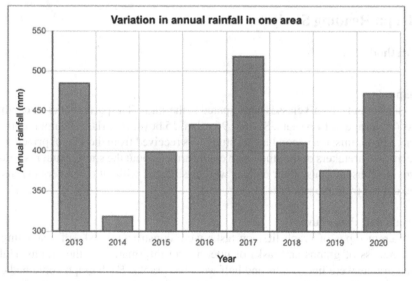

Fig. 1. Example of an evaluation task: the y-axis of the graph does not start from zero

Procedure: The study was conducted in a web-based environment during regular school hours and a teacher administered the activities. First, students filled in the demographics questionnaire. The rest of the activities were storified. The used story was inspired by the results of the literature review (i.e. act as fake news detectors). Accordingly, in the beginning students were informed that they will act as fact checker trainees in a media

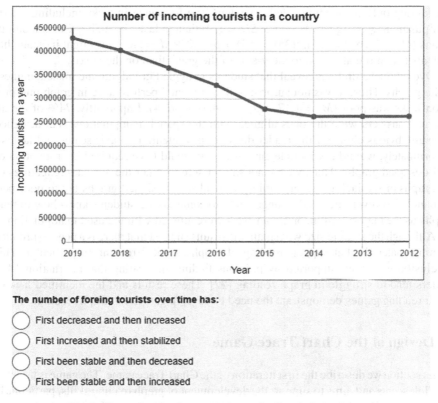

Fig. 2. Example of an interpretation task: the x-axis is reversed

company and their task is to ensure that misleading graphs do not end up in production. Students got some basic information about misleading graphs before the actual tasks. After that students completed the 32 evaluation tasks following the four interpretation tasks. Finally, a few days after completing the study, the teacher gave a debriefing session in which students got feedback about their performance (based on log files) and some of the tasks were discussed in detail.

3.2 Results

A paired-samples t-test was run to investigate students' abilities to evaluate the trustworthiness of the graphs (evaluation tasks). The analyses indicated that the students ability to identify well-formed graphs ($M = .56$, $SD = .14$) did not differ from their ability to identify misleading graphs ($M = .55$, $SD = .13$), $t(35) = 0.352$, $p = .727$, $d = 0.05$. Their overall performance was only slightly above chance indicating huge challenges to evaluate the trustworthiness of graphs. On the other hand, it is also possible that the tasks confused students and they based their evaluations on irrelevant details of the graphs (e.g., they may have considered how suitable bar and line graphs were for presenting the used data set or judged the graphs based on the credibility of the used data set). When considering only misleading graphs, students' performance in tasks including y-axis manipulations was higher ($M = .61$, $SD = .19$) than in tasks including x-axis manipulations ($M = .45$, $SD = .27$), $t(35) = 2.786$, $p = .009$, $d = .46$. This might indicate that students paid more attention to the y-axis of the graph than on the x-axis.

Overall, these findings reveal that students struggled in judging the misleadingness of the graphs. Thus, it was not surprising that students' performance in graph interpretation tasks was poor ($M = 1.17$, $SD = 1$; max score 4). Importantly, 74% of the all incorrect answers were the ones aligned with the spatial manipulations (i.e. designed to be an obvious choice if the reader does not pay attention to axis scales and labels). Unfortunately, we did not include any tasks that would have required interpretation of well-designed graphs. Thus, we cannot say for sure whether the misleading features of the graphs or the lack of general ability to read well-designed graphs led to poor performance. However, the results suggest that to some extend students knew how to read graphs as the majority of incorrect answers were aligned with the used manipulations.

Although the sample size was small, the results suggest that there is a need to produce learning materials that support reading of graphs, critical reading in particular. This conclusion is further supported by previous findings indicating that international 8th graders tend to struggle in graph reading [22]. These results and the identified lack of graph reading games demonstrate the need to develop games for graph reading.

4 Design of the Chart Trace Game

In this section we describe the first iteration of the Chart Trace game. The game is targeted for adolescents and aims to support the development of graph reading skills, particularly critical evaluation of the graphs. With respect to the graph reading framework, the game focuses on the steps of reading the data and reading between the data [8]. Based on our graph reading study we decided to map game mechanics to graph interpretation tasks and include both well-formed and misleading graphs in the game. We used performance results of the study in balancing the difficulty level of the game.

To facilitate the development work, we used the Number Trace game [23] as a starting point for the Chart Trace game. In Chart Trace, the player controls a dog character on a walkable platform located in the forest and tries to collect bones shown on the platform. Moving in the forest consumes energy and the challenge is to collect the bones with minimum energy consumption. Roughness of the terrain in different parts of the platform varies and moving in rougher terrain consumes more energy. The amount of energy required to get to different locations on the platform is presented with a graph (see Fig. 3). In other words, the energy consumption presented in graphs is mapped to the game world (roughness of the platform) and to moving on the platform (energy consumption). Consequently, as the player has only a limited amount of energy, the ability to interpret the graphs is an essential part of the gameplay and continuous graph reading is needed to make right decisions and succeed in the game.

In practice, the graphs include seven data points that are labeled with letters (A, B, C, D, E, F). In the case of bar graphs, the platform is divided evenly into six sections marked with the same letters starting from A (example in Fig. 3). For line graphs, the platform is divided evenly into five sections. In bar graph tasks the data points (bars) indicate how much energy is spent by walking through the whole section (Fig. 3). By figuring out how much energy is required to cross each section, the student must decide the best route to the bone. Since the dog always starts from the leftmost position on the platform, the player effectively has two options: walk towards right until the bone is reached, or use the teleport skill (arrow button on top of the screen) to instantly move (without losing any energy) to the rightmost position on the platform and then walk towards left to the bone. For example, Fig. 3 shows a task that includes a misleading graph. If the player does not notice that the x-axis is reversed, he might assume that it would take less energy to walk to the bone through sections A to C as the first bars in the graph are shorter. However, as the x-axis is reversed, the best solution is to teleport the dog to the right side of the platform and walk through sections F to D to the bone (total sum of energy consumption 9 compared to 21). Line graphs work similarly as bar graphs except that the energy consumption of each section is defined as an average of section's start and end point values. In practice, the energy consumption between two consecutive data points is linear.

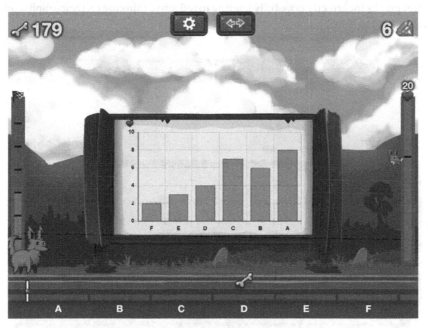

Fig. 3. Bar graph task with a reversed y-axis.

We implemented several mechanics to make the decision making more complex. Figure 4 shows an example of a task in which the bar graph shows the energy consumption for both walking and jumping on the platform. Based on the graph the player has to decide whether he activates the jumping shoes or tries to reach the bone by walking. That is, to correctly solve a task, players have to infer that they need to calculate the sum of the sections' energy values needed to reach the bone from left and right and for both jumping and walking to be able to make the needed comparisons. If needed the decision space can be further extended by providing special skills to the player. In the example task, there is a special skill available that allows the player to reset the energy consumption of one segment to zero. The activation of special skills requires diamonds that the player has a certain amount in each level. Thus, also the manipulation of available diamonds can be used in determining the difficulty level of the game. The game also includes scaffolding features that can be activated to help players to realize the misleading elements of the graphs.

One game level consists of 6–10 tasks (graphs) and the player has certain amount of energy points in each task. Half of the tasks are balanced in the way that if the player does not select the right route to collect the bone, the player will run out of energy. In each level the player can gain 1–3 stars depending on their playing performance (economical energy consumption). This creates clear goals for the player and focuses the player's attention on energy consumption, i.e. to the graphs describing the consumption. As the graphs are mapped to energy consumption, the energy bar provides continuous feedback for the player. This approach allows players to experience the data that the graphs display. In general, the aim of the game is to create perceivable cognitive conflicts when players interpret graphs incorrectly hopefully leading to reflective thinking on their graph reading behavior and strategies.

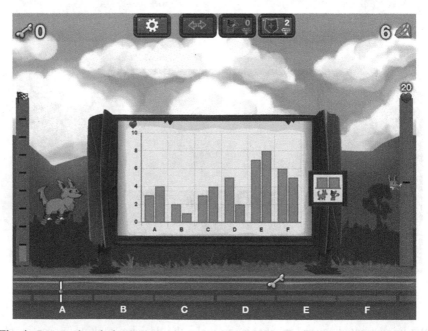

Fig. 4. Bar graph task that includes two movement ways and on-demand energy reset skill

5 Conclusions

The aim of the presented work was to report the first iteration of the evidence-based development of a game that addresses critical reading of graphs. We followed a multi-step approach. First, by analysing the literature on the use of games to foster critical reading skills, we found that research has focused on adult populations and none of the articles examined games that address graph reading but most applied a storified approach by putting players in the shoes of a fake news detector or creator. Although we could not identify any game mechanics used to support graph reading, the results indicated that game-based approaches have been successfully used to support critical reading of written information. Next, we ran an empirical study on graph reading with adolescents using a similar storified approach (i.e. act as fact checker in a media company) that was successfully used in several of reviewed articles. Our results indicated that adolescents lacked the necessary competences to adequately read and interpret graphs, particularly misleading graphs. Accordingly, in a final step, we designed and developed a game for adolescents which aims to foster graph reading competencies including identification of misleading graphs. As our empirical study revealed that graph interpretation tasks provide clearer information about graph reading abilities than credibility evaluation tasks, we used graph interpretation as a main learning mechanic of the game. Next, we will run small-scale studies to evaluate the quality of the game design and to define a blueprint for the next iteration of the Chart Trace game. It is possible that several iterations are needed before it is reasonable to evaluate the effectiveness of the game at a large scale in classrooms.

Acknowledgments. This research is funded by the Strategic Research Council (SRC).

References

1. Kendeou, P., Robinson, D.H., McCrudden, M.: Misinformation and Fake News in Education. Information Age Publishing, Charlotte, NC (2019)
2. Bursztyn, L., Rao, A., Roth, C., Yanagizawa-Drott, D.: Misinformation during a pandemic. University of Chicago, Becker Friedman Institute for Economics Working Paper (2020)
3. Kiili, C., Leu, D.J., Marttunen, M., Hautala, J., Leppänen, P.H.T.: Exploring early adolescents' evaluation of academic and commercial online resources related to health. Read. Writ. 31(3), 533–557 (2017). https://doi.org/10.1007/s11145-017-9797-2
4. Kiili, C., Coiro, J., Räikkönen, E.: Students' evaluation of online texts during online inquiry: Working individually or in pairs. Aust. J. Lang. Lit. 42(3), 167–183 (2019)
5. Hämäläinen, E.K., Kiili, C., Marttunen, M., Räikkönen, E., González-Ibáñez, R., Leppänen, P.H.: Promoting sixth graders' credibility evaluation of web pages: an intervention study. Comput. Hum. Behav. 110, 106372 (2020)
6. Leu, D.J., Forzani, E., Rhoads, C., Maykel, C., Kennedy, C., Timbrell, N.: The new literacies of online research and comprehension: rethinking the reading achievement gap. Read. Res. Q. 50(1), 37–59 (2015)
7. Galesic, M., Garcia-Retamero, R.: Graph literacy: a cross-cultural comparison. Med. Decis. Making 31, 444–457 (2011)
8. Ciccione, L., Dehaene, S.: Can humans perform mental regression on a graph? Accuracy and bias in the perception of scatterplots. Cogn. Psychol. 128, 101406 (2021)

9. Okan, Y., Garcia-Retamero, R.G., Galesic, M., Cokely, E.T.: When higher bars are not larger quantities: on individual differences in the use of spatial information in graph comprehension. Spat. Cogn. Comput. **12**(2–3), 195–218 (2012)

10. Bråten, I., Braasch, J.L.G.: Key issues in research on students' critical reading and learning in the 21st century information society. In: Ng, C., Bartlett, B. (eds.) Improving Reading and Reading Engagement in the 21st Century, pp. 77–98. Springer, Singapore (2017). https://doi.org/10.1007/978-981-10-4331-4_4

11. Wouters, P., van Nimwegen, C., van Oostendorp, H., van Der Spek, E.D.: A meta-analysis of the cognitive and motivational effects of serious games. J. Educ. Psychol. **105**, 249–265 (2013)

12. Clever, L., et al.: FakeYou! - a gamified approach for building and evaluating resilience against fake news. In: van Duijn, M., Preuss, M., Spaiser, V., Takes, F., Verberne, S. (eds.) MISDOOM 2020. LNCS, vol. 12259, pp. 218–232. Springer, Cham (2020). https://doi.org/10.1007/978-3-030-61841-4_15

13. Huang, L.-Y., Yeh, Y.-C.: Meaningful gamification for journalism students to enhance their critical thinking skills. Int. J. Game-Based Learn. **7**, 47–62 (2017)

14. Katsaounidou, A., Vrysis, L., Kotsakis, R., Dimoulas, C., Veglis, A.: MAthE the game: a serious game for education and training in news verification. Educ. Sci. **9**, 155 (2019)

15. Literat, I., Chang, Y.K., Hsu, S.-Y.: Gamifying fake news: engaging youth in the participatory design of news literacy games. Convergence **26**, 503–516 (2020)

16. Maertens, R., Roozenbeek, J., Basol, M., van der Linden, S.: Long-term effectiveness of inoculation against misinformation: three longitudinal experiments. J. Exp. Psychol. Appl. **27**, 1–16 (2021)

17. Maze, C., Haye, A., Sarre, J., Galaup, M., Lagarrigue, P., Lelardeux, C.P.: A board game to fight against misinformation and fake news. In: Marfisi-Schottman, I., Bellotti, F., Hamon, L., Klemke, R. (eds.) GALA 2020. LNCS, vol. 12517, pp. 326–334. Springer, Cham (2020). https://doi.org/10.1007/978-3-030-63464-3_31

18. Pimmer, C., Eisemann, C., Mateescu, M.: Fake news resilience through online games? Tentative findings from a randomized controlled trial in higher education. In: Proceedings of the 17th International Conference on Cognition and Exploratory Learning in the Digital Age (CELDA 2020). IADIS Press (2020)

19. Roozenbeek, J., van der Linden, S.: The fake news game: actively inoculating against the risk of misinformation. J. Risk. Res. **22**, 570–580 (2019)

20. Scheibenzuber, C., Nistor, N.: Media literacy training against fake news in online media. In: Scheffel, M., Broisin, J., Pammer-Schindler, V., Ioannou, A., Schneider, J. (eds.) EC-TEL 2019. LNCS, vol. 11722, pp. 688–691. Springer, Cham (2019). https://doi.org/10.1007/978-3-030-29736-7_67

21. Yang, S., Lee, J.W., Kim, H.-J., Kang, M., Chong, E., Kim, E.: Can an online educational game contribute to developing information literate citizens? Comput. Educ. **161**, 1040–1057 (2021)

22. TIMSS 2011 Assessment. International Association for the Evaluation of Educational Achievement (IEA) (2013). https://nces.ed.gov/times/pdf/TMSS2011_G8Math.pdf

23. Lindstedt, A., Koskinen, A., McMullen, J., Ninaus, M., Kiili, K.: Flow experience and situational interest in an adaptive math game. In: Marfisi-Schottman, I., Bellotti, F., Hamon, L., Klemke, R. (eds.) GALA 2020. LNCS, vol. 12517, pp. 221–231. Springer, Cham (2020). https://doi.org/10.1007/978-3-030-63464-3_21

Technology Used for Serious Games

The Potential of Functional Near-Infrared Spectroscopy (fNIRS) for Motion-Intensive Game Paradigms

Thomas Kanatschnig[1]([⊠]) [iD], Guilherme Wood[1,2] [iD], and Silvia Erika Kober[1,2] [iD]

[1] Institute of Psychology, University of Graz, Universitaetsplatz 2/III, 8010 Graz, Austria
{thomas.kanatschnig,guilherme.wood,silvia.kober}@uni-graz.at
[2] BioTechMed-Graz, Mozartgasse 12/II, 8010 Graz, Austria

Abstract. Functional near-infrared spectroscopy (fNIRS) is gaining popularity as a non-invasive neuroimaging technique in a broad range of fields, including the context of gaming and serious games. However, the capabilities of fNIRS are still underutilized. FNIRS is less prone to motion artifacts and more portable in comparison to other neuroimaging methods and it is therefore ideal for experimental designs which involve physical activity. In this paper, the goal is to demonstrate the feasibility of fNIRS for the recording of cortical activation during a motion-intensive task, namely basketball dribbling. FNIRS recordings over sensorimotor regions were conducted in a block-design on 20 participants, who dribbled a basketball with their dominant right hand. Signal quality for task-related concentration changes in oxy-Hb and deoxy-Hb has been investigated by means of the contrast-to-noise ratio (CNR). A statistical comparison of average CNR from the fNIRS signal revealed the expected effect of significantly higher CNR over the left as compared to the right sensorimotor region. Our findings demonstrate that fNIRS delivers sufficient signal quality to measure hemispheric activation differences during a motion-intensive motoric task like basketball dribbling and bare indications for future endeavors with fNIRS in less constraint settings.

Keywords: Functional near-infrared spectroscopy · fNIRS · Contrast-to-noise ratio · CNR · Basketball · Sensorimotor cortex · Motor activity · Serious games · Gaming

1 Introduction

The use of neurophysiological methods for the measurement of brain activity during gaming is an ever-increasing field of interest in psychological research. Especially promising is the use of neurophysiological methods in the context of serious games, which, due to the ubiquity of gaming as a leisure activity in recent decades, is a factor of increasing importance. Game elements are continuously being implemented into new applications in the context of learning, as well as rehabilitation, to optimize the user experience and to increase engagement [1, 2]. In addition, a review by Ninaus et al. [3] demonstrates the importance of using neurophysiological methods such as functional near-infrared

© Springer Nature Switzerland AG 2021
F. de Rosa et al. (Eds.): GALA 2021, LNCS 13134, pp. 91–100, 2021.
https://doi.org/10.1007/978-3-030-92182-8_9

spectroscopy (fNIRS), functional magnetic resonance imaging (fMRI), or the electroen-cephalogram (EEG) to validate behavioral results of gaming on a neuronal level. Due to constant technological improvements, especially fNIRS is gathering more and more research interest, because it gives researchers flexibility in their experimental designs, that could not be achieved before. FNIRS has already been utilized in different settings in the context of gaming [1–4]. However, the main advantages of fNIRS, i.e., its portability and robustness against motion artifacts, are still quite underutilized. Our aim in this work is to use the example of basketball dribbling to show, that with fNIRS the monitoring of cortical activity is possible even during motion-intensive paradigms. Furthermore, we discuss the advantages that fNIRS can bring to the research of gaming and serious games.

1.1   FNIRS in Gaming Research

The monitoring of cortical activity with fNIRS functions non-invasively through the measurement of concentration changes of hemodynamic parameters, mainly the oxy-genated hemoglobin (oxy-Hb) and deoxygenated hemoglobin (deoxy-Hb) in the cortical blood flow [5]. Proof-of-concept investigations show that it is possible to monitor cortical activity with fNIRS during light exercising like cycling and table tennis and also during artistic performances like piano and violin playing [6, 7]. Furthermore, the advance-ments in portable fNIRS technology make it possible for subjects to move around freely and wirelessly. Additional advantages are the easy and fast montage of the fNIRS setup, which does not require abrasive gel on the scalp like with EEG and the possibility of hyperscanning on multiple subjects. Since the number of exergames (motion-intensive exercise games), as well as virtual reality (VR) applications with motion tracking tech-nology is rising, where active movements of the users are essential, these advantages of fNIRS over other neurophysiological methods such as fMRI or EEG make fNIRS a valuable tool for gaming research.

Another field that is gaining more and more research interest is the field of fNIRS-based brain computer interfaces (BCI). Several studies have investigated the feasibility of fNIRS as a means to control digital devices and machines with promising results [8]. In that regard, fNIRS also shows highly promising results for the development of neurofeedback (NF) paradigms, to let users influence their own brain activity [9]. Such fNIRS based BCI and NF applications are also suited for the implementation of gaming elements, which has already been demonstrated in the past [10].

1.2   Quantifying fNIRS Signal Quality

Multiple examinations on fNIRS signal quality have been conducted (e.g., [11, 12]). A constant finding in these examinations is the compelling performance of wavelet filtering, which was first introduced for the use in fNIRS by Molavi and Dumont [13]. The wavelet filter smooths the signal and thereby eliminates motion artifacts with great efficiency [11–13]. Furthermore, wavelet filtering increases the overall quality of the signal, which can be seen by considerable improvements of the contrast-to-noise ratio (CNR) [12]. CNR is an objective indicator for the signal quality of neurophysiological methods, such as fMRI and fNIRS [12, 14, 15]. It is a standardized measure for the relationship between task-related activation levels and noise in the measurement. The higher CNR, the higher the signal quality. Further, because it is a standardized measure, it allows findings from different examinations to be compared to each other. In the study by Cooper et al. [12] wavelet filtering, compared to other common correction techniques, produced the highest average increase of CNR (39%). Another capable technique for fNIRS signal improvement is the use of so-called short-separation channels [16, 17]. These are channels that can be recorded in addition to the standard long-separation channels of every common fNIRS system to monitor general hemodynamic changes that occur outside of the cerebral cortex. These measurements can then be regressed out of the fNIRS signal to only leave information about the underlying cortical activation in the signal. As Gagnon et al. [16] showed, utilizing short-separation measurements can lead to considerable improvements in CNR (oxy-Hb: 50%; deoxy-Hb 100%).

1.3 The Present Study

FNIRS studies investigating sensorimotor cortex (SMC) activity during simple hand movement tasks like clenching or finger tapping generally show the expected patterns of higher contralateral compared to ipsilateral sensorimotor activation [18, 19]. In a recent study, Carius et al. [20] successfully administered fNIRS for the measurement of SMC activity during a complex and motion-intensive motoric task in the form of basketball dribbling. However, to this point little is known about the signal quality in such settings. The main goal of the present study is to investigate fNIRS signal quality during a motion-intensive task, namely basketball dribbling. FNIRS data was taken from another yet unpublished study from the authors of this paper, where basketball dribbling was used as a motoric task. Participants were split into two groups, with one group dribbling a basketball with the left hand, the other with the right hand. For the demonstrative purpose of this study, only the data from the right-hand-dribbling group were analyzed. First, significantly active channels were identified by means of the false discovery rate (FDR) proposed by Singh and Dan [21] for the use with fNIRS data. Then, CNR calculations were conducted channel-wise for oxy-Hb and deoxy-Hb for each participant. Further, regions-of-interest (ROI) were identified to compare average CNR across different ROI in the SMC and across brain hemispheres. Based on the findings on SMC activity during motor execution [18, 19] right hand dribbling should elicit higher activation and thus a stronger signal in SMC regions of the left hemisphere (LH) compared to the right hemisphere (RH). Therefore, it is hypothesized, that average CNR is significantly higher in regions of the LH compared to the RH for oxy-Hb and deoxy-Hb, respectively. We assume that we will reach a high signal quality while playing basketball to demonstrate that fNIRS is a useful tool to measure brain activation patterns while performing motion-intensive tasks.

2 Method

2.1 Sample and Procedure

In the present study, the fNIRS measurements from 20 participants (10 men and 10 women) aged between 18 and 26 years ($M = 23.10$, $SD = 2.53$) were analyzed. Prerequisites for participation in the original study were right-handedness as well as the absence of neurological and psychological conditions. All participants were right-handed as assessed by the Edinburgh Handedness Inventory ($M = 79.00$, $SD = 15.27$) [22].

Participants had to dribble a standard (size 7) basketball 16 times for 10 s each, while sitting on a chair. Every dribbling trial was followed by a randomized resting period of 10, 12, 13 or 15 s, where the participants held the ball still on their lap with both hands. The signals to start and stop the dribbling were given by auditory cues, that were programmed into a script using PsychoPy3 [23], which ran on a laboratory PC. While dribbling with one hand, the other hand should lay flat on the lap. The overall duration of the intervention was approx. 6 min.

2.2 FNIRS Recording and Pre-Processing

The hemodynamic response of the participants during dribbling was recorded with a NIRSport2 system (NIRx Medizintechnik GmbH, Berlin, Germany). The probe-layout consisted of eight source- and seven detector-optodes (one detector used for short-separation measurements), that had been mounted on measuring-caps (standard EEG electrode positions, according to the international 10–20 system) over the SMC. A sampling frequency of 10.2 Hz was used. The eight source-optodes of the NIRS system emit light at 760 nm and 850 nm wavelengths, corresponding to oxy-Hb and deoxy-Hb, respectively. Distance-holders were used to ensure a 30 mm distance between each source-detector-pair, which corresponded to long-separation channels. In addition, short-separation channels were implemented as well (8 mm distance to source-optodes). Figure 1 shows the probe-layout used with every participant, as well as a channel sensitivity profile of the probe-layout projected on the "Colin27" digital brain atlas [24]. Visualizations were generated within AtlasViewer (Ver. 2.11.3) [25], a free software package suited for the use with the Homer2 [26] fNIRS data processing software, based on MATLAB (MathWorks, Natick, MA, USA). The sensitivity profile in Fig. 1 (A and B) was calculated by means of a Monte Carlo program, which simulates the path that photons travel through the cortical tissue to give an estimation of the measured cortical regions. Projections of the measured regions on the cortical surface were extracted channel-wise within AtlasViewer by means of automated anatomical labeling (AAL) [27] and are listed in Table 1.

The recorded fNIRS signal has been pre-processed using Homer2 (Ver. 2.3) [26]. For the sake of conciseness, a detailed description of the processing pipeline was omitted. If the interest exists, the original Homer2 processing-file is available upon request from the corresponding author of this paper. For further statistical analysis block averages were calculated and exported for each participant.

2.3 FDR and Statistical Analysis

To examine which channels showed significant task-related activation, a FDR-analysis was calculated according to the procedure described by Singh and Dan [21]. Average activation across all participants during the task interval was compared to a baseline interval within the oxy-Hb and deoxy-Hb measurements, respectively. For the calculation of the activation averages (because of the delay in the hemodynamic response to cortical activation) a timeframe starting a few seconds after dribbling onset was chosen for

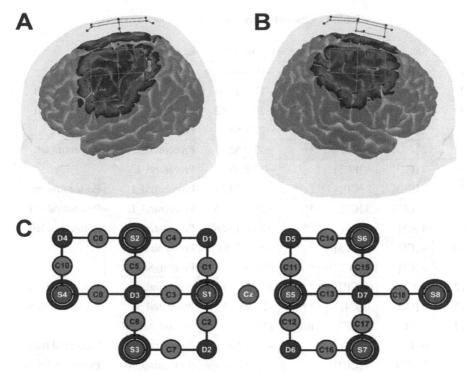

Fig. 1. Projection of the probe-layout over (A) the left and (B) the right hemisphere, respectively. Corresponding to the sensorimotor cortex, precentral as well as postcentral regions are illuminated in the sensitivity profile (red regions) bilaterally. (C) Illustration of the probe-layout displaying numbers and positions of the sources (S1–8, red circles), detectors (D1–7, blue circles; blue rings mark short-separation detectors) and channels (C1–18, yellow circles), as well as the "Cz" position (EEG 10–20 system) as a reference point for the probe location (Color figure online).

the task interval (5 to 12 s), after visual inspection of the HRF in Homer2 revealed this interval to contain the peak of the hemodynamic response. The timeframe of five seconds before dribbling onset was taken as the baseline interval (−5 to 0 s). The FDR analysis revealed significant activation for channels: 1, 3, 5, 6, 7, 8, 9, 10, 13, 15, 16, 17 and 18 in oxy-Hb, as well as for channels: 3, 5, 8, 9, 11, 12 and 13 in deoxy-Hb ($p <$ FDR 0.05). The remaining channels did not reach significance ($p >$ FDR 0.05). Table 1 lists all 18 long-separation channels of the used probe-layout with the corresponding source and detector numbers, as well as the MNI (Montreal Neurological Institute) coordinates and AAL brain region labels obtained with AtlasViewer. Table 1 also shows the ROI assignment of selected channels that form symmetrical patterns across both hemispheres, which were based on the AAL labeling and used for the ensuing statistical analysis.

CNR calculations were performed based on the procedure used in previous studies [14, 15], the formula is displayed in Eq. 1. CNR values were calculated using the same timeframes as during the FDR analysis. The term "dur" refers to task (5 to 12 s, where participants dribble the basketball with their right hand, which should lead to a signal increase over the LH), "pre" refers to baseline (−5 to 0 s, where participants do nothing

Table 1. Channel information for the probe-layout.

Ch.	Src.	Det.	Sig.	Coord. MNI	Label AAL	ROI
1	1 [C1]	1 [FC1]	*	−19 −6 64	Frontal_Sup_L	
2	1 [C1]	2 [CP1]	n.s	−17 −24 66	Precentral_L	Precentral left
3	1 [C1]	3 [C3]	**	−29 −15 62	Precentral_L	Precentral left
4	2 [FC3]	1 [FC1]	n.s	−27 7 58	Frontal_Mid_L	
5	2 [FC3]	3 [C3]	**	−45 2 62	Precentral_L	Precentral left
6	2 [FC3]	4 [FC5]	*	−37 8 36	Precentral_L	
7	3 [CP3]	2 [CP1]	*	−23 −34 54	Postcentral_L	Postcentral left
8	3 [CP3]	3 [C3]	**	−39 −24 55	Postcentral_L	Postcentral left
9	4 [C5]	3 [C3]	**	−55 −14 56	Postcentral_L	Postcentral left
10	4 [C5]	4 [FC5]	*	−55 −2 40	Postcentral_L	
11	5 [C2]	5 [FC2]	*	30 0 73	Frontal_Sup_R	
12	5 [C2]	6 [CP2]	*	28 −26 70	Precentral_R	Precentral right
13	5 [C2]	7 [C4]	**	42 −14 73	Precentral_R	Precentral right
14	6 [FC4]	5 [FC2]	n.s	27 6 49	Frontal_Mid_R	
15	6 [FC4]	7 [C4]	*	49 −3 60	Precentral_R	Precentral right
16	7 [CP4]	6 [CP2]	*	36 −38 61	Postcentral_R	Postcentral right
17	7 [CP4]	7 [C4]	*	53 −27 65	Postcentral_R	Postcentral right
18	8 [C6]	7 [C4]	*	44 −16 42	Postcentral_R	Postcentral right

Ch.: Channel number; Src.: Source number (approx. EEG position in brackets); Det.: Detector number (approx. EEG position in brackets); Sig.: Channel significance according to FDR (* = sig. in oxy-Hb or deoxy-Hb; ** = sig. in oxy-Hb and deoxy-Hb; n.s. = not significant); Coord. MNI: Coordinates in MNI space; Label AAL: Region label according to automated anatomical labeling (AAL); ROI: Region of interest.

in particular, in order to record background noise). The terms "mean" and "var" refer to the mean and the variance of the corresponding timeframes of the fNIRS signal, respectively.

$$CNR = \frac{mean(dur) - mean(pre)}{\sqrt{\mathrm{var}(dur) + \mathrm{var}(pre)}} \tag{1}$$

Higher CNR values indicate that the task-related signal is higher in relation to the baseline noise, meaning better signal quality. Channel-CNR values were averaged across the corresponding ROI. To test the hypothesis of higher CNR in the LH compared to the RH, a 2 × 2 × 2 ANOVA for repeated measures was calculated with the within-subject factors *Hb-Type* (oxy-Hb vs. deoxy-Hb), *Hemisphere* (LH vs. RH) and *ROI* (precentral vs. postcentral). Alpha was set to 0.05. Statistical calculations were performed using IBM SPSS Statistics 27 (IBM Corp., Armonk, NY, USA).

3 Results

Descriptive statistics for the CNR calculations are presented in Table 2. Typically, deoxy-Hb is showing a decrease in concentration in the fNIRS signal during cortical activation. This is why the sign of the CNR values for deoxy-Hb was switched for easier comparison, which is also the procedure applied in previous CNR examinations [14, 15]. This also ensures a valid comparison of the CNR values of oxy-Hb and deoxy-Hb in the ANOVA. The $2 \times 2 \times 2$ ANOVA yielded a significant main effect for the factor *Hemisphere*, indicating higher average CNR in the LH ($M = 3.50$, $SD = 1.86$) compared to the RH ($M = 2.50$, $SD = 1.88$; $F (1, 19) = 8.74$, $p = .008$, $\eta_p^2 = .315$). No other main or interaction effects reached significance (*Hb-Type*: $F (1, 19) = 3.26$, $p = .087$, $\eta_p^2 = .146$; *ROI*: $F (1, 19) = 0.01$, $p = 919$, $\eta_p^2 = .001$; *Hb-Type * Hemisphere*: $F (1, 19) = 0.14$, $p = .711$, $\eta_p^2 = .007$; *Hb-Type * ROI*: $F (1, 19) = 3.66$, $p = .071$, $\eta_p^2 = .161$; *Hemisphere * ROI*: $F (1, 19) = 0.84$, $p = .371$, $\eta_p^2 = .042$; *Hb-Type * Hemisphere * ROI*: $F (1, 19) = 0.01$, $p = .936$, $\eta_p^2 < .001$).

Table 2. Descriptive statistics for the CNR calculations.

ROI	Oxy-Hb		Deoxy-Hb		Avg. hemisphere	
	M	SD	M	SD	M	SD
Precentral left	4.00	3.52	2.78	3.43	3.50	1.86
Postcentral left	5.06	3.01	2.18	3.67		
Precentral right	3.11	3.73	2.22	3.85	2.50	1.88
Postcentral right	3.56	3.61	1.11	3.79		
Avg. Hb-Type	3.93	2.48	2.07	3.22		

Oxy-Hb: CNR for oxy-Hb; Deoxy-Hb: CNR for deoxy-Hb; ROI: Region of interest; Avg. Hemisphere: Average CNR over ROI of the left and right hemispheres; Avg. Hb-Type: Average CNR over all ROI for oxy-Hb and deoxy-Hb; M: Mean; SD: Standard deviation.

4 Discussion

With this paper our goal was to demonstrate the feasibility of fNIRS for the measurement of cortical activation during a motion-intensive paradigm, to show its potential value for gaming and serious game research. We analyzed fNIRS data from an experiment in which participants dribbled a basketball with their dominant right hand. The signal quality has been examined by means of CNR calculations.

On first inspection of Table 2 it stands out, that CNR is tendentially higher in the precentral and postcentral regions of the LH compared to the RH, corresponding to the expected pattern of sensorimotor activation. This observation is further corroborated by the results of the ANOVA, which yielded a significant effect for the factor *Hemisphere*. Thus, the hypothesis of higher CNR, due to higher activation, in the LH compared to the RH has been confirmed and is in line with the results found in the literature [18, 19]. We also compared our results to the previous findings in terms of overall CNR levels. Cui et al. [15] report average CNR values of 0.36 for BOLD, as well as 0.12 and 0.13 for oxy-Hb and deoxy-Hb, respectively. In that study fNIRS measurements were conducted during cognitive tasks and simultaneously to BOLD measurements. In their other investigation, Cui et al. [14] report average CNR values of 1.31 for oxy-Hb and 1.28 for deoxy-Hb during a finger-tapping task. Compared to that our results display overall higher CNR levels, with an average of 3.93 for oxy-Hb and 2.07 for deoxy-Hb. Due to finger-tapping being a motoric task, a comparison to our results would be more appropriate, although finger-tapping is still a less motion-intensive task compared to basketball dribbling. Thus, it is difficult to classify our results, because to our knowledge there are no similar studies examining CNR of the fNIRS signal during basketball playing (or similar motion-intensive tasks), to which we could compare our results to. Nevertheless, the relatively high levels of CNR in our results compared to previous studies, are a promising indicator that high fNIRS signal quality can be achieved also during motion-intensive paradigms like basketball playing.

In conclusion we were able to demonstrate the feasibility of using fNIRS in a motion-intensive paradigm in the form of basketball dribbling. Our findings have implications for future endeavors with fNIRS in new and less constrained settings. Using cortical activation patterns of bodily movement could be implemented into gaming paradigms to control virtual characters or to interact with a virtual environment. Furthermore, creators of future BCI- and NF-systems in the context of rehabilitation, could benefit from the implementation of fNIRS in the development of new applications that involve movement, thereby potentially increasing the level of engagement and improving the user experience.

References

1. Kober, S.E., Wood, G., Kiili, K., Moeller, K., Ninaus, M.: Game-based learning environments affect frontal brain activity. PLoS One **15**, e0242573 (2020). https://doi.org/10.1371/journal. pone.0242573
2. Wang, Z., et al.: Effects of three different rehabilitation games' interaction on brain activation using functional near-infrared spectroscopy. Physiol. Meas. **41**, 125005 (2020). https://doi. org/10.1088/1361-6579/abcd1f
3. Ninaus, M., et al.: Neurophysiological methods for monitoring brain activity in serious games and virtual environments: a review. Int. J. Technol. Enhanced Learn. **6**, 78–103 (2014). https:// doi.org/10.1504/IJTEL.2014.060022
4. Witte, M., Ninaus, M., Kober, S.E., Neuper, C., Wood, G.: Neuronal correlates of cognitive control during gaming revealed by near-infrared spectroscopy. PLoS One **10**, e0134816 (2015). https://doi.org/10.1371/journal.pone.0134816
5. Pinti, P., et al.: The present and future use of functional near-infrared spectroscopy (fNIRS) for cognitive neuroscience. Ann. N. Y. Acad. Sci. **1464**, 5–29 (2018). https://doi.org/10.1111/ nyas.13948
6. Piper, S.K., et al.: A wearable multi-channel fNIRS system for brain imaging in freely moving subjects. Neuroimage **85**, 64–71 (2014). https://doi.org/10.1016/j.neuroimage.2013.06.062
7. Balardin, J.B., et al.: Imaging brain function with functional near-infrared spectroscopy in unconstrained environments. Front. Hum. Neurosci. **11**, 1–7 (2017). https://doi.org/10.3389/ fnhum.2017.00258

8. Naseer, N., Hong, K.-S.: fNIRS-based brain-computer interfaces: a review. Front. Hum. Neurosci. **9**, 1–15 (2015). https://doi.org/10.3389/fnhum.2015.00003

9. Kohl, S.H., Mehler, D.M.A., Lührs, M., Thibault, R.T., Konrad, K., Sorger, B.: The Potential of functional near-infrared spectroscopy-based neurofeedback—a systematic review and recommendations for best practice. Front. Neurosci. **14**, 594 (2020). https://doi.org/10.3389/fnins.2020.00594

10. Ninaus, M., et al.: Neurofeedback and serious games: In: Connolly, T.M., Hainey, T., Boyle, E., Baxter, G., Moreno-Ger, P. (eds.) Psychology, Pedagogy, and Assessment in Serious Games, pp. 82–110. IGI Global (2014). https://doi.org/10.4018/978-1-4666-4773-2.ch005

11. Brigadoi, S., et al.: Motion artifacts in functional near-infrared spectroscopy: a comparison of motion correction techniques applied to real cognitive data. Neuroimage **85**, 181–191 (2014). https://doi.org/10.1016/j.neuroimage.2013.04.082

12. Cooper, R.J., et al.: A systematic comparison of motion artifact correction techniques for functional near-infrared spectroscopy. Front. Neurosci. **6**, 1–10 (2012). https://doi.org/10.3389/fnins.2012.00147

13. Molavi, B., Dumont, G.A.: Wavelet-based motion artifact removal for functional near-infrared spectroscopy. Physiol. Meas. **33**, 259–270 (2012). https://doi.org/10.1088/0967-3334/33/2/259

14. Cui, X., Bray, S., Reiss, A.L.: Functional near infrared spectroscopy (NIRS) signal improvement based on negative correlation between oxygenated and deoxygenated hemoglobin dynamics. Neuroimage **49**, 3039–3046 (2010). https://doi.org/10.1016/j.neuroimage.2009.11.050

15. Cui, X., Bray, S., Bryant, D.M., Glover, G.H., Reiss, A.L.: A quantitative comparison of NIRS and fMRI across multiple cognitive tasks. Neuroimage **54**, 2808–2821 (2011). https://doi.org/10.1016/j.neuroimage.2010.10.069

16. Gagnon, L., Cooper, R.J., Yücel, M.A., Perdue, K.L., Greve, D.N., Boas, D.A.: Short separation channel location impacts the performance of short channel regression in NIRS. Neuroimage **59**, 2518–2528 (2012). https://doi.org/10.1016/j.neuroimage.2011.08.095

17. Brigadoi, S., Cooper, R.J.: How short is short? Optimum source–detector distance for short-separation channels in functional near-infrared spectroscopy. Neurophotonics **2**, 025005 (2015). https://doi.org/10.1117/1.NPh.2.2.025005

18. Franceschini, M.A., Fantini, S., Thompson, J.H., Culver, J.P., Boas, D.A.: Hemodynamic evoked response of the sensorimotor cortex measured noninvasively with near-infrared optical imaging. Psychophysiology **40**, 548–560 (2003). https://doi.org/10.1111/1469-8986.00057

19. Robinson, N., et al.: Real-time subject-independent pattern classification of overt and covert movements from fNIRS signals. PLoS One **11**, 1–21 (2016). https://doi.org/10.1371/journal.pone.0159959

20. Carius, D., Seidel-Marzi, O., Kaminski, E., Lisson, N., Ragert, P.: Characterizing hemodynamic response alterations during basketball dribbling. PLoS One **15**, e0238318 (2020). https://doi.org/10.1371/journal.pone.0238318

21. Singh, A.K., Dan, I.: Exploring the false discovery rate in multichannel NIRS. Neuroimage **33**, 542–549 (2006). https://doi.org/10.1016/j.neuroimage.2006.06.047

22. Oldfield, R.C.: The assessment and analysis of handedness: the Edinburgh inventory. Neuropsychologia **9**, 97–113 (1971). https://doi.org/10.1016/0028-3932(71)90067-4

23. Peirce, J., et al.: PsychoPy2: experiments in behavior made easy. Behav. Res. Methods **51**(1), 195–203 (2019). https://doi.org/10.3758/s13428-018-01193-y

24. Collins, D.L., et al.: Design and construction of a realistic digital brain phantom. IEEE Trans. Med. Imaging **17**, 463–468 (1998). https://doi.org/10.1109/42.712135

25. Aasted, C.M., et al.: Anatomical guidance for functional near-infrared spectroscopy: atlasviewer tutorial. Neurophotonics **2**, 020801 (2015). https://doi.org/10.1117/1.NPh.2.2.020801

26. Huppert, T.J., Diamond, S.G., Franceschini, M.A., Boas, D.A.: HomER: a review of time-series analysis methods for near-infrared spectroscopy of the brain. Appl. Opt. **48**, D280 (2009). https://doi.org/10.1364/AO.48.00D280

27. Tzourio-Mazoyer, N., et al.: Automated anatomical labeling of activations in SPM using a macroscopic anatomical parcellation of the MNI MRI single-subject brain. Neuroimage **15**, 273–289 (2002). https://doi.org/10.1006/nimg.2001.0978

Adapting Autonomous Agents for Automotive Driving Games

Gabriele Campodonico, Francesco Bellotti$^{(\boxtimes)}$, Riccardo Berta, Alessio Capello,
Marianna Cossu, Alessandro De Gloria, Luca Lazzaroni, Tommaso Taccioli,
and Federico Davio

DITEN, University of Genoa, Via Opera Pia 11A, 16145 Genoa, Italy
{francesco.bellotti,riccardo.berta,alessandro.degloria}@unige.it

Abstract. This article investigates the feasibility of implementing a reinforcement learning agent able to plan the trajectory of a simple automated vehicle 2D
model in a motorway simulation. The goal is to use it to implement a non-player
vehicle in serious games for driving. The agent extends a Deep Q Learning agent
developed by Eduard Leurent in Stable Baselines by adding rewards in order to
better meet the traffic laws. The motorway environment was enhanced as well, in
order to increase realism. A multilayer perceptron model, processing cinematic
inputs from the ego and other vehicles, was tested in different traffic conditions
and outperformed the original model and other policies such as a heuristic and a
minimal-reward one. Our experience stresses the importance of defining episode
metrics to assess agent behavior, keeping into accounts factors related to safety
(e.g., keeping a safe time to collision) and consumption (e.g., limiting accelerations
and decelerations). This is key to define rewards and penalties able to properly
train the model to meet the traffic laws while keeping a high-speed performance.

Keywords: Reinforcement learning · Automotive driving · Serious games ·
Deep Q learning · Stable baselines · Metrics · Rewards and penalties ·
Autonomous agents

1 Introduction

Automotive driving is a very important activity for several people in the world. On the
one hand, it allows people to move quite freely and efficiently, on the other hand it
also has negative impacts in terms of accidents, costs (fuel), pollution. This stresses the
importance of driving well, particularly in a safe and consumption-savvy way [1].

To this end, digital technologies, simulations and also serious games, are being
employed (e.g., [2]). In a realistic driving environment, a key role is played by non-
player vehicles (NPVs) that represent the surrounding traffic with which the ego (player)
vehicle has to interact on the road lanes.

As literature is lacking of descriptions, NPVs in games may be typically implemented
through heuristic algorithms. Reinforcement learning (RL) techniques are acquiring ever
more relevance in decision making for automated driving functions (ADFs), and tools

© Springer Nature Switzerland AG 2021
F. de Rosa et al. (Eds.): GALA 2021, LNCS 13134, pp. 101–110, 2021.
https://doi.org/10.1007/978-3-030-92182-8_10

are appearing to support this research, for instance Car Learning to Act (CARLA), an open-source driving simulator (relying on the Unreal engine) developed for automated driving research and which provides specific support for RL [3, 4].

A significant contribution in this direction, particularly in the gaming context, comes from "An Environment for Autonomous Driving Decision-Making", the PhD thesis of Eduard Leurent, University of Lille, which developed a set of environments for decision-making in autonomous driving [5]. The current publicly available version of the Leurent models seem more suited for games than for serious games (SGs), as the goal of the developed autonomous agents seem to concern maximizing the number of kilometers driven with no concern, for instance, of avoiding right overtaking.

In this context, our research intends investigating the feasibility of a RL autonomous agent implementing a behavior more consistent with the basic traffic laws. This involves addressing research questions concerning the choice of the most suited rewards and penalties to achieve the goal. Other fundamental questions concern the architecture of the neural network to train the RL model, and the type of inputs to provide to it.

The remainder of the article is organized as follows. Section 2 presents some related work, while Sect. 3 provides background information on RL and the Leurent environments. Our system adaptations are presented in Sect. 4, while Sect. 5 discuss the experimental results. Conclusions are drawn in the final section.

2   Related Work

Several SGs have been implemented to support driving instruction. [6] presents the implementation of an educational game on traffic behavior awareness through the main stages of analysis, design, development, and evaluation, aiming at investigating the contribution of gamification in traffic safety. Results reveal that a properly developed educational game could enhance traffic awareness through experiential and mediated learning. [7] presents a virtual reality SG providing players the knowledge of driving or getting ready for the basic driving lessons and rules before they drive a real car on the real road. User tests revealed that the game can combine enjoyment with learning basic driving skills and knowledge. [8] investigates the effects of the use of SG in eco-driving training. The results demonstrate that the serious game influences positively the behavior of inexperienced drivers in ecological driving.

[9] presents a set of fuzzy logic models that process signals from basic vehicular sensors (e.g., speed and throttle position) in order to compute an estimation of fuel consumption, then usable in reality-enhanced SGs. As a complementary tool, Edgine supports smart configuration of limited-resource edge devices in order to send the proper information to a cloud-based measurement management system [10].

[11] presents a set of three classes of neural networks for RL algorithms to face the issue of driving a car in a simple racing game. [12] provides a comprehensive overview of artificial intelligence (AI) for serious games. Particularly, it presents a set of advanced game AI components that enable pedagogical affordances and that can be easily reused across game engines and platforms. All components have been applied and validated in serious games that were tested with real end-users.

3   Reinforcement Learning and the Leurent Environments

Reinforcement Learning (RL) is a branch of Machine Learning (ML) that deals with facing the problem of an agent free to take certain actions to achieve a goal in an environment, interacting with it. Born in the area of video games, with the most famous example of the victory of the system called "AlphaGo" against Lee Sedol, world champion of the game "Go", RL is currently applied to a wide range of application domains, thanks also to the application of Deep Learning techniques [13].

Unlike supervised and unsupervised learning, the RL agent uses trial and error mechanics, in which it observes the environment around him and performs actions within it, and in return receives a reward: he exploits the previous experience, which he acquired by trial and error, to improve his learning in such a way as not to repeat certain mistakes. The main objective is to maximize the reward function, as it represents an index of the goodness of learning. The main elements of the RL are the agent (agent) and the environment (environment), where the environment represents the world in which the agent is located and with which it interacts. At each step of the interaction, the agent observes the state of the environment and makes a decision on how to behave; the environment can change as a result of the agent actions or it can also evolve autonomously. A fundamental element of the RL is the reward function (also called reinforcement function), which is a function that, given a certain feedback from the environment, provides a reward in the form of a real numerical value that indicates the quality of the agent's state. interior of the environment. If the feedback is positive, then the reinforcement function assigns a positive real value; if instead the feedback is negative, the reinforcement function assigns a negative real value, which represents a penalty. The agent's goal is to maximize the return value which, as will be explained, includes the sum of the rewards.

As anticipated in the introduction, our research builds upon the PhD project by Eduard Leurent. The project has been developed in Stable Baselines [14], which is a series of implementations of RL algorithms based on OpenAI Baselines. The goal of Stable Baselines is to create an interface providing common methods such as training, saving, loading and forecasting for RL algorithms. Stable Baselines relies on Tensorflow, the most widespread open source library to develop and train ML models [15]. In the Tensorflow Toolkit, we have made extensive use of Tensorboard, which supports easy visualization for Machine Learning model training and optimization.

A key to the implementation of effective RL projects is given by the availability of (customizable) simulated environments. For this, the Leurent project relies on the popular "Gym" toolkit. All the test environments made available by this toolkit have a common interface allowing users to test their algorithms in multiple scenarios without having to make significant changes to the code.

Leurent also developed a set of deep Q learning autonomous agents, taking as input (observations) either kinematics values (position and speed of the ego vehicle and of the others) or a grayscale image of the landscape surrounding the vehicle. The first possibility is particularly suited for a simulation/gaming environment, where all information is available. This second option is interesting also because it somehow reflects the availability of information from cameras and lidars, as in the case of real vehicles.

For the first type of inputs, a straightforward model is represented by a multilayer perceptron (MLP), with 2 hidden layers (64 neurons each), a dueling architecture (one network for the state value function and one for the state-dependent action advantage function [16]) and an additional target network [13]. For the second type of input, Leurent implemented a model based on a convolutional network [17], which processes a grayscale image of 84 × 84 pixels surrounding the vehicle.

As the main development tool, we used the Google Colaboratory (Colab) site [18]. Colab is an alternative to Jupyter Notebook that allows users to write and run Python code in the browser providing two major advantages: no configuration is needed, and free access is provided to GPUs. The environment, however, has two main drawbacks: the 12 h continuous use limit and a suspension of the GPU availability in case of prolonged use.

4   System Adaptation

The Leurent project code consists of several Python modules divided into three groups:

- Envs: contains modules used to configure and create all the various environments implemented, such as highway (e.g., Fig. 1), intersection, merge, roundabout, parking. It also contains the abstractions to interact with all the environments;
- Road: containing the modules used to create roads usable in the environments;
- Vehicle: in which there are modules that deal with the creation, properties and actions concerning the vehicles running in the environments.

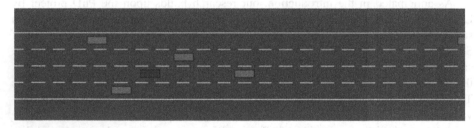

Fig. 1. Highway (Color figure online)

Our work focused on the highway environment, in which the ego vehicle (green rectangle in Fig. 1) moves on a multi-lane freeway with the objective of traveling as many kilometers as possible, while avoiding accidents. At each simulation step, the deep Q learning model developed by Leurent produces one of the following discrete actions: lane left, idle, lane right, slower, faster. The rewards provided by the highway environment are the following.

- Collision_reward: a penalty (negative reward) given in case of accident with one of the non-player vehicles.
- Right_Lane_Reward: reward given when the ego vehicle travels in the rightmost lane;

- High_Speed_Reward: reward given when the vehicle travels in a certain speed range close to the upper limit.

The reward function is calculated at each step using the "_reward" method contained in the reference class of the environment. The method receives as input the action that the vehicle did in the previous step. Once an episode is finished, the rewards of the various steps are added up and the reward normalized between zero and one. There are two possible end of episode conditions: accident and maximum duration limit, that we set to 1 min.

A fundamental step for controlling the behavior of the vehicle under train is the definition of an assessment method for each simulated episode, in order to tune and compare the various attempted behavior policies. This tool was useful to us in two different ways: to adjust the rewards looking for the best set of rewards among those tested and as a comparison tool between the various tested policies. We decided to have an assessment over a total of 60 episodes, thus 1 h of simulation.

Table 1 reports the 17 metrics that have been chosen to evaluate the simulations. Each metric was assigned a threshold to define the saturation value. Displacements from the saturation value are rewarded/penalized with a linear rule. A weight was also assigned according to the importance of the metric in question: the sum of all weights is 100 and corresponds to the maximum achievable score.

Table 1. Implemented metrics

Type of metrics	Metrics
Collisions	Number of collisions (up to one per episode)
Distance	Traveled distance
Overtakes	Left overtaking and right overtaking
Longitudinal control	Time to collision (avg and stdev); avg, stdev acceleration and deceleration
Latitudinal control	Avg(lane_occupancy function), where lane_occupancy penalizes improper (e.g., also considering overtaking preparation) occupancy of non-rightmost lanes; lane changes; hazardous cut-in by the ego vehicle; avg, stdev steering activity
Speed	Difference from the speed limit

The weight of the dimensions in the metric was chosen empirically and arbitrarily on the basis of the importance we have given to each single dimension and observing the videos of the resulting outcomes. Several tests were made to ensure that the weight of the metrics lead to a suited behavior of the agent. The set of weights we have employed in the tests reported in this article are the following:

- 24% kms driven
- 20% Number of collisions

- 16% Number of right overtaking
- 9% Lane occupancy function
- 5% avg Time To Collision (TTC), avg distance from speed limit (DSL), number of lane changes (LC), number of hazardous LC
- 2% avg acceleration, avg deceleration, avg steering
- 1% stdev TTC, stdev DSL, stdev acceleration, stdev deceleration, stdev steering
- 0% Number of left overtaking

In order to increase the realism of the model and make it more suited to address issues related to the traffic law, we made some modifications. Particularly, in the IDMVehicle class (in the Abstract module) we have implemented methods for recognizing events such as the left and right overtake event and the ego-vehicle cut-in, which is considered an hazardous behavior to be avoided.

In the Kinematics module, we upgraded the generation of the NPVs. In the original version, which was suited for testing a player reaction ability in a game, but with little attention to traffic realism and law, vehicles were generated also in the left-most lane, with a limited speed. We have implemented a vehicle creation distribution function, giving a higher probability density to right lanes. Also the speed of the NPVs now depends on the lane.

Other major changes were made in the statistics module, in order to take into account the metrics and make a proper reporting of each episode. We also added a new json config module, which allows customizing rewards and metrics without any modification in the code.

For the sake of analysis, we implemented a set of alternative policies, that we outline in the following. For the RL policy, we prepared in the environment a set of 11 reward functions, corresponding to the episode metrics reported in Table 1. Some rewards are continuous (i.e., given at every time step), while other (e.g., overtaking) are given on specific events. The definition of the optimal reward values turned out to be quite complicated and required a lot of tuning, together with simulation video inspection. After an initial empirical attempt, we set up a random search of about 50 different rewards sets, followed by a limited grid search in the proximity of the best set. Final results, employed in our model, are reported in Table 2. An Early Stopping algorithm [13] was also used to prevent overfitting. Our RL policy was implemented by training the above mentioned MLP model available in the Leurent implementation, as anticipated above.

We also defined a "minimal" RL policy, where there is only the traveled kms reward, and the episode is terminated not only in case of an accident, but also of a right overtaking, as of the traffic law. Another policy is a heuristic one, which implements a set of reasonable rules that define the action to be undertaken by the vehicle at each step, based on the current observation. Finally, a random policy selects the next action at random, for each step.

Table 2. Reward set for the RL policy

Reward name	Value
Right_Lane_Reward	−0,075
High_Speed_Reward	0,075
Speed_Reward	−0,5
Right_Overtaking_Reward	−0,9
Unsafe_Distance_Reward	−0,65
Left_Overtaking_Reward	0,9
Long_Accel_Reward	−0,1
Long_Decel_Reward	−0,2
Hazardous_Lane_Change_Reward	−0,65
Steering_Reward	−0,02
Collision_Reward	−1
Lane_Hazardous_Reward	0,5

5   Results

The system was implemented with a 2-layer multilayer perceptron (MLP) neural network and the algorithm used was deep Q learning.

Reported results concern an environment with the following main parameter values:

- Number of lanes: 3;
- Number of vehicles: 15;
- Traffic density: variable 0.3/0.7/0.9;
- Starting lane: 2;
- Length (maximum duration): 60 s;
- Initial speed Ego_vehicle: 30 m/s;
- Max speed Ego_vehicle: 30 m/s;

Figure 2 shows the performance comparison on some of the defined metrics and on the overall score between our RL policy and the original Leurent model. Results show that the introduction of specific metrics based on traffic law, and implementing a more realistic traffic behavior leads to better outcomes under all dimensions, including the number of traveled kilometers.

Figure 3 shows the comparison among our RL policy and other policies we have defined for the sake of the analysis. Not surprisingly we see that the random policy has a huge number of collisions. It is also apparent that the RL policy outperforms all the others in most of the considered dimensions, which is clearly reflected in the overall score. Random policy has a lower number of right overtaking because of the much lower number of kms driven. On the other hand, the good result obtained by the minimal RL policy in terms of number of right overtaking shows that a focused training allows

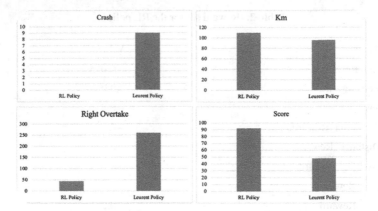

Fig. 2. Comparison between our RL and Leurent policies

achieving better results in the few considered dimensions, because of the simplification of the problem. This is however not confirmed by the number of collisions, in which the minimal RL is outperformed by the much more complex RL policy.

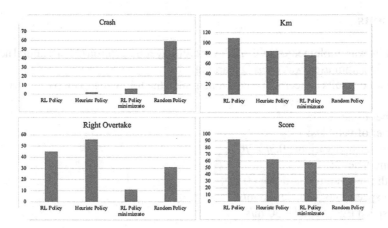

Fig. 3. Comparison between RL and other policies.

The overall score is arbitrary because of the weights we assigned to the considered dimensions, but also the analysis on the single dimensions shows the superiority of our RL policy. Also the minimal RL model, focused on the two basic traffic rules (avoid collisions and right overtaking) outperforms the Leurent basic policy, with our metrics. Finally, the heuristic policy has somehow acceptable performance, indicating a certain possibility of identifying rules for managing the behavior of a vehicle.

Considering the training of the model, [19] reports issues, mainly related to the order of vehicles in the observation, for training the MLP model with kinematics inputs, but we did not find this difficulty. The training of the 24,077 model parameters required several hours on a Tesla V100 board, for a total of 1.75 M steps (i.e., decided actions).

We also tried a deeper solution with a 5 layer MLP model, but without any improvement. We also tried employing the Nature CNN model on a grayscale image input, but the model involves 3.4 M parameters, and the training required is quite longer, and we could not go farther than 400 K steps, reaching a performance level lower than the original MLP model.

We also tried some different configurations of the environment, while keeping the MLP model trained in a 3 lane highway in mixed traffic conditions. Considering the traffic density, test scores increase as the traffic decreases, and the average speed comes significantly closer to the limit. Considering the road configuration, performance clearly degrades with a number of lanes different from 3. Particularly, we observed a steep increase in number of lane changes in the 4-lane case, and of right overtaking in the 2-lane case.

6   Conclusions and Future Work

This article has demonstrated the feasibility of implementing a RL agent able to plan the trajectory of a simple automated vehicle 2D model in a motorway simulation, thus usable as a NPV in SGs for driving. The agent extends a Deep Q Learning agent developed by Eduard Leurent in Stable Baselines by adding rewards in order to better meet the traffic laws. The motorway environment was enhanced as well, in order to increase realism. A MLP model, processing cinematic inputs from the ego and other vehicles, was tested in different traffic conditions and outperformed the original model and other policies such as a heuristic and a minimal-reward one. Our experience stresses the importance of defining episode metrics to assess agent behavior, keeping into accounts factors related to safety (e.g., keeping a safe time to collision) and consumption (e.g., limiting accelerations and decelerations). This is key to define rewards and penalties able to properly train the model to meet the traffic laws while keeping a high-speed performance. A convolutional neural network model was quite more difficult to train and did not provide valid results.

As future work, we intend to improve the model, so to make it better able to adapt to different road configurations and traffic conditions. We are also interested in improving the training of the convolutional network, and to study a Monte Carlo tree search model which is available in the Leurent's highway environment.

References

1. Massoud, R., Berta, R., Poslad, S., De Gloria, A., Bellotti, F.: IoT sensing for reality-enhanced serious games, a fuel-efficient drive use case. Sensors. 21(10), 3559 (2021). https://doi.org/10.3390/s21103559
2. Renault group, The Good Drive, a serious game to learning to drive, available online at: https://www.renaultgroup.com/en/news-on-air/news/the-good-drive-a-serious-game-for-learning-to-drive/
3. Dosovitskiy, A., Ros, G., Codevilla, F., Lopez, A., Koltun, V.: CARLA: An Open Urban driving simulator. In: 1st Conference on Robot Learning (CoRL 2017). Mountain View, USA (2017)
4. Carla community: Carla simulator. Version 0.9.11. https://carla.readthedocs.io/en/latest/. Accessed 23 April 2021

5. Leurent, E.: An environment for autonomous driving decision-making, github repository, Available at: https://github.com/eleurent/highway-env (2018)
6. Gounaridou, A., Siamtanidou, E., Dimoulas, C.: A serious game for mediated education on traffic behavior and safety awareness. Educ. Sci. **11**, 127 (2021). https://doi.org/10.3390/edu csci11030127
7. Likitweerawong, K., Palee, P.: The virtual reality serious game for learning driving skills before taking practical test. In: 2018 International Conference on Digital Arts, Media and Technology (ICDAMT), pp. 158–161 (2018). https://doi.org/10.1109/ICDAMT.2018.837 6515.
8. Hrimech, H., et al.: The effects of the use of serious game in eco-driving training. Front. ICT (2016). https://doi.org/10.3389/fict.2016.00022
9. Massoud, R., Poslad, S., Bellotti, F., Berta, R., Mehran, K., De Gloria, A.: A fuzzy logic module to estimate a driver's fuel consumption for reality-enhanced serious games. Int. J. Serious Games **5**(4), 45–62 (2018). https://doi.org/10.17083/ijsg.v5i4.266
10. Lazzaroni, L., Mazzara, A., Bellotti, F., De Gloria, A., Berta, R.: Employing an IoT framework as a generic serious games analytics engine. In: Marfisi-Schottman, I., Bellotti, F., Hamon, L., Klemke, R. (eds.) GALA 2020. LNCS, vol. 12517, pp. 79–88. Springer, Cham (2020). https://doi.org/10.1007/978-3-030-63464-3_8
11. Aldape, P., Sowell, S.: Reinforcement learning for a simple racing game. https://web.stanford. edu/class/aa228/reports/2018/final150.pdf/ Retrieved 14 Sept 2020
12. Westera, W., et al.: Artificial intelligence moving serious gaming: presenting reusable game AI components. Educ. Inf. Technol. **25**(1), 351–380 (2019). https://doi.org/10.1007/s10639-019-09968-2
13. Geron, A.: Hands-On Machine Learning With Scikit-Learn and Tensorflow. O'Reilly (2017)
14. Stable baselines: Available online at: https://stable-baselines.readthedocs.io
15. Tensorflow: Available online at: https://www.tensorflow.org/
16. Wang, Z., Schaul, T., Hessel, M., Van Hasselt, H., Lanctot, M., De Freitas, N.: Dueling network architectures for deep reinforcement learning. In: Proceedings of the 33rd International Conference on International Conference on Machine Learning, vol. 48 (ICML'16). JMLR.org (2016)
17. Mnih, V., et al.: Human-level control through deep reinforcement learning. Nature **518**, 529–533 (2015). https://doi.org/10.1038/nature14236
18. Colab: https://colab.research.google.com/
19. Leurent, E., Mercat, J.: Social attention for autonomous decision-making in dense traffic. In: Machine Learning for Autonomous Driving Workshop at the Thirty-third Conference on Neural Information Processing Systems (NeurIPS 2019). Montreal, Canada arXiv:1911. 12250 (2019)

Sex Differences in User Experience in a VR EEG Neurofeedback Paradigm

Lisa M. Berger[1]([✉]) [iD], Guilherme Wood[1,2] [iD], Christa Neuper[1,2] [iD],
and Silvia E. Kober[1,2] [iD]

[1] Institute of Psychology, University of Graz, Universitaetsplatz 2/III, 8010 Graz, Austria
`{lisa.berger,guilherme.wood,christa.neuper,`
`silvia.kober}@uni-graz.at`
[2] BioTechMed-Graz, Mozartgasse 12/II, 8010 Graz, Austria

Abstract. In brain-computer interface applications such as neurofeedback (NF), traditional 2D visual feedback has been replaced frequently by more sophisticated 3D virtual reality (VR) scenarios. VR is considered to be more motivating and to increase NF training success. However, hard evidence on user experience in set-ups combining VR-EEG NF has been scarcely reported. Hence, we evaluated user experience on cybersickness, discomfort/pain, technology acceptance and motivational factors and compared them between a 3D and a 2D VR scenario. Additionally, we focused on possible sex differences. 68 subjects received one VR-neurofeedback session with either a 3D or 2D VR paradigm. Statistical analyses showed that sickness was higher after the VR-NF training than before, and women experienced higher sickness values than men. Further, women reported more subjective pressure sensations on the head, eye burning and headache, as well as higher technology anxiety, less perceived usefulness of the used technology and less perceived technology accessibility. No dimensionality or sex differences regarding subjective feeling of flow and presence were found. Moreover, no differences between the 3D and 2D VR scenarios were observed. Our results indicate sex differences in user experience in VR-based NF paradigms, which should be considered when using VR as feedback modality in future NF applications. In contrast, 3D or 2D presentation of the VR scenario did not affect user experience, indicating that more immersive 3D VR scenarios do not cause more negative side effects than the less immersive 2D VR scenario.

Keywords: Virtual reality · Neurofeedback · EEG

1 Introduction

Neurofeedback is a brain-computer interface (BCI) where the aim is to learn how to alter voluntarily one's own brain activity. Here, brain activation patterns are acquired mostly by measuring cortical electric current fluctuations with Electroencephalography (EEG). Activation is then preprocessed in real-time and fed back to the user [15]. Modulating brain activation patterns in a desired direction using NF is used to improve cognitive

© Springer Nature Switzerland AG 2021
F. de Rosa et al. (Eds.): GALA 2021, LNCS 13134, pp. 111–120, 2021.
https://doi.org/10.1007/978-3-030-92182-8_11

or motoric performances in the context of neurorehabilitation and neuropsychological training [17], sports [33], acting performance [6], or improving sleeping quality [23].

Neurofeedback often requires multiple training sessions, sometimes even up to 70–100 sessions [17, 29]. Having to complete the same task all over again can be tiresome and demotivating in the long run. Paradigms mostly consist of visual feedback, showing bars or circles that should be increased in size during the training session [12]. As neurofeedback is strongly dependent on psychological factors such as motivation [9], subjective feeling of presence [7] and locus of control [32], it seems desirable to investigate factors increasing those subjective states, to make the training less tiresome and more engaging. Virtual Reality thereby poses as a modern tool to give more immersive feedback and maybe increase training motivation [11], as well as training success [12].

Besides possible positive effects of VR-based feedback, negative effects on NF training should be investigated. For example, cybersickness can occur in 25–80% of the participants related to the usage of virtual environments [2, 26]. Symptoms of discomfort in virtual environments are quite common and disappear after about 2–6 min after usage [1]. They can, however, attenuate for example the feeling of presence [30], which can in turn influence training success of neurofeedback [7]. Hence, we designed two different VR paradigms, a 3D environment with a moving viewer perspective and the other with a static 2D environment, to investigate cybersickness.

Additionally, in a VR-EEG set-up, the head-mounted VR-system (VR goggles) is placed over the electrodes. What has never been reported in previous studies using a similar set-up is that this combinational set-up could cause headache or pressure sensations, since VR-goggles press against the electrodes on the head, as before mostly CAVE™-like surround projection screens have been used for VR induction. Therefore, we wanted to investigate pain and discomfort with visual analogue scales (VAS).

Further, sex differences in the user experience need to be considered, as men still perceive technology as more positive, than women [3]. Also, it has been reported that women experience less subjective feeling of control over technology usage and experience less self-efficacy [22]. Control beliefs can predict the upregulation of the sensorimotor rhythm [32], hence the neurofeedback success.

In this study, we therefore investigated different aspects of user experience and psychological constructs in 2D vs. 3D VR paradigm groups. Dimensionality and sex differences concerning technology perception, cybersickness and motivation were tested in healthy young adults in an EEG-based neurofeedback study.

2 Methods

2.1 Subjects

Seventy-six healthy participants were tested in this study and were randomly assigned to the 2D or 3D group. Inclusion criteria were the absence of neurological or psychiatric diseases and age of participants to be between 18–34 years old. Eight participants were excluded due to bad EEG data quality, technical problems and not fulfilling inclusion criteria. 68 subjects (Mean age = 23.21, SD = 3.41) were left for further analysis. As a reward, every participant could try out Google Earth in the Virtual Reality after the experiment and psychology students would get course credits for their participation.

All participants gave their written informed consent. The study was approved by the local ethics committee of the University of Graz, Austria and is in accordance with The Code of Ethics of the World Medical Association (Declaration of Helsinki) for experiments involving humans (WMA (World Medical Association), 2009).

2.2 Questionnaires

Technology Usage Inventory (TUI). This questionnaire [14] asks for the acceptance of technologies and psychological factors concerning the usage of technology. The items are divided into eight scales: curiosity, anxiety, interest, user friendliness, immersion, usefulness, scepsis and accessibility. Sum scores are calculated and transformed to stanines, ranging from 1 to 9, where higher values represent higher manifestations. Cronbach's Alpha shows an intern validity between .70 and .89.

Questionnaire for Current Motivation (FAM). The FAM [21] evaluates the momentary learning motivation in four scales: fear of failure, interest, success probability and challenge. Sum scores are calculated for interpretation, where higher values represent higher manifestations. Cronbach's Alpha range from .66 to .90.

Flow Short Scale (FKS). The Flow scale [20] evaluates the extent to which participants experienced flow with the three factors: Smooth automated procedure, absorbedness, and worry. A total sum score can be calculated as well as the sum scores of the three subscales. For the analysis, t-values were taken from the according norm-table. Internal consistency of Cronbach's Alpha lies at .90.

Igroup Presence Questionnaire. This questionnaire evaluates the grade in which people feel present in a VR [19]. The IPQ consists of three subscales: spatial presence, involvement and experienced realism and an additional item, not associated to any subscale. A sum score over all items can be calculated, as well as the scores for the three subscales. Higher values indicate higher manifestations. Cronbach's Alpha was tested in two studies, the first reported an Alpha between .80 and .85. The second study shows similar Alpha with .77–.87.

Simulator Sickness Questionnaire (SSQ). The SSQ [8] covers several physical symptoms such as nausea and headache The sum score is calculated, the higher the score, the higher the symptoms. Also, three subscales can be calculated: nausea (e.g. sweating, stomach awareness), oculomotor (e.g. blurred vision, eye strain), and disorientation (e.g. dizziness). This questionnaire was filled out before and after the neurofeedback training. The sum score and subscores each need to be multiplicated by weights, described elsewhere [8].

Visual Analogue Scale (VAS) on Physical Condition. This VAS was self-constructed to identify whether participants experienced headache or pain due to VR-googles and electrodes. Pain intensity levels could vary between values of 0 up to 100, the higher the values the greater the pain/discomfort.

Evaluation of Training Enjoyment. At the end of the neurofeedback session participants were asked in a single question, whether they had fun during the training. Frequencies were calculated.

2.3 Neurofeedback

After filling out questionnaires and having the EEG and VR montage done, participants had to undergo seven feedback-runs of 3 min each with short breaks in-between. The first run was a baseline run where they were told to just watch the target objects without trying to alter their brain activation in order to identify individual frequency-band thresholds for SMR (12–15 Hz), Theta (4–7 Hz) and Beta (16–30). SMR had to be kept high, whereas Theta and Beta should be held as low as possible, to avoid artifacts such as blinks or movements [28] as target objects would turn red and stop moving when they were too high.

The 2D paradigm showed one green two-dimensional vertically moving bar (see Fig. 1A) [12] in the virtual space. The bar would increase in its height, whenever the trained EEG-frequency was over the individually identified threshold and would decrease, whenever the frequency was below that threshold.

The 3D paradigm showed a forest environment (downloaded from TriForge Assets in the Unity Asset Store), where a green ball was rolling along a predefined path, collecting light blue floating objects. The ball would move, whenever the predefined threshold of the trained EEG-frequency was exceeded and it would stand still, whenever the frequency was below that threshold (see Fig. 1B). Half of the participants received the 2D paradigm and the other half received the 3D paradigm.

The HTC Vive Pro-System was used, and the VR environments were programmed in the game engine Unity 3D, Version 2018.3.1.4. The lab streaming layer LSL4Unity plugin, freely available at https://github.com/labstreaminglayer/LSL4Unity, was implemented to stream the incoming EEG data.

The gUSBamp RESEARCH EEG-amplifier from g.tec medical engineering was used for the EEG-acquisition. Feedback was given over the Cz electrode [11]. Real-time preprocessing was done via OpenViBE Version 2.2.0.

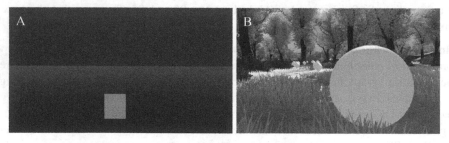

Fig. 1. A) 2D VR paradigm and B) 3D VR paradigm. Both were presented via the HTC-Vive Pro head-mounted VR goggles.

2.4 Statistical Analysis

To evaluate dimensionality and sex differences in cybersickness, an ANOVA with the between-subject factors dimensionality (2D vs. 3D) and sex, as well as one within-subjects factor time taking pre- and post-training into account, was conducted.

To analyze subjective values on physical condition and technology acceptance, ANOVAs with the between-subject factors dimensionality and sex were calculated for each VAS and subscales.

To investigate current motivation, we only took the between-subjects variable sex and calculated a Mann-Whitney-U Test. Finally, we checked for dimensionality and sex differences concerning enjoyment with a Chi-Square test.

2.5 Results

Simulator Sickness. SSQ sum score was higher after the training ($M = 102.19$, $SE = 2.86$) than before ($M = 93.23$, $SE = 1.62$). Women showed higher sickness (Pre: $M = 97.68$, $SE = 2.57$; Post: $M = 110.77$, $SE = 4.79$) than men (Pre: $M = 88.77$, $SE = 1.67$; Post: $M = 93.61$, $SE = 2.43$) at both time points. Oculomotor problems ($M = 69.00$, $SE = 1.79$) increased after the training ($M = 80.59$, $SE = 3.07$). Women showed higher values at both timepoints (Pre: $M = 74.69$, $SE = 2.95$; Post: $M = 90.51$, $SE = 5.11$) compared to men (Pre: $M = 63.32$, $SE = 1.53$; Post: $M = 70.67$, $SE = 2.49$) and disorientation ($M = 105.22$, $SE = 1.47$) was also significantly higher after the training ($M = 119.55$, $SE = 3.10$; see Table 1). Women showed higher levels at both timepoints (Pre: $M = 107.68$, $SE = 2.37$; Post: $M = 129.37$, $SE = 4.79$) than men (Pre: $M = 102.76$, $SE = 1.66$, Post: $M = 107.76$; $SE = 3.21$). Also, there was a significant interaction of sex and time (see Table 1) All other effects were non-significant.

Physical Condition. Women experienced more pressure sensations ($M = 31.94$, $SE = 4.52$) on the head than men ($M = 18.35$, $SE = 2.76$), more headache ($M = 13.50$, $SE = 3.30$) after the training than men ($M = 3.47$, $SE = 1.47$) and higher symptoms of eye burning ($M = 14.97$, $SE = 3.74$) than men ($M = 5.71$, $SE = 1.50$), with higher values of women in the 3D group ($M = 22.18$, $SE = 6.56$), compared to the 2D group ($M = 7.76$, $SE = 2.86$; see Table 1). Everything else was tested non-significant.

Technology Usage Inventory. Women reported less perceived usefulness of technology ($F(1, 64) = 4.55$, $p = .037$, $\eta_p2 = .066$), higher technology anxiety ($F(1, 64) = 5.49$, $p = .022$, $\eta_p2 - .079$) and less subjective accessibility of technology ($F(1, 64) = 4.89$, $p = .031$, $\eta_p2 = .071$) than men. Finally, women reported significantly less interest ($F(1, 64) = 38.52$, $p = .000$; $\eta_p2 = .376$; see Fig. 2). No other effects were shown.

Motivation/Enjoyment. The subscale fear of failure showed a tendency of higher fear in women ($M = 12.03$, $SE = 1.03$), compared to men ($M = 9.15$, $SE = 0.76$; $Z = -1.951$, $p = .051$). The effects of all the other subscales were non-significant.

Flow and Presence. No significant main effects of dimensionality (Presence: $F(1, 64) = .79$, $p = .377$, $\eta_p2 = .012$; Flow: $F(1, 64) = .67$, $p = .548$, $\eta_p2 = .006$) or sex (Presence: $F(1, 64) = 53$, $p = .468$, $\eta_p2 = .008$; Flow: $(F(1, 64) = .37$, $p = .548$, $\eta_p2 = .006$) were found, as well as no interaction effects of dimensionality vs. sex (Presence: $(F(1, 64) = .02$, $p = .892$, $\eta_p2 = .000$; Flow: $(F(1, 64) = .01$, $p = .915$, $\eta_p2 = .000$).

116   L. M. Berger et al.

Table 1. F-statistics for sickness, physical condition, presence, and flow.

Analysis	Factors	$F(1,64)$	p	$\eta_p 2$	Sig.
SSQ	Time	14.71	.000	.187	**
	Sex	12.16	.001	.160	*
Oculomotor	Time	20.76	.000	.245	**
	Sex	15.34	.000	.193	**
Disorientation	Time	29.59	.000	.316	**
	Sex	10.53	.002	.141	*
	Time × sex	7.44	.008	.104	*
Heachache	Sex	8.03	.006	.112	*
Pressure	Sex	6.94	.011	.098	*
Eye Burning	Sex	5.74	.020	.082	*
	Sex × dimensionality	4.10	.047	.060	*

Note. ** p < .001; * p < .05.

The majority of the participants (88.2%) had fun during the training, for 2.9% the training was not fun 8.8% had partly fun with the training. There are no group differences between 2D and 3D design ($X^2(2, N = 68) = .50, p = .779$) but more women (33) reported fun during the training than men (27; $X^2(2, N = 68) = 6.6, p = .037$).

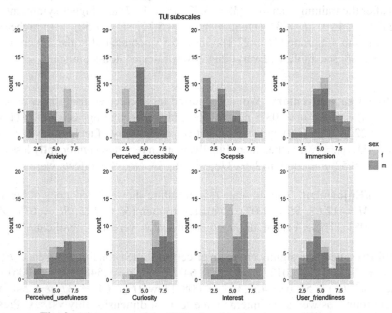

Fig. 2. Histograms of the TUI subscales showing sex differences.

2.6 Discussion

In the present study, the differences of a 3D and 2D VR-NF paradigm on user experience and possible sex differences were evaluated. Participants completed a single EEG-NF session while wearing VR goggles. Here, we found several sex differences in terms of user experience.

Cybersickness was higher after the VR-NF training than before. One previous study on motion sickness in virtual environments reported that subjective sickness values were much higher, when questionnaires were given pre and post exposure to the virtual environment, as if they were only given post-exposure [34]. Hence, asking participants twice might bias their answers to higher sickness values. However, participants from the 3D group did not report higher cybersickness than those, from the 2D feedback. Hence, more dynamic paradigms do not necessarily result in higher values of cybersickness, being applicable in terms of NF interventions.

Women reported higher sickness than men, appearing to be more easily affected by VR training concerning sickness. In fact, such sex-differences can be biologically hardwired or generated through differences in VR-experiences [4]. Women have a higher field of view [31], there is a greater non-fit of the interpupillary distance of the VR goggles in female participants [27]. Additionally, female hormones increase susceptibility to simulator sickness [13]. Nevertheless, previous studies suggested that VR-experience accounts at least as much as sex to the development of sickness-symptoms [25]. Video-game experience has not been assessed in this study, however, we tried to find different aspects that could represent user experience. Women reported lower levels of subjective accessibility of the technology, which could indicate that the female participants had less VR-experience. Furthermore, women also experience higher technology anxiety than men, which also has been found elsewhere [24]. Trait-anxiety can be a driving factor in the generation of cybersickness [18]. This is an important indicator that participants need to get used to the technology in for example introduction sessions, to secure the best possible training success and reduce anxiety to a minimum.

What is more, women rated the VR technology as less useful. As stated in the Technology Acceptance Model (TAM) of Davis [5], perceived usefulness is a crucial point in the acceptance of technology, entailing a higher intention to use in participants. This implicates that Virtual Reality and its possibilities in usage as well as its possible consequences should be communicated at the beginning of the neurofeedback session more directly to the participants, so that even less-experienced individuals can grasp the usefulness of the used technology. However, women did not have a solely negative user experience. The less perceived accessibility of the technology might be the reason, why women reported more fun during the training as maybe less women previously had the chance to try VR compared to male participants.

No group differences in subjective feeling of presence, however, were apparent between 3D and 2D groups. One reason for that is that even in the 2D group, three dimensional effects could not completely be ruled out. The dark space around the 2D bar target object, evokes a feeling of presence due to the stereoscopic effect of the VR goggles. Also, bigger screens result in higher feelings of presence [10] when using stereoscopic projection screens to display VR scenarios, but in the present study, both paradigms were shown with Virtual Reality goggles, therefore, did not differ in presentation size. They therefore had the same level of immersion which also correlates with presence [16]. Therefore, both groups were very similar in the technical aspects, wherefore no differences in presence could emerge.

Also, no group differences in the subjective flow-experience were found, which was also recorded previously in a NF study comparing a computer screen vs. VR projection screen paradigm [6]. This may be explained by episodes of successful feedback-moments that were too short to lead to a flow sensation. The target object was green and moving into the desired direction only when SMR exceeded, and Beta and Theta remained under the individually pre-defined thresholds. Therefore, sequences where all three factors were in equilibrium were comparably short, so that no feeling of flow could develop.

2.7 Conclusion

User experience in combinational VR-EEG neurofeedback designs differs between male and female participants, showing that instructional sessions for the VR would be beneficial for women to get used to the technology they perceive as less accessible. Additionally, the results show that more immersive 3D paradigms do not cause any more side effects than 2D designs. Generally, one strength in this paper is a comparably big sample size, which is rare in neurofeedback studies, and the moderate to big effect sizes. Hence our results point toward generalizability. Nevertheless, more research on this topic is needed.

References

1. Pesudovs, K.: The development of a symptom questionnaire for assessing virtual reality viewing using a head-mounted display. Optom. Vision Sci. **82**(7), 571 (2005). https://doi.org/10.1097/01.opx.0000171186.02468.b7
2. Brooks, J.O., et al.: Simulator sickness during driving simulation studies. Accid. Anal. Prev. **42**(3), 788–796 (2010). https://doi.org/10.1016/j.aap.2009.04.013
3. Cai, Z., Fan, X., Du, J.: Gender and attitudes toward technology use: a meta-analysis. Comput. Educ. **105**, 1–13 (2017). https://doi.org/10.1016/j.compedu.2016.11.003
4. Davis, S., Nesbitt, K., Nalivaiko, E.: A systematic review of cybersickness. In: Blackmore, K., Nesbitt, K., Smith, S.P. (eds.) Proceedings of the 2014 Conference on Interactive Entertainment, pp. 1–9. ACM, New York, NY, USA (2014)
5. Davis, F.D., Bagozzi, R.P., Warshaw, P.R.: User acceptance of computer technology: a comparison of two theoretical models. Manage. Sci. **35**, 982–1003 (1989)
6. Gruzelier, J., Inoue, A., Smart, R., Steed, A., Steffert, T.: Acting performance and flow state enhanced with sensory-motor rhythm neurofeedback comparing ecologically valid immersive VR and training screen scenarios. Neurosci. Lett. **480**(2), 112–116 (2010). https://doi.org/10.1016/j.neulet.2010.06.019
7. Juliano, J., et al.: Embodiment is related to better performance on a brain–computer interface in immersive virtual reality: a pilot study. Sensors **20**(4), 1204 (2020). https://doi.org/10.3390/s20041204
8. Kennedy, R.S., Lane, N.E., Berbaum, K.S., Lilienthal, M.G.: Simulator sickness questionnaire: an enhanced method for quantifying simulator sickness. Int. J. Aviat. Psychol. **3**(3), 203–220 (1993). https://doi.org/10.1207/s15327108ijap0303_3

9. Kleih, S.C., Nijboer, F., Halder, S., Kübler, A.: Motivation modulates the P300 amplitude during brain-computer interface use. Clin. Neurophysiol. **121**(7), 1023–1031 (2010). https://doi.org/10.1016/j.clinph.2010.01.034

10. Kober, S.E., Kurzmann, J., Neuper, C.: Cortical correlate of spatial presence in 2D and 3D interactive virtual reality: an EEG study. Int. J. Psychophysiol. **83**(3), 365–374 (2012). https://doi.org/10.1016/j.ijpsycho.2011.12.003

11. Kober, S.E., Reichert, J.L., Schweiger, D., Neuper, C., Wood, G.: Effects of a 3D Virtual Reality Neurofeedback Scenario on User Experience and Performance in Stroke Patients. In: Bottino, R., Jeuring, J., Veltkamp, R.C. (eds.) GALA 2016. LNCS, vol. 10056, pp. 83–94. Springer, Cham (2016). https://doi.org/10.1007/978-3-319-50182-6_8

12. Kober, S.E., Reichert, J.L., Schweiger, D., Neuper, C., Wood, G.: Does feedback design matter? A neurofeedback study comparing immersive virtual reality and traditional training screens in elderly. IJSG **4**(3) (2017). doi:https://doi.org/10.17083/ijsg.v4i3.167

13. Kolasinski, E.M.: Simulator Sickness in Virtual Environments, Bd 1995. Alexandria, VA (1995)

14. Kothgassner, O.D., Felnhofer, A., Hauk, N., Kastenhofer, E., Gomm, J., Kryspin-Exner, I.: TUI – Technology Usage Inventory. Manual (2013)

15. Marzbani, H., Marateb, H.R., Mansourian, M.: Neurofeedback: a comprehensive review on system design, methodology and clinical applications. Basic Clin. Neurosci. **7**(2), 143–158 (2016). https://doi.org/10.15412/J.BCN.03070208

16. Oh, S.Y., Bailenson, J.: Virtual and augmented reality. In: Rössler, P., Hoffner, C.A., van Zoonen, L. (eds.) The International Encyclopedia of Media Effects, pp. 1–16. John Wiley & Sons Inc, Chichester, West Sussex, Malden, MA (2017)

17. de Barros, P., França, F.: Follow-up to case study: neurofeedback as a first choice treatment in an adhd and comorbidities. KLS (2018). https://doi.org/10.18502/kls.v4i8.3285

18. Paillard, A.C., et al.: Motion sickness susceptibility in healthy subjects and vestibular patients: effects of gender, age and trait-anxiety. J. Vestibular Res. **23**(4–5), 203–209 (2013). https://doi.org/10.3233/VES-130501

19. Regenbrecht, H.T., Schubert, T.W., Friedmann, F.: Measuring the sense of presence and its relations to fear of heights in virtual environments. Int. J. Hum. Comput. Interact. **10**(3), 233–249 (1998). https://doi.org/10.1207/s15327590ijhc1003_2

20. Rheinberg, F., Vollmeyer, R., Engeser, S.: FKS – Flow-Kurzskala. ZPID (Leibniz Institute for Psychology Information) – Testarchiv (2019)

21. Rheinberg, F., Vollmeyer, R., Burns, B.D.: FAM – Fragebogen zur aktuellen Motivation. ZPID (Leibniz Institute for Psychology) – Open Test Archive (2021)

22. Salisbury, D.B., Dahdah, M., Driver, S., Parsons, T.D., Richter, K.M.: Virtual reality and brain computer interface in neurorehabilitation. Baylor Univ. Med. Center Proc. **29**(2), 124–127 (2016)

23. Schabus, M., et al.: Enhancing sleep quality and memory in insomnia using instrumental sensorimotor rhythm conditioning. Biol. Psychol. **95**, 126–134 (2014). https://doi.org/10.1016/j.biopsycho.2013.02.020

24. Schmidt, M., Kafka, J.X., Kothgassner, O.D., Hlavacs, H., Beutl, L., Felnhofer, A.: Why does it always rain on me? Influence of gender and environmental factors on usability, technology related anxiety and immersion in virtual environments. In: Reidsma, D., Katayose, H., Nijholt, A. (eds.) ACE 2013. LNCS, vol. 8253, pp. 392–402. Springer, Cham (2013). https://doi.org/10.1007/978-3-319-03161-3_29

25. Shafer, D., Korpi, M., Carbonara, C.P.: Modern Virtual reality technology: cybersickness, sense of presence, and gender. Media Psychol. Rev. **11**, 1–13 (2017)

26. Sharples, S., Cobb, S., Moody, A., Wilson, J.R.: Virtual reality induced symptoms and effects (VRISE): comparison of head mounted display (HMD), desktop and projection display systems. Displays **29**(2), 58–69 (2008). https://doi.org/10.1016/j.displa.2007.09.005

27. Stanney, K., Fidopiastis, C., Foster, L.: Virtual Reality is sexist: but it does not have to be. Front. Rob. AI **7**, 4 (2020). https://doi.org/10.3389/frobt.2020.00004
28. Tatum, W.O., Dworetzky, B.A., Schomer, D.L.: Artifact and recording concepts in EEG. J. Clin. Neurophysiol. **28**(3), 252–263 (2011). https://doi.org/10.1097/WNP.0b013e31821c 3c93
29. Van Doren, J., Arns, M., Heinrich, H., Vollebregt, M.A., Strehl, U., Loo, S.K.: Sustained effects of neurofeedback in ADHD: a systematic review and meta-analysis. Eur. Child Adolesc. Psychiatry **28**(3), 293–305 (2018). https://doi.org/10.1007/s00787-018-1121-4
30. Weech, S., Kenny, S., Barnett-Cowan, M.: Presence and cybersickness in virtual reality are negatively related: a review. Front. Psychol. **10**, 158 (2019). https://doi.org/10.3389/fpsyg. 2019.00158
31. Williams, J.M., Thirer, J.: Vertical and horizontal peripheral vision in male and female athletes and nonathletes. Res. Quarterly Am. Alliance Health Phys. Educ. Recreation **46**(2), 200–205 (1975). https://doi.org/10.1080/10671315.1975.10615324
32. Witte, M., Kober, S.E., Ninaus, M., Neuper, C., Wood, G.: Control beliefs can predict the ability to up-regulate sensorimotor rhythm during neurofeedback training. Front. Hum. Neurosci. **7**, 478 (2013). https://doi.org/10.3389/fnhum.2013.00478
33. Xiang, M.-Q., Hou, X.-H., Liao, B.-G., Liao, J.-W., Hu, M.: The effect of neurofeedback training for sport performance in athletes: a meta-analysis. Psychol. Sport Exercise **36**, 114–122 (2018). https://doi.org/10.1016/j.psychsport.2018.02.004
34. Young, S.D., Adelstein, B.D., Ellis, S.R.: Demand characteristics in assessing motion sickness in a virtual environment: or does taking a motion sickness questionnaire make you sick? IEEE Trans. Visualization Comput. Graphics **13**(3), 422–428 (2007). https://doi.org/10.1109/ TVCG.2007.1029

Validity of a Content Agnostic Game Based Stealth Assessment

Vipin Verma[1]([⊠]) [iD], Ashish Amresh[2] [iD], Scotty D. Craig[1] [iD], and Ajay Bansal[1] [iD]

[1] Arizona State University, Mesa, AZ, USA
{vverma9,scotty.craig,ajay.bansal}@asu.edu
[2] Arizona State University, Tempe, AZ, USA
amresh@asu.edu

Abstract. In an attempt to predict the learning of a player during a content agnostic educational video game session, this study used a dynamic bayesian network in which participants' game play interactions were continuously recorded. Their actions were captured and used to make real-time inferences of the learning performance using a dynamic bayesian network. The predicted learning was then correlated with the post-test scores to establish the validity of assessment. The assessment was moderately positively correlated with the post-test scores demonstrating support for its validity.

Keywords: Game based assessment · Sensor-free · Stealth assessment · Dynamic bayesian network · Educational games

1 Introduction

Serious games are prodding the education domain to delineate the meaning of learning and assessment which are both challenging in nature [1,9]. While developing a game itself takes a lot of time, adding assessment adds another time-consuming process to it. To ease this process, our study used the content agnostic game engineering (CAGE) architecture [2] embedded with stealth assessment [15,16,18,19].

Baron [2] created CAGE architecture to facilitate the development of multiple educational games at once. It develops game mechanics that are independent of the learning content taught in the game and is called content agnostic mechanics. This allows using a single game to teach multiple learning contents, saving time and money which would otherwise be used to create multiple games to teach all of them. Further, Shute and colleagues [16] developed stealth assessment strategies for learning games that use player interactions as evidence that can aid in inferring learning while the player is actively playing the game. Our study used stealth assessment within CAGE to create a content agnostic game based assessment strategy. We present our results with validating the assessment so that it can be adopted as an effective strategy for educational games [8].

© Springer Nature Switzerland AG 2021
F. de Rosa et al. (Eds.): GALA 2021, LNCS 13134, pp. 121–130, 2021.
https://doi.org/10.1007/978-3-030-92182-8_12

2   Content Agnostic Game Engineering

Usually an educational game is designed to teach a specific learning content and to teach another content it is required to develop another game specific to that content. However, designing and developing an educational video games is a time and cost intensive process [2]. Therefore, teaching multiple content would mean creating multiple different games, leading to more effort, more time and money requirements. CAGE can alleviate this problem by using content agnostic mechanics that separates the game mechanics from the learning content. This is not only beneficial for researchers, but also benefits industry due to savings in terms of time and money.

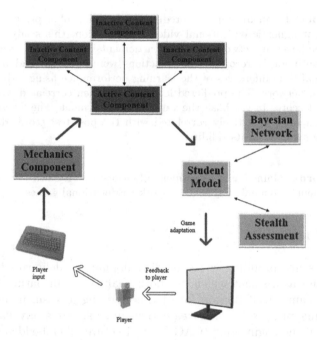

Fig. 1. CAGE model for educational game development.

CAGE follows a component-based architecture consisting of three components; mechanics component, content component, and student model as depicted in Fig. 1. The mechanics component is designed to be content agnostic. CAGE consists of multiple content components which can be switched at anytime. Student model creates a model of the student learning using an embedded stealth assessment by utilizing the player interactions within the game. Multiple stealth assessment strategies can be combined to create a student model [18]. These three components are held together with the help of the underlying framework that connects the player input with the game mechanics.

3   Dynamic Bayesian Network

A Bayesian Network (BN) uses probabilistic graph to model several variables which are conditionally dependent on each other [7]. A Dynamic Bayesian Network (DBN) is a type of BN that allows modeling time-series and sequences using variables that have probabilistic dependence over a period called lag or time-steps [13,14]. A simple DBN called as knowledge tracing [6] was used as a basis for the current study, shown in Fig. 2. The Figure shows a 2-quiz series that consists of three nodes; a participant node (S), a question node (Q), and a knowledge node (K). There are four performance parameters which are prior knowledge, slip rate, learn rate, and guess rate, that model the network.

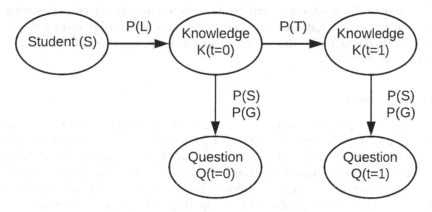

Fig. 2. Two time slices of the knowledge tracing model [6].

An individual learner (S) is represented using the student node and regulates the prior knowledge parameter P(L) which depicts the prior knowledge level of a learner before they start playing the game [12]. A diagnostic pre-test can be used to obtain the parameter value. State of learner's knowledge at any point in time is modeled using the latent knowledge node (K). This node is replicated across each time-step and is termed as a temporal node. At any time-step, the knowledge node is conditionally dependent on the knowledge node from the previous time-step. This dependence of knowledge node with itself across time-steps is depicted using learn rate which is also called as transition rate P(T). It determines the probability that the learner will transition from an unlearned state to a learned state when moving to the next time-step. The question node (Q) depicts the question which was asked to measure learner's knowledge. It consists of two states, true and false, which represents learner's answer being correct or incorrect. It is conditionally dependent on the time-specific knowledge level of the participant. The question node is replicated across all the time-steps and is therefore temporal. It consists of two parameters, slip rate P(S) and the guess rate P(G). Slip rate models the probability of answering incorrectly when a learner possess the knowledge, while guess rate accounts for guessing correctly despite not having the required knowledge.

4 Method

4.1 Participants

The current study was conducted online due to the Covid-19 pandemic. It recruited 172 undergraduate students of which 61 students did not complete the study due to potential bugs in the game or the issues with the game interface when playing on devices with different resolutions. A total of 111 participants completed the study (91 male, 20 female, average age 21.6 years, standard deviation of 6.17). Sixty-one participants reported having played games with an average play time of sixteen hours per week and a standard deviation of fifteen hours. Their participation lasted up to 2 h (mean playtime of 95 min, standard deviation of 29.5 min).

4.2 Background

CAGE architecture [2,3] was used to create a 2D platformer game titled "Chemo-o-crypt" in Unity3D (v2018.1.9f2). In CAGE, the game play mechanics were designed in such a manner that they were not tightly connected to the educational content. This allowed the same mechanics to be used to teach multiple subjects without significantly modifying the game play mechanics. Educational games that follow this architecture are getting popular as content dependent mechanics make the game development costly and time-consuming [4].

Game Mechanics. In Chemo-o-crypt, the game play mechanics allowed left and right player movement, jumping, and ladder climbing. Three different types of enemies patrolled certain areas within the game environment. It reduced a portion of the player health when they collided with an enemy. The game environment also consisted of two different types of static hazards, spikes and water. On falling into these hazards, the player health was immediately reduced to zero.

The game consisted of two learning contents, chemistry and cryptography. Each learning content had 4 distinct levels representing a learning problem for that given level. During each level, the player was tasked with collecting the required number of elements corresponding to the goal of that level. The game map had coins and heart-shaped items (1-up) which were scattered at various locations. A player initially had three lives which could be increased by collecting one hundred coins or a 1-up.

Game Content. For the cryptography content, the players were required to collect the alphabetical letters corresponding to the encryption/decryption of a given text using the encryption key provided to them. However, there were either excess or different letters present in the game map which would act as a distractor. This was deliberately done to see if a player is collecting everything instead of collecting only required letters. It was also expected to make the game more stimulating for learners. All the collectible letters were displayed in white color. However, the distractor letters became red when picked while the rest were shown in glowing green ink signaling that they were not distractors. Operant conditioning was implemented to prevent the players from collecting distractors [17]. On picking up a distractor, players received a kickback and some health loss which was governed by the content level. For example, during the first content level, there was no health loss, during the second content level there was some health loss, but during the last content level the player instantly died on collecting a distractor. A collectible element randomly became either a required letter or a distractor when the player came into its proximity. On collecting all the required letters, the "GO" (completion text) appeared. But if there were distractors which were not yet collected, there was a 50% chance that a collectible would become a distractor instead of becoming a completion text. On collecting the completion text, the same encryption/decryption problem appeared (as a quiz) which they solved with the help of game play mechanics. The next content level was loaded on answering the quiz, irrespective of the answer being right or wrong. The game had four content levels, each having their own background music which got more intense as the player moved to higher and more complex content levels. The task along with solutions for each level are enumerated below:

1. Encrypt the Plain Text: "ATTACK AT DAWN" using the Key: 2
   Resulting encryption = "CVVCEMCVFCYP"
2. Decrypt the Cipher Text: "EFGFOE UIF DBTUMF" using the Key: 1
   Resulting decryption = "DEFENDTHECASTLE"
3. Encrypt the Plain Text: "PURA VIDA" using the Key: 13
   Resulting decryption = "CHENIVQN"
4. Decrypt the Cipher Text: "URON RB KNJDCRODU" using the Key: 9
   Resulting decryption = "LIFEISBEAUTIFUL"

For the chemistry content, players were tasked with collecting the exact number of molecules that partake in a given chemical reaction to balance it. The chemical equation for the first content level require 3 Oxygen (O_2) and 2 Ozone (O_3) molecules to balance. The excess of these molecules would act as a distractor. The balanced equation for each content level is listed below:

1. $2\,O_3 \longrightarrow 3\,O_2$
2. $N_2 + 3\,H_2 \longrightarrow 2\,NH_3$
3. $ZnS + 2\,HCl \longrightarrow ZnCl_2 + H_2S$
4. $Al_2O_3 + 6\,HCl \longrightarrow 2\,AlCl_3 + 3\,H_2O$

Stealth Assessment. The DBN used for assessment in the game is shown in Fig. 3. To implement the network in the game, Bayes Server 8.17 [5] was used. The network had eleven nodes, of which five were temporal (Knowledge1, Distractor10, Distractor11, Distractor12, and Question1). In addition to the Prior Knowledge, and Question node from the knowledge tracing model [12], the network consisted of several distractor nodes. Each of them represented the event of picking up a distractor. Distractor0x nodes denoted the evidence that player has collected this distractor at time-step $t = 0$ (i.e. content level 1). However, Distractor1x nodes designated the evidence for time-steps $t = 1, 2, 3$ (i.e. content level 2, 3, 4 respectively). To assign the value to Prior node, a pre-test containing twenty questions was used which would serve as evidence for the Knowledge0 node which is conditionally dependent on it. Knowledge0 node has two states, true and false, indicating the presence or absence of knowledge required to achieve the level aim. It expresses the probability that the player possess the required knowledge at the time-step $t = 0$ while Knowledge1 if for the time-steps $t = 1, 2, 3$. The probabilities for the first content level were intentionally made different from the rest of the content levels with the help of the complex DBN structure. This allowed for learning the game mechanics on the first content level, since players were not initially aware that they were not allowed to collect distractors. While learning the game mechanics during first content level, the probabilities of collecting the distractor were expected to be higher when compared to the rest of the content levels. The conditional probabilities of the network were estimated using a combination of parameter learning [11] and expert raters advice. An earlier experiment consisting of 107 participants was used to collect the data for parameter learning. The estimated probabilities are depicted in Table 1 and 2.

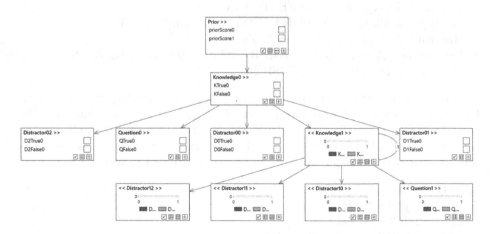

Fig. 3. DBN used for assessment in the Chem-o-crypt.

Table 1. Conditional probabilities used for Prior and Knowledge0 node.

Prior score states (pre-test score)		0	1	2	3	4	5	6	7	8	9	10
Knowledge0		.01	.01	.01	.03	.04	.05	.05	.08	.30	.37	.05
	True	.40	.42	.44	.46	.48	.50	.52	.54	.56	.58	.60
	False	.60	.58	.56	.54	.52	.50	.48	.46	.44	.42	.40

Table 2. Conditional probabilities used for Distractor, Knowledge1, and Question nodes.

Knowledge0	Distractor00		Distractor01		Distractor02		Question0		Knowledge1	
	True	False	True	False	True	False	True	False	True	False
True	.52	.48	.01	.99	.00	1.00	.97	.03	.53	.47
False	.99	.01	.94	.06	.28	.72	.58	.42	.34	.66
Knowledge1	Distractor10		Distractor11		Distractor12		Question1		Knowledge1	
	True	False	True	False	True	False	True	False	True	False
True	.34	.66	.00	1.00	.00	1.00	.92	.08	.80	.20
False	1.00	.00	.64	.36	.20	.80	.75	.25	.11	.89

External Assessment. The experiment consisted of pre and post-test which were isomorphic in nature. They consisted of 20 multiple choice questions and randomized the order or the questions as well the available choices within each question. Pre-test was used as a diagnostic assessment for evaluating the state of the prior node while post-test was used as a summative assessment to be compared with the inference of knowledge from the DBN at the end of the game play.

4.3   Procedure

Participants downloaded the game and instructions upon consenting to partake in the study. Figure 4 shows a typical participant workflow during the game. On starting the game, player walked through a tutorial level where the basic game play mechanics to navigate the gaming environment were introduced. After the tutorial level, they went through the reading material for the first learning content, followed by the pre-test and the actual game play. On finishing the four content levels for the first learning content, they completed the post-test and survey and went to the reading material for the second learning content. Each learning content consisted of four content levels. The game ended when player finished all the 4 × 2 levels. After finishing the workflow they were rewarded course-completion credits.

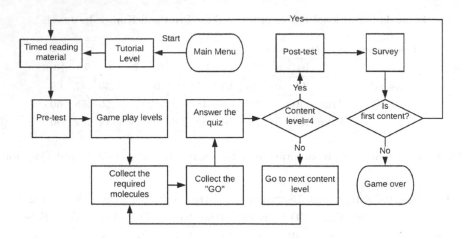

Fig. 4. Typical participant workflow for the experiment.

5   Results

To check the relationship between the post-test scores and the knowledge inferred from the DBN, a correlation analysis was conducted. The probability value of the Knowledge1 node at the end of game play was treated as the inferred knowledge for the purpose of comparison with the post-test scores. Cryptography post-test score was found to be positively correlated to the knowledge inferred from the DBN, $r_s(111) = .46$, $p < .001$. Chemistry post-test score was positively correlated as well, $r_s(111) = .36$, $p < .001$. The overall post-test scores for the two contents combined were also positively correlated to the knowledge inferred from DBN, $r_s(222) = .31$, $p < .001$. Overall, DBN showed a small but significant correlation of knowledge with the post-test scores for both the contents.

6   Discussion

Correlations observed between the post-test score and the knowledge level inferred from the DBN were significant and small to moderately positive. This shows validity for using the BNs to model learner beliefs in the CAGE based games. Previously BNs have been used to predict students' final grades in university education [10]. The current experiment demonstrated that the game based stealth assessment based on DBN can be applied in a content agnostic way as the same network was used for both the learning contents in the game. Thus, DBN acts as a valid instrument to create a content agnostic game based stealth assessment.

There are possible avenues for improving the DBN constructed for use in this study. For example, the current game used only three distractors to keep it simple. Instead of a fixed number, a variable number of distractors could be employed in the game and the network structure be modified to reflect that.

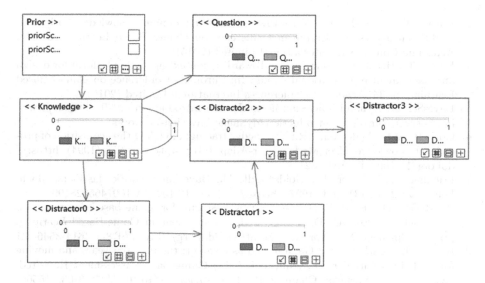

Fig. 5. A possible DBN with a different structure.

Apart from this, there are alternate network structures which could be employed to model the current scenario in the game such as one depicted in Fig. 5. This network consists of four distractors. Only the first distractor in this structure has conditional dependence on knowledge, while rest of the distractors are conditionally dependant on the previous distractor that was collected.

7   Conclusion

A significant small to moderately positive correlation between the post-test scores and knowledge inferred from the DBN demonstrated support for the validity of the content agnostic game based assessment using DBN. CAGE helps in reducing the time and cost requirement for creating an educational video game. The current evidence in support of the validity of the DBN further adds to the aim of the CAGE games by embedding a content agnostic assessment within the game. Using the current findings, educational games can support embedding the assessment within CAGE games to provide for a holistic educational environment that not only supports learning but also assess it.

References

1. Amresh, A., Verma, V., Baron, T., Salla, R., Clarke, D., Beckwith, D.: Evaluating gamescapes and simapps as effective classroom teaching tools. In: European Conference on Games Based Learning, p. 22-XII. Academic Conferences International Limited (2019)
2. Baron, T.: An architecture for designing content agnostic game mechanics for educational burst games. Ph.D. thesis, Arizona State University (2017)

3. Baron, T., Amresh, A.: Word towers: assessing domain knowledge with non-traditional genres. In: European Conference on Games Based Learning, p. 638. Academic Conferences International Limited (2015)
4. Baron, T., Heath, C., Amresh, A.: Towards a context agnostic platform for design and assessment of educational games. In: European Conference on Games Based Learning, p. 34. Academic Conferences International Limited (2016)
5. BayesServer: Dynamic Bayesian networks - an introduction (2020). https://www.bayesserver.com/docs/introduction/dynamic-bayesian-networks
6. Corbett, A.T., Anderson, J.R.: Knowledge tracing: modeling the acquisition of procedural knowledge. User Model. User-Adap. Inter. 4(4), 253–278 (1994). https://doi.org/10.1007/BF01099821
7. Friedman, N., Geiger, D., Goldszmidt, M.: Bayesian network classifiers. Mach. Learn. 29(2–3), 131–163 (1997). https://doi.org/10.1023/A:1007465528199
8. Ifenthaler, D., Eseryel, D., Ge, X.: Assessment for game-based learning. In: Ifenthaler, D., Eseryel, D., Ge, X. (eds.) Assessment in Game-Based Learning, pp. 1–8. Springer, New York (2012). https://doi.org/10.1007/978-1-4614-3546-4_1
9. Kim, Y.J., Ifenthaler, D.: Game-based assessment: the past ten years and moving forward. In: Ifenthaler, D., Kim, Y.J. (eds.) Game-Based Assessment Revisited. AGL, pp. 3–11. Springer, Cham (2019). https://doi.org/10.1007/978-3-030-15569-8_1
10. Mouri, K., Okubo, F., Shimada, A., Ogata, H.: Bayesian network for predicting students' final grade using e-book logs in university education. In: 2016 IEEE 16th International Conference on Advanced Learning Technologies (ICALT), pp. 85–89. IEEE (2016)
11. Neapolitan, R.E.: Learning Bayesian Networks, vol. 38. Pearson Prentice Hall, Upper Saddle River (2004)
12. Pardos, Z.A., Baker, R.S., San Pedro, M.O., Gowda, S.M., Gowda, S.M.: Affective states and state tests: investigating how affect and engagement during the school year predict end-of-year learning outcomes. J. Learn. Anal. 1(1), 107–128 (2014)
13. Reichenberg, R.: Dynamic Bayesian networks in educational measurement: reviewing and advancing the state of the field. Appl. Measur. Educ. 31(4), 335–350 (2018)
14. Reye, J.: Student modelling based on belief networks. Int. J. Artif. Intell. Educ. 14(1), 63–96 (2004)
15. Rheem, H., Verma, V., Becker, D.V.: Use of mouse-tracking method to measure cognitive load. In: Proceedings of the Human Factors and Ergonomics Society Annual Meeting, vol. 62, pp. 1982–1986. SAGE Publications Sage, Los Angeles (2018)
16. Shute, V.J., Ventura, M., Bauer, M., et al.: Melding the power of serious games and embedded assessment to monitor and foster learning: flow and grow. In: Serious Games, pp. 317–343. Routledge (2009)
17. Skinner, B.F.: The Behavior of Organisms: An Experimental Analysis. BF Skinner Foundation, Cambridge (2019)
18. Verma, V., Baron, T., Bansal, A., Amresh, A.: Emerging practices in game-based assessment. In: Ifenthaler, D., Kim, Y.J. (eds.) Game-Based Assessment Revisited. AGL, pp. 327–346. Springer, Cham (2019). https://doi.org/10.1007/978-3-030-15569-8_16
19. Verma, V., Rheem, H., Amresh, A., Craig, S.D., Bansal, A.: Predicting real-time affective states by modeling facial emotions captured during educational video game play. In: Marfisi-Schottman, I., Bellotti, F., Hamon, L., Klemke, R. (eds.) GALA 2020. LNCS, vol. 12517, pp. 447–452. Springer, Cham (2020). https://doi.org/10.1007/978-3-030-63464-3_45

Serious Game Usage

A Digital Companion to Assist the Game Master for the Orchestration of a Mixed-Reality Game

Catherine Bonnat$^{(\boxtimes)}$ and Eric Sanchez$^{(\boxtimes)}$

TECFA, University of Geneva, 40 Bd du pont de l'Arve, CH-1211 Geneva 4, Switzerland
{catherine.bonnat,eric.sanchez}@unige.ch

Abstract. The control of the game world by the game master during the activity requires a precise monitoring of the activity which increases in a mixed-reality game context due to the multiplicity of possible interactions with the tangible and digital game elements. This article deals with the design of a digital companion to help a game master to orchestrate a game. This companion is integrated in a game, *Geome*, a mixed-reality game dedicated to museum school visits, that combines tangible and digital elements. This companion is based on the collection of multimodal traces from different interactions set up during the whole game scenario. This paper addresses the issue of the traces to collect to help the game master in the configuration and the monitoring of the activity. The presented prototype is the result of a co-design process between researchers, practitioners, and computer scientists. Thus, we present the first results from 3 experiments conducted with students (12–15 years old) in a natural museum. The results show the types of interactions tracked during the game use and the needed information for the game orchestration. However, while the players play the game as intended using most of the features, the game master makes little use of his dashboard and does not interact with the players through the dedicated interface.

Keywords: Game-master · Mixed-reality game · Orchestration

1 Introduction

Games integration in an educational context, especially for role-playing learning games, escape games and mixed-reality games that combine digital game elements and physical and social aspects of traditional game play [1], shifts the students and teacher's roles. Indeed, the roles of the students and the teacher evolve, respectively as players and game master. From the game-master perspective, the teacher is responsible for setting the fictional contract [2], delivering narrative control through interacting with players, ensuring that all players know and understand the game rules and ensuring players engagement by providing constant challenges [3]. Many studies have been carried out to assist the teacher for monitoring learning activities with dashboards [4] and orchestration tools [5] i.e. the means given to the teacher to organize and manage, in real time, activities and the various interactions that result from it. However few papers address this issue for game-based learning and research on the role of the teacher in game-based learning

© Springer Nature Switzerland AG 2021
F. de Rosa et al. (Eds.): GALA 2021, LNCS 13134, pp. 133–142, 2021.
https://doi.org/10.1007/978-3-030-92182-8_13

is still in its infancy [6]. The control of the game world by the game master during the activity requires a precise monitoring of the activity which increases in a mixed-reality game context due to the multiplicity of possible interactions with the tangible and digital game elements.

This paper addresses the issue of the recording of players' activity for mixed-reality games, and the information needed by the game master for the monitoring of the activity. Thus, we present *DigitComp*, a digital companion dedicated to the monitoring of mixed-reality games. The presented prototype is the result of a co-design process between researchers, practitioners, and computer scientists.

2   Context: *Geome*, a Mixed-Reality Game Dedicated to Museum School Visits

Our research deals with the monitoring of *Geome*, a mixed-reality game dedicated to museum school visits in a nature museum. We want to identify the information and the tools needed by the game master for the game orchestration.

Geome (Fig. 1b) is a two-parts mixed-reality game played in teams with digital tablets in the Nature Museum located in Sion (Switzerland). The game is dedicated to museum school visits tailored for secondary school students (12–15 years old). *Geome* encourages the students to question their relationship with nature. Thus, the expected learning outcomes are linked with the understanding of the Anthropocene, a geological period in which human beings do not longer considered themselves as part of nature but over-exploits it with many consequences on biodiversity and climate change. Another expected learning outcome of the game concerns the students' relationship to knowledge. During the game, they are expected to question the nature of knowledge (certainty and complexity), and the way it is produced (source and justification).

The design of the game scenario takes into account the museography in order to promote interactions between players and the museum tangible elements, but also to settle a coherent game narrative. Indeed, the permanent exhibition of the Nature Museum includes collections of fauna, flora, and geology of the local environment, distributed in several rooms and two floors (Fig. 1a). The exhibition discourse focuses on the historical evolution of the relationship between human beings and its environment.

Fig. 1. *Geome*, a game played with digital tablets in the Nature Museum

The game lasts about 1 h30 including two distinct parts and debriefings that follow each part of the game. The players play as teams of 3 or 4 players. They play the role of a wildlife expert who lives in an alpine valley. In the first part of the game, the character they play is stuck in the valley because of the winter weather conditions (Fig. 1c). He needs to gather resources to survive. For the players, this means scanning the stuffed animals displayed in the museum. A QR code provides access to information related to the scanned animal such its name and scientific description. Each animal is then captured, killed, or domesticated. They can also trade the collected resources with another team. In collecting resources, they collectively lose by depleting the energy of the "tree of life", a metaphor of the quality of the environment (Fig. 2c). This first part of the game lasts 10 to 15 min and the students cannot win.

In the second part of the game, freed from the constraints of winter, the character can resume his work. He is called, as a wildlife expert, to solve fake news, rumors or polemics related to the natural environment (Fig. 2b). The museography provides clues (Fig. 2a) that allow to address the issues and make visible the complexity of the natural ecosystem interactions. The victory depends on the capacity of the players to identify the complexity of the relationships between animals and to develop critical thinking regarding the information provided.

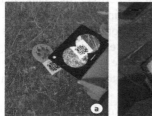

Fig. 2. *Geome*, a two-parts mixed-reality game

Thus, the player adopts successively two postures during the 2 parts of the game: that of the predator who exploits his natural environment, then that of the investigator who brings to light the complex interspecific relations within the ecosystem. During the debriefings, the students are led to question their relationship with nature, but also to analyze their relationship with the media and information.

Due to the complexity of interactions during the game and the constraints generated by the museum (rooms distributed on two levels), the role of game master (taken by the museum staff) is crucial, and our work consists of: (1) Identifying the different interactions that take place to provide the game-master with relevant information about: what the players do? what they perceive? what they feel? and what they learn? (2) Providing the game-master with the tools needed for the game orchestration.

In the next section we describe the different levels of interaction that need to be considered.

3 Game-Based Learning: Different Levels of Interactions

Game-based learning results from the implementation of different categories of inter-actions. The first category consists of interactions between the player and the game or his opponents. These interactions are competitive in nature and result in what Salen and Zimmerman refer to as an "artificial conflict" [7]. The player attempts to meet challenges by implementing strategies that evolve based on successes and failures. The player may therefore have to change the way he thinks and acts depending on the feedback from the game or opponents. For example, by playing *Geome*, a player may notice that collecting resources in the museum decreases the energy level of the tree of life (Fig. 2c). He is expected to make a causal link between exploitation of natural resources and the ecosystem degradation. This is an *action situation* according to Brousseau [8].

A second level of interaction concerns the interactions between the players themselves. This level consists of collaboration between teammates. Each player is led to communicate, to teammates, the winning solutions and strategies that will allow them to overcome the challenge. These verbal interactions lead the players to formulate and establish the validity of the knowledge needed to win. Brousseau describes these situations as *formulation and validation situations*. This is what happens when players who solve the puzzles in *Geome* discuss and decide to stop collecting resources to stop the decrease of the tree of life's energy or when they trade resources.

The third level of interaction concerns the exchanges between the game master (teacher or museum staff) and the players. Depending on the information collected, the game master makes decisions that allow the game to run smoothly. These decisions are of different kinds. They enable to control the game rules, to encourage storytelling or even to stop the game. For example, in the case of *Geome*, the game master can send a message to the different teams to tell them that they have lost, to ask them to meet in the room where the debriefing will take place.

These situations, competition (action), collaboration (formulation and validation) and orchestration are thus distinguished by the nature of the interactions that take place and by who is involved in these interactions: player-game, player-player or game master-player. They can be represented in the form of 3 nested interaction levels (Fig. 3a). This representation is inspired by Margolinas' work [9]. It allows us to distinguish the different categories of interactions that can be traced and to qualify the interactions that concern the game master. We use this model to design the *DigitComp*.

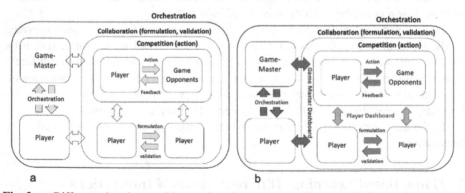

Fig. 3. a. Different situations and interactions for game-based learning. b. Interactions tracked and enabled by *DigitComp* (Color figure online)

4   Research Methods

The research work consists of a Design-Based Research methodology [10–12]. This multidisciplinary approach (learning sciences and computer science) relies on the collaboration of researchers with teachers and museum staff for the co-design and the co-evaluation of the *DigitComp*. Practitioners and researchers are both involved in the design (co-design) and the testing of the prototype, and the interpretation of the data collected (co-evaluation). The process is also iterative. It includes different cycles for the design and evaluation of the prototype, with the possibility, for each iteration, to modify the prototype and the theoretical models on which it is based. For this purpose, the prototype is tested in a naturalistic context, i.e. at the Museum of Nature, with 12 to 15 years old students. Figure 4 describes the design-based approach and the articulation of two processes: the co-design of the prototype and its co-evaluation.

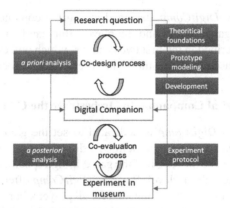

Fig. 4. Research method: an articulation of two processes

The co-designs of the game and the digital companion was carried out in parallel during 16 workshops organized in three phases. In this paper we present the work carried out for the design and testing of *DigitComp*. The first phase consists in positioning our research problem according to existing works. This step leads to the choice of a theoretical framework [9] necessary to model the interactions within the game. The chosen model is described in Sect. 3 (Fig. 3a). The second step focuses on the design of the *DigitComp*, which supports the interactions of the game master within the game: i.e. the tracking of the players' interactions (player-player, player-game interface and player-museum exhibition) and the interactions with players in terms of game orchestration (the decisions taken by the game master). This step allows the identification of the traces to be collected, the way to make them accessible to the game master for the synchronous monitoring of the players' activity and the way to use them. The third phase consists of the development of *DigitComp* and also the connection of all the game elements, in order to collect and visualize the interaction traces. The *a priori* analysis consists of a detailed review of the design of *DigitComp* to ensure that it is in accordance with the theoretical model.

The co-evaluation phase consists of 3 different experiments (64 players divided in 21 teams of 3–4 players) that took place in February 2021 at the Nature Museum. The experiments enabled for the data collection from students' interactions and to test the digital companion functionalities. A workshop was dedicated to co-analyze data and to discuss what type of interactions have been set up and tracked during the game, but also their nature, according to the ones identified in Fig. 3a. Data has been converted (into a csv format), cleaned and pre-processed in order to create understandable visualizations of the actions performed by the players. Besides, the use of *DigitComp* by the museum staff was discussed. The observations made during the experiments and the discussions during the co-evaluation workshop were reported. The co-evaluation process also contributes to review the prototypes and the research protocol.

5   Results

The digital companion, *DigitComp*, designed during the co-conception process, is an interface between the game master and the players that can be used anytime. It offers different functions described in the first two sections, which will evolve and be enriched for the next iteration based on the result of the co-evaluation process.

5.1   *DigitComp*, a Digital Companion to Orchestrate the Game

Before the game starts, *DigitComp* is dedicated to set the game parameters (Fig. 5a b). For example, the game master can define/modify the game objectives (number of resources to collect), choose the length of the game, assign specific quests to the different teams depending on their ability level. Besides, *DigitComp* offers the game master the possibility to set automatic feedback intended for all players. For example, an automatic message can be sent if the energy level of the "tree of life" (Fig. 2c), which represents the points earned or lost by the players, reaches a threshold that the game master considers as critical. Currently, these parameters cannot be changed after the game starts.

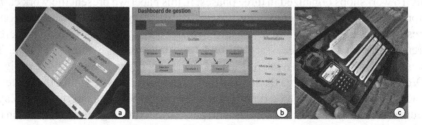

Fig. 5. *DigitComp*, an interface between the game master and players

DigitComp also includes a text-chat which enables synchronous communication between the game-master and players (Fig. 5c). The text-chat is integrated as an element of the game narrative. As a result, the game master takes a specific and active role in the game narrative (as the head of the wildlife experts) in the game world. At any time, the game master can help one team of players or another. For example, the help may take the form of a clue needed for solving the puzzle. Teams of players are notified via a smartwatch (Fig. 6c) that they received a message readable on the tablet. Players are free to use the text-chat if they need to answer and/or ask the game master at any time. The text-chat allows the game master to overcome the difficulty to communicate with the players displayed in the different museum's rooms spread over two floors. In addition, it offers the opportunity to provide the players with tailored assistance. *DigitComp* is a toolbox dedicated to support the interactions between the game master and the players (situation of orchestration). This support requires real-time tracking of the players' activity described in the next section.

5.2 *DigitComp*, a Digital Companion to Track Player Interactions

DigitComp allows for the recording in a database of multimodal traces in JSON format. The traces come from the player (physiological parameters collected by the smartwatch such as the heart rate) (Fig. 6c), the interactions of the players with the tablet (Fig. 6a), and the interactions with the tangible elements of the museum exhibition (scan of stuffed animals) (Fig. 6b).

Fig. 6. Multimodal traces from different interactions during the game

These traces are made available to the researcher (raw data), but also, for some of them, to the game master with an interface dedicated to the orchestration of the game [4].

Different traces are processed and made available to the game master (Fig. 7a). These traces reflect the game variables, such as the evolution of the energy of the "tree of life" according to the gain or loss of points. They also reflect actions performed by players with the tablet, which may or may not interact with the tangible elements of the museum. For example, during the game, players are asked to investigate elements of the museum (stuffed animals). Each element of the museum is identified by a particular QR code and the use of the "scan" function in the game (Fig. 6b) allows the game master to know the elements the player interacts with. Finally, regarding the issue of assessing the player engagement into the game, emotions [13], a smartwatch worn by one of the players of each team, collects physiological data (heart rate).

With the dashboard, the game master can review the interactions of a single player, a group of players or all the groups (Fig. 7a). Currently, the data available to the game master results from a basic processing of the nature and number of actions performed (e.g., number of "scans" of the stuffed wolf). These traces have been selected and processed in order to provide the game master with an account of the players' activity. A dashboard is also made available to the players (Fig. 7b). It provides an overview of the actions performed, the resources collected, the points earned or lost and the smartwatch display the state of the "tree of life" (Fig. 6c).

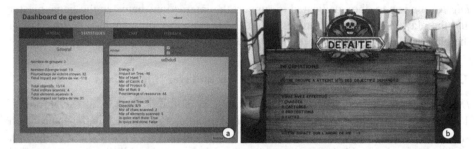

Fig. 7. Dashboard for the game master (a) and players (b)

Figure 3b summarizes the interactions tracked or enabled by *DigitComp*. *DigitComp* tracks the interactions from the action situation (in blue, i.e. scan of an animal, loss of points). It also tracks the interaction between players through the interface (in green i.e. trading of resources between two teams). *DigitComp* makes available this information for the player (in light grey) and the game master (in dark grey) through the player and game master dashboards. However, oral interactions between players (formulation and validation situation) are not tracked. At last, *DigitComp* enables interactions for the orchestration of the game (in red, i.e. sending or receiving a message).

5.3   Interactions Tracking: Lessons Learned from the Experiments

This section is an overview of the types of interactions [7–9] implemented and tracked during the experiments to discuss the limits and perspectives of evolution of the artifacts (*Geome* and *DigitComp*) for the next iteration.

Concerning the first level of interaction (the action situation) (Fig. 3a, 3b), the data show that all the functionalities have been used according to what was expected from the *a priori* analysis. It means that the players play the game as originally planned. This is notably reflected by the animal scans to collect a maximum of resources for the survival of the character in the first part of the game. However, the teams adopted different strategies in terms of number and selected animals and selected action (hunting, domesticating…). In addition, some teams stopped to collected resources before the end of the first part which may be interpreted as they become aware that the energy of the "tree of life" decrease.

The collaboration in the game (formulation and validation situations), is reflected by the trading of resources. Few trading was performed, and 3 teams did not trade any resource. We consider that it is due to the complexity and the design of this game mechanics, as well as the limited time dedicated to the first part of the game (10 min.

However, it does not mean that players did not collaborate. Indeed, though the traces do not reflect the collaboration between players during the game, the interactions between teammates and the different teams were reported by the observers. In particular, they reported that, in the first part of the game, some players understood the causal relationship between their actions (hunting, domesticating…) and the collective loss of points. They shared this information with other teams and stopped to collect resources. Thus, the interpretation of the collected traces can only be interpreted by adding complementary data (videos, observations…). We point out here one of the limits of the interactions tracking set up during the game. The experiment protocol is now revised as we plan to collect complementary data enabling multi-modal analysis in order to reduce the subjective interpretation of the trace's co-analysis.

Regarding the 3rd level of interaction, between the players and the game master, we notice a gap between what was planned (during the digital companion features design) and what happened. First, the game-master made little use of the *DigitComp*. The chat module was not used by the game master who preferred to interact directly with players. Besides, despite a conclusive pilot test (in the laboratory), the smartwatch did not work due to the disconnections from the internet network of the museum when the players move. This issue, which has not yet been solved, prevented the collection of data on physiological parameters. Furthermore, the game master dashboard (Fig. 7a) was not used during the game, nor during the debriefing though useful information is made available (Fig. 7b). The game master preferred to ask the players about the data available on their own dashboard. The discussions during the co-evaluation workshop revealed that the dashboard is unattractive and that information is missing. For example, the number and the nature of the trading of resources is not available for the game master. In addition, though this is an important learning outcome and crucial for carrying out the debriefing, the information about the link between the animal identified by the players are missing as well. As a result, the *DigitComp* will be revised for the next iteration in order to offer a better support for the game master.

6   Conclusions and Perspectives

DigitComp is a first step towards a systematic and holistic tracking of the players' interactions and the support of the game master for the orchestration of a mixed-reality game. *DigitComp* is based on the observation of players' activity through the collection of interactions traces and functionalities enabling the game master to orchestrate the game. Regarding the issue about *what the players did*, *DigitComp* managed to capture the digital traces of the players and offers a good overview of its activity in the Museum. However, these traces capture a limited part of the players' activity and need to be completed (audio or text recordings when they solve the puzzles). We expect to collect traces from the formulation and validation situations. Regarding the issue about *what the players perceived*, the digital traces enable to know which animals were scanned in the museum. However, it is again a limited part of what they perceived since the players interact with stuffed animal without scanning them. The issues *what the players felt* is not yet well addressed due to technical challenges, but we expect to find a solution and we plan to offer the players, for to the next version of *DigitComp*, the opportunity to express their feelings (happy, frustrated, anxious...) by a single click on a symbol available on the tablet. Regarding *what the players learnt, DigitComp* provides limited information (such as the relationships between the animals represented by a map) but we expect to define some indicators that may be useful for the game master. For example, when the players stop to scan the animal during the first part of the game, it probably means that they learnt the causal relationship between the exploitation of resources and its consequences on the environment. The modeling of the players' experiences according to these 4 issues mentioned above may constitute an innovative approach for the representation of the activity of a player and the design of the game master interface.

The next iteration of the project will be also dedicated to re-think the information needed by the game-master. Indeed, during experiments, the game master did not use the interface to communicate with the players, but also to build his debriefing. The ergonomics, but also the lack of familiarity with such an interface may be the reason for this result.

References

1. Cheok, A., et al.: Touch-Space: Mixed-Reality Game Space Based on Ubiquitous, Tangible, and Social Computing. Personal Ub Comp **6**, 430–442 (2002)
2. Tychsen, A.: Tales for the Many: Process and Authorial Control in Multi-player Role-Playing Games. In: Spierling, U., Szilas, N. (eds.) ICIDS 2008. LNCS, vol. 5334, pp. 309–320. Springer, Heidelberg (2008). https://doi.org/10.1007/978-3-540-89454-4_38
3. Tychsen, A., Hitchens, M., Brolund, T., Kavakli, M.: The game master. ACM Int. Conf. Proceeding Ser. **123**, 215–222 (2005)
4. Dabbebi, I.: Conception et génération dynamique de tableaux de bord d'apprentissage contextuels. PhD Thesis, Université du Maine (2019)
5. Dillenbourg, P.: Design for classroom orchestration. Comput. Educ. **69**, 485–492 (2013)
6. Molin, G.: The Role of the Teacher in Game-Based Learning: A Review and Outlook. In: Ma, M., Oikonomou, A. (eds.) Serious Games and Edutainment Applications, pp. 649–674. Springer, Cham (2017). https://doi.org/10.1007/978-3-319-51645-5_28
7. Salen, K., Zimmerman, E.: Rules of play, game design fundamentals. MIT Press (2004)
8. Brousseau, G.: Théorie des situations didactiques. La Pensée sauvage, Grenoble (1998)
9. Margolinas, C.: La structuration du milieu et ses apports dans l'analyse a posteriori des situations. In: Margolinas, C. (ed.) Les débats de didactique des mathématiques, pp. 89–102. La Pensée sauvage, Grenoble (1995)
10. Design-Based Research Collective: Design-based research: an emerging paradigm for educational inquiry. Educ. Res. **32**(1), 5–8 (2003)
11. Wang, F., Hannafin, M.J.: Design-based research and technology-enhanced learning environments. Education Tech. Research Dev. **53**(4), 5–23 (2005)
12. Sanchez, É., Monod-Ansaldi, R.: Recherche collaborative orientée par la conception. Un paradigme méthodologique pour prendre en compte la complexité des situations d'enseignement-apprentissage. Éducation et didactique **9**(2), 73–94 (2015). https://doi.org/10.4000/educationdidactique.2288
13. Blikstein, P.: Multimodal learning analytics. In: Proceedings of the Third International Conference on Learning Analytics and Knowledge, 102 (2013)

Towards an Immersive Debriefing of Serious Games in Virtual Reality: A Framework Concept

Jonathan Degand$^{(\boxtimes)}$, Guillaume Loup$^{(\boxtimes)}$, and Jean-Yves Didier

Université Paris-Saclay, Univ Evry, IBISC, 91020 Evry-Courcouronnes, France
guillaume.loup@univ-evry.fr

Abstract. Debriefing and simulation are two complementary and indivisible phases for the use of serious game. However, practices of debriefing vary depending on the objectives and the context. With the advent of new virtual reality simulations, it is interesting to identify methods of debriefing for the trainer and learner in this situation. This paper provides a global review of debriefing in a serious game context and considers the findings tied to a virtual reality context. The purpose of this analysis is to find a proper solution and to use virtual reality technology to improve the debriefing experience. We finally propose a tool for virtual reality simulations that provides an immersive debriefing system that includes a replay system of the simulation occurred as well as a possibility to restart at any moment of the replay. As such, we think that the participant can have a better understanding and reflection of what he/she has experienced as well as a possibility to explore other choices.

Keywords: Debriefing · Simulation · Virtual reality · Game engine

1 Introduction

With the advent of serious games in which, contrary to the instructor, learners are equipped with virtual reality helmets, researches on new practices for these serious games are needed. Virtual reality brings a more concrete environment to the learner, whenever organizing such an environment in reality is difficult. However, it is necessary that the learner earns new skills, remembers and interprets a virtual environment so that it can profit for future similar experiences in reality. Thus, a significant amount of simulations integrates at least one debriefing phase.

The concept of debriefing according to Sawyer et al. is associated to an interactive, bidirectional, and reflective discussion or conversation [1]. However, Jody S. Piro and Catherine O'Callaghan [2] separate the discussion and reflection part in their uncommon definition of debriefing. According to them, a simulation is divided into 3 steps: the *Doing* (the performance of the learner during the simulation), the *Debriefing* (the immediate analysis behind the doing process), the *Deliberation* (Reflexive discussion upon the analysis).

© Springer Nature Switzerland AG 2021
F. de Rosa et al. (Eds.): GALA 2021, LNCS 13134, pp. 143–152, 2021.
https://doi.org/10.1007/978-3-030-92182-8_14

We define debriefing as a post-hoc analysis, of a series of events and situations, performed individually or in groups that involve observation, feedback, discussion and reflection. Debriefing is thus a phase in which learners meet the actions and the context of their experience and analyzes them.

Debriefing and simulation are considered as two complementary and indivisible phases [3]. However, David Crookal highlighted in an editorial published in 2010 [4] the lack of new tools and methods of debriefing in many studies on serious games. Indeed, a deep learning is associated with a debriefing that allows to share, review and analyse the actions of the learner. The article from Chinedu Obikwelu and Janet C Read published in 2012 [5] mentions that debriefing allows learners to reflect upon their experience by reviewing their action. Debriefing is considered as necessary in nursing education [6] as well as any serious game that is in a medical education context [7].

Debriefing is also tied with the notion of engagement [8]. According to Crookal, engagement and debriefing are tied to a point that there is a specific engagement for the game and for the debriefing. Thus, the learner experiences better motivation and concentration not only during the simulation, but also during the debriefing. Whereas serious games can involve strong emotions such as joy, fear or anger, a debriefing phase allows the learner to externalize his/her feelings.

Thereafter, a comparative study between a simulation with and without debriefing has been realized by Ryoo et Ha [9]. The result of this study shows clearly that debriefing brings a significant improvement in learners' skills learning and knowledge.

In a virtual simulation debriefing context study, Verkuyl suggested areas for future research [10] such as the efficiency of a debriefing reduced only to questions and feedbacks, or the timing of debriefing. We can thus observe a need to explore different methods of debriefing.

In this article, we will first present the different characteristics of debriefing. Then, we will focus on the different digital tools used for debriefing. Finally, we will propose a solution following the review made.

2 Characteristics of Debriefing

Following these ideas of research, many studies has begun to emerge on this subject [11]. This section will first focus on studies that present different types of debriefing, then on articles that study the place of the debriefing in the simulation, and finally, on the different debriefing practices.

2.1 Types of Debriefing

There are various qualifiers to describe the different types of debriefing. We retained 4 main types of debriefing which form 2 modalities: the *instructor-led debriefing* in opposition to *peer-led debriefing* and the *self-debriefing* in opposition to *group debriefing*.

Instructor-Led Debriefing. Instructor-led debriefing includes all debriefings that involve an instructor. Such a debriefing can be performed:

- *Individually:* each participant has his/her own individual session with an instructor [12].
- *In groups:* all the participants from a group are in the same session [13].

The instructor can help the learner to have a better learning and skill gain. Thus, for pre-operative care simulation, it has been proved that the quality of debriefing as well as the learner's skills were higher after an instructor-led debriefing, compared to a debriefing without instructor [12]. However, such a debriefing needs a well-trained instructor, which is costly [14].

Peer-Led Debriefing. A debriefing handled by the learners themselves. It can be performed either individually, as a written debriefing [15] by seeing a review [3] (for example a video [16]) of the simulation, or in groups by discussing with other learners [1]. This method does not need an instructor training, which reduces the cost involved [14]. If the simulation is performed within team, a within team peer-led debriefing improves significantly the team performance [17]. Such a debriefing method still has satisfying results, as long as it does not require learning specific skills [18].

Group Debriefing. A group debriefing is performed simultaneously with multiple learners. This debriefing method can improve learners' communicative skills and can allow learning from others as thoughts can "resonate" between learners [19]. Although group debriefing has better results in knowledge gain and self-efficacy [13], the larger the group is, the more passive the students are [20]. Finally, such a debriefing is more adapted for team-based simulations if the debriefing is peer-led [17].

Self-debriefing. A self-debriefing is performed individually. The main tools of this debriefing method are based on series of questions [21], summary of their own performance or even video of the learner [22]. Studies of self-debriefing have been carried out on design variations [24] and also on comparison between face-to-face and asynchronous debriefing [25]. Self-debriefing can also be performed with an instructor, which provides a safe space in which a discussion occurs between the learner and his/her instructor only [11].

Debriefing Combinations. The most adapted debriefing methods to a specific simulation depends on many aspects such as the context, the cost or the objectives. However, many studies has begun to be interested in debriefing combinations and in particular the combination of self-debriefing and group debriefing [26]. By comparing them with a group debriefing only [27], there is a better appreciation and engagement observed [20]. Furthermore, learners have also better self-awareness [19] as well as an improvement in communication skills [28]. Generally, learners consider that doing a self-debriefing immediately after a simulation allow them to prepare the group debriefing process [29]. Thus, because they are more prepared, they can express themselves better on what they have experienced.

2.2 Debriefing Timing

The article from Sawyer et al. [1] presents two main debriefing timings: either after simulation, which is called a "post-event debriefing" or during the simulation, which is called a "within-event debriefing". In the latter case, it can consist in interrupting the simulation event to debrief, when needed, and then continuing on with the simulation. Thus, the learner can correct an error made before processing to the next step. We observe in the literature an implicit preference on post-event debriefing in a medical context. However, in a business intelligence context [30], better results on learning and motivation are observed for a within-event debriefing in comparison to a post-event debriefing. It is also specified that an integrated debriefing is appreciated if the simulation is longer.

3   Debriefing's Digital Tools

3.1   Debriefing with Traditionnal Tools

In the study from Lapum et al. [21] on self-debriefing, virtual simulation is defined as any simulation performed with a virtual technology, for example a computer. Thus, it is not focused on a specific type of virtual technology.

In 2017, a study from Verkuyl et al. [10] stated that there is a lack of research in debriefing for virtual simulation. Indeed, many articles listed best debriefing practices for simulation in general but not for virtual simulation. According to Verkuyl's study, virtual simulations have specific attributes. Thus, it is not sufficient to use the result for simulation in general only and new specific studies are needed.

In a following comparative study of debriefing combinations for virtual simulation from the same authors [29], participants suggested to integrate the self-debriefing to the simulation. An immersive tool such as virtual reality can be adapted in this situation, as the immersion provided can help to integrate the debriefing in the simulation and thus, improve learners' engagement.

3.2   Debriefing with Immersive Tools

Debriefing in virtual simulation and virtual reality (VR) are two emerging concepts, it is difficult to find, at the moment, a clear method of debriefing that applies to virtual reality simulation. However, there are findings on the use of immersive tools for debriefing such as the 360° video or interactive VR.

A study from Nicholson et al. is focused on the use of 360° videos in debriefing and its "record and review" perspective [31]. It has already been proven that the use of video in debriefing as a replay can be useful [16]. Thus, the study follows this statement and questions what an immersive tool such as the 360° video can bring to debriefing. Participants from the study asserted that VR has provided a more immersive debriefing environment, in which they were more engaged in their performances and experienced a better view of the simulation events.

Interactive VR is mostly the use of interactive feedbacks during a VR simulation. Feedbacks and debriefing are sometimes confused [32]. However, feedbacks are defined as information about performance provided to participants during the simulation [1], whereas debriefing is above all a facilitated reflective conversation.

3.3 Design Constraints for Immersive Debriefing Environments

VR an immersive experience at least similar to a 360° video, as well as more interactions. As such, learner's immersion, presence and affordance can be improved in the debriefing as well, which can enhance the engagement in an active debriefing. In this sense, we aim to facilitate the design of an immersive debriefing environment in VR. To achieve this goal, we focus on the design constraints of an immersive VR debriefing environment using the main game engines.

To achieve this objective, it is necessary that the game engine is, in a first step, able to store a set of information and, in a second step, to exploit this data to place the user in conditions similar to the first one at the chosen moment. However, the architectures of the main game engines are based on different modules such as AI, scripts, animation, physics engine, networking and multimedia rendering [33]. No module is totally dedicated to a database or even to an exchange protocol. Only libraries are linked to saving but limited to those of scores and object positions. However, each module of the game engine has many different structural parameters that can vary with each frame. Thus our objective of restoring an interactive virtual environment from a previous state requires the proposal of a new framework.

4 An Immersive Debriefing Tool in Virtual Reality

4.1 Goals of the Immersive Debriefing Tool

As we prioritize the application of our solution to medical education, the tool we propose will provide a post-event debriefing. Indeed, such a debriefing practice is often used in medical education. Like a video record debriefing, this debriefing will feature a replay of the simulation. As such, learners will experience a better reflection and observation of their performance and emotions. The difference however, is in the representation of this replay system, as the replay will happen directly in the simulation scene and will offer an immersion at least similar to a 360° video. Thus, we combine the advantages provided by a video replay system on the debriefing with a more immersive aspect to reinforce some of these advantages. The debriefing purpose is to move across the learning cycle towards assimilation and accommodation for transfer of learning to future situations [23]. We think that adding further immersion will make the debriefing fulfill its purpose more efficiently.

Furthermore, contrary to a 360° video, the point of view for reviewing will not be unique. It is envisaged that the users of this system can move freely in the scene during the replay. The learner can thus see his/her own actions, performed by an avatar of himself/herself, from a third person perspective.

We also know from the literature that instructor-led debriefing is the most used in medical education, whereas a peer-led self-debriefing before an instructor led group debriefing has its advantages. This solution proposes to realize both of these practices at once. Indeed, it is envisaged that this solution will include a collaborative aspect: the instructor will be able to be with the learner in the scene during the debriefing phase. Thus, the learner can express more easily his/her feelings and decisions to the instructor, whereas the instructor will have better tools to show to the learner in the scene what are the objectives and the choices to make.

Above all, this solution is a tool for different debriefing practices in virtual reality. The purpose of this tool is to simplify and feature a debriefing phase with different parameters depending of the simulation's objectives. The targets of this tool are the simulation developers. Because adding a debriefing system to an already finished simulation needs time and resources, we propose this independent tool to help them save time and quickly include a debriefing system, without changing drastically the simulation's implementation. Even if the first tests are done with the Oculus Quest 2 using Unity, our goal is to propose an architecture compatible with other game engines such as Unreal Engine but also other VR devices contributing to the avatar's fidelity.

4.2 Proposed Architecture

The recording could be realized with different methods. A first method can consist in recording each information of the scene on each frame. This solution can achieve a replay system that reflects the reality very closely but with the cost of high memory usage. A second method can be based only on the recording of inputs. However, if the simulation involves randomness, this method may end up not providing an accurate replay. A third method can be a recording of events, but involves listening to predefined events. For a tool that is meant to be useable by most VR simulation, it is difficult to listen to all specific events.

By using a scenario based design, the method we propose will only take into account the initial state of the scene, the involved players and the objects, as well as listening the events of the activities. Thus, the recording system uses elements of the first and third method and will mainly focus on the properties of objects and players, as well as the events subject to user interactions.

Spatial data, animations, physics and renderers are all taken into account during the recording of the sequence (see Fig. 1). To ensure the correspondence between the users, which are mainly learners and eventually instructors, and their avatars, it can be useful to record the information from the microphone and sensors of the virtual reality devices.

It should be noted that the simulators take into account factors such as human behavior, the random selection of values, responses to machine performance or variable information from external databases. Thus a new plugin to the game engine will allow to add a script to record the properties of components that are directly or indirectly dependent on external factors. The data of these registrations must be collected and stored on server in order not to be limited by the memory constraints of virtual reality headsets (see Fig. 2).

4.3 Replay Mode and Redo Mode

A module added to the scene will implement the solution. The module will first record each important element of the scene and will then provide an interface that features a replay mode. This interface will be visible during the entire replay process. As such, a redo mode can be performed at any time during the replay process.

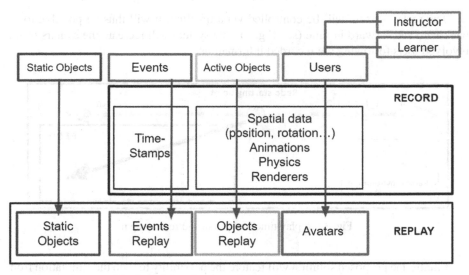

Fig. 1. Information recorded for the replay system

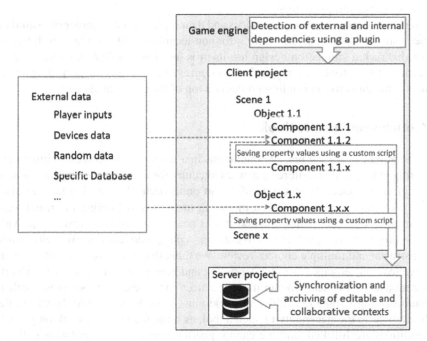

Fig. 2. Protocol and architecture of recordings dedicated to virtual reality debriefing

The replay system will be controlled via a timeline. It will thus be possible to go backward and forward in time (see Fig. 3). The system will recreate the avatars of the involved users following the recorded information.

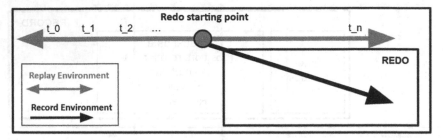

Fig. 3. Replay timeline system and redo system

Finally, the proposed solution will feature the possibility to redo the simulation from any time of the replay. With the instructor nearby, the learner will be able to play the simulation again differently. This is especially useful for simulations that need to be repeated until the right choice is made. We want to meet the needs of the instructors that want to redo the simulation from a key point for a guided run. What's more, as soon as the redo is performed, a new record can also be performed. Thus, it will allow learners to review their different choices.

The idea of featuring multiple choices and their replays for the learner in a simulation has been studied by Melody Laurent [3] for non-technical skills simulations. It has been shown that such a simulation design has its pros for non-technical skills learning. The difference with our tool is mainly the redo system available during the debriefing process, featuring thus an active debriefing process on top of the different choices.

5   Conclusion and Outlook

With the advent of virtual reality simulations in a serious game context, virtual reality debriefing is a topic that requires a new architecture for a tool supporting an innovative pedagogical approach. After a state of the art on theoretical debriefing in a simulation context, we propose a new solution that is an immersive debriefing in virtual reality. Because there is no debriefing method that is adapted to every context, we provide a tool that proposes multiple features: recording, replay, redo, collaborative environment with instructor and multiple choices review. We think that virtual reality and its features improve learners' engagement in a debriefing and help them to remember their performance more easily, which will facilitate the reflection process. Our tool aims to enhance different existing simulations efficiently and must as such, be generic. However, there are limitations to the generecity of such a tool, as some features can work only if a few preconditions are fulfilled, and we cannot guarantee that every simulation will fulfill them. That's why our approach will focus on matching with the most common virtual simulations that need a debriefing system. Furthermore, experimentation will be needed to evaluate our tool's effectiveness.

References

1. Sawyer, T., et al.: More than one way to debrief. Simul. Healthc. **11**, 9 (2016)
2. Piro, J., O'Callaghan, C.: Constructive destabilization in the liminal space: doing, debriefing and deliberating in mixed reality simulations. **21**, 178–208 (2020)
3. Laurent, M.: La scénarisation sous l'emprise de la métaphore spatiotemporelle: approche réflexive en environnement virtuel. 183 (2017)
4. Crookall, D.: Serious games, debriefing, and simulation/gaming as a discipline. Simul. Gaming **41**, 898–920 (2010)
5. Obikwelu, C., Read, J.C.: The serious game constructivist framework for children's learning. Procedia. Comput. Sci. **15**, 32–37 (2012)
6. Rim, D., Shin, H.: Effective instructional design template for virtual simulations in nursing education. Nurse Educ. Today **96**, 104624 (2021)
7. Thompson, D., et al.: Serious video games for health how behavioral science guided the development of a serious video game. Simul. Gaming **41**, 587–606 (2010)
8. Crookall, D.: Engaging (in) gameplay and (in) debriefing. Simul. Gaming **45**(4–5), 416–427 (2014)
9. Ryoo, E.N., Ha, E.-H.: The Importance of Debriefing in Simulation-Based Learning (2015)
10. Verkuyl, M., et al.: An exploration of debriefing in virtual simulation. Clin. Simul. Nurs. **13**, 591–594 (2017)
11. Kim, Y.-J.: The utilization of debriefing for simulation in healthcare A literature review. Nurse Educ. Pract. 10 (2020)
12. Kim, S.S., De Gagne, J.C.: Instructor-led vs. peer-led debriefing in preoperative care simulation using standardized patients. Nurse Educ. Today **71**, 34–39 (2018)
13. Verkuyl, M., et al.: Comparison of debriefing methods after a virtual simulation: an experiment. Clin. Simul. Nurs. **19**, 1–7 (2018)
14. Isaranuwatchai, W., Alam, F., Hoch, J., Boet, S.: A cost-effectiveness analysis of self-debriefing versus instructor debriefing for simulated crises in perioperative medicine in Canada. J. Educ. Eval. Health Prof. **13**, 44 (2016). https://doi.org/10.3352/jeehp.2016.13.44
15. Ha, E.-H.: Effects of peer-led debriefing using simulation with case-based learning: written vs. observed debriefing. Nurse Educ. Today **84**, 104249 (2020). https://doi.org/10.1016/j.nedt.2019.104249
16. Dudas, K., Wheeler, J.: Faculty re-enactment videos as a tool in simulation debriefing. Clin. Simul. Nurs. **40**, 25–30 (2020)
17. Boet, S., et al.: Within-team debriefing versus instructor-led debriefing for simulation-based education: a randomized controlled trial. Ann. Surg. **258**, 53–58 (2013)
18. Boet, S., et al.: Looking in the mirror: Self-debriefing versus instructor debriefing for simulated crises. Crit. Care Med. **39**, 1377–1381 (2011)
19. Verkuyl, M., et al.: Exploring Self-Debriefing plus group-debriefing: a focus group study. Clin. Simul. Nurs. **43**, 3–9 (2020)
20. Verkuyl, M., et al.: Comparison of self-debriefing alone or in combination with group debrief. Clin. Simul. Nurs. **37**, 32–39 (2019)
21. Lapum, J.L., et al.: Self-Debriefing in Virtual Simulation: Nurse Educator **44**, E6–E8 (2019)
22. Kun, Y., Hubert, J., Bin, L., Huan, W.X.: Self-debriefing model based on an integrated video-capture system: an efficient solution to skill degradation. J. Surg. Educ. **76**, 362–369 (2019)
23. Reed, S.J.: Measuring learning and engagement during debriefing: a new instrument. Clin. Simul. Nurs. **46**, 15–21 (2020). https://doi.org/10.1016/j.ecns.2020.03.002
24. Miller, E.T., Farra, S., Simon, A.: Asynchronous online debriefing with health care workers: lessons learned. Clin. Simul. Nurs. **20**, 38–45 (2018). https://doi.org/10.1016/j.ecns.2018.04.007

25. Atthill, S., Witmer, D., Luctkar-Flude, M., Tyerman, J.: Exploring the impact of a virtual asynchronous debriefing method after a virtual simulation game to support clinical decision-making. Clin. Simul. Nurs. **50**, 10–18 (2021)
26. Verkuyl, M., et al.: Combining self-debriefing and group debriefing in simulation. Clin. Simul. Nurs. **39**, 41–44 (2020)
27. Verkuyl, M., et al.: Adding self-debrief to an in-person simulation: a mixed-methods study. Clin. Simul. Nurs. **47**, 32–39 (2020)
28. Rueda-Medina, B., et al.: A combination of self-debriefing and instructor-led debriefing improves team effectiveness in health science students. Nurse Educ. **46**, E7 (2021)
29. Verkuyl, M., et al.: Exploring debriefing combinations after a virtual simulation. Clin. Simul. Nurs. **40**, 36–42 (2020)
30. Grund, C.K., Schelkle, M.: Developing serious games with integrated debriefing: findings from a business intelligence context. Bus Inf Syst Eng **62**, 87–101 (2020)
31. Nicholson, J., Gillespie, R., Bickerdike, S., et al.: OP13 Immersive video for simulation debriefing: 'record and review' in 360-degrees using a virtual reality headset. BMJ Simul. Technol. Enhanc. Learn. **5** (2019)
32. Voyer, S., Hatala, R.: Debriefing and feedback: two sides of the same coin? Simulation in Healthcare: The Journal of the Society for Simulation in Healthcare **10**, 67–68 (2015)
33. Messaoudi, F., Ksentini, A., Simon, G., Bertin, P.: Performance analysis of game engines on mobile and fixed devices, ACM Transactions on Multimedia Computing, Communications, and Applications. 13(4), pp. 57:1–57:28 (2017)

Exploring Higher Education Teachers' Attitudes Towards Gamification

Giada Marinensi[1] (✉) and Marc Romero Carbonell[2]

[1] Link Campus University, Via del Casale di San Pio V, 44, 00165 Rome, Italy
g.marinensi@unilink.it
[2] Universitat Oberta de Catalunya, Rambla Poblenou, 156, 08018 Barcelona, Spain

Abstract. The purpose of this study is to gain a better understanding of university teachers' attitudes toward gamification. A broader goal is to lay the groundwork for a better understanding of how university teachers gaming habits and preferences might be leveraged in efforts to introduce gamification in Higher Education (HE). Building on previous research, showing no differences in teachers' attitudes towards gamification by age, gender or type of institution (public or private), this exploratory study tries to assess whether teachers' level of familiarity with games may have an influence on their attitudes and their expectations about the use of a gamified approach in a Higher Education course. The data were collected through focus groups, involving 13 teachers all in-service in a private Italian university, and were analysed through qualitative content analysis. Participants were divided into three groups according to their playing habits and preferences (well-rounded gamers, casual gamers and non-gamers). Results show that, even though the participants' overall attitude towards gamification was favourable, there were some differences between the three groups. For instance, teachers in the "well-rounded gamers" group expressed the highest level of concern about the possible negative effects of the use of gamification in HE, while "casual gamers" and "non-gamers" seemed to be less cautious and more focused on the possible advantages of a gamified educational strategy. "Non-gamers" were the group more concerned about the time and guidance needed to really be able to use this new pedagogical approach in their courses.

Keywords: Gamification · Higher education · Teachers' attitudes · Gamer types

1 Introduction

Engagement in learning activities and motivation to learn play an important role in students' academic achievement and performance, both in traditional [1–3] and online classroom settings [4, 5]. Students who possess a strong motivation to learn and show a high level of academic task engagement are more likely to carry out successfully their learning experience [6], are more resilient [7] and less likely to drop out [8] or adopt negative behaviours including academic cheating [9].

Several studies referred to gamification, which can be defined as the "use of game design elements to motivate user behavior in non-game contexts" [10], as a possible strategy to foster students' engagement and motivation in educational contexts [11–13].

© Springer Nature Switzerland AG 2021
F. de Rosa et al. (Eds.): GALA 2021, LNCS 13134, pp. 153–163, 2021.
https://doi.org/10.1007/978-3-030-92182-8_15

In particular, the use of gamification in Higher Education Institutions (HEIs), which has increased considerably over the past few years, seems to have led to the achievement of positive results in relation to the improvement of students' engagement and motivation [14–21].

The fact that previous studies about the use of gamification in HEIs have achieved promising results is consistent with the fact that the use of game elements in learning contexts can be appealing for the new generations of students, which are digital natives, have a high level of familiarity with the video games language [22], and are open to the concept of learning from this medium [23].

However, a crucial factor affecting the adoption of this new pedagogical practice, as any other one, is teachers' willingness to implement it [24–26]. In fact, even though experimenting with a new teaching methodology can represent an opportunity, it is also a challenge comporting risks and requiring an investment in terms of time (i.e., to prepare new learning materials) or even money (i.e., to buy technical equipment).

Therefore, exploring teachers' attitudes towards gamification can be helpful since attitude is a significant predictor of teachers' intention to use gamification [26, 27].

Nevertheless, teachers' attitudes towards gamification are still a neglected research area. So far, even if some studies highlighted that not all teachers accept gamification or have the same expectations about this approach [28, 29], no relevant factors influencing the teachers' willingness to adopt gamification have been identified.

In particular, the results of the study carried out by Martí-Parreño et al. [27] show no differences in teachers' attitudes towards gamification/educational games by gender or age, so other studies should try to identify the factors influencing teachers' attitudes toward gamification. One of these factors could be the teachers' level of familiarity with games and their gaming practices and preferences.

According to data about gamers and games (especially digital games), in the last couple of decades, a shift has happened, and the average age of a video game player is now between 35 and 44 years in the U.S. [30] and 31 in Europe [31]. Moreover, gamers are almost equally distributed between males and females: in the U.S., 41% of gamers are female, and 59% are male [30], while in Europe, 45% of gamers are female, and 55% are male [31].

So, if nowadays university students are likely to be gamers, the same is true for teachers as well. Can their gaming habits and preferences affect their attitude toward gamification and their willingness to adopt it in their courses?

1.1 Research Questions

This study aims to better understand teachers' attitudes towards gamification and to understand if their gaming practices and preferences can influence their attitude about gamification, their expectations about the use of a gamified approach in a HE course and their willingness to adopt this methodology.

Therefore, the main research questions are as follows:

R1: Do teachers serving in HEIs show a positive attitude towards gamification?
R2: Does the level of familiarity with games affect attitude towards gamification for teachers serving in HEIs?

2 Methodology

The data were collected through three focus groups in which the objective was to collect information about teachers' point of view about four main topics: (a) perception of students' level of motivation and engagement, and approaches currently adopted to foster their active participation in the learning process; (b) level of familiarity with games, gaming habits and general opinion about games; (c) willingness to adopt a new pedagogical practice to foster students' motivation and engagement; (d) attitude towards gamification and the use of game elements to foster students' motivation and engagement.

An interview guide (Table 1) was prepared and previously validated by two educational experts with experience in the field of pedagogical innovation in HE.

Informed consent was obtained from all participants before the focus groups were held. Two researchers were present during each focus group, one acting as a moderator and the other as an assistant moderator.

Each focus group began with an introduction and description of the purpose of the discussion and by a brief presentation of each participant. Then, the moderator, following the interview guide, asked the participants several open-ended questions.

The focus groups lasted for 70–95 min, were audio-recorded and transcribed verbatim.

Table 1. Interview guide.

Introduction questions	Thoughts about the level of engagement and motivation of university students Will you describe them as motivated? Have you ever struggled to keep them engaged? What kind of approach do you generally use to foster their motivation and engagement?
Transition questions	Thoughts about the role of games in participants' everyday life Will you describe yourself as a gamer? Do you prefer digital or analogical games? How much time do you spend playing games? What genre of games do you play the most?
Key questions	Are you familiar with the concept of "gamification"? Have you ever used a gamified application (i.e., for learning a new language or for adopting a new habit)? What is your general attitude toward the use of game elements in learning contexts? Would you be willing to adopt a gamified approach in your classes?
Additional questions	Reflection on what was said during the discussion Does anyone have something further to add?

2.1 Participants

At the focus groups participated a total of 13 teachers, all in-service at Link Campus University, a private university based in Rome, Italy, both in bachelor's and master's degree programs. Participants' age range is between 33 and 56; 4 are male, and 9 are female. Table 2 summarises the demographic of the sample.

Table 2. Demographic data of the sample

		Percentage	Means
Gender	Male	31	–
	Female	69	–
Age		–	39
Degree program	Only bachelor's degree program	39	–
	Only master's degree program	23	–
	Both bachelor's degree and master's degree programs	38	–
Year of experience in teaching in HEIs		–	5

N = 13

Moreover, the information that each participant provided answering the question about the role of games in their everyday life were used to associate them to one of the following categories, as defined by Manero et al. [32]: (a) well-rounded, playing all kinds of games with a high frequency; (b) casual, who play less frequently and mostly mobile, social and party games; (c) hardcore, who prefer first-person shooters and sport games; (d) non-gamers, who do not usually play games of any kind.

The "well-rounded" group includes 4 teachers (31%) who showed a higher level of familiarity with games: they play games both for entertainment and for learning purposes, play different kinds of games (both digital and analogical).

The "casual" group includes 5 teachers (38%) who played mostly mobile games or party games, just for entertainment purposes.

The "non-gamers" group includes 4 teachers (31%) who show the lowest level of familiarity with games and an overall negative attitude toward games.

Finally, none of the teachers matched the profile of the hardcore gamer.

Of the thirteen participants, only 1 (included in the "well-rounded" group) had previously adopted a structured gamified approach in some HE courses. However, 7 participants have already used gamified applications (with different aims, such as personal improvement, physical rehabilitation, learning, etc.), and 8 of the participants reported having implemented some game-based activities in their teaching practice.

3 Data Analysis

Data were analysed through qualitative content analysis [33–36], which has been defined by Hsieh and Shannon [35] as "a research method for the subjective interpretation of the content of text data through the systematic classification process of coding and identifying themes or patterns". The analysis performed aimed to compile the data to highlight teachers' attitudes towards gamification (RQ1) and if their level of familiarity with games and their gaming habits affected their attitudes towards gamification (RQ2).

The approach adopted consisted of six main phases: reading and re-reading data to become familiar with them, identifying the analysis units, organising the analysis units into categories (themes) based on the common aspects they share [36], reviewing themes, defining and naming themes, producing the report of the study findings.

The first part of the analysis was performed in the original language (Italian), but the themes were defined and named in English. Data were analysed using CAQDAS software NVivo 12.

4 Findings

After coding the data, a matrix was built in order to identify which of the three gamers' categories show the most positive attitude towards the use of gamification in HE (Table 3). Even though the participants' overall attitude towards gamification was favourable and the positive comments outnumbered the negative ones, it was possible to highlight some differences between the three groups.

Table 3. Negative attitude vs positive attitude toward gamification.

	Drawbacks of adopting gamification in HE	Benefits of adopting gamification in HE
Non-gamers (4 teachers)	4	13
Casual gamers (5 teachers)	4	16
Well-rounded gamers (4 teachers)	7	6
Total	15	35

In particular, teachers in the "well-rounded gamers" group expressed the highest level of concern about the negative effects of the use of gamification in HE, such as the overtaking of competition on collaboration, the diminishing of teacher's authority or subject importance in the eyes of the students, the risks of letting behind students that are shy or less at ease in a more interactive classroom context. One teacher, for instance, stated: "Due to the general perception of games as childish activities, with the sole aim of entertaining the players, students may perceive educational delivered through games as less serious, less valuable than contents delivered in more traditional ways" (male, 43), while another one commented: "A more playful classroom atmosphere may have a negative impact on the way the subject I teach is perceived by students as if it were somehow less serious" (female, 35).

Conversely, "casual gamers" and "non-gamers" seemed to be less cautious, valuing more the expected benefits than the possible negative impacts of adding game elements to their teaching practice. Some of the participants, for instance, stated: "In my opinion, it is absolutely true that the game affects the teachers' authority, but it is a side effect that is worth experiencing, because the students gain a greater awareness of the study matter" (female, 37, casual gamer); "Game it's very effective as icebreaking, and it can help students to know each other better and form strong social bonds" (female, 45, non-gamer).

Looking more deeply at the comments of the participants, it was also possible to identify the benefits (Table 4) and risks (Table 5) of adopting a gamified approach in HE that the teachers perceived as the most relevant.

Table 4. Most relevant benefits of adopting gamification in HE.

Most relevant benefits	Number of comments		
	Non-gamers	Casual	Well-rounded
Monitoring students' progress throughout the course	2	1	1
Guiding the students in their learning process (by providing them with short and medium-term goals and constant feedback)	2	3	2
Linking the summative evaluation with students' performance throughout the course	2	1	
Creating a stronger and more positive relationship with the teacher	2	2	
Easing the creation of social bonds among students	2	4	1
Enhancing engagement and fostering motivation	3	3	2
Promoting a higher level of contents retention		2	
Total	13	16	6

Table 5. Most relevant drawbacks of adopting gamification in HE.

Most relevant drawbacks	Number of comments		
	Non-gamers	Casual	Well-rounded
Overtaking of competition on collaboration			3
Diminishing of teacher's authority		2	2
Diminishing of subject importance in the eyes of the students		2	1
Requiring guidance and technical support to be implemented	2		
Time-consuming to implement	2		
Creating classroom dynamics difficult to manage			1
Total	4	4	7

5 Discussion

Coherently with previous research carried out on this topic [27, 37, 38], the results of this study show the existence of an attitude-use gap in educational gamification. In fact, even though the overall attitude towards gamification of the teachers participating in this study is positive, only 1 of them (and belonging to the "well-rounded gamers" category) already uses gamification on a regular basis.

Common barriers preventing teachers from adopting pedagogical innovations, especially technology-related innovations, such as lack of time, lack of training/guidance [39], were mentioned only by the teachers belonging to the "non-gamers" group. The hesitancy of "non-gamers" can be understood in the broader framework of their relationship with technologies and with technology-related pedagogical innovation. In fact, according to Hayes and Ohrnberger [40], non-gamers are significantly less inclined to perceive themselves as innovators or one of the first to use new technologies if compared with gamers.

On the other hand, "well-rounded" and "casual" gamers, who have more experience with games, expressed concerns about the fact that merging gaming and teaching/learning activities could draw the latter inside the "magic circle" of game, therefore casting an entertainment light on the educational process, and possibly diminishing the seriousness of it in the eyes of the students. These results are coherent with previous research, which focuses on teachers' behaviours and beliefs regarding digital game-based language learning and highlights a discrepancy between personal and pedagogical media usage, including gaming [38].

Teachers belonging to the "well-rounded" and "casual" gamers groups didn't share the same views about the risks of playing competitive aspects. In fact, "well-rounded" gamers were the only ones stating that adding game elements into the educational context may lead to excessive competition among students and to the creation of classroom dynamics difficult to manage. This difference between "well-rounded" and "casual" gamers can possibly be explained in the light of the different kinds of games that each group is more likely to play. The element of competition, in fact, is usually highly mitigated by game mechanics fostering collaboration and communication in the vast majority of mobile games and party games, which are the kind of games preferred by "casual gamers".

Differences emerged in this study between "well-rounded" and "casual" gamers seem to be worthy of further investigations and, more generally, to support the fact that a simple dichotomy between gamers and non-gamers cannot provide enough depth to the analysis.

6   Conclusions

The main goal of this research was to gain a better understanding of teachers' attitudes towards gamification (RQ1) and to evaluate if their level of familiarity with games and their gaming habits had an influence on their expectations about the use of a gamified approach in HE courses and on their willingness to adopt this methodology (RQ2).

Although the findings are related to a small group of teachers and cannot be generalised, they offered interesting insights.

As for the RQ1, the results of this study highlighted a general positive attitude of HE teachers towards gamification and the use of game elements as part of the teaching practice. There were indeed more than twice as many positive comments as negative ones (35 comments highlighted the benefits of gamification, while only 15 highlighted drawbacks). None of the teachers declared to be opposed to the idea of adopting a gamified approach in their courses, and more than half of the teachers have already tried implementing some game-based activities in their teaching practice (9 teachers out of 13).

Analysing the comments of each teacher, it was also possible to identify some differences in their expectations about the use of gamification based on their gaming habits and their level of familiarity with games (RQ2). Teachers in the "well-rounded gamers" group were more concerned about the negative impacts that gamification and game-elements can have on classroom dynamics, such as moving the focus from the learning to the competitive aspects of the game and diminishing the teacher's authority alongside the perceived importance of the discipline he teaches.

Teachers in the "casual gamers" and "non-gamers" groups were more focused on the benefits related to the adoption of a gamified approach in HE, such as easing the creation of social bonds among students (mentioned six times), enhancing engagement and fostering motivation (mentioned six times) and guiding the students in their learning process (mentioned five times). Casual gamers, in particular, pointed out that the power of games to foster the creation of social bandings among students and with the teacher outweighed the risk of a change in the balance of teacher-student authority relation.

"Non-gamers" were the group more concerned about the time needed to learn the new approach in order to really be able to use it in their courses.

Due to the limitations of this study, in particular the small number of participants, further research should deeper explore this topic, building on these preliminary results. A larger and more diverse sample of participants could also allow to explore the correlation between the discipline thought by each teacher and their gaming habits, and to further verify if the results of the study carried out by Martí-Parreño et al. (2017), showing in teachers' attitudes towards gamification/educational games by gender or age.

References

1. Schnitzler, K., Holzberger, D., Seidel, T.: All better than being disengaged: student engagement patterns and their relations to academic self-concept and achievement. Eur. J. Psychol. Educ. **36**(3), 627–652 (2020). https://doi.org/10.1007/s10212-020-00500-6
2. Sedova, K., Sedlacek, M., Svaricek, R., et al.: Do those who talk more learn more? The relationship between student classroom talk and student achievement. Learn. Instr. **63**, 101217 (2019). https://doi.org/10.1016/j.learninstruc.2019.101217
3. Christenson, S.L., Wylie, C., Reschly, A.L.: Handbook of Research on Student Engagement (2012)
4. Dixson, M.D.: Measuring student engagement in the online course: the online student engagement scale (OSE). Section II: Faculty Attitudes and Student Engagement. Report (2015). Online Learn. J. **19**, 143
5. Robinson, C.C., Hullinger, H.: New benchmarks in higher education: student engagement in online learning. J. Educ. Bus. **84**(2), 101–109 (2008). https://doi.org/10.3200/JOEB.84.2. 101-109
6. Hughes, J.N., Luo, W., Kwok, O.M., Loyd, L.K.: Teacher-student support, effortful engagement, and achievement: a 3-year longitudinal study. J. Educ. Psychol. **100**(1), 1–14 (2008). https://doi.org/10.1037/0022-0663.100.1.1
7. Finn, J.D., Rock, D.A.: Academic success among students at risk for school failure. J. Appl. Psychol. **82**(2), 221–234 (1997). https://doi.org/10.1037/0021-9010.82.2.221
8. Finn, J.D.: Withdrawing from school. Rev. Educ. Res. **59**(2), 117–142 (1989). https://doi.org/ 10.3102/00346543059002117
9. Finn, K.V., Frone, M.R.: Academic performance and cheating: moderating role of school identification and self-efficacy. J. Educ. Res. **97**(3), 115–121 (2004). https://doi.org/10.3200/ JOER.97.3.115-121
10. Deterding, S.: Situated motivational affordances of game elements: a conceptual model, pp. 3–6 (2011)
11. Contreras-Espinosa, R.S., Eguia Gomez, J.L.: How could the use of game elements help students' affective and cognitive engagement during game play? J. Inf. Technol. Res. **13**(1), 17–29 (2020). https://doi.org/10.4018/JITR.2020010102
12. Majuri, J., Koivisto, J., Hamari, J.: Gamification of education and learning: a review of empirical literature. In: CEUR Workshop Proceedings, vol. 2186, pp. 11–19 (2018)
13. Xi, N., Hamari, J.: Does gamification satisfy needs? A study on the relationship between gamification features and intrinsic need satisfaction. Int. J. Inf. Manag. **46**, 210–221 (2019). https://doi.org/10.1016/j.ijinfomgt.2018.12.002
14. Ab Rahman, R., Ahmad, S., Hashim, U.R.: The effectiveness of gamification technique for higher education students engagement in polytechnic Muadzam. Int. J. Educ. Technol. High. Educ. **15**, 1–16 (2018)
15. Alsawaier, R.S.: The effect of gamification on motivation and engagement. Int. J. Inf. Learn. Technol. **35**(1), 56–79 (2018)
16. Campillo-Ferrer, J.M., Miralles-Martínez, P., Sánchez-Ibáñez, R.: Gamification in higher education: impact on student motivation and the acquisition of social and civic key competencies. Sustainability **12**, 4822 (2020). https://doi.org/10.3390/SU12124822
17. Dicheva, D., Irwin, K., Dichev, C.: Exploring learners experience of gamified practicing: for learning or for fun? Int. J. Serious Games **6**, 5–21 (2019)

18. Huang, B., Hew, K.F., Lo, C.K.: Investigating the effects of gamification-enhanced flipped learning on undergraduate students' behavioral and cognitive engagement. Interact. Learn. Environ. 27(8), 1106–1126 (2018). https://doi.org/10.1080/10494820.2018.1495653

19. Lopes, R.P.: An award system for gamification in higher education. In: 7th International Conference of Education, Research and Innovation (2014)

20. Sánchez-Martín, J., Cañada-Cañada, F., Dávila-Acedo, M.A.: Just a game? Gamifying a general science class at university: collaborative and competitive work implications. Think. Skills Creat. 26, 51–59 (2017). https://doi.org/10.1016/j.tsc.2017.05.003

21. Kovácsné Pusztai, K.: Gamification in higher education. Teach. Math. Comput. Sci. 18, 87–106 (2021). https://doi.org/10.5485/tmcs.2020.0510

22. Glover, I.: Play as you learn: gamification as a technique for motivating learners. In: Proceedings of World Conference on Educational Multimedia, Hypermedia and Telemcommunications (2013)

23. Prensky, M.: Don't Bother Me Mom: I'm Learning: How Computer and Video Games are Preparing Your Kids for 21st Century Success and How You Can Help. St Paul: Paragon House, Minnesota (2003)

24. Teo, T.: Pre-service teachers' attitudes towards computer use: a Singapore survey. Australas. J. Educ. Technol. (2008). https://doi.org/10.14742/ajet.1201

25. Ketelhut, D.J., Schifter, C.C.: Teachers and game-based learning: improving understanding of how to increase efficacy of adoption. Comput. Educ. 56(2), 539–546 (2011). https://doi.org/10.1016/j.compedu.2010.10.002

26. Asiri, M.J.: Do teachers' attitudes, perception of usefulness, and perceived social influences predict their behavioral intentions to use gamification in EFL classrooms? Evidence from the middle east. Int. J. Educ. Pract. 7(3), 112–122 (2019). https://doi.org/10.18488/journal.61.2019.73.112.122

27. Martí-Parreño, J., Seguí-Mas, D., Seguí-Mas, E.: Teachers' attitude towards and actual use of gamification. Procedia Soc. Behav. Sci. 228, 682–688 (2016). https://doi.org/10.1016/j.sbspro.2016.07.104

28. Browne, K., Anand, C., Gosse, E.: Gamification and serious game approaches for adult literacy tablet software. Entertain. Comput. 5(3), 135–146 (2014). https://doi.org/10.1016/j.entcom.2014.04.003

29. Chung, C.H., Shen, C., Qiu, Y.Z.: Students' acceptance of gamification in higher education. Int. J. Game-Based Learn. 9(2), 1–19 (2019). https://doi.org/10.4018/IJGBL.2019040101

30. Entertainment Software Association: 2020 Essential Facts About the Video Game Industry. Cision, pp. 1–2 (2020)

31. ISFE: Europe Video Game Industry Key Facts 2020, pp. 1–20 (2020)

32. Manero, B., Torrente, J., Freire, M., Fernández-Manjón, B.: An instrument to build a gamer clustering framework according to gaming preferences and habits. Comput. Hum. Behav. 62, 353–363 (2016). https://doi.org/10.1016/j.chb.2016.03.085

33. Weber, R.P.: Basic Content Analysis, 2nd edn (1990)

34. Shelley, M., Krippendorff, K.: Content analysis: an introduction to its methodology. J. Am. Stat. Assoc. (1984). https://doi.org/10.2307/2288384

35. Hsieh, H.F., Shannon, S.E.: Three approaches to qualitative content analysis. Qual. Health Res. 15, 1277–1288 (2005). https://doi.org/10.1177/1049732305276687

36. Bardin, L.: L'analyse de contenu (2013)

37. Sánchez-Mena, A., Martí-Parreño, J.: Gamification in higher education: teachers' drivers and barriers. In: ICFE (2016)

38. Blume, C.: Games people (don't) play: an analysis of pre-service EFL teachers' behaviors and beliefs regarding digital game-based language learning. Comput. Assist. Lang. Learn. 33, 109–132 (2020). https://doi.org/10.1080/09588221.2018.1552599

39. Mumtaz, S.: Factors affecting teachers' use of information and communications technology: a review of the literature. J. Inf. Technol. Teach. Educ. **9**(3), 319–342 (2000). https://doi.org/10.1080/14759390000200096

40. Ohrnberger, M.: The gamer generation teaches school: the gaming practices and attitudes towards technology of pre-service teachers. J. Technol. Teach. Educ. **21**, 153–177 (2013)

Democratizing Game Learning Analytics
for Serious Games

Víctor M. Pérez-Colado$^{(\boxtimes)}$ ⓘ, Iván J. Pérez-Colado ⓘ, Iván Martínez-Ortiz ⓘ,
Manuel Freire-Morán ⓘ, and Baltasar Fernández-Manjón ⓘ

Department of Software Engineering and Artificial Intelligence, Complutense University
of Madrid, C/ Profesor José García Santesmases, 9, 28040 Madrid, Spain
victormp@ucm.es

Abstract. Interest in the field of serious games (SGs) has grown during the last few years due to its multiple advantages. For example, SGs provide immersive learning environments, where risky or complex scenarios can be tested in safety while keeping players engaged. Moreover, the highly interactive nature of serious games opens new opportunities for applying learning analytics to the interaction data gathered from the gameplays. These interaction data can be used, for example, to measure the impact of serious games on their players. At e-UCM, we have developed open code tools to support serious game learning analytics (GLA), especially an xAPI tracker that collects the player interactions and sends them to a cloud analytic store, SIMVA. Although this tracker uses the xAPI specification as a basis, it includes extensions tailored to our tools. However, not all game developers have the knowledge to operate our analytics infrastructure or are willing to use our tools. We present the design of a GLA system based on existing software modules, focused on collecting and storing analytics generated by SGs in xAPI format. The main elements of this lean architecture are the Learning Record Store (LRS) and the xAPI tracker. With this work, we aim to facilitate and lower the barrier of applying learning analytics in serious games.

Keywords: Game learning analytics · Serious games · xAPI · Tracker

1 Introduction

The growth in interest in serious games (SGs) is due to their multiple advantages, such as greater attention retention capacity, the ability to teach skills through fun mechanics, or to simulate real environments safely, ensuring more authentic learning. Additionally, SGs that include assessment capabilities can produce evidence-based assessments.

However, few SGs include assessment and, even when present, it is rare to have scientifically validated the assessment with enough learners and in real environments. In most cases, SGs are developed as black box systems [1, 2]. That is, the SG only provides a result (e.g., score), and although they may have a complex internal logic that responds to the interactions and educational needs of the learner, this is not observable from the outside. This implies that there is no evidence of the learning process produced with the game, limiting its educational usefulness, and hindering its scientific validation [1, 3].

© Springer Nature Switzerland AG 2021
F. de Rosa et al. (Eds.): GALA 2021, LNCS 13134, pp. 164–173, 2021.
https://doi.org/10.1007/978-3-030-92182-8_16

At best, the game provides scores, progress, or evaluations as output data; but there is a lack of specific data about the player's process to obtain these results.

To improve the usefulness and reliability of SGs, work has been done mainly on formal game validation [4] and a white-box evaluation or reporting model [5]. Through validation it is possible to ensure that the game produces the expected outcome and, therefore, its application in a real setting should be effective. The most popular method used for validation of SGs is through questionnaires applied before and after using the game in which the desired change is reflected (usually this change is also compared with a control group) [4]. On the other hand, through a white box evaluation, the game sends out the meaningful interactions of the player with the game. This exhaustive report adds meaning or extra information to the activity and can be monitored in real time or analyzed a posteriori to assess the player and even to predict the player's outcome. A particular use case of application of this approach is stealth assessment [6]. We consider that, by combining both methods, formal validation and learning analytics (LA) could be a method capable of providing both assessment and scientific validations.

The open issue is that, despite recognizing the usefulness and potential of LA in the SG community, its application is still limited [7]. Usually, in those cases where analytics are implemented, it is done ad-hoc and from scratch. But implementing LA in games requires specific skills (software development or data analytics) that are not very common in small or medium-sized development studios, which are the ones that usually develop SGs. The use of LA requires not only the deployment of a complex software infrastructure often only within reach of experts, but also meeting both the general and specific educational needs of each game and the regulatory needs for the treatment of information (e.g., EU GDPR privacy law). It is, therefore, necessary to develop methodologies and software modules that simplify this complex task.

To systematize and democratize the application of game learning analytics (GLA), the responsibilities of SG developers should be clearly delimited, with a primary focus on selecting relevant in-game events to be analyzed by data analytics experts. To achieve this goal, two aspects need to be considered from the very beginning: the data exchange format (to achieve common semantics on which to perform the analysis), and the Application Program Interface (API) to be used to communicate formatted data, so SGs can be easily deployed in different environments. Both aspects can be simplified with software modules to both assist with formatting and communicating this information outside the game (i.e., a tracker) and receiving and storing it somewhere (usually in the cloud) securely, while providing at least basic query and analysis functionalities.

Our approach is centered on the use of an e-learning standard designed to capture user interaction as part of an educational scenario such as xAPI (eXperience API), that in the specific case of SGs, provides a format to represent user interactions within the game and that will allow us to record the user traces within the game. The xAPI specification (version 2.0 will become an IEEE standard during 2021) is a specification that provides a statement-based data model that is generic and extensible. The structure of a basic statement consists of the following elements: an actor (*who* performs the action), a verb (*what* action is performed) and an object (the action's *target*). The purpose of this basic structure is to enable communities of practice to define precisely, through custom application profiles, specific vocabularies for each of the elements of statements.

For example, there is an application profile for SGs (xAPI-SG), created by e-UCM in collaboration with ADL as part of the European H2020 RAGE project [8].

As part of previous projects, we developed an open-source tool (tracker) that implements xAPI-SG and simplifies the communication of user traces between the game and an external store, without requiring the SG developer to be an xAPI expert. Until now, this tracker communicated SGs with our analytics tools such as SIMVA and T-Mon, which simplify the management of SG experiments and deployments and automate some aspects of data analysis on xAPI traces [9]. Although these tools are free and open-source, technical knowledge is required for their use and deployment. On the other hand, the xAPI specification also defines a standard API that focuses mainly on sending and querying xAPI *statements*. This standardized API allows an educational tool, such as a SG, to communicate with a generic xAPI Learning Record Store (LRS).

The present work describes how we have combined and adapted our technology (primarily the tracker) to interact with any standard LRS. This should democratize GLA by making it more accessible to game developers, allowing SG developers, educational organizations, and teachers to use the LRSs that best suits their specific needs. For example, some will opt to use an LRS that is already integrated with their existing institutional Learning Management System (LMS), while others may chose a commercial or open-source LRS offered as SaaS. With these enhancements, we can maximize the benefits of using our tracker during SG development (by being able to interact with our SG validation tools) while allowing choice regarding the LRS to use once deployed.

The following sections describe the current model for collecting GLA using the e-UCM group tools; how SG LA can be collected using reusable generic software components; the modifications to our tools to further the democratization of analytics for SGs; and finally, present conclusions and future work.

2   A Tailor-Made Scalable Learning Analytics Ecosystem

Systematization of LA in SGs requires software to store analytics, simplify the collection of analytics within the SG, and communicate it with the analytics store. This section describes our experience developing tools for these problems.

The e-UCM group has developed different tools related to the collection and analysis of data generated by SGs. The most recent is the SIMple VAlidator (SIMVA) platform [9]. SIMVA's main objective is the creation and orchestration of SG validation experiments using GLA. Usually, SGs are validated by using questionnaires before and after the activity in which participants play the SG. SIMVA includes an integrated questionnaire management tool to simplify this process. In addition, during the game activity, SIMVA takes care of collecting the LA generated by the SG [7, 10].

Using SIMVA it is possible to design different user experiments (called studies) for different games with full control over the flow of the experiment, offering, for example, the possibility of comparing two versions of the same game (A/B testing). As part of the management of the experiments, SIMVA allows us to generate a list of experiment participants identified exclusively by anonymized identifier tokens, which allow the actions of each participant in the different activities of a study to be linked together, while complying with regulations related to privacy and data protection. Likewise, the

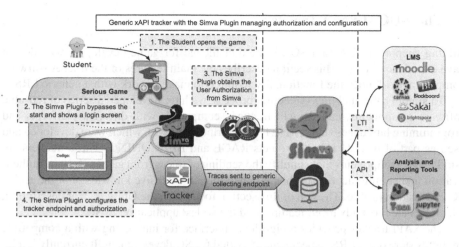

Fig. 1. Interaction flow of a SG with SIMVA, and of SIMVA with other tools such as T-Mon.

researcher or teacher involved in the experiment can monitor the progress of participants in each activity. Finally, SIMVA offers an API that can be used by data analysis experts to download and analyze the data collected during the experiment. This API is compatible with AWS S3, which is one of the APIs commonly supported by big data and data analytics tools such as Jupyter Notebooks.

From a game development perspective, SIMVA provides a plugin compatible with the Unity platform that simplifies authentication and trace submission for study participants/players. The usual process of interaction of a SG with SIMVA is as follows (Fig. 1): 1) players launch the game; 2) the game displays a simplified login interface, where players enter their 5-letter participant code; 3) the game connects to SIMVA by sending the study code and participant code, verifying that the user is assigned to the study and that the activity to be performed is to play the game (for instance, studies may require their participants to complete a survey before playing; in this case, an informative message with a link to the survey would be displayed, and the game would not start); 4) the game obtains the necessary configuration data to use the xAPI tracker and gameplay would start, during which analytics will be sent to SIMVA.

Once the experiment is finished, it is time for data science experts to analyze the data generated during the experiment. To simplify this task, we have created the T-Mon tool built on top of Jupyter Notebooks. T-Mon is a data analysis tool specialized on xAPI data compatible with the xAPI-SG profile, and provides a set of generic analyses and predefined visualizations adapted to this xAPI-SG profile.

Game learning analytics is a complex and error-prone process, requiring skills not always present in a game studio. Collecting game analytics data alone requires linking the game to a data store, identifying the user who is playing the game, and considering many other aspects of security and reliability. The following sections discuss the current capabilities of our analytics tracker, and the design changes needed to extend it so that user traces can be sent to xAPI-standard data stores such as the Learning Record Store (LRS).

3   The e-UCM xAPI Tracker

Adding support for LA to a SG can be a challenge for game developers who do not have experience in LA. This section describes the main features of the tracker software component to identify the functionality required to make it work with a generic LRS.

To simplify the analytics collection process, we have developed a series of reusable software components, called xAPI trackers, compatible with different platforms and programming languages (Unity, .NET, JavaScript, and Java), which were developed and used as part of the EU H2020 projects RAGE and BEACONING. These trackers are middleware components that simplify the sending of traces from games (solving authentication and communication problems), avoiding an extensive knowledge of the xAPI-SG application profile. The rest of this section focuses on the Unity tracker description, which has the most advanced features and the widest application in SGs.

The xAPI tracker provides a high-level interface for interacting with a compatible analytics store (e.g., LRS), specifically targeted for SG development. It currently implements the xAPI-SG application profile and includes another xAPI application profile for creating geopositioned games [11]. In addition, the tracker has other features that differentiate it from other existing xAPI support modules (see Fig. 2):

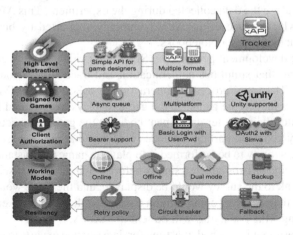

Fig. 2. e-UCM xAPI Tracker functionalities. Its five key aspects are shown on the left.

The first and main feature of the tracker is to provide a high-level and simplified interface so that developers and designers do not have to be experts in the xAPI format to record the game session or send interaction information. In fact, it allows traces to be created in multiple formats. For example, in addition to xAPI format, it is also possible to generate the traces using the more compact CSV format. For example, this is the format used to store a local backup of the traces inside the gaming device (if the backup mode of the tracker is enabled).

The tracker is implemented using Unity's primitives (such as network access), without which it would be more complex to create cross-platform SGs. In addition, the tracker has an interface to build partial traces to maintain the logical order of events even considering the internal logic of the game and its possible interactions.

The tracker supports authentication and privacy aspects. The current xAPI specification mandates only basic web authentication and OAuth1, neither of which is without problems. Basic authentication only authenticates tools, but not users; and, if game privileges are desired, different credentials for the same game must be created, complicating its use. On the other hand, OAuth1 has been discouraged for some time due to protocol security flaws. Thus, our tracker has been updated to support the new OAuth2 and OpenID connect standards, which are considered secure and allow not only to identify the tool but also the user who is using it. This improves security and minimizes the possibility that a user can access or send data on behalf of another user.

The tracker currently provides three modes of operation: online, offline, and with backups. These modes reflect our experience and the complexities of the actual use and application of SGs in real educational environments, where technical limitations and limited network reliability in schools or institutions where games are deployed games are a frequent occurrence. In online mode the tracker sends the data to an analytics store such as SIMVA, in offline mode the tracker stores the data on the gaming device, and in backup mode both strategies are combined to achieve greater reliability.

The tracker must be robust to be able to operate in non-reliable environments where technical problems may emerge. To this end, the tracker incorporates different strategies, such as exponential back off retry, bulkhead isolation, or circuit-breaker. For example, if the tracker detects that the analytics store is not responding properly for a certain period (which is configurable), it automatically switches to offline mode, and after a certain period it will retry the pending operations.

Despite the advanced features described above, before this work our tracker only implemented the xAPI-SG application profile, and due to issues with authentication and authorization was not designed to interact directly with a standard LRS.

4 DA Standard-Based Scalable Generic Game Learning Analytics Infrastructure

The creation of a platform to support LA for SGs requires different components depending on intended goals and required functionalities. Basic analytics support which includes only the collection of traces from a single game for later analysis is very different from a complete system that supports multiple games and also supports real-time user interaction analysis (e.g., H2020 BEACONING or RAGE); or a complete system to support experimentation with SGs such as SIMVA, where playing a game is only one of multiple activities that can be built into a study.

Game analytics processes are complex and fragile, with many sources of potential errors, such as communication, latency or availability – and it is not always possible to develop a fully integrated approach. The present work describes a strategy for implementing a GLA system based on existing software modules, focusing on the collection and storage of analytics generated by SGs in xAPI format. The main elements of this lean architecture are the Learning Record Store (LRS) and the xAPI tracker.

By adopting the full xAPI specification, which includes both a data format and programming interface for standards-compliant LRSs, we can reduce development costs and allow analytics collected in different deployment environments to share a conforming LRS, or the use of existing xAPI API-compatible services to interact with those LRSs. At the time of this writing, several popular LRSs are available:

- **ADL LRS** is an open source LRS by ADL, supporting OAuth1. However, this LRS is a reference implementation, designed only to carry out proof-of-concept activities with small numbers of users.
- **Learning Locker** is an open source LRS with support for basic data analysis and visualization and a business rules layer for easier integration with other systems. It also has an enterprise-oriented SaaS version.
- **Rustici LRS** is the main reference LRS, as Rustici works closely with ADL; and is offered as part of SCORM Cloud, an LMS for xAPI activities that can act as a mediator between traditional LMSs that support SCORM 1.2 or LTI and CMI-5 packages. This LRS supports similar data processing and business rules to Learning Locker, but offloads reports, analysis and visualizations to SCORM Cloud.
- **Yet Analytics LRS** is a commercial LRS that is offered in three versions: as a Cloud deployment, as a self-contained LRS compatible with a SQL interface installable on-premises, and as a hardware appliance that can even be deployed in experiments or field activities. To provide analytics and visualizations, Yet Analytics offers an xAPI Sandbox, a free platform based on its Yet Pro v2 LRS that provides on-demand LRSs and supports multiple dashboards.
- **Watershed LRS** is a commercial LRS that provides reports, performs data conversion to different formats and allows editing trace data or metadata. Watershed's LRS is currently free, although features such as dashboards, analysis, or visualizations require paid licenses.
- **Apereo OpenLRW** is an open source project that provides an xAPI-compliant LRS, as well as other analytics specifications such as IMS Caliper or IMS OneRoster. To analyze data, it can be connected with Apereo OpenDashboard-API, a framework for creating dashboards and visualizations.

An LRS is only useful if it receives traces that it can store for later analysis. We have identified three open-source trackers that can be used for development of SGs in Unity:

- **TinCan.NET** by Rustici Software is developed on.NET Framework 3.5, and can therefore be used from within the Unity platform. However, due to the peculiarities of Unity's.NET support, development of cross-platform games presents several issues. In addition, its use of synchronous communication clashes with the Unity game development model. Rustici also provides a JavaScript version: TinCan.JS.
- **UnityGBLxAPI** (formerly GBLxAPI) by Dig-iT! Games is a wrapper for TinCan.NET, with several improvements: i) better setup and compatibility, since it is Unity-specific; ii) an asynchronous queue approach to send the statements, which avoids game freezes while sending data; and iii) cross-platform compatibility of the generated games by using the specific network primitives offered by Unity. As a limitation, this tracker loses the ability to interpret LRS certain responses, preventing

developers from relating traces to each other via xAPI StatementRefs; also, it may be difficult to update if the underlying TinCan.NET library changes.

- Unity-xAPIWrapper by ADL is a lightweight tracker, with less dependencies and easier to use than the above alternatives. It uses Unity primitives for network communication, with similar advantages to those of UnityGBLxAPI. Its main limitations are that it is very simple, and requires more work from developer to achieve a flexible, secure, and resilient tracker; and a low rate of updates.

To use the xAPI API to communicate with an LRS from a game, certain configuration parameters must be known: base URL of the LRS, and usernames and passwords for the LRS. The xAPI specification does not detail how activities obtain these parameters. Fortunately, this problem has already been addressed in the CMI-5 specification [12]. CMI-5 is considered to be a natural evolution of SCORM, but using xAPI to communicate activity interactions with an LRS. This specification addresses several aspects: packaging, launching (including the exchange of credentials and configuration parameters needed to communicate with an LRS), and an xAPI application profile (xAPI-CMI5) that provides insight into the status and progress of an activity. Despite its benefits, CMI-5 adoption is currently very limited, especially by LMSs.

5   Adaptation of the Tracker for Use in the Generic Architecture

The use of a standard LRS can have advantages, especially for the actual exploitation of SGs in real educational settings, for example, by integrating them with a pre-existing e-learning infrastructure. We believe that our tracker has several unique and desirable characteristics, but we are also aware that to lower the entry barrier of applying LA we should be compatible with xAPI-compliant LRSs. In this regard, we have identified the following modifications to achieve this compatibility with our tracker: i) improve adherence to the xAPI specification, ii) provided support for the CMI-5 protocol, and iii) implement different modes of operation that allow running both SIMVA and a generic LRS configured either manually or via CMI-5 release.

Two additional modifications allow the standard to be followed more closely. On the one hand, integration with SIMVA extends the standard with additional services such as user authentication or retrieval of game configuration. We replaced them with traces following the CMI-5 profile. On the other hand, the generated traces were intended to be stored in a specific storage associated with the specific activity created in SIMVA to represent the game session. However, standard LRSs do not partition data like this. Using the *context.contextActivities* property of a statement, it is possible to specify the context in which it has been generated, for example, specifying in which SG the trace was generated, the educational activity that represents the session (or sessions) where the SG is used, or even the course where the educational activity is being included. Additionally, by using the *context.registration* property we can identify statements that belong to each attempt of a player.

Moreover, implementing the CMI-5 launch protocol allows the tracker to receive both the location of the LRS where information should be sent, as well as the authentication of the user who is developing the activity. Should CMI-5 not be available, the tracker can read this configuration from locations chosen at development time.

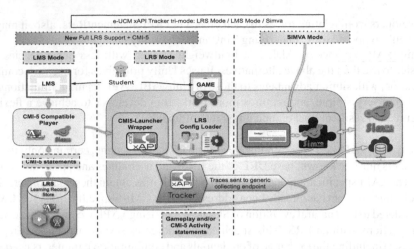

Fig. 3. Tracker working modes, internal components and interaction with external systems

Finally, in addition to the operating modes described in Sect. 3 (online, offline, backup), three working modes have been established: the SIMVA mode (the current mode), the standard LRS mode and the LMS-CMI-5 mode (Fig. 3). The SIMVA mode represents the tracker behavior prior to proposed modifications, and uses specific capabilities provided by SIMVA to simplify validation of SGs. In the standard LRS mode, the tracker will be configured to use the xAPI API exclusively, obtaining the configuration parameters for the LRS from the pre-established locations configured during development. Finally, in LMS-CMI-5 mode, LMS support will be used to launch the SG as a CMI-5 activity, retrieving configuration parameters directly from the LMS.

6   Conclusions and Future Work

Learning analytics is a decisive step forward in adopting serious games as reliable tools in the learning process. Analytics provides evidence beyond simple results, and allows insights into how players achieved those results. However, GLA implementations are still complex and fragile, and require significant technical skills to deploy.

In previous work, we proposed a SG analytics architecture that relies on the use of xAPI as a data standard and on a set of software modules to capture SG information (tracker) and communicate it to a data warehouse in the cloud for secure storage and analysis (SIMVA, T-Mon). However, our approach is difficult to integrate with existing infrastructure. To decrease the cost of entry and increase reliability and adoption, this work proposes a similar architecture using pre-existing software components in the xAPI ecosystem (e.g., trackers and LRS). Thanks to the use of standards, both xAPI and LRS, it is possible to swap some of the software components without causing vendor lock-in. Furthermore, it is possible to reuse components such as LRS, which are increasingly already deployed in existing e-learning infrastructure.

Since the e-UCM tracker was, until now, strongly coupled with e-UCM tools such as SIMVA and did not offer full support for third-party LRSs, we are implementing two new standards-compatible modes for the tracker: an LRS mode to connect to any standards-based LRS, and an LMS mode to allow our newly CMI-5 compliant tracker to convert SGs into packages that can be easily deployed as activities in LMSs.

Acknowledgements. This work has been partially funded by Regional Government of Madrid (eMadrid S2018/TCS4307, co-funded by the European Structural Funds FSE and FEDER) and by the Ministry of Education (TIN2017-89238-R, PID2020-119620RB-I00).

References

1. Chaudy, Y., Connolly, T.: Specification and evaluation of an assessment engine for educational games: empowering educators with an assessment editor and a learning analytics dashboard. Entertain. Comput. **27**(September), 209–224 (2018). https://doi.org/10.1016/j.entcom.2018.07.003
2. Freire, M., Serrano-Laguna, Á., Manero-Iglesias, B., Martínez-Ortiz, I.: Game learning analytics: learning analytics for serious games. Learn. Des. Technol. https://doi.org/10.1007/978-3-319-17727-4
3. Marchiori, E.J., Torrente, J., Del Blanco, Á., Moreno-Ger, P., Sancho, P., Fernández-Manjón, B.: A narrative metaphor to facilitate educational game authoring. Comput. Educ. **58**(1), 590–599 (2012). https://doi.org/10.1016/j.compedu.2011.09.017
4. Boyle, E.A., et al.: An update to the systematic literature review of empirical evidence of the impacts and outcomes of computer games and serious games. Comput. Educ. **94**, 178–192 (2016). https://doi.org/10.1016/j.compedu.2015.11.003
5. Hauge, J.B., et al.: Implications of learning analytics for serious game design. In: Proceedings of the IEEE 14th International Conference on Advanced Learning Technologies, ICALT 2014, pp. 230–232 (2014). https://doi.org/10.1109/ICALT.2014.73
6. Shute, V.J.: Stealth assessment in computer-based games to support learning. Comput. Games Instr. **55**(2), 503–524 (2011)
7. Alonso-Fernández, C., Calvo-Morata, A., Freire, M., Martínez-Ortiz, I., Fernández-Manjón, B.: Applications of data science to game learning analytics data: a systematic literature review. Comput. Educ.**141**(June), 103612 (2019). https://doi.org/10.1016/j.compedu.2019.103612
8. Serrano-Laguna, Á., Martínez-Ortiz, I., Haag, J., Regan, D., Johnson, A., Fernández-Manjón, B.: Applying standards to systematize learning analytics in serious games. Comput. Stand. Interfaces **50**, 116–123 (2017). https://doi.org/10.1016/j.csi.2016.09.014
9. Perez-Colado, I.J., Calvo Morata, A., Alonso-Fernández, C., Freire, M., Martínez-Ortiz, I., Fernández-Manjón, B.: Simva: simplifying the scientific validation of serious games. Proceedings of the IEEE 14th International Conference on Advanced Learning Technologies, ICALT 2014, pp. 113–115 (2019). https://doi.org/10.1109/ICALT.2019.00033
10. Alonso-Fernández, C., Martínez-Ortiz, I., Caballero, R., Freire, M., Fernández-Manjón, B.: Predicting students' knowledge after playing a serious game based on learning analytics data: a case study. J. Comput. Assist. Learn. **36**(3), 350–358 (2020). https://doi.org/10.1111/jcal.12405
11. Perez-Colado, V.M., Rotaru, D.C., Freire, M., Martinez-Ortiz, I., Fernandez-Manjon, B.: Learning analytics for location-based serious games. In: 2018 IEEE Global Engineering Education Conference (EDUCON), vol. 2018, pp. 1192–1200, April 2018. https://doi.org/10.1109/EDUCON.2018.8363365
12. Bakhouyi, A., Dehbi, R., Lti, M.T., Hajoui, O.: Evolution of standardization and interoperability on E-learning systems: an overview. In: 201716th International Conference on Information Technology Based Higher Education and Training, ITHET 2017 (2017). https://doi.org/10.1109/ITHET.2017.8067789

The App Magic House: Assessing Updating in Young Children

Sabrina Panesi[✉], Laura Freina, and Lucia Ferlino

National Research Council, Institute for Educational Technology, Genova, Italy
panesi@itd.cnr.it

Abstract. Several cognitive assessment tools have been developed to measure Executive Functions in pre-schoolers, most of them in an analogue form. Since specifically developed apps would allow the assessment to be more accessible, valid, and fun for young children, "The Magic House" app was implemented. The app offers a simple game to measure *updating*, one of the Executive Functions. A first test was performed involving a small sample of 61–77 months old children. Results show that the internal consistency is acceptable. Non-significant differences related to gender and younger (61–70 months old) and older (71–77 months old) children were found. Furthermore, a comparison with a previous analogue version of the same task was done showing that children performance were better in the analogue version. This may also be due to the difference between actively interacting with virtual objects in a bidimensional world, from playing with real toys.

Keywords: Executive functions · App · Preschoolers · Updating · Serious games

1 Introduction

Several analogue cognitive assessment tools have been developed to investigate cognitive processes and abilities in children starting from a young age (e.g. [1–4]). Among these the Executive Functions (EFs), which are a set of general-purpose control processes that regulate one's thoughts and behaviors [5], but despite our digital era, new technologies, apps in particular, are seldom addressed [6–8]. To fill this gap, in the context of ShareFUN project [9], we developed the "The Magic House" app [10] to assess EFs, in particular the updating ability, in preschoolers. In line with previous studies (e.g. [7, 8]), the app was implemented in an effort to make cognitive assessments more accessible, valid, and fun for young children.

The term *updating* refers to the cognitive ability to monitor and code incoming information, and to update the content of memory by replacing old items with newer, more relevant, information [11]. In the model proposed by Miyake and colleagues [12, 13] updating is considered as one of EFs, along with *inhibition* (the ability to deliberately override dominant or prepotent responses) and *shifting* (the ability to switch flexibly between tasks or mental sets). Terminological and conceptual discrepancies, however, lead to confusion on the definition of updating in preschoolers.

© Springer Nature Switzerland AG 2021
F. de Rosa et al. (Eds.): GALA 2021, LNCS 13134, pp. 174–183, 2021.
https://doi.org/10.1007/978-3-030-92182-8_17

In the developmental literature, updating is often considered as a synonym of *working memory*, usually referred to a system that can store and process information simultaneously (i.e., hold mental representations available for processing [14]), thus defining working memory as an EF [15], which is not the case in Miyake and colleagues [12] and in all adult research. On the other hand, recently some researchers clarified the difference between the concepts of updating and working memory [16] focusing especially on young children [17]. According to their work, updating is considered as an EF, while working memory as a general-domain cognitive resource, in line with Miyake and Friedman [5].

The different definitions create some problems in the research context when cognitive tasks are created to measure these cognitive abilities; furthermore only a few instruments have been developed with the aim to investigate updating in preschoolers.

An example is the "Keep Track" task, adapted for preschoolers by Traverso, Viterbori and Usai [18].The task was originally defined for assessing the updating ability both in adults [12] and children [11]. In the adapted version, the child is shown some pictures, belonging to one of five categories: animals (dog, cat, fish, bird), sky (sun, moon, stars, cloud), fruit (strawberry, grapes, pear, apple), vehicles (train, bicycle, motorbike, car), and clothes (socks, skirt, t-shirt, shoes). Before each trial, the child is asked to pay attention to one (in the first three trials) or two (in the last three trials) target categories. The pictures are shown in a sequences of six. During the presentation of each sequence, the child has to name each picture. At the end of the sequence, the child is asked to recall the last seen item belonging to the target categories. The task requires managing the interference caused by the other pictures that were named while watching the sequence. The number of target categories increased from one to two. Small pictures representing the target categories are shown as a reminder at the bottom of the screen all the time.

More recently, Cheng and Kibbe [19] created the "Hide-and-Seek" task for preschoolers to investigate updating in young children. In the task, children first view sets of cards with animal illustrations, which are then covered by occluders. In the static block, the objects remain in their original position, while in the swap block, the occluders swap location one or more times. In order to successfully track the objects in the array, children have to remember the bindings between the objects and their location in working memory (static block) or *update* the objects' location as their occluders move in space (swap block). During the study, the experimenters systematically manipulated both the number of objects children had to encode and the number of times the objects swapped locations in order to investigate the effects of increasing storage and updating load on children's performance.

Finally, in the Italian context, "The Magic House", an analogue task to investigate updating in preschoolers, was created [20]. Sequences of three, four or five toy animals are sequentially placed in a cardboard toy house; then, the child is asked to recall the last two animals that entered the house. Nine fixed sequences are shown to the child, and a score is computed counting the number of animals that are correctly recalled. Each sequence can therefore score from a minimum of 0 points (no animals are correctly recalled) to a maximum of 2 (when both the last and the second last animals are correctly identified), giving an overall score ranging from 0 to 18.

"The Magic House" was tested with 118 preschoolers and results showed that: the task has an acceptable internal consistency; performance in the task is related to inhibition and, to a lesser degree, on working memory capacity; performance in the task shows qualitative changes with increasing working memory capacity.

2 The Magic House App

Starting from the analogue version of "The Magic House", a digital version in the form of an app was implemented, with the aim of making it directly accessible to the child on a Tablet or Smartphone.

Apps can be a useful tool to assess updating in preschoolers because: apps are familiar and motivating for preschoolers who start using them at an early age for leisure purposes [21]; children are more highly engaged by apps that present dynamic and immersive stimuli allowing to better capture their cognitive abilities [22]; the tactile-based interface of touchscreens enables the introduction of digital interaction at an early age since they do not require the use of mouse and keyboard [21, 23–25]; apps have the advantages to have lightweight design, portability, relatively intuitive interfaces, communication features, and affordability [26]. Furthermore, an app to measure updating in preschoolers could be easily used by any clinician, researcher or teacher, guaranteeing a certain level of objectivity in the collected data. Finally, it could be installed on any smartphone or tablet and would not require the use of physical toys.

The choice to implement an app for measuring EFs in young children is in line with recent studies that highlighted the importance to shift away from traditional cognitive testing to more fun, accessible, and easy approaches [7, 8, 25], but, to the best of our knowledge, "The Magic House" app is the first app developed with the aim to investigate in preschoolers a specific EF: updating.

2.1 Detailed Description of the Magic House App

"The Magic House" app is a digital game developed to measure the updating ability in preschoolers. The app shows a magic house and eight young animals. The animals are friends and wish to go and play together in the house, but, since the house is magic, only the last two friends that enter the house can play together (Fig. 1).

When the app starts, an introduction presenting the characters and explaining the game to the child is offered, but can be skipped when not needed. During the game, some animals (a random number between 3 and 6) enter the house one at a time. After the last one has entered, all the animals are shown again and the child has to tap on the last one that entered, and then on the second last one.

The app shows nine fixed sequences. A small number in the bottom right corner shows the number of the sequence and no feedback is given to the player as the aim is testing the child's performance. One point is given to each correct answer, for a maximum score of 18. At the end of the game, the player's id and his final score are shown, and then a new session can be started.

The app was developed using Unity 3D, version 219.2.10f, and tested on Android tablets. It could also be used on a standard PC, but since the use of the mouse requires eye-manual coordination that is not yet sufficiently mature in the target age, a touch interface

Fig. 1. "The Magic House" app

is needed. A configuration file is stored locally giving the possibility to pause the game and restart it again from where it was paused. This featured was added because of the young age of the target children, but was never used during the study here presented.

The game is designed to be used with an active internet connection, allowing to store play data directly on the cloud server for future analysis. Nevertheless, when the internet connection is not available, play data is temporarily saved locally to be uploaded at the beginning of the following game session. Should this not be possible, data can be collected directly from the used device. Each player action is logged in a JSON format file that is then imported in an Excel sheet for later analysis.

As the game is developed to be used by the children under the constant supervision of an adult tutor, to guarantee the player's privacy, no personal data is logged on the web server. A unique id code is assigned to each player and is then managed by the tutor who types it in at the beginning of the game, and is responsible for the association between the player's id code and all the other relevant data.

After each shown sequence, the system automatically logs the id code, date and time, reaction time, sequence number and the list of animals belonging to the sequence, the chosen animal, the specific task (i.e. if the child is identifying the last or the second last character that entered the house), the type of answer (correct, the chosen animal was in the sequence, but it was not the correct one, the chosen animal was not in the sequence), the total score.

3   The Pilot Study

3.1   Research Questions and Hypothesis

The present work presents a pilot study conducted with the main aim to explore the first prototype version of "The Magic House" app, a game implemented to investigate updating in young children. The research questions guiding the present study, and the corresponding hypotheses are:

RQ1: Is the internal consistency of "The Magic House" app acceptable?
Hypothesis 1: Following Panesi and Morra [20] who found an acceptable internal consistency in the analogue version of "The Magic House" task, it is hypothesized that the internal consistency of "The Magic House" app will be acceptable (according with literature, Alpha Chronbach value $\geq$ 0.7 [27, 28]).

RQ2: Are there gender differences in "The Magic House" app performances?
Hypothesis 2: In line with literature [29], where no differences were found in performance in an updating tasks between male and female children in preschool years, no gender differences are hypothesized.

RQ3: Are there qualitative changes in "The Magic House" app performance with age growth?
Hypothesis 3: In line with literature that suggests that the updating ability increases through infancy [19, 20], qualitative changes in "The Magic House" app performance are hypothesized with age growth.

RQ4: Are performance in "The Magic House" app similar to those from the traditional version of the task?
Hypothesis 4: Studies with adults comparing traditional and digitized cognitive tests found similar performances [30]. Due to the COVID-19 health pandemic, it was not possible to use the analogue version of the The Magic House" task with the children, therefore results from the app are hypothesized to be similar to findings reported by Panesi and Morra [20].

3.2 Participants

A total of 21 preschoolers from 61 to 77 months old (M = 70.00; SD = 3.82) took part in the study. 11 were male (52%) and 10 were female (48%). All participants were Italian with typical development (no formal diagnosis of disability, language impairment, or behavior disorder).

3.3 Procedure

A unique id code was assigned to each child and managed by an adult tutor. Personal data as age, gender, and any other relevant information was managed by the tutor externally to the system. Each child played individually with "The Magic House" app using a tablet in a quiet room, supervised by the tutor that typed the id code and guided the child during the game. In order to guarantee that all the participants had a similar experience, they all started the game looking at the introduction that provided instructions on how to play. After the introduction, the game was immediately started, and all the participants played the game without pausing. When the game finished, the total score appeared on the screen and a positive reinforcement was given to the child.

3.4   Data Analysis and Results

Data collected in the pilot study was then analyzed with the aim of finding an answer to the research questions. The SPSS 20.0 software program [31] was used for all the analysis. To explore the internal consistency of "The Magic House" app, developed to measure updating in preschoolers, the Cronbach's Alpha was computed, resulting in .75, a value that can be considered acceptable.

Descriptive statistics were then calculated for the performance scores (ranging from 0 to 18) from the whole sample and splitting the sample by gender (male and female), and by age (61–70 months old and 71–77 months old). Table 1 shows the descriptive statistics referred to the whole sample, male and female subsamples, and younger and older preschoolers. No significant differences between male and female subsamples and between younger and older preschoolers subsamples were found (in all cases, p > .05). The t test was then computed to compare means between male and female groups, and younger and older groups.

Table 1. Descriptive statistics and t-test

	Whole sample	Male	Female	Younger (61–70 months old)	Older (71–77 months old)
Mean	10.86	11.54	10.10	10.73	11
SD	2.92	2.73	3.07	2.33	3.59
Min.	3	8	3	8	3
Max.	15	15	14	15	15
t		1.141		.209	
p		.268		.837	

Qualitative changes in performance between younger and older preschoolers was also analyzed using a contingency table and the X^2 test. Starting from Panesi and Morra [20], a threshold overall score of 9 was identified to differentiate between relatively low performance and average or good performance. A score of 9 implies that, on average, 1 animal only per sequence was correctly identified by the child, while a score of 10–18 indicates that more than half responses are correct. Table 2 reports the contingency table, showing that most children reached an average/good performance level, and no significant differences were found between younger and older groups, as shown by the not significant chi-square test ($X^2 = .095$ p = .757).

Finally, through an exploratory investigation, we compared the mean performance measured with "The Magic House" app, with the mean performance measured with the analogue "Magic House" task, as reported by Panesi and Morra [20]. Table 3 reports data, showing that using "The Magic House" app, gets a mean performance that is slightly lower than the one related to the analogue version of the same task.

Table 2. Contingency table by age groups

Overall score	Younger	Older	Total
10–18	7	7	14
≤9	4	3	7
Total	11	10	21

Table 3. "The Magic House" app vs. Analogue Magic House Task

	The Magic House app	Analogue Magic House Task*
Mean	10.86	13.75
SD	2.92	3.04
10° percentile	8	10
1° quartile	9	11
Median	10	14
3° quartile	13.50	16
90° percentile	14.80	18

*Source: [20]. Results related to preschoolers 61–73 months old (N = 28).

4   Discussion

The present study reports the preliminary findings related to a first pilot study of "The Magic House" app, a newly implemented digital tool to assess EFs, in particular updating, in preschoolers. In line with previous research [7, 8, 25], "The Magic House" app can contribute to the shift from traditional cognitive testing to a more enjoyable and accessible tool to assess EFs in young children.

Within this shift, it is of fundamental importance that digital tools guarantee the validity of EFs assessment when compared with the more traditional and validated tools [8]. The pilot study presented in this paper aimed at investigating "The Magic House" app and comparing it to the traditional, analogic version of that same task.

Results from the pilot study confirmed Hypothesis 1: internal consistency of data from the digital version of the task is acceptable, as it was with the analogue version of that same task [20].

Gender differences were then analyzed and, as predicted by Hypothesis 2, no significant differences were found both in the digital and in the analogue versions of the task [29].

In order to confirm Hypothesis 3, differences between data from younger children (61–70 months old) and older ones (71–77 months old) were investigated. Literature suggests that the updating ability increases throughout infancy [19, 20], therefore qualitative changes in performance with age growth were expected. This was not the case with the collected data: Hypothesis 3 was not confirmed. There may be several explanations for this finding. Several previous studies exploring the development of EFs in preschool years [32–34] identified the age of 4½ (54 months old) as an important threshold separating younger children (aged 3–4½) and older ones (added 4½–6). In this view, all the children who participated in this pilot study belonged to the older group, which appears to be internally rather homogeneous. Furthermore, the use of digital games to assess EFs needs to take into account the child's familiarity with the use of tablets. Performance may be impacted and an older child who is not so familiar with tablets may have a lower performance when compared to a younger child used to digital games. Future studies will be organized to explore the impact of the child's familiarity with tablets.

The fourth and last research question hypothesized that results from Panesi and Morra [20] related to performance in the analogue version of the Magic House task would be similar to the ones in "The Magic House" app. The hypothesis was not confirmed, and the digital version of the task resulted having a lower mean performance when compared to the analogue version of that same task. As with Hypothesis 3, the child's familiarity with the use of tablets could play an important role. Future studies will have to take this into account, also by using both the analogue and the digital version of the test with the same children and addressing a larger sample of preschoolers.

5 Conclusions

The present paper presents a first pilot study aiming at comparing a digital version of a previously existing analogue task to assess the updating ability in young children. While data internal consistency and lack of gender differences were confirmed, it was not so with respect to qualitative changes related to age growth and the similarity of results between the two versions of the same task. Several explanations are possible, among which previous familiarity with the digital tools may play an important role that needs to be further investigated in future research. Furthermore, according to several researchers, representational systems emerge relatively late in infancy [35], therefore, interacting with virtual bidimensional objects can be more demanding than manipulating real toys.

Moreover, relations between "The Magic House" and other different tasks for preschoolers measuring the updating function need to be explored, for example the adapted version of the "Keep Track" task for preschoolers [18] and the "Hide-and-Seek" task from Cheng and Kibbe [19].

Finally, the present pilot study opens future reflections on the practical implications of using a digital app to assess EFs in young children. Apps like "The Magic House", as well as EYT [6] and eFun [7, 8], are easy to use tools, available for clinicians, researchers, but also for teachers and parents, allowing them to explore young children's cognitive development in different contexts. These tools are very important especially in those cases when children have difficulty in moving from home, as was the case during the COVID-19 health pandemic [10], but also in those cases when a child has particular disabilities and a tele-assessment may be fundamental.

References

1. Morra, S.: Issues in working memory measurement: testing for M capacity. Int. J. Behav. Dev. **17**(1), 143–159 (1994)

2. Carlson, S.M.: Developmentally sensitive measures of executive function in preschool children. Dev. Neuropsychol. **28**, 595–616 (2005)
3. Isquith, P.K., Crawford, J.S., Espy, K.A., Gioia, G.A.: Assessment of executive function in preschool-aged children. Ment. Retard. Dev. Disabil. Res. Rev. **11**(3), 209–215 (2005)
4. Morra, S., Gandolfi, E., Panesi, S., Prandelli, L.: A working memory span task for toddlers. Infant Behav. Dev. **63**, 101550 (2021)
5. Miyake, A., Friedman, N.P.: The nature and organization of individual differences in executive functions: four general conclusions. Curr. Dir. Psychol. Sci. **21**(1), 8–14 (2021)
6. Howard, S.J., Melhuish, E.: An early years toolbox for assessing early executive function, language, self-regulation, and social development: validity, reliability, and preliminary norms. J. Psychoeduc. Assess. **35**(3), 255–275 (2017)
7. Berg, V., Rogers, S.L., McMahon, M., Garrett, M., Manley, D.: A novel approach to measure executive functions in students: an evaluation of two child-friendly apps. Front. Psychol. **11**, 1702 (2020)
8. Berg, V.: A game-based online tool to measure cognitive functions in students. Int. J. Serious Games **8**(1), 71–87 (2021)
9. Sharefun Project Homepage. http://www.sharefun.it. Accessed 29 June 2021
10. Panesi, S., Freina, L., Ferlino, L.: A kit of apps to improve and assess executive functions and working memory capacity in preschoolers. In: Proceedings of 17th International Conference on Cognition and Exploratory Learning in Digital Age (CELDA 2020), pp. 18–20. Lisbon, Portugal (2020)
11. van der Sluis, S., de Jong, P.F., van der Leij, A.: Executive functioning in children, and its relations with reasoning, reading, and arithmetic. Intelligence **35**, 427–449 (2007)
12. Miyake, A., Friedman, N.P., Emerson, M.J., Witzki, A.H., Howerter, A., Wager, T.D.: The unity and diversity of executive functions and their contributions to complex "FrontalLobe" tasks: a latent variable analysis. Cogn. Psychol. **41**, 49–100 (2000)
13. Miyake, A., Friedman, N.P.: The nature and organization of individual differences in executive functions: four general conclusions. Curr. Dir. Psychol. Sci. **21**(1), 8–14 (2012)
14. Engle, R.W., Cantor, J., Carullo, J.J.: Individual differences in working memory and comprehension: a test of four hypotheses. J. Exp. Psychol. Learn. Mem. Cogn. **18**, 972–992 (1992)
15. Garon, N., Bryson, S.E., Smith, I.M.: Executive function in preschoolers: a review using an integrative framework. Psychol. Bull. **134**(1), 31–60 (2008)
16. Morra, S., Panesi, S., Traverso, L., Usai, M.C.: Which tasks measure what? Reflections on executive function development and a commentary on Podjarny, Kamawar, and Andrews (2017). J. Exp. Child Psychol. **167**, 246–258 (2018)
17. Panesi, S., Morra, S.: Executive functions and mental attentional capacity in preschoolers. J. Cogn. Dev. **21**(1), 72–91 (2020)
18. Traverso, L., Viterbori, P., Usai, M.C.: Improving executive function in childhood: evaluation of a training intervention for 5-year-old children. Front. Psychol. **6**, 525 (2015)
19. Cheng, C., Kibbe, M.M.: Development of updating in working memory in 4–7-year-old children (2021)
20. Panesi, S., Morra, S.: La Casetta Magica. Un nuovo strumento per indagare l'aggiornamento (updating) della memoria di lavoro in età prescolare. Psicol. Clin. dello sviluppo **21**(3), 443–462 (2017)
21. Dini, S., Ferlino, L.: Knowledge at their fingertips: kids' learning and playing in the app age. TD Tecnologie Didattiche **24**(3), 147–155 (2016)
22. Howard, S.J., Okely, A.D.: Catching fish and avoiding sharks: investigating factors that influence developmentally appropriate measurement of preschoolers' inhibitory control. J. Psychoeduc. Assess. **33**(6), 585–596 (2015)

23. Plowman, L., Stevenson, O., Stephen, C., McPake, J.: Preschool children's learning with technology at home. Comput. Educ. **59**(1), 30–37 (2012)
24. Panesi, S., Ferlino, L.: Using apps in formal education to improve executive functions in preschoolers. In: Proceedings of INNODOCT 2019, International Conference on Innovation, Documentation and Education, Valencia, 6th–8th, November 2019
25. Howard, S.J., Melhuish, E.: An early years toolbox for assessing early executive function, language, self-regulation, and social development: validity, reliability, and preliminary norms. J. Psychoeduc. Assess. **35**(3), 255–275 (2017)
26. Vavoula, G., Karagiannidis, C.: Designing mobile learning experiences. In: Bozanis, P., Houstis, E.N. (eds.) PCI 2005. LNCS, vol. 3746, pp. 534–544. Springer, Heidelberg (2005). https://doi.org/10.1007/11573036_50
27. Konting, M.M., Kamaruddin, N., Man, N.A.: Quality assurance in higher education institutions: exit survey among Universiti Putra Malaysia graduating students. Int. Educ. Stud. **2**(1) (2009)
28. Tavakol, M., Dennick, R.: Making sense of Cronbach's alpha. Int. J. Med. Educ. **2**, 53–55 (2011). https://doi.org/10.5116/ijme.4dfb.8dfd
29. Panesi, S., Morra, S.: Association between drawing and language in preschoolers: the role of working memory and executive functions. Cogn. Dev. (under review)
30. Björngrim, S., van den Hurk, W., Betancort, M., Machado, A., Lindau, M.: Comparing traditional and digitized cognitive tests used in standard clinical evaluation–a study of the digital application minnemera. Front. Psychol. **10**, 2327 (2019)
31. Arbuckle, J.L.: IBM SPSS Amos 20 User's Guide. Amos Development Corporation, SPSS Inc (2011)
32. Panesi, S.: Relationship between drawing and language in toddlers and preschoolers: the role of working memory and executive functions. Unpublished doctoral thesis, University of Genova (2017)
33. Wiebe, S., Scheffield, T., Nelson, J.M., Clark, C.A., Chevalier, N., Espy, K: The structure of executive function in 3-year-olds. J. Exp. Child Psychol. **108**, 436–452 (2011)
34. Usai, M.C., Viterbori, P., Traverso, L., De Franchis, V: Latent structure of executive function in five-and six-year-old children: a longitudinal study. Eur. J. Dev. Psychol. **11**, 447–462 (2014)
35. Piaget, J.: Play, Dreams, and Imitation. Norton, New York (1962)

Serious Games Design

Cards and Roles: Co-designing Privacy Serious Games with an Online Role-Playing Boardgame

Patrick Jost[1]([✉]) [iD] and Andreas Künz[2] [iD]

[1] Department of Computer Science, Norwegian University of Science and Technology,
Trondheim, Norway
patrick.jost@ntnu.no
[2] Research Centre for User-Centred Technologies, Vorarlberg University of Applied Sciences,
Dornbirn, Austria

Abstract. The increasing digitalisation of daily routines confronts people with frequent privacy decisions. However, obscure data processing often leads to tedious decision-making and results in unreflective choices that unduly compromise privacy. Serious Games could be applied to encourage teenagers and young adults to make more thoughtful privacy decisions. Creating a Serious Game (SG) that promotes privacy awareness while maintaining an engaging gameplay requires, however, a carefully balanced game concept. This study explores the benefits of an online role-playing boardgame as a co-designing activity for creating SGs about privacy. In a between-subjects trial, student groups and educator/researcher groups were taking the roles of player, teacher, researcher and designer to co-design a balanced privacy SG concept. Using predefined design proposal cards or creating their own, students and educators played the online boardgame during a video conference session to generate game ideas, resolve potential conflicts and balance the different SG aspects. The comparative results of the present study indicate that students and educators alike perceive support from role-playing when ideating and balancing SG concepts and are happy with their playfully co-designed game concepts. Implications for supporting SG design with role-playing in remote collaboration scenarios are conclusively synthesised.

Keywords: Role play · Digital boardgame · Serious game design · Online co-design · Remote co-creation · Design card set · Privacy

1 Introduction

By increasing data services integration in our daily routine, we are faced with ubiquitous data sharing decisions. However, specifically, teenagers/young adults are susceptible to making less reflected privacy judgments [1]. Serious Games represent a promising strategy to reach this target audience and encourage better privacy choices. Yet, creating a Serious Game (SG) that keeps an entertaining game flow and at the same time succeeds to raise awareness about real-world privacy choices requires a sensibly balanced game concept. As Dörner et al. [2] emphasised, SGs have the intention to entertain and to achieve at least one or more additional goals. Concerning privacy decision-making,

© The Author(s) 2021
F. de Rosa et al. (Eds.): GALA 2021, LNCS 13134, pp. 187–197, 2021.
https://doi.org/10.1007/978-3-030-92182-8_18

factors such as risk behaviour or social group influences may be assessed in the SG. Thereby the entertainment goal is complemented not only by the educational goal to encourage better privacy choices but also by the researching goal to learn about privacy choice influences for improving the SG efficacy.

Balancing these different perspectives in an early ideation phase is essential to avoid both interrupting the players' engaging game flow [3] and extraneous cognitive impact from game interaction on pedagogical and scientific assessments. Considering the perspectives of different stakeholders in a role-playing co-design activity may help to create such balanced SG concepts.

1.1   Related Work – Role-Play as Support in Design Activities

In 1956, Mann [4] defined role-play as situations where an individual takes a new role or his usual role in a "setting not normal for the enactment of the role". In a more recent definition by Mäkelä et al. [5], role-playing is seen as "any act in which an imaginary reality is concurrently created, added to and observed". While role-playing is often used for learning and training [6, 7], it can also enhance design processes [8]. A literature review by Seland [9] found the rationales for using role-play in design are understanding/involving users and exploring and communicating ideas. Burns et al. [10] showed in the early 1990s how designers role-playing as users can improve idea finding by fostering conversations between stakeholders. Various research works from the last 30 years further proved the potential of role-playing for design processes, especially for the ideation phase [11–13], including online applications using virtual 3D worlds [14].

Role-play elements can further be combined with games for idea finding and design creation to enhance the communication by defining the roles of participants and specific rules and pushing a creative, exploratory and visionary mindset [15]. Vaajakallio and Mattelmäki [16] promote the so-called design games as playful co-creation tools – in accordance with Brandt [17] non-competitive scenarios with specific rules – that can bring designers, researchers and users/non-experts together (e.g. for idea finding) and foster reflection upon experiences and knowledge.

The potential of games for the early design phase depends on a balance between restrictive structure and creative aspects [18]. Brandt and Messeter [19] and Finke et al. [20] also point out the importance of restrictions in the ideation phase and the great capability of design games to improve idea finding outcomes. The outlined suggestions are considered by the design game described in this paper that investigates the purported benefits of role-playing in the currently underexplored online/remote co-design context.

1.2   Research Objectives

This study introduces a digital role-playing boardgame that aims to support students, teachers, and researchers in co-creating an engaging SG about privacy. The game is evaluated in collaborative video conference sessions with student groups and international educators/researcher groups playing the different roles and co-designing privacy SGs with a playboard and a selection of cards. The research questions that guided the investigation were:

1. How does role-playing with an online boardgame support students and educators in collaboratively ideating and balancing SG concepts?
2. How do students and educators perceive the applicability of boardgame role-playing for online co-designing SG concepts?

2 Research Approach

The research follows the cyclic design science approach [21]. The presented evaluation cycle examines the qualities of the designed digital boardgame artefacts (Sect. 2.1) for supporting online co-creation of SG concepts. The role-playing boardgame design was oriented on the card-based SG design toolset developed by Jost and Divitini [22]. The toolset features design cards for the roles of *player*, *teacher*, *researcher* and *designer,* a playboard to lay out privacy game challenges and stepwise instructions to balance each role-oriented part of a SG to a complete game concept. For example, such a privacy game could aim to raise awareness about third-party data sharing or tracking behaviours by integrating engaging game qualities (e.g. storytelling) and pedagogical/research strategies (e.g. reflection, evaluation of privacy decisions) into a balanced SG.

In online user trials, student and educator groups played the boardgame via video conferencing to co-create SG concepts. Perceived support from playing the roles and using the design cards/board was investigated (Sect. 2.2). Therefore, the online game sessions were evaluated by in-game ratings of the individual role-players' satisfaction with the game concept and a post-game questionnaire where the participants rated their perceived support for ideating, balancing, and the perceived applicability of the role-playing boardgame. According to the *two research objectives*, the null hypotheses established for the empirical study were:

H_{0A}: 'There are no significant differences in perceived ideation and balancing support between students and educators when using the online role-playing boardgame for co-designing SG concepts.'
H_{0B}: 'There are no significant differences in perceived applicability between students and educators when using the online role-playing boardgame for co-designing SG concepts.'

2.1 Artefacts and Features of the Online Role-Playing Boardgame

The digital boardgame is based on the affordance-oriented SG design toolset – the Challenge Game Frame (CGF) [22]. The toolset features cards with SG design suggestions for the roles of player, teacher, researcher and designer – 12 decks with 150 cards in total. In addition, it includes four role-independent card decks to define the context of who will play the game when and where, and a dedicated card deck with privacy challenges to define the domain/educational goal. For creating balanced SG concepts in a multi-perspective dialogue, a playboard and time-restricted, stepwise instructions are provided to lay out each of the parts and discuss conflicts between the roles. The game is intended to be used by remote groups of two to six players that are connected in a videoconference and play the game in a web browser.

Roles and Cards. Each of the four different roles was implemented with a cartoon illustration and two rating sliders ranging from 0 to 100% (Fig. 1). These sliders allow players to rate their satisfaction with the currently laid out game concepts at any time.

Fig. 1. The four roles and two rating sliders for rating satisfaction with concept A or alternative B

There are two alternate game challenge streams that can be rated. The main game challenge A and an optional concept stream B that can be used to place alternative design suggestions (Sect. 2.2, Fig. 2). Based on the ratings, the group can decide to change their focus from main to alternative. Being able to try out alternate design representations can support creativity, as pointed out by Fischer [23]. At the same time, the two streams provide a guiding structure that may help narrow down choices from the comprehensive card decks and focus on ideas [19, 20]. Rating the current satisfaction with the concepts provides a quality success criterion for the role-players [24], complemented by supporting the remotely collaborating players to give emotional feedback. Therefore, the pictured avatars change their facial expression according to the ratings.

The role-independent context cards and the privacy challenge (i.e. the domain goal) are selected in the beginning stages and can be placed by all players. The role-oriented cards, on the other hand, are chosen and placed goal-driven by each role separately and discussed for conflicts in a stepwise process. Thereby the player role chooses how the game affords *achieving* (e.g. maximising score), *acting* (e.g. collaborating teams), *progressing* (e.g. narrative, story), *engaging* (e.g. awards, curiosity) and *adapting* (e.g. extending game world). The teacher role includes design suggestions for *reflecting* (e.g. in-game questions, journal) and *examining* (e.g. answer time, patterns). The researcher is deciding how the game is *researching* privacy decision influences (e.g. risk behaviour), *reporting* (e.g. by questionnaire) and *monitoring* (e.g. logging team decisions). Finally, the designer is responsible for the *interacting* and *presenting* qualities of the game and chooses if the game world is, for example, represented in a 2D or 3D visualisation and can be operated by touch, mouse pointer, voice or any other modality.

Board and Rules. The goal of the game is to reach a balanced SG concept about the domain challenge, in this case, better privacy decisions. The group has six timed co-designing steps (Sect. 2.2) to reach that goal which are explained/read-out-loud by a character before each segment. This follows the suggestions of other research to provide clearly defined goals, a step-by-step process and guiding restrictions in co-design activities [19, 20, 24]. Players play the boardgame in their own browser with all interactions (e.g. movement of cards, markers) synchronised over the web while discussing the game concept connected in a video conference.

2.2 Online Co-design Sessions with Educators and Students

The created digital game was subsequently applied in online game sessions with students, researchers and educators (Fig. 2).

Participants. A class of Computer Science students ($n = 32$) at the first authors' university was selected to play the boardgame in groups.

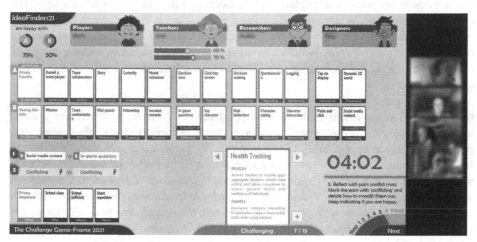

Fig. 2. Online role-playing sessions with student or educator groups – here in step 5, marking and discussing conflicts (red bands)

Twenty-six researchers/educators ($n = 26$) participated in randomly assigned groups after responding to an e-mail invitation sent out to universities in Norway, Austria, and Ireland. The participants from various scientific fields had experience in both research ($M = 6.5$ years) and teaching ($M = 7.3$ years). However, for better readability, we will refer to the group hereafter as educators. Students and educators reported a comparable skill average in game design (students $M = 2.7$, educators $M = 2.3$; Likert scale: 1, none; 7, professional).

Procedure and Data Collection. In the two-hour sessions, players were first introduced to SG design theory by the researcher/facilitator. After the interface and rules of the boardgame were explained, the game session took one hour. The step-by-step instructions were displayed and read aloud by a voiceover before the designated group manager clicked the start button that started each step synchronised. The steps were:

1. Agree on who plays the role of either player, teacher, researcher or designer
2. Define the context of the game: domain, target group, location/time of play
3. Individually read through role-assigned cards and pick favourites
4. Co-create/balance a game challenge: starting from left to right, discuss ideas from the role-oriented cards or create custom cards and fill all slots of at least one challenge stream (A or B). Each role places/argues its proposals while rating the whole concept

5. Identify conflicting pairs of cards in the game concept and balance out the potential flow breaks by discussing alternative picks or another group agreement
6. Agree on the final picks, define a working title and write a game plot summary

The players kept their role for the entire game and had the decisional authority over their card decks. In step three, all role-players were studying their cards in detail so they could explain them to the others. Role-players were also instructed to advocate their chosen design proposals and explain their reasoning to the other roles when sorting out conflicts in stage five. When a placed card pair was marked as conflicting, it was resolved in group discussion. The role-players had to either agree to keep the current cards or one or both respective roles switched to other design suggestions to balance the game concept. During the game, the role-players rated their satisfaction with the concept using the rating sliders.

After the game session, all participants individually filled out the post-game questionnaire. A 7-point Likert scale (1, strongly disagree; 7, strongly agree) was used to appraise the players' impressions. The players rated perceived ideation/balancing support and perceived applicability of the role-playing game, cards, roles and playboard. Ideation and application dimensions consisted of 4 items each, and balancing support was assessed with 8 items. Exemplary statements included: *'I had ideas I would not have had without the cards.' (ideation); 'The roles helped identifying conflicts between the game parts.' (balancing); 'I can imagine using the boardgame to co-design games for research (e.g. investigate decisions, risk-taking).' (application).*

3   Results

Data analysis showed non-normal but similar distributions (Kolmogorov-Smirnov-Z test $p > .05$) and homogeneity of variance (Levene's test $p > .05$) for the groups. Thus, following Field [25] and Hart [26], non-parametric Mann-Whitney U analysis ($\alpha = 0.05$) was performed to compare the distribution medians.

3.1   Ideating and Balancing

As regards *ideation,* students and educators reported support from playing the boardgame with a median rating of at least 5 (somewhat agree) on the Likert scale for all four items. Educators thereby perceived more guidance to develop new ideas from playing the game with 92% agreeing at least partly compared to 69% of the students, $U = 589.5, z = 2.82, p = .005, r = .37$ (Fig. 3).

Similarly, educators felt more ideation support from the role-oriented design cards, with 92% largely agreeing that they had ideas they would not have had without cards, whereas 72% of students reported that, $U = 581, z = 2.67, p = .008, r = .35$. To the same significant difference and percentages except the students' median rating being 5.5, educators felt more that the cards helped them focusing on ideas, $U = 541, z = 2.03, p = .043, r = .27$. Most students (75%) and educators (65%) agreed that the cards helped them fine-tune already existing ideas, $U = 406.5, z = -.15, p = .878$ with an equal median rating of 5.

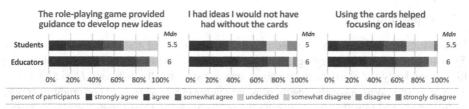

Fig. 3. Perceived *ideating* support by the role-playing game – significantly different ratings between students and educators

Concerning the *balancing* support, students and educators experienced support largely similar (Table 1) with median ratings of at least 5 for all eight items. However, educators statistically felt more supported structuring and visualising the game concept balance using the playboard than the students (effect size $r = .29$).

Table 1. Perceived *balancing* support by the role-playing game

	Agreeing % S/E	Mdn S/E	Mode S/E	U	z	p
Using the boardgame helped balancing game to domain goal	70/96	5/6	7/6	501.0	1.38	.169
Using the boardgame helped balancing the SG concept parts	78/77	5/6	6/6	468.0	0.84	.399
Using the cards helped balancing the SG concept parts	75/85	5.5/6	6/6	467.0	0.84	.410
Playing the roles helped identifying conflicts	75/88	5/6	6/6	493.0	1.26	.208
Playing the roles helped balancing game to domain goal	66/92	5/6	5/5	504.5	1.43	.154
Playing the roles helped balancing the SG concept parts	69/81	5/6	7/6	418.0	0.03	.974
Using playboard helped balancing game to domain goal	66/77	5/5	6/5	432.5	0.27	.790
Using playboard helped structuring and visualising SG balance	84/88	6/6	6/7	551.5	2.23	.026

Note. S = Students, E = Educators; agreeing percentage includes strongly agreeing, agreeing, and somewhat agreeing

While the median for both groups was equal and the percentage of overall agreement was similar, the rating difference is represented in detail by the mode (i.e. the most frequent rating). Educators considerably more often (42% of educators vs 15% of students) rated structuring and visualising support with the maximum rating of 7. As educators and students perceived ideating and balancing support differently, analysis suggests rejecting H_{0A}.

3.2 Applicability

Regarding the *applicability*, most educators (77%, *Mdn* = 6) and students (66%, *Mdn* = 5) expressed to have fun playing the role-playing game. While educator ratings showed a higher tendency for enjoyment, the result was not statistically different, $U = 537.5, z = 1.95, p = .051$. With a similar result, most educators (85%, *Mdn* = 6) and students (66%, *Mdn* = 5) stated that they can imagine using the game by themselves for co-designing SG concepts, $U = 538, z = 1.96, p = .051$.

Expectedly, the educators were significantly more confident (81%, *Mdn* = 6) than the students (59%, *Mdn* = 5) when agreeing that they can imagine using the role-playing boardgame to create research-oriented games, $U = 553.5, z = 2.21, p = .027, r = .29$. Most educators (88%, *Mdn* = 6) and students (75%, *Mdn* = 5) also expressed to be well satisfied with the co-designed game concept in the questionnaire, $U = 526, z = 1.79, p = .074$.

This is confirmed by analysis of the in-game role slider ratings. Both students and educator role-players showed a high level of satisfaction with their final SG concept, with a median rating of 80% or higher for every role (Fig. 4).

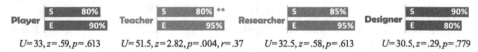

Player	S 80%	Teacher	S 80% **	Researcher	S 85%	Designer	S 90%
	E 90%		E 95%		E 95%		E 80%

$U=33, z=.59, p=.613$ $U=51.5, z=2.82, p=.004, r=.37$ $U=32.5, z=.58, p=.613$ $U=30.5, z=.29, p=.779$

Fig. 4. Role-oriented satisfaction (*Mdn*) with the final co-designed SG concept; S = Students, E = Educators

Educators playing the role of the teacher were thereby significantly more comfortable (*Mdn* = 95%) with the co-created SG concept than their student peers with an already high-level 80% median. Since the groups differ in perceived applicability, the analysis suggests rejection of H_{0B}.

4   Discussion

Regarding the *first research question*, the trials showed that both students and educators were well supported in ideating and balancing SG concepts by the online boardgame. Our results confirm previously found positive influences of role-playing with a structured, time guided [19, 20] and stepwise process [17] for remote/online co-design scenarios. The role-oriented card decks helped students and educators finding and focusing on ideas. For both groups playing the game provided guidance to develop new ideas as the playboard helped structuring and visualising the SG balance. The results suggest that integrating quality feedback criteria such as instant ratings of design alternatives and emotional feedback cues can support role-oriented co-creation of design solutions in remote/online scenarios and thus align with recommendations of Maaravi et al. [24].

Comparative analysis showed that educators felt even more supported than students, with 88% agreeing in general and 42% strongly agreeing that the playboard helped SG balancing, and more than 90% perceiving support for ideating SG concepts. It is conceivable that the pedagogical and scientific background of the educators facilitated role-playing, linking design proposals and resolving conflicts regarding the teacher and researcher roles. The synthesised results on role-playing support for ideation/balancing of SG parts Fig. 3/Table 1 and role-oriented satisfaction shown in Fig. 4 support this conception. The findings imply that educators joining student groups for playing the teacher/researcher role in the co-design game could help ideation and improve the balance of a SG concept. However, further trials are required with such integrated scenarios to investigate the influences of the teacher-student relationship.

When looking at the *second research question*, the perceived ideation and balancing support is also backed by applicability. Most students and educators enjoyed playing the role-playing game and were satisfied with the final SG concept to a high degree. The role-oriented analysis confirmed this contentment with all median ratings at or above 80%. This indicates that the role-playing game is applicable for co-designing SGs with non-experts feeling comfortable playing expert roles when supported with design cards and structured gameplay. Additionally, educators reported strong confidence to use the game for co-creating SG concepts in a privacy education and research context. The results suggest the role-playing design game approach is applicable by educator/research groups to playfully co-design privacy SG concepts in initial development phases to integrate and balance privacy research objectives with engaging game ideas. As students also showed confidence playing the roles and satisfaction with the outcome, their sense of enjoyable experiences can be fostered in joint gaming sessions. Thereby they can complement research groups/educators by taking the roles of players or designers. The ability to participate remotely adds to this utility in research scenarios where international cooperation is obligatory even in the absence of a pandemic.

5   Conclusion

This study investigated supporting collaboratively ideating and balancing SG concepts in online/remote scenarios using a role-playing browser game and video conferencing. The results provide valuable insight on co-design strategies and benefits of a multi-perspective approach, especially relevant in times of pandemics that previous research rarely covered. All in all, the introduced online role-playing game proved as a supportive co-design tool. It represents a playful activity that enables co-designing balanced SG concepts with physically distanced participants.

The study shows that non-experts can confidently engage in role-playing with digital expert design suggestion cards, an associated playboard and guided gameplay to successfully ideate and balance SG concepts in a dialogical approach. Students and educators were having fun playing the design game while also being satisfied with the final game concepts. Mixed co-design groups are suggested as future research trail for online role-playing investigations to learn more about SG multiperspectivity and foster the outlined potential for balancing SG designs.

Acknowledgements. This research was funded by the NFR IKTPLUSS project ALerT, #270969. We thank the participating students and educators, Tobias Werner for being the voice of the game and Monica Divitini for helping to organise the game sessions.

References

1. Jost, P.: The Quest Game-Frame: Balancing Serious Games for Investigating Privacy Decisions. In: Ahlin, K., Mozelius, P., Sundberg, L. (eds.) Proceedings of the 11th Scandinavian Conference on Information Systems (SCIS2020), pp. 1–17. AIS, Atlanta (2020)
2. Dörner, R., Göbel, S., Effelsberg, W., Wiemeyer, J. (eds.): Serious Games. Springer, Cham (2016). https://doi.org/10.1007/978-3-319-40612-1
3. Nakamura, J., Csikszentmihalyi, M.: Flow theory and research. In: Snyder, C.R., Lopez, S.J. (eds.) Handbook of Positive Psychology, pp. 195–206. Oxford University Press, Oxford (2009)
4. Mann, J.H.: Experimental evaluations of role playing. Psychol. Bull. **53**, 227–234 (1956)
5. Mäkelä, E., Koistinen, S., Siukola, M., Turunen, S.: The process model of role-playing. In: Bøckman, P., Hutchison, R. (eds.) Dissecting LARP: Collected papers for Knutepunkt the 9th annual Nordic Conference on LARP, pp. 205–236. Grimshei Trykkeri, Oslo (2005)
6. van Ments, M.: The Effective Use of Role-play: Practical Techniques for Improving Learning, 2nd edn., vol. 4, pp. 400–402. International Career Development (1999)
7. Zowghi, D., Paryani, S.: Teaching requirements engineering through role playing: lessons learnt. In: Proceedings. 11th IEEE International Requirements Engineering Conference, pp. 233–241. IEEE, Washington (2003)
8. Boess, S.: Rationales for Role playing in design. Presented at the 3rd International Conference UNIDCOM/IADE, Lisbon, Portugal, 1 November 2006
9. Seland, G.: System designer assessments of role play as a design method: a qualitative study. In: Proceedings of the 4th Nordic Conference on Human-Computer Interaction: Changing Roles, pp. 222–231. ACM, New York (2006)
10. Burns, C., Dishman, E., Verplank, W., Lassiter, B.: Actors, hairdos and videotape—informance design. In: Conference Companion on Human Factors in Computing Systems, pp. 119–120. ACM, New York (1994)
11. Buchenau, M., Suri, J.F.: Experience prototyping. In: Proceedings of the 3rd Conference on Designing Interactive Systems, pp. 424–433. ACM, New York (2000)
12. Karwowski, M., Soszynski, M.: How to develop creative imagination?: assumptions, aims and effectiveness of role play training in creativity. Think. Ski. Creat. **3**, 163–171 (2008)
13. Strömberg, H., Pirttilä, V., Ikonen, V.: Interactive scenarios-building ubiquitous computing concepts in the spirit of participatory design. Pers. Ubiquitous Comput. **8**, 200–207 (2004)
14. Rudra, A., Jæger, B., Aitken, A., Chang, V., Helgheim, B.: Virtual team role play using second life for teaching business process concepts. In: Sprague, R.H. Jr. (ed.) Proceedings of the 44th Annual Hawaii International Conference on System Sciences, pp. 1–8. IEEE, Washington (2011)
15. Vaajakallio, K.: Design games as a tool, a mindset and a structure. Ph.D. thesis, Aalto University School of Arts, Design and Architecture, Aalto (2012)
16. Vaajakallio, K., Mattelmäki, T.: Design games in codesign: as a tool, a mindset and a structure. CoDesign **10**, 63–77 (2014)
17. Brandt, E.: Designing exploratory design games: a framework for participation in participatory design? In: Proceedings of the ninth Conference on Participatory Design, pp. 57–66. ACM, New York (2006)
18. Hannula, O., Irrmann, O.: Played into collaborating: design games as scaffolding for service co-design project planning. Simul. Gaming. **47**, 599–627 (2016)

19. Brandt, E., Messeter, J.: Facilitating collaboration through design games. In: Proceedings of the Eighth Conference on Participatory Design: Artful Integration: Interweaving Media, Materials and Practices - Volume 1, pp. 121–131. ACM, New York (2004)
20. Finke, R.A., Ward, T.B., Smith, S.M.: Creative Cognition: Theory, Research, and Applications. The MIT Press, Cambridge (1992)
21. Hevner, A.R.: A three cycle view of design science research. Scand. J. Inf. Syst. **19**, 4 (2007)
22. Jost, P., Divitini, M.: The challenge game frame: affordance oriented co-creation of privacy decision games. In: Fotaris, P. (ed.) Proceedings of the 14th International Conference on Game Based Learning (ECGBL 2020), pp. 277–286. ACI, Reading (2020)
23. Fischer, G.: Social creativity: turning barriers into opportunities for collaborative design. In: Proceedings of the Eighth Conference on Participatory Design: Artful Integration: Interweaving Media, Materials and Practices-Volume 1, pp. 152–161. ACM, New York (2004)
24. Maaravi, Y., Heller, B., Shoham, Y., Mohar, S., Deutsch, B.: Ideation in the digital age: literature review and integrative model for electronic brainstorming. Rev. Manag. Sci. **15**, 1431–1464 (2021)
25. Field, A.: Discovering Statistics Using IBM SPSS Statistics. SAGE Publications, Thousand Oaks (2017)
26. Hart, A.: Mann-Whitney test is not just a test of medians: differences in spread can be important. BMJ **323**, 391–393 (2001)

The Role of Metaphor in Serious Games Design: the BubbleMumble Case Study

Mario Allegra[1], Antonella Bongiovanni[4], Giuseppe Città[1],
Antonella Cusimano[4], Valentina Dal Grande[1], Manuel Gentile[1,3]([⊠]),
Annamaria Kisslinger[6], Dario La Guardia[1], Giovanna Liguori[5],
Fabrizio Lo Presti[1], Salvatore Perna[1,2], Sabrina Picciotto[4],
Simona Ottaviano[1], Carla Sala[7], and Alessandro Signa[1,2]

[1] Institute for Educational Technology (ITD), National Research Council
of Italy (CNR), Palermo, Italy
manuel.gentile@itd.cnr.it
[2] Department of Engineering, University of Palermo, Palermo, Italy
[3] Department of Computer Science, University of Turin, Turin, Italy
[4] Institute for Research and Biomedical Innovation (IRIB),
National Research Council of Italy (CNR), Palermo, Italy
[5] Institute of Genetics and Biophysics (IGB), National Research Council of Italy
(CNR), Naples, Italy
[6] Institute of Experimental Endocrinology and Oncology (IEOS),
National Research Council of Italy (CNR), Naples, Italy
[7] Zabala Innovation Consulting, Pamplona, Spain
http://www.itd.cnr.it/

Abstract. Metaphors represent a powerful cognitive tool through which
it is possible to facilitate the understanding of abstract concepts or concepts belonging to unfamiliar domains. In the field of Serious Games
(SGs), metaphors connect the user's previous experience in the game
domain to the information load that is intended to be conveyed. This
paper presents a prototype of a model for the design of SGs based on the
extensive use of the concept of metaphor. As a case study, the design of
the digital SG BubbleMumble is introduced. BubbleMumble is intended
to convey the fundamental concepts behind the extracellular vesicle biogenesis and production processes exploiting metaphor-driven SG design.

Keywords: Serious game design · Metaphors · Extracellular vesicles

1 Introduction

Metaphor is a cognitive process that eases the human mind's understanding of
new concepts. The metaphor in fact allows to create similarities and parallelisms
between a new concept (abstract or belonging to a new domain) and a concept
already known (more concrete or already belonging to the cultural and experiential baggage of the person). It creates a bridge from the source domain (the
known concept) to the target domain (the new concept) [6].

© Springer Nature Switzerland AG 2021
F. de Rosa et al. (Eds.): GALA 2021, LNCS 13134, pp. 198–207, 2021.
https://doi.org/10.1007/978-3-030-92182-8_19

Metaphor has been used since remote times to facilitate education, and research has begun to indicate why it has proved so enduringly successful [16]. Several studies [5,7,8,11,15,22] show that the use of metaphors allows students to generate inference processes in relation to the topics covered in class by teachers. Metaphors also facilitate communication between teachers and students both when the information to be conveyed is axiomatic and when it is the product of critical thinking [7,15]. There is further evidence that the use of metaphors can also have a positive impact towards students' ability to memorize information [4,10].

In addition, some studies [17,23] show that students can improve their problem solving and critical thinking skills if they are actively involved in constructing the analogies themselves. However, there are also those who draw attention to the negative effects that some metaphors can have. If, in fact, they excessively simplify the concepts they are intended to convey, this could lead to the misinterpretation of the said concepts [21]. The assumptions made so far are practically reflected in the science lessons done in school. In that context, in fact, metaphors are much more frequent than in scientific articles. Teachers exploit them to ensure an appropriate level of complexity in dealing with the most difficult topics facing an audience of non-experts. In fact, one of the educational missions of teachers is to motivate students by proposing concepts within their grasp [20].

In the Serious Games (SGs) field, some studies have shown that metaphors in the design phase are an excellent educational approach to introduce the learning of concepts and contents [12]. Lankford and Watson [14] argue that the design of a game and its gameplay allow for establishing a relationship between a metaphorical reality, the game world, and the complex reality constituted by the real world. The game designer can distil the essential features of human and ecological processes into a virtual conceptual model such as the SG by implementing a metaphorical process that links the two realities.

In this context, the use of metaphors allows structuring visual scenarios that are cognitively stimulating for the learner because it allows connecting the user's previous experience to the specific experience of the game through the use of well-structured analogies [3].

According to literature [4,9,12], younger children cannot work with analogies and metaphors unless (a) the metaphors are presented explicitly, (b) Source–Target correspondences are given, and (c) the children have an adequate understanding of the Source domain before the metaphor is given. This study underlines how important it is to provide a solid knowledge base in order for the user to be able to use metaphors as an effective learning tool. In order to make this benefit accessible to the majority, it was decided to use some of the most popular game mechanics as metaphors. The paper aims to contextualise and introduce the role that metaphor can play in SG design and what are the specific dynamics of metaphor that allow connecting the domain of a game with the real domain of knowledge that is to be represented in the game. This role is outlined to propose a metaphor-driven design model in a prototype form. Two case studies are given as initial arguments to support the proposed prototype model.

2   A Metaphor-Driven Serious Games Design Process

Exploiting the metaphorical process as a cognitively valid approach able to stimulate learning and to anchor the game experience to the previous experience of the player, we designed the BubbleMumble game as a metaphor of a specific biological process: the genesis and extraction of vesicles (see Sect. 3; Fig. 2). The first step in this process was the analysis of the process and extraction of the key features of the actual process that was intended to be represented in the game model (*Process analysis and key features extraction*). According to Lankford and Watson [14] this process of analysis has allowed on the one hand to "distill" the essential characteristics of the phenomenon to be represented and on the other hand to make a series of initial comparisons between the two domains involved (the domain of the game and the domain of the reality to be represented). Thanks to the structuring of these analogies between the two domains involved (*Identification of main analogies*) it was possible to select the primary Game Mechanics (GMs) most suitable for the purpose (*GMs selection*). The selection of the mechanics has involved reconnaissance and an in-depth analysis of existing games (mainly commercial games) and their most relevant and appropriate features (*Identification and analysis of existing games*). Once we selected mechanics and existing games, we structured the game model of BubbleMumble (*Metaphor refinement*). The steps of selection of mechanics, identification and analysis of existing games, and metaphor refinement have constituted a cyclic process that, applied repeatedly, has allowed us to build a suitable metaphor of a biological process. Once we obtained a suitable metaphor, we proceeded with the game implementation (*Game implementation*) (see Fig. 1).

3   Ves4US Project

VES4US is a new European project funded by the Horizon 2020-Future and Emerging Technology (FET) Open program, which aims to develop an innovative platform for the efficient production of extracellular vesicles (EVs) from a renewable bio-source, enabling their exploitation as tailor-made products in the fields of nanomedicine, cosmetics and nutraceutics (https://ves4us.eu). A core aspect of the project is to focus on microalgae as identified natural source to constitute a cost-effective and sustainable source of EVs. The project lasts for three years (2018–2021) with six organizations from six European countries (Italy, Germany, Swiss, Ireland, Slovenia, Spain). The project unfolds in three phases: the first phase, focused on the selection of the natural source and the optimization of culture condition at pre-industrial scale [18]. The second phase is centered on the isolation and physio-chemical characterization of the extracellular vesicles. In the third phase, the functionalization and load of the EVs is approached. Safe, efficient and specific nano-delivery systems are essential to

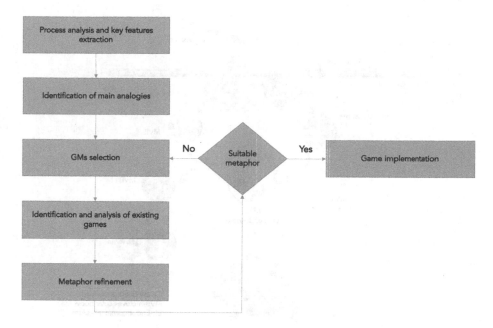

Fig. 1. A flowchart of the metaphor-driven serious game design process

current therapeutic medicine, cosmetic and nutraceutics sectors. The ability to optimise the bioavailability, stability, and targeted cellular uptake of a bioactive molecule while mitigating toxicity, immunogenicity and off-target/side effects is of the utmost priority. In this perspective, VES4US aims to create a fundamentally new bioprocessing approach to generate and functionalize EVs from microalgae, which will enable for their exploitation in the fields of nanomedicine, cosmetics and nutraceutics.

Within the context of the VES4US project, we developed two games designed according to the prototype model presented above. These games, described in the following sections, will aim to disseminate the contents and results of the project to non-specialist users with a particular focus on secondary school students.

3.1   BubbleMumble Kart

We designed the first game to allow the user to acquire the core concepts linked with the extracellular nanovesicles' biogenesis process. The Fig. 2 shows this process and its main elements in abstract terms. In particular, this representation highlights the circular nature of the process and the need for specific conditions for its success. To simplify, the formation of multivesicular bodies and the inclusion of specific components like lipids, proteins and nucleic acids represent the essential facilitating conditions that allow the biogenesis process.

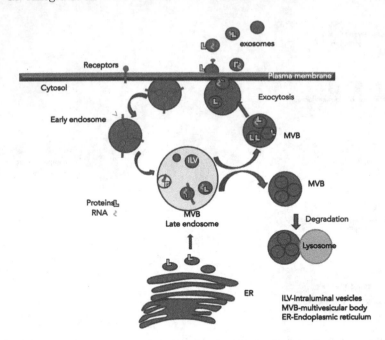

Fig. 2. A representation of the vesicles biogenesis process

Starting from the analogy of the process as a pathway, we have identified moving along a path as a possible first game mechanic. This first analogy led to the idea of a game in line with the famous commercial game *Mario Kart*™.

Mario Kart is a motor racing video games series by Nintendo. It is, as of today, one of the most famous and best-selling video games in the industry. In *Mario Kart*, the player may choose among several playable characters of the Mario series and may compete against opponents (human and virtual players) both locally or online. The main strengths of the title are the captivating graphics, the level of entertainment, the low level of complexity and the possibility to compete with other people. The identification of *Mario Kart* as a reference game produces other possible analogies. The kart can assume the role of the Multivesicular body which is formed in the cytosol and moves through the cellular environment. Consequently, it seemed natural to set this race in a cellular environment, where the track is the representation of the circularity of the process. The Fig. 3 shows the machine (the Multivesicular body) controlled by the player and intent on collecting the elements necessary for the biogenesis of the vesicles. From the image it is noticeable that the environment is an abstraction whose purpose is to strengthen the idea of being inside a cell: the hexagon-shaped walls represent the endoplasmic reticulum, the spiky spherical objects represent lysosomes, while other elements, such as the checkpoint rings present along the track, resemble the double helix conformation of the nucleic acids.

Moreover, we adapted the classical *Mario Kart* mechanics of collecting elements to simulate in the Multivescicular body the inclusion in intraluminal vesicles of those elements (lipids, proteins and nucleic acids) necessary for the process of bio-genesis.

In BubbleMumble Kart, the player can collect the necessary components for the biogenesis process by passing onto them. Once the player manages to collect three organic components a vesicle will be created and stored. The same feature has been used for creating obstacles: other than the three aforementioned items, red virus-like objects (Lysosome, cell organelle in charge of degradation) are scattered on the track. Their retrieval causes the kart to skid and lose control for a few seconds.

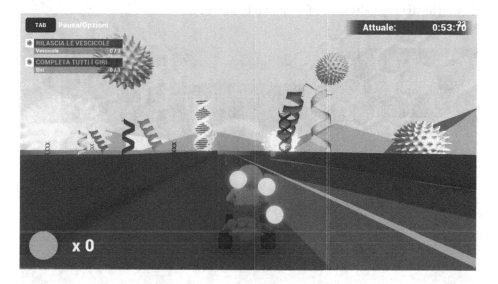

Fig. 3. A screenshot of the BubbleMumble Kart game

3.2   BubbleMumble Lab

The second game was designed to illustrate the research work behind the Ves4us project and its main results. The process of culture isolation and characterization of nanovesicles consists of a series of steps [1]. The specification of controlled parameters for each step is the primary outcome of the project. The main analogy that guided the design process was to consider the process as a recipe. With this in mind, we identified *Overcooked*™as a possible reference point for the creation of the game. *Overcooked* is a multiplayer-based Action/Indie video game, in which the player has to team up with friends for cooking, arranging and serving a variety of dishes for an audience of impatient customers. The main feature that makes the game extremely entertaining is the constant state of "frenzy" that forces the player to sharpen its reflexes and to always maintain a certain degree of attention. It is, as a consequence, extremely difficult to focus on other activities while playing and, at the same time, the constant commitment provides the player with a feeling of satisfaction once the rush is over. The flow of the level is characterised by a series of basic operations (i.e. slicing the onion) that have to be accomplished in a subsequent fashion so that the final recipe may be ready to be served. The ingredients have to be carried across the space to proceed with the recipe and the necessary steps are listed with a minimal but effective UI.

Bubble Mumble relies on many of the previously presented features, trying to achieve the level of immersivity of *Overcooked*, while providing the knowledge for which the original project was intended.

Bubble Mumble is set in a laboratory for nanovesicles production. Figure 4 shows the 3D reproduction of a classic laboratory.

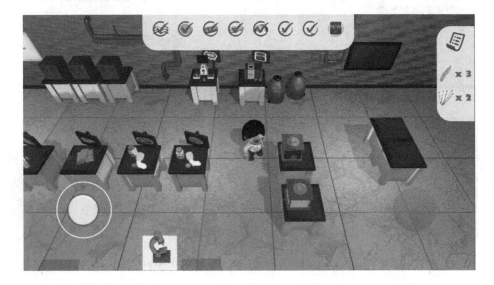

Fig. 4. A screenshot of the BubbleMumble Lab game

Extracellular Vesicles produced by microalgae cells are proposed as novel biogenic nanotechnology useful in fields such as pharmaceuticals and customer care. The player plays the role of a new researcher who is introduced to the manufacturing process: starting with the choice of a certain microalgae strain, he or she will have to create a high-quality culture by supplying the nutritional components necessary for its growth, then extrapolate the vesicles and carry out a quality check before delivering them.

The same flow of play that characterises Overcooked has been implemented in Bubble Mumble: in order to produce the nanovesicles the player must follow a number of subsequent tasks, each one comprehensive of a mini-game whose score will directly impact the quality of the culture. To maintain a certain degree of attention and devotion to the objective, an approach that is similar to the one aforementioned is used: a group of researchers, represented by some balloons on the screen, will demand for specific orders; the time slot in which it is allowed to satisfy these requests is limited and represented with the changing color of the balloon (it will turn from white to yellow and finally to red, with a consequent decrease of the final score for that delivery).

In order to merge in a proper manner the entertaining aspect of the game and the scientific purpose of sharing the knowledge behind the mentioned process, the game provides two different modes: the *Internship Mode* and the *Production Mode*. In the *Internship Mode*, there is no time limit to fulfill the requests. Moreover, an NPC supports the player during the process, highlighting the key concepts of each production step (Fig. 5). The purpose of this mode is to provide the player with the detailed, often numeric, knowledge that is needed to perform the correct steps: he or she will have to select, for example, the correct amount of vitamins for the culture medium, adjust the pH and remember if a certain microalga needs a mixture of metals to support its growth. The tutorial of the game also takes place here, so that the player can start to get acquainted with the game mechanics and controls.

The *Production Mode* was created to make spice up the game. For this to happen, we introduce the time limits as a critical design choice like in Overcooked.

Another feature that has been introduced in this game mode is the random generation of obstacles inside the scene. During the game, sometimes a flask may fall down and create a slippery puddle of chemical material. If the player tramples upon it, they will stumble and be unable to move for a few seconds.

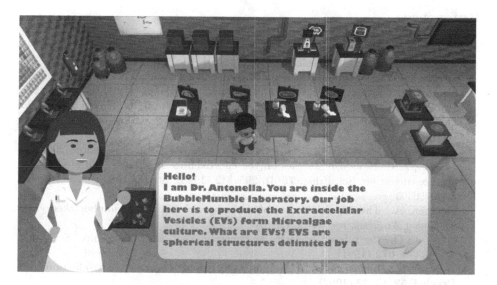

Fig. 5. The NPC avatar in BubbleMumble Lab game

4   Discussion and Future Works

In this article, we have presented a prototype of a model for the design of serious games based on the extensive use of the concept of metaphor. The model has been tested in developing two serious games, realised within the European project Ves4us. Starting from the didactic objectives and identifying the main characteristics of the process on which a serious game is to be created, the model identifies the fundamental steps necessary for creating a game. The construction of the metaphor is presented as an iterative process in which the analysis of existing games (mainly commercial games) supports the definition of the basic similarities and game mechanics. The two case studies, representing one of the outputs of the Ves4us project, were qualitatively tested during the 2020 European Researchers' Night promoted by the SHAring Researchers' Passion for Engaging Responsiveness and will be subjects of future field trials. In particular, we will test how the games engage students in critical thinking about vesicles concepts by generating their own analogies. Moreover, once this prototype of a metaphor-driven model has been systematised and formalised, we aim to compare it with other design models proposed in the field of SG [2,13,19] and assess the extent of the novelty introduced by the concept of metaphor as a catalyst for learning and as the organisational fulcrum of the relationship between game mechanics and learning contents.

Acknowledgements. Funding: The authors acknowledge financial support from the VES4US project funded by the European Union's Horizon 2020 research and innovation program under grant agreement No 801338.

References

1. Adamo, G., et al.: Nanoalgosomes: introducing extracellular vesicles produced by microalgae. J. Extracell. Vesicles **10**(6) (2021). https://doi.org/10.1002/jev2.12081
2. Arnab, S., et al.: Mapping learning and game mechanics for serious games analysis. Br. J. Edu. Technol. **46**(2), 391–411 (2014). https://doi.org/10.1111/bjet.12113
3. Buendía García, F., García-Martínez, S., Navarrete-Ibañez, E.M., Cervelló-Donderis, M.: Designing serious games for getting transferable skills in training settings. Interact. Des. Archit.(s) **19**, 47–62 (2013)
4. Cameron, L.: Metaphor in Educational Discourse. A&C Black, London (2003)
5. Dagher, Z.R.: Review of studies on the effectiveness of instructional analogies in science education. Sci. Educ. **79**(3), 295–312 (1995). https://doi.org/10.1002/sce.3730790305
6. Deignan, A.: The cognitive view of metaphor: conceptual metaphor theory. In: Metaphor Analysis, pp. 44–56 (2010)
7. Duit, R.: On the role of analogies and metaphors in learning science. Sci. Educ. **75**(6), 649–672 (1991)
8. Gentner, D., Holyoak, K.J.: Reasoning and learning by analogy: introduction. Am. Psychol. **52**(1), 32 (1997)
9. Gentner, D., Toupin, C.: Systematicity and surface similarity in the development of analogy. Cogn. Sci. **10**(3), 277–300 (1986)

10. Harris, R.J., Tebbe, M.R., Leka, G.E., Garcia, R.C., Erramouspe, R.: Monolingual and bilingual memory for English and Spanish metaphors and similes. Metaphor. Symb. **14**(1), 1–16 (1999)
11. Holyoak, K.J., Holyoak, K.J., Thagard, P.: Mental Leaps: Analogy in Creative Thought. MIT Press, Cambridge (1995)
12. Jemmali, C., Kleinman, E., Bunian, S., Almeda, M.V., Rowe, E., El-Nasr, M.S.: Using game design mechanics as metaphors to enhance learning of introductory programming concepts. In: Proceedings of the 14th International Conference on the Foundations of Digital Games. ACM, August 2019. https://doi.org/10.1145/3337722.3341825
13. Lameras, P., Arnab, S., Dunwell, I., Stewart, C., Clarke, S., Petridis, P.: Essential features of serious games design in higher education: linking learning attributes to game mechanics. Br. J. Educ. Technol. **48**(4), 972–994 (2016). https://doi.org/10.1111/bjet.12467
14. Lankford, B., Watson, D.: Metaphor in natural resource gaming: insights from the RIVER BASIN GAME. Simul. Gaming **38**(3), 421–442 (2007). https://doi.org/10.1177/1046878107300671
15. Lawson, A.E.: The importance of analogy: a prelude to the special issue. J. Res. Sci. Teach. **30**(10), 1213 1214 (1993)
16. Low, G.: Metaphor and Education. The Cambridge Handbook of Metaphor and Thought, pp. 212–231 (2008)
17. Middleton, J.L.: Student-generated analogies in biology. In: The American Biology Teacher, pp. 42–46 (1991)
18. Picciotto, S., et al.: Isolation of extracellular vesicles from microalgae: towards the production of sustainable and natural nanocarriers of bioactive compounds. Biomater. Sci. **9**(8), 2917–2930 (2021). https://doi.org/10.1039/d0bm01696a
19. Rooney, P.: A theoretical framework for serious game design. Int. J. Game-Based Learn. **2**(4), 41–60 (2012). https://doi.org/10.4018/ijgbl.2012100103
20. Skorczynska, H.: Metaphor and education: reaching business training goals through multimodal metaphor. Procedia. Soc. Behav. Sci. **116**, 2344–2351 (2014)
21. Spiro, R.J.: Multiple analogies for complex concepts: antidotes for analogy-induced misconception in advanced knowledge acquisition. Center for the Study of Reading Technical Report; no. 439 (1988)
22. Sutton, C.: Figuring out a scientific understanding. J. Res. Sci. Teach. **30**(10), 1215–1227 (1993)
23. Wittrock, M.C., Alesandrini, K.: Generation of summaries and analogies and analytic and holistic abilities. Am. Educ. Res. J. **27**(3), 489–502 (1990)

Transforming Game Premise: An Approach for Developing Cooperative Serious Games

Supara Grudpan[1]([⊠]), Jakob Hauge[2], Jannicke Baalsrud Hauge[2,3], and Rainer Malaka[1]

[1] Digital Media Lab, TZI, University of Bremen, Bremen, Germany
{sgrudpan,malaka}@uni-bremen.de
[2] BIBA-Bremen Institute for Production and Logistics Gmbh, Bremen, Germany
{baa,hau}@biba.uni-bremen.de
[3] KTH-Royal Institute of Technology, Stockholm, Sweden

Abstract. Developing cooperative serious games has specific challenges of enabling players to achieve both gaming and learning goals in a cooperative fashion. The complexity of handling game and learning requirements leads to the lack of guidance for systematically developing cooperative serious games (SGs). To overcome the challenges, we propose a systematic approach to utilize elements of entertainment cooperative games to foster player engagement in SGs. The guideline, which consists of steps to transform the existing cooperative entertainment games into cooperative SGs, is proposed. To demonstrate the guideline application, we developed a game prototype follow the steps. To validate our guidelines, we conducted a user study to verify games for their learning potential. Learning objectives related to urban logistics are defined and limited the scope of our research. We ask participants to do pretest and posttest to measure their memorization. The study showed that the game developed followed by our method could support players to achieve learning objectives.

Keywords: Serious games development · Cooperative games · Cooperative serious games · Game premise

1 Introduction

Developing cooperative SGs have complexity with unique requirements. The gameplay has to fulfill the requirements of traditional multiplayer games (players' engagement and players' interaction), overcome challenges in SGs design (inclusion of learning content and adaptation & personalization [14]). Further, since the main characteristic of cooperative games is to communicate and cooperate to achieve a goal [16], this needs to find specific consideration in the design.

Increasing players' motivation is a significant challenge for designing and developing SGs [5]. SGs developers have to consider fulfilling functional requirements to find the suits formal game elements for given learning goals. However, developers also have to include non-functional requirements, which is the fun/entertaining aspect to engage players in the long term [4]. Additionally, SGs are tailored to learning objectives, leading

© Springer Nature Switzerland AG 2021
F. de Rosa et al. (Eds.): GALA 2021, LNCS 13134, pp. 208–219, 2021.
https://doi.org/10.1007/978-3-030-92182-8_20

to low flexibility in redesign and reusability of the products and high cost and time consuming [4, 12]. Therefore, it is vital to explore the systematic way to develop SGs to minimize the cost and time consuming of the development project. At the same time, still, fulfill serious and entertainment purpose of the games [4]. To overcome the complexity of cooperative SGs development, we proposed a guideline that systematically converts cooperative entertainment games to cooperative SGs by modifying the premise.

In the next section, we describe the background and related work for the design and development of cooperative SGs. In Sect. 3, we explain a method for elaborating our guideline. In Sect. 4, we propose a three-phase approach to the guideline. The phases are Selecting a reference game, Develop a game blueprint, and Reframing the game premise. To validate the practical application of our guideline, we apply it to a real-world example. We conduct a user study to verify the educational value of the game prototype that developed follow our guidelines. Details of guideline application and the user study are presented in Sect. 5.

2 Background and Related Works

2.1 Challenges of Cooperative SGs Design and Development

Serious games are software that has its specific requirements and design process. The design and development of SGs require a development team consisting of both game designers and education experts. However, due to this multi-disciplinarity, the team members often do not share a common vocabulary and domain viewpoints [2–4]. Therefore, to improve the method of the SGs development, the pedagogical contents have to be translated and implemented into the game mechanics [4]. One of the biggest challenges in the SGs design and development is to study the relationship between learning mechanics (LM) and game mechanics (GM) to improve the game design process [9].

Cooperative SGs are games that all players have a common goal to accomplish together. The players have to communicate and cooperate to operate or make the decision. Each member can have an individual role or ability needed for achieving a common goal. Designing and developing cooperative SGs is difficult due to the complexity of the mentioned characteristics. The players have to cooperate or make decisions together for the maximum team. Additionally, to complete the game missions, the game must provide the environment for engaging the whole group of players [1, 11, 13]. Thus, the construction of the setting for cooperative SGs is an essential part. The learning process occurs during their interactions towards the gameplay. Therefore, the game environment should be designed to support interactions among players, notably, to their cooperative aligning with characteristics of the game.

2.2 Elements of SGs

Understanding game elements and their potential interrelationships are the basis of game design [11, 21]. We can use the principle together with creativity to design the new type of gameplay. Deterding [5] mentioned that using game design elements in non-game contexts can motivate and increase user activity and retention in gamification.

However, designing SGs is more complicated because they have full-fledged game characteristics [5] and specific requirements to fulfill pedagogical goals [4, 12]. Generally, the learning objectives or serious contents are used for determining elements of SGs. The process can limit creativity and the flexibility of SGs designers, which affect the player motivation of the games. Therefore, it is essential to pay attention to integrating learning content into the gameplay ingeniously. Adding proper dramatic elements into SGs can be another option that can provide meaningful experiences and enable games to be more emotionally engaging [1, 5, 16].

In this paper, we proposed a systematic approach to develop cooperative SGs. Our approach applies the concept of using the potential of commercial-off-the-shelf games (COTS) for learning purposes [14] to ensures that the game mechanics are well balanced to avoid players' engagement problems. Additionally, our guideline includes the steps for selecting, adding learning contents of existing games to confirm that formal elements of the games chosen can fulfill learning objects.

2.3 Game Premise

The game premise is one of the dramatic elements which are commonly used in many games. The premise establishes meaning to the players' actions through a setting or metaphor [8]. Game premise helps players to understand and operate essential features in the games efficiently. The game premise differs from the story in the narrative aspect. A premise stays the same. It is not changed by players' actions. In comparison, the story builds upon the setting or theme and is altered by the game's progression. According to the definition of the game premise, we define *game premise* as the meaning or reason for players to act in games. In the aspect of SG developers, it is interesting to utilize the effect of game premise in developing effective SGs.

This paper suggests transforming existing cooperative entertainment games into cooperative SGs by modifying the premise of the existing games. The game premise is defined based on the scenario set by the learning contents.

3 Research Approach

To elaborate guidelines for transforming the game premise of cooperative games to cooperative SGs, we performed an iterative process that alternated between literature reviews and user testing to identify points for refinement.

To overcome challenges in cooperative SGs' complexity, we employed the concept of using games design elements to improve the player's motivation in the game for learning purposes and non-gaming context systems [5]. We explored game elements that influence the player experience. We found that dramatics elements can be used as a set of tools for engaging players emotionally by creating a dramatic context for the formal elements [6, 10]. Then, we looked at the dramatic elements that can be modified without changing the core gameplay. We found that the game premise is a possible candidate. Then, we conducted a user study and found that game premise affects player experience on competence, relatedness, and players' cooperation in cooperative games [7]. The finding motivated us to develop cooperative SGs by modifying the premise of the game. Subsequently, we produced an initial set of guidelines on transforming the game premise of existing cooperative games to cooperative SGs from the lesson learn of our development team. The guideline has been iteratively improved during the development process. The details of the guidelines are shown in Sect. 4. We conducted a user study (N = 74) to verify that the approach to modifying the premise of existing cooperative games can be an option to simplify the process of cooperative SGs development. The objective of the study is to confirm that the game developed using our guideline can support players to achieve learning objectives embedded in the game premise. The application of our framework and the results of the user study are presented in Sect. 5.

4   A Guideline: Transform Cooperative Games to Cooperative SGs

Our guideline includes workflow and documents for collaboration among the developer team, including game designers, game programmers, and experts who developed learning content. The guideline consists of a three-phase approach which is 1)—selecting game reference, 2)—Developing a game blueprint (ATMSG), and 3)—Reframing game premise (Extension of ATMSG). The method for elaborate each phase describes as follows.

Phase1: Selecting a Reference Game
To explore the existing COTS games that can be used as a reference game for initially developing cooperative SGs, we suggest that developers conduct *Selection Criteria*. The selection criteria have to contain information describing learning activities that instruction intends to add into SGs [4]. Thus, our guideline suggests developing selection criteria by considering three topics as follows.

- *The similarity of game and learning activities*: Generally, formal elements (rule, gameplay, character) of SGs are built based on the learning objectives. Therefore, to select the COTS game which can be a candidate for transforming to SGs. We have to look at the formal elements of the games. At this point, we have to consider the games that have game activities (actions, tools, goals) similar to the learning activity. For example, we have to consider utilizing a cooperative board game to train players to collaborate among stakeholders involved in urban logistics planning [8].
- *The similarity of real-world scenario and game scenario:* We suggest considering the games with a similar environment with the learning contents. With this criterion, the developers' team can minimize to design process. For example, a game that includes networking or map graphics and traveling activities can be a prominent candidate for developing a logistics game.
- *Characteristics of cooperative activities:* We suggest looking at the interaction between players to ensure that the activities support learning objectives which are the main requirements. For example, to develop multiplayer rehabilitation games, we should look for the existing cooperative games that require players to cooperate in the gameplays and consider the game, which includes physical activities such as the cooperative mode of the Guitar Hero game.

Phase2: Develop a Game Blueprint

In this phase, the game blueprint of cooperative SGs is developed to ensure that the game chosen can fulfill learning requirements. This phase consists of two steps. The first step is to analyze the game activities of the game chosen. The second step is to brainstorm for adding learning content to the individual state of the game. The details of each step are described as follows.

Step 2.1: Analysis of the game chosen: For this step, the selected games are analyzed using the Activity Theory-based Model for Serious Games (ATMSG) [4]. ATMSG is a model for SGs analysis. The model allows the developers' team to deconstruct the architecture of SGs. The architecture consists of a flow chart and a table of gaming, learning, and instruction activities (see Table 1). This step aims to analyze the structure of the games chosen to identify game elements and game states that are suitable with assigned learning objectives. We follow the guideline of ATMSG to illustrate the game flow and game activities of the selected games. In this step, the development team can use the initial parts of the ATMSG diagram, which consist of a flow chart (game flow) and game activity taxonomies (actions, tools, goals) to select the suitable reference games. Game designers and programmers should involve in this step to support the team in drawing flowcharts and tuning game mechanics.

Step 2.2: Brainstorm to add learning activity: We continued to fill out the game's learning elements and intrinsic instruction elements (see Table 1). In this phase, game flow, game elements, learning elements, and intrinsic instruction elements are illustrated. The table can help the team have a clear picture of how players cooperate and interact. The team can consider adjusting formal elements of the game while still clearly seeing how the elements affect the other elements.

These two steps support the developer team in selecting reference games and creating the initial game blueprint. The game blueprint allows the team to have a common view of game architecture and identify the game element suitable for the defined learning objectives.

Phase3: Reframing Game Premise

In this phase, we focus on the implementation process. Our guideline supports the iterative development process. We suggest developing a game prototype based on the game blueprint from the previous phase for the first iterative of developing a game prototype. Programmers can focus on implementing formal elements, which are gameplay, rules. After that, we propose the steps to modify the dramatic elements which relate to the game premise. Thus, we advise programmers to arrange source code in a way that is flexible for rephasing objects. All the text embedded in the game should be able to export in a format that educational experts can edit easily to modify learning content.

The guideline in this stage includes the steps of documenting and keeping track of transforming the original game's premise to SGs. To ensure that the game is documented systematically, we describe the four steps of game document support communication among game designers, educational experts, and programmers as follows.

Step 3.1: Labeling game elements derived from the game premise: In this step, we labeled game elements, gaming tools, which are a row in gaming activity in the ATMSG table.

Step 3.2: Listing game elements of the original game into the Version table: To keep track of the naming of game elements of the original game version with our modified version, we recommend creating a *Version table* to document changes. In this step, game designers and game programmers need to cooperate to extract all the game elements into the table. The storyboard and user interface of the original game are the additional documents which require in this step.

Step 3.3: Phasing game elements: The game elements in Step 3.2 are phased and added in the column next to the original game of Version table. The Version table is not only a checklist for game designers and programmers to modify the naming of game elements. The document also helps educationists/experts who have no technical background to change entertainment games to SGs without dealing with technical problems. We recommend that programmers flexibly organize source code to import the new version of the text file back to the game project.

Step 3.4: Adding modified game elements back to the ATMSG table: We added another layer to the bottom of the ATMSG table. This last layer helps the developer team track-back to the original design of the game, which can be used later when the team needs to redesign or change the learning contents of the game.

5   Application of the Guideline

We implemented cooperative games using our proposed guideline to verify that the procedure is repeatable and can be one option for developing cooperative SGs. Urban logistics is selected to use as a scope for developing the prototype.

Phase1: Selecting a Reference Game
We began with analyzing the scenarios of urban logistics from the literature and identified the learning objectives. Then, we created the selection criteria for choosing reference games. We investigated the popular cooperative commercial games then develop the following criteria to filter the number of games.

The main criteria used in the selection of the reference games were as follows:

i). Games, where players need to deal with a map or network like this, match the type of environment required for logistics game. ii). Multiplayer games require the players to help each other complete the game goal. iii). Games which mandate the players to cooperate on the decision level. iv). Games where the players need to make decisions based on their roles. We found that the Pandemic board game [15] was one of the most promising games that could be used as a reference game for implementing our prototype as it satisfied all the requirements in our criteria.

Originally, Pandemic [15] is a turn-based multiplayer cooperative game where the goal is to stop spreading diseases on the map before the Pandemic occurs. The players need to cooperate to make decisions to win the game. **Gameplay:** The game starts with the spreading of infections. In one turn, the player needs to take action, which consists of three phases. Action-phase: the player needs to execute movement actions and the actions for treating/ discovering. Draw-phase: the player draws the cards that allow movement and cure actions from the player deck. Infection-phase: The player draws cards from the infection deck and the infection progress on the map. **Win/Lose conditions:** The game ends when one of the following lose conditions occurs. i). The player runs out of cards from the player deck, ii). all infection markers are set on the map and, iii). an outbreak occurred more than eight times (a city has more than three infection items which lead to a cascade spreading to adjacent cities). To win the game, players need to discover a cure for all diseases. The game is designed so that the more turns the players use, the higher the chances of losing the game by running out of cards or by the outbreak. The game design forces players to work cooperatively to discover cures for the diseases within limited game turns. The gameplay of Pandemic enforces players to cooperate in making the decision that is similar to the situation requires in urban logistics planning. Thus, the game is selected to be a reference game.

Phase2: Develop a Game Blueprint
We deconstructed the Pandemic game by using the ATMSG [4]. Based on the ATMSG methodology, we identified subjects and activities from the urban logistics scenarios. Then, we created the game blueprint that shows game elements' relations with the learning objectives follows ATMSG procedures (see Table 1).

Table 1. Game blueprint.

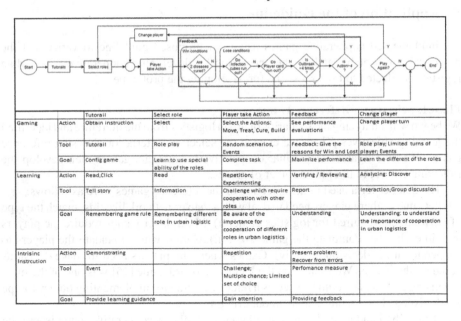

		Tutorail	Select role	Player take Action	Feedback	Change player
Gaming	Action	Obtain instruction	Select	Select the Actions: Move, Treat, Cure, Build	See performance evaluations	Change player turn
	Tool	Tutorail	Role play	Random scenarios, Events	Feedback: Give the reasons for Win and Lost	Role play; Limited turns of player; Events
	Goal	Config game	Learn to use special ability of the roles	Complete task	Maximize performance	Learn the different of the roles
Learning	Action	Read,Click	Read	Repetition; Experimenting	Verifying / Reviewing	Analyzing: Discover
	Tool	Tell story	Information	Challenge which require cooperation with other roles	Report	Interaction;Group discussion
	Goal	Remembering game rule	Remembering different role in urban logistic	Be aware of the importance for cooperation of different roles in urban logistics	Understanding	Understanding: to understand the importance of cooperation in urban logistics
Intrisinc Instrcution	Action	Demonstrating		Repetition	Present problem; Recover from errors	
	Tool	Event		Challenge; Multiple chance; Limited set of choice	Perfomance measure	
	Goal	Provide learning guidance		Gain attention	Providing feedback	

Phase3: Reframing Game Premise
We developed versions of the original Pandemic game for our user study and reduced it to only core mechanics. We downscale the mechanic of the original Pandemic game to ensure that the game can be played within 30 min, which is the requirement of the lecturers who will apply the game to the class. Consequently, we took out some game

elements, downsized the map from 48 nodes to 24 nodes. Then, we named the nodes as the street names of the city that conducted the user study. We changed the goal based on the urban logistics scenario. Thus, instead of discovering the cure, the goal is to solve traffic congesting and pollution by building Urban Distribution Center (UDC).

We reduce the number of achievements from 4 to 2. Game strategies were added into tutorials and embedded the learning contents derived from urban logistics scenarios. In addition to reducing the game's complexity, we added an option to introduce a subset of game mechanics of the additional game mechanics from the original. These elements would not affect the game's play but add the dramatic elements like a story mode required to make a stronger connection with the game premise. We used 3 of 5 roles from the original game related to the task and requirements of stakeholders in urban logistics, namely, operational expert, dispatcher, and medic role.

We modified the game premise, which is the setting behind the game, the name of the players' actions, and players' roles also need to be adapted as they are different from the original Pandemic game version.

Our learning goal is to understand the concept and relation of stakeholders in urban logistics. Thus, we applied urban logistics scenarios to the game. In the game, the players are the stakeholders in the city who are Mayor, Logistic Service Provider (LSP), and Shop owner. The players have to cooperate for solving the traffic congestion and pollution problems caused by delivering goods from manufacturers located outside the city (Table 2).

Table 2. Phased game element

Game elements	Naming of game element in different versions of games	
	Pandemic version	Urban logistics versin
Game actions	Treat	Release traffic jam
	Cure disease	Construct a UDC
	Build research station	Located a UDC Landmark
	Share knowledge	Share solutions
Other elements	Outbreaks rate	Pollution rate
	Infection rate	Procurment rate
	Epidemic card	Market Expansiiom
Roles	Medic	Shop owner
	Dispatcher	Logistics Service Provider (LSP)
	Operations expert	Mayor

In our design process, we mainly paid attention to alter the naming of the game elements (actions, roles of the players, phrasing in the tutorial) while keeping the game mechanics consistent across both game versions. The story mode is added before tutorial mode to show all stakeholders' roles, requirements, and relationships.

6 Game Validation

6.1 Measures

We measured improved players' scores to ensure that the game implemented follows our method achieves its intended purpose and outcome. To assess the learning improvement of players, we used a set of 15 multiple choice questions for measuring the knowledge of participants before and after the game session. The questions were derived from the learning objectives embedded in the game: 1). To understand the concept of urban logistics, 2). To understand the requirements of stakeholders in urban logistics, and 3). To understand the roles of stakeholders in urban logistics. There are five questions for measuring each objective.

We used the same set of questions to investigate memory retention. We asked the participants again after they joined the study for ten days. Additionally, we conducted a semi-structured interview with 14 inquiries related to their attitude and memorization regarding the learning content and game premises.

To explore the effect of the premise, we conducted a semi-structured interview with eight questions related to participants' attitudes toward the game premise and player roles and learning contents of the game after the play session for the first study.

6.2 Procedure

Two participants were randomly paired as a team in each session and randomly assigned to one game version. First, the participants were informed about the study and asked to complete a consent form followed by a demographic's questionnaire assessing their learning style, their experience with board games, digital games, and their current gaming habits. After that, participants were asked to fill out a personality test, and pretest (multiple choices) asked questions related to knowledge of concepts of urban logistics and the stakeholders. Subsequently, they performed the game session include a story mode, two parts of the tutorial. After completing the tutorial, the participants played the game in normal mode, then with special abilities. After finished playing two modes of the game, the subjects answered posttest. Finally, the examiner conducted a semi-structured interview by asking questions related to the premise and satisfaction of learning content.

Ten days after the first study had been completed, we asked the participants who are university students in the Logistics and Management class (n = 52) to join the second study to evaluate memory retention. The participants were asked to do pretest, perform game session, and posttest again for this session. In the end, the examiner conducted a semi-structured interview by asking questions related to memorization.

6.3 Participants

We recruited 74 students (46 female) who registered for Supply Chain Economics and Logistics (n = 52) and Management course (n = 22) in our study. Most subjects were between 18 and 34 years old.

6.4 Results and Analysis

We first conducted a paired sample t-test to indicate that our game design was successive in foster learning based on three learning objectives embedded in the game.

The results from the pretest (M = 6.32, SD = 3.12) and posttest (M = 7.47, SD = 2.75) indicate that the addition of premises can foster learning, $t(36) = 2.745$, $p = .008$.

After that, we investigated the effect of the game premise on memory retention by comparing two studies with ten days gap. Finally, we explored the impact of the game premise with player cooperation by measuring the number of cooperative actions that player takes in the game (as share action) and players conversation during the gameplay.

6.5 Effect of the Game Premise on Memory Retention

In the first round, we began by conducted paired sample t-tests (only student from Management course, n = 52) between the two rounds' overall pretest scores, posttest scores, and improved scores of all participants:

Pair 1: Pretest scores of round 1 and 2 (M = 2.25, SD = 3.15) The analysis revealed significant improvement in round 2, t(54) = 5.152, p = .000.
Pair 2: Posttest scores of round 1 and 2 (M = 0.808, SD = 308) The analysis revealed no-significant difference, t(54) = 1.89, p = .064.
Pair 3: Round 2's posttest scores and round 1's pretest scores (M = 3.135, SD = 2.82) The analysis revealed significant improvement in round 2, t(54) = 8.01, p = .000.
Pair 4: improved scores of round 1 and 2 (M = −1.442, SD = 4.18) The analysis revealed significant decrease or scores in round 2, t(54) = −2.49, p = .016 (Fig. 1).

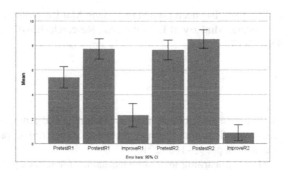

Fig. 1. The average score of pre and post test

6.6 Semi-structure Interview

In the second round of the study (after ten days), we asked participants *if they still remember the learning contents of the game? If yes, what reminds you of the learning contents?* We conduct a Chi-square test to examine the relation of the frequency of participants who answer *"Yes"* in the questions related to learning and memorization. The relation between these variables was significant, (4, N = 52) = 10.658, p = .031.

We then asked them to identify components/objects/phases in the game, reminding them of the contents. We found that 32 of 52 participants mentioned that Ability, Goal, and Story are the game components that recalled their memory. There are components derived from the game premise. Moreover, P34, P62, and P78 mentioned that playing a role as logistics stakeholders help them to remember the urban logistics planning conditions.

7 Conclusion and Future Work

We proposed the guideline for transform cooperative entertainment games into cooperative SGs. Our design method includes the set of guidelines that helps SGs development team to select existing cooperative entertainment games. The procedure is to develop an initial design (game blueprint) that shows the relation of learning and game elements and transfer entertainment premise to serious premise while keeping track of modified version. The main contribution is to provide method for converting the full-fledged game, then, modifying the game's premise instead of reusing elements/parts of the games, which is the regular practice for developing SGs. Our study was only a limited and primary study to evaluate our outline by measuring the learning improvement of players. In the next step, we want to assess the usability and usefulness of the design method with SGs designers and SGs programmers. Additionally, we will compare our approach with other approaches based on the issues. We showed the example of using our design method to implement an urban logistics game for learning. The findings showed that the developed game fulfills the learning purpose in understanding and memory retention of the players.

Acknowledgement. This work has been funded by Chiang Mai University and has been partly funded by the German Federal Ministry of Education and Research (BMBF) through the project DigiLab4U (No. 16DHB2113).

References

1. Antle, A.N., et al.: Futura: a design for collaborative learning and gameplay on a multi-touch digital tabletop. In: Proceedings of the Fifth International Conference on Tangible, Embedded, and Embodied Interaction, pp. 93–100 (2010)
2. Arnab, S., et al.: Mapping learning and game mechanics for serious games analysis. Br. J. Educ. Technol. **46**(2), 391–411 (2015). https://doi.org/10.1111/bjet.12113
3. Bellotti, F., et al.: Designing serious games for education: from pedagogical principles to game mechanisms. In: Proceedings of the European Conference on Games-Based Learning (2011)
4. Carvalho, M.B., et al.: An activity theory-based model for serious games analysis and conceptual design. Comput. Educ. (2015). https://doi.org/10.1016/j.compedu.2015.03.023
5. Deterding, S., et al.: Gamification: Using Game Design Elements in Non-Gaming Contexts
6. Fullerton, T.: Game Design Workshop: A Playcentric Approach to Creating Innovative Games. AK Peters/CRC Press, Boca Raton (2018)
7. Grudpan, S., Alexandrovky, D., Baalsrud Hauge, J., Malaka, R.: Exploring the effect of game premise in cooperative digital board games. In: van der Spek, E., Göbel, S., Do, E.-L., Clua, E., Baalsrud Hauge, J. (eds.) ICEC-JCSG 2019. LNCS, vol. 11863, pp. 214–227. Springer, Cham (2019). https://doi.org/10.1007/978-3-030-34644-7_17
8. Grudpan Supara Hauge, J.B., Malaka, R.: Playful training for understanding activities, roles, and stakeholder in urban logistics. In: Supply Chain Networks vs Platforms: Innovations, Challenges and Opportunities, pp. 306–315 (2019)

9. Kiili, K.: Call for learning-game design patterns. In: Educational Games: Design, Learning and Applications, pp. 299–311 (2010)
10. Lim, T., et al.: Narrative serious game mechanics (NSGM)--insights into the narrative-pedagogical mechanism. S. 23--34. In: Wiemeyer, J. (ed.) Games for Training, Education, Health and Sports. In: Proceedings of the 4th International Conference on Serious Games, GameDays, pp. 1–5 (2014)
11. Oksanen, K., Hämäläinen, R.: Game mechanics in the design of a collaborative 3D serious game. Simul. Gaming **45**(2), 255–278 (2014)
12. Proulx, J.-N., et al.: Learning mechanics and game mechanics under the perspective of self-determination theory to foster motivation in digital game based learning. Simul. Gaming **48**(1), 81–97 (2017)
13. Terzidou, T., Tsiatsos, T.: Designing a 3D collaborative game to support game based learning. In: Proceedings of the 5th European Conference on Games Based Learning, pp. 573–581 (2011)
14. Wendel, V., et al.: Designing collaborative multiplayer serious games. Educ. Inf. Technol. **18**(2), 287–308 (2013)
15. Z-Man Games, I.: Matt Leacock: Pandemic (2008)
16. Zagal, J.P., et al.: Collaborative games: lessons learned from board games. Simul. Gaming (2006). https://doi.org/10.1177/1046878105282279

Employing Social Interactions of Multiplayer Role-Playing Games in a Serious Game
The Case of maSters of AIR (SAIR)

Varvara Garneli[✉] and Konstantinos Chorianopoulos

Ionian University, Corfu, Greece
vgarneli@ionio.gr

Abstract. Collaborative games prompt players to work together, communicating, coordinating, and assisting each other; such features make them suitable for learning purposes. Although several suggestions have been made to design serious collaborative games, the RPGs' social interactions have not yet been explored in the context of science learning. This study evaluated a multiplayer game that integrates chemistry content in the gameplay mechanics of adventure games and RPGs. Twelve game testers participated in the evaluation process, constructing five groups: two groups of three persons and three groups of two. The players downloaded and installed the game on their computers, and then they played it. The results from the qualitative data confirmed that the clearly defined rules system facilitated teamwork through constant coordination and communication, making playing a pleasant experience. In addition, each player progressed his/her character through individual activities, promoting active collaboration in the missions' accomplishment. Thus, the social character of RPGs has the potential to support the design of collaborative learning settings.

Keywords: Collaborative games · Role-Playing games · Science education

1 Introduction

A collaborative learning setting promotes several interactions among the participants. Parameters, such as group size, group structure, role-based scenarios, rule systems, interactions' monitoring, and regulation, might increase the probability of triggering learning mechanisms [1]. On the other hand, collaborative games encourage players' interactions, focusing on teamwork, coordination, and assisting each other; such features make them suitable for teaching, training, and assessing. A collaborative game design should split the work among players, develop heterogeneous resources, assign distinct tasks and abilities, and encourage communication and teamwork [2]. In this direction, the potential of employing Role Playing Games (RPGs) features to promote interactions among players in an educational setting needs further exploration and evaluation.

RPGs are a popular game genre that has its roots in the 1970s. Multiplayer RPGs include various features that facilitate group work [3]. The Multiplayer Serious Game Methodology (MSGM) provides guidelines to integrate the educational content in the

© Springer Nature Switzerland AG 2021
F. de Rosa et al. (Eds.): GALA 2021, LNCS 13134, pp. 220–229, 2021.
https://doi.org/10.1007/978-3-030-92182-8_21

gameplay mechanics of adventure games and RPGs, blending the entertaining character of video games with collaborative learning techniques [4]. MaSters of AIR (SAIR) [5] is a multiplayer chemistry game designed according to MSGM guidelines. SAIR aims to motivate and enhance science learning to 14 years old students. The integrated educational content regards oxygen, an essential component of the atmospheric air. Therefore, SAIR encourages players to perform several game activities that promote group work. Additionally, personal growth and character progression are achieved through individual activities as the work is split to all members to acquire skills and resources. Finally, those unique players' achievements facilitate collaboration, as they relate with the missions' completion. Although MSGM guidelines emphasize the multiplayer character of the game in various ways, there is no evaluation of players who used the game.

This study aims to evaluate the multiplayer component of SAIR, a game that integrates chemistry content in the gameplay mechanics of RPGs. The experimental procedure included participants who read the online instructions [6], downloaded and installed the game to play it in groups of two or three persons. Participants worked from a distance, using their equipment. Players had to keep notes on the process, describing them, underlying difficulties, and suggesting improvements. Moreover, there were two synchronous sessions and constant asynchronous communication with the researchers to ask questions and solve technical problems. In addition, that gave additional data to the researchers to evaluate the process of downloading, installing, and connecting to the game. The significance of this assessment is great as the teachers' acceptance to implement a serious game in a typical learning setting is influenced by several factors, such as the need for technical and organizational support, training on using them, previous gaming experience, and more [7]. Therefore, this study:

[1]: evaluated the interactions among players while using the game
[2]: recorded potential difficulties that players might encounter
[3]: provided future improvements to the game design

2 Related Work

Designing digital games that can engage people in collaborative activities is a challenging process. Zagal [8] suggests the use of different roles and abilities that need coordination and decision-making. Another suggestion regards the use of quite tricky problems that need players to collaborate. Therefore, players must work together to share knowledge and resources and identify the best strategy to apply. Wendel [9] designed the "Escape of the Wilson Island," to underline the features of collaborative multiplayer games. The game employs requirements of the traditional single-player games, such as fun, narration, challenges of multiplayer games design, such as concurrent gaming, interaction, and finally, the serious game design, such as the inclusion of learning content. Nevertheless, extraordinary coordination is needed to solve the collaborative tasks.

From a different perspective, employing RPGs features could also support collaborative interactions among players. The "pen and paper" RPGs go back to the 1970s; players sit around a table, interacting with the game world through their characters. Another player undertakes the role of the game master, who is responsible for the game world beyond the players' characters. Playing the game involves verbal description by the players or by the game master. Written materials determine the rules, aims, and character descriptions. Finally, a character sheet describes the character in quantitative terms, allowing the character's progression. Pen and paper RPGs are social affairs; players often get together to spend time in role-playing activities with their friends and maximize their character's effectiveness in a structural context [3, 10]. Dillembourg's instructions [1] for designing adequate collaborative learning settings suggest using role-based scenarios and a clearly defined rule system.

On the other hand, digital RPGs have similarities and differences with pen and paper RPGs. Digital RPGs also provide players a virtual world to move and explore through their characters, in a freeway. Players still interact with the game world through interactions that include battles, dialogues, and object interactions. There is even the concept of the game master, one or more characters who control the game rules but in a quantitative way. A clearly defined rule system manages players' actions [3], facilitating collaboration [1].

3   Methodology

3.1   Research Design

The "maSters of AIR" (SAIR) is a chemistry game for three players. The multiplayer component was designed using the MSGM guidelines. The SAIR supports three different types of activities: individual, cooperative, and collaborative activities. Therefore, each player, through his Playable Character (PC), is assigned several individual activities. Responsible for those assignments are the Non-Playable Characters (NPCs) which guide players throughout the game. In addition, the individual activities reward PCs with skills stored in their inventories, increasing their growth with different skills (see Fig. 1).

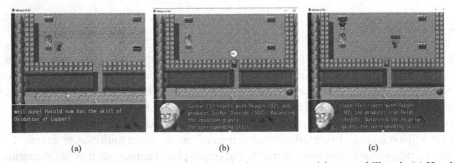

Fig. 1. Individual activities: players progress their characters, acquiring one skill each. (a) Harold acquired the copper oxidation skill. (b) Therese is assigned to balance the sulfur oxidation to acquire the sulfur oxidation skill. (c) Marsha is assigned to balance the iron oxidation

Those skills have a significant meaning as they empower collaboration in the game; the NPCs assign missions that require each character to use his/her individual skills to complete the assigned missions (see Fig. 2).

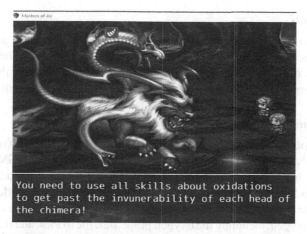

Fig. 2. Battles force players to collaborate, using their acquired skills to eliminate their enemy.

Additionally, some activities promote group work differently. In this viewpoint, PCs are on the same map, attending the same events. However, these cooperative activities have a free character meaning that one PC can perform the assigned tasks or watch the others complete them [4, 5] (Fig. 3).

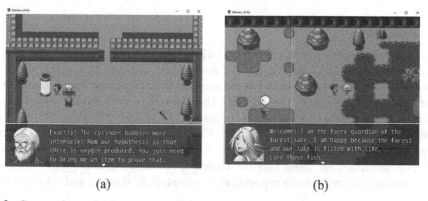

(a)   (b)

Fig. 3. Cooperative activities promote teamwork through coordination and communication. (a) Players observe the experiment. (b) Players walk in the forest to observe and learn content.

This study explored the interactions among players while they were performing the various game activities. Moreover, we assessed the process of downloading, installing, and connecting to the game. The evaluation was conducted in May 2021 in Greece. The research followed all necessary procedures to be in alignment with institutional rules and ethics.

3.2 Participants

We assessed the multiplayer component of SAIR with twelve master's degrees in "Digital Applications and Innovations" students (six females and six males). Their average age was 35.8 years old (SD = 8.03). Students optionally participated in the study. They constructed five groups: two groups of three persons and three groups of two.

3.3 The Chemistry Game

SAIR is a multiplayer educational game that integrates chemistry content in the gameplay mechanics of adventure and Role-Playing Games, according to the MSGM methodology guidelines. The integrated curriculum follows the policies of the introductory chemistry book [11]. In addition, the game connects the content with real-world applications, supporting meaningful collaborative learning. The integrated chemistry content regards the chapter on oxygen, including the oxygen properties, the oxides, and the combustions, as described in the introductory chemistry book [11]. The game can be used by students who are 14 years old or by people who would like to learn chemistry in an alternative way.

The game was developed with RPG MAKER MV, a role-playing game development engine published by Degica and developed by Kadokawa Games [12]. Instructions for installing and using the game are available online. Additionally, the game's code is available on the internet for further improvements, modifications, and content updating [6].

3.4 Procedure

We organized the game's evaluation in the following steps. First, we informed the participants about the content and the aim of the study. Then, we asked them to read the online instructions and download and install the game on their computer. Participants worked remotely due to the Covid-19 pandemic. Therefore, they followed the instructions to create a virtual network for two or three persons. We additionally suggested the use of online collaborative tools to communicate. Then, participants connected to those virtual networks to play the game. They kept notes of the process as well as the various problems they encountered. They could also use asynchronous communication tools or/and two synchronous sessions with the researchers to solve technical issues and ask questions.

3.5 Measures and Data Analysis

We based the evaluation process on the data from the participants' notes and their questions during the process. The researchers used these data to assess the game's installation and use, emphasizing the multiplayer component. Our first step was to remove all the personal information before digitizing them. Then, we performed an inductive content analysis to identify properties, attributes, and embedded patterns. Finally, we highlighted interesting phrases and discussed our data to develop the study's coding schema. In particular, this study explored three coding categories, social experience, technical issues, game use. Although the inductive analysis could give more coding categories, we did not use them as the age of participants was not appropriate to assess the educational perspective.

3.6 Results

The inductive content analysis of the qualitative data revealed some interesting coding patterns regarding the multiplayer component and its implementation in the SAIR's gameplay mechanics (see Table 1).

Table 1. Inductive content analysis

Coding categories	Description	Examples
Social experience	The way the game forces players to collaborate and cooperate	"All players must collaborate to complete an assigned mission" "The game did not provide an in-game communication tool, and therefore we needed to use other communication channels" "The game did not permit a single player to use it; one or two more players needed to join him/her"
Technical issues	Issues that occur due to the multiplayer component	"I could not join the game at a later time." We did know how to advance to the following map"
Game use	Game content, such as stats, names, and supplementary information that guides players	"I could not understand some game statistics, such as HP "I would like an introduction to my character and his/her role in the game." "I did not know the steps to leave the game without affecting the other players"

Participants underlined the need to connect two or three players in a virtual network to play the game (20%), while they also noticed the need for collaboration/coordination (56%) and communication (16%).

Although the participants' notes did not clearly describe the multiplayer game component, the various technical issues concerned connectivity. Furthermore, the coordination issue due to the multiplayer component appeared in 60% of the cases. For example, the "waiting players" warning message, meaning that one or more group members have not finished assigned tasks, so the others should wait for them (48%). In addition, 16% of them underlined the need for in-game communication. Finally, 56% mentioned technical problems to join the virtual network. Therefore, participants asked for better guidance in using the game, especially in the beginning (36%). Moreover, this guidance also concerned specific features, such as the battle feature (36%) or the characters and their statistics (20%).

4 Discussion

This study evaluated SAIR, a chemistry game for two or three players who want to practice introductory chemistry content. The evaluation process provided valuable insights into the potential of multiplayer digital games and RPGs elements in the context of science education.

4.1 Social Experience

Most participants clearly described SAIR as a digital chemistry game that "forces" two or three players to collaborate. They noticed from the beginning that "the game does not allow one player to start playing unless one or two more players join the game world. "On the other hand, some observations reflect the game's individual, cooperative, and collaborative activities that enrich the gameplay. For example, one participant realized that the game's instructions were not always the same as those of her peers". Individual cognition does not stop in peer interaction. Additional to the cognitive mechanisms that occur in collaborative settings, there are still individual activities, such as reading, building, predicting, and more, which trigger some learning mechanisms, such as induction, deduction, compilation, and more [1]. Individual activities are additionally crucial for the gameplay as they facilitate characters' evolution and collaboration. In particular, individual activities reward players with skills (character progression) to use them coordinately in the battle's challenge. Character progression and the battle challenge are basic RPGs features that can support collaboration [10]. Following the MSGM guidelines, collaborative activities facilitate group work, promoting players to assist each other [2]. Therefore, players "enjoyed working together as active members of the group." They were very excited, suggesting "the enrichment of the game with more activities that promote active participation."

The players relied on "constant communication and coordination" to advance the game plot and avoid unexpected game stops. "It was common sense that "one player's actions depended on the steps of the others". The game demanded coordination to complete the assigned missions, which included the battle challenges. They could not progress to the next level or eliminate an enemy unless they coordinated their effort. As a result, they all needed communication tools, suggesting in-game communication features to improve the gameplay. Meanwhile, all groups used familiar synchronous communication tools to play the game. Coordination and communication processes are essential in collaborative gameplays [8].

4.2 Technical Issues

The cooperative character of some activities prompted players to act as a group. In this case, all of them should participate in activities, such as taking instructions and observing experiments, meaning that they could not advance the game plot without their peers. The message "waiting players" appeared to point out this need. However, 48% of the players thought that the game unexpectable stopped, and they did not realize that some peers needed more time to complete an action (see Fig. 4). It seems that the game design needs to employ alternatives to improve this issue.

Fig. 4. Warning message

Players mentioned that "in case of not coordinated actions, they should start all over again," as the need for coordination influences the game track advancement. Players who use the SAIR must transfer all together to the following map [5]. Adventure games allow a serial game plot, according to the content of a book [2]. In this direction, the MSGM suggests the integration of the science's book educational content in the gameplay mechanics [4]. Therefore, the game design wants all players to move to the following map together. However, it seems that the "group traveling" needs a more careful design.

Another technical issue concerned the game battle, a collaborative activity that also requires coordination and communication to successfully eliminate an enemy. Such problems made the gameplay difficult for those who had no game experience. On the other hand, the groups that involved one player with such knowledge successfully managed to deal with such problems. Thus, previous gaming experience seems to be important in implementing a multiplayer game [7]. A way to deal with such issues is to structure heterogeneous groups that involve experienced and inexperienced players [1].

Some other technical issues concerned the failure of participants to reconnect to the virtual network or join it later. However, the game does not permit changes to the group's structure due to its collaborative learning character. Such issues need the host to save the game and restart the session with all participants.

4.3 Game Use

Most of the aforementioned technical issues made players ask for more instructions, especially regarding the battle's use, the characters' statistics and skills, and the gameplay. Players suggested some manageable levels, aiming to teach players the gameplay, the battle's process, and show to save their work for future use. Gee [14] argues that games include excellent methods to teach all players, even the inexperienced ones, how to play the game.

The last players' suggestion does not concern the multiplayer component. Instead, players underlined the luck of providing players with more information about their virtual character and its role in the game. They needed to feel more "connected to their character and even have the option to choose it". The players of digital RPGs move in the game world through their character, gaining new skills and abilities to overcome obstacles and fulfill their quests. Therefore, the game could employ a more prosperous storytelling element to connect players with their character and facilitate their progression [10].

4.4   Limitations and Future Work

The study presented in this paper has some limitations too. Although the evaluation process gave us evidence of the RPGs multiplayer component and its implementation in a serious game with science content, the game targets 14 years old students who learn introductory chemistry concepts. Therefore, we did not evaluate the influence of the multiplayer component on the learning experience and learning performance. Moreover, we assessed the game only remotely due to the Covid-19 restrictions. Nevertheless, we had the chance to have an overall picture of downloading, installing, and playing the game by groups of two or three persons.

Future work will improve SAIR, empowering the storytelling element to connect players with their characters and roles. Furthermore, manageable levels will be added to introduce players with the gameplay. Finally, the game needs an evaluation that involves 14 years old students and their teachers with the use of quantitative and qualitative methods, such as voice-chat or text-chat discussions analysis.

5   Conclusions

This study evaluated the multiplayer component of SAIR, which is a digital game for up to three persons. The game relies on complex gameplay that includes different types of activities which promote individual effort, character progression, coordination, and collaboration between players. Significantly, the collaborative activities need the active participation of all players. As a result, players enjoy working together in such pleasant environments, influenced by the RPGs elements.

References

1. Dillenbourg, P.: What do you mean by collaborative learning? In: Dillenbourg, P. (ed.) Collaborative-learning: Cognitive and Computational Approaches, pp. 1–19. Elsevier, Oxford (1999)
2. Wendel, V., Konert, J.: Multiplayer Serious Games. In: Dörner, R., Göbel, S., Effelsberg, W., Wiemeyer, J. (eds.) Serious Games, pp. 211–241. Springer, Cham (2016). https://doi.org/10.1007/978-3-319-40612-1_8
3. Hitchens, M., Drachen, A.: The many faces of role-playing games. Int. J. Role-playing 1(1), 3–21 (2009)
4. Garneli, V., Patiniotis, K., Chorianopoulos, K.: Designing multiplayer serious games with science content. Multimodal Technol. Interaction 5(3), 8 (2021). https://doi.org/10.3390/mti5030008
5. Garneli, V., Patiniotis, K., Chorianopoulos, K.: Game mechanics of a character progression multiplayer role-playing game with science content. In: Marfisi-Schottman, I., Bellotti, F., Hamon, L., Klemke, R. (eds.) GALA 2020. LNCS, vol. 12517, pp. 415–420. Springer, Cham (2020). https://doi.org/10.1007/978-3-030-63464-3_40

6. SAIR: A Multiplayer Chemistry Game. https://www.notion.so/SAIR-A-Chemistry-Multip layer-Game-bf4a108cc89440349e20658e54a0e6b9. Accessed 17 July 2021
7. Sánchez-Mena, A., Martí-Parreño, J.: Teachers acceptance of educational video games: a comprehensive literature review. J. e-Learning Knowl. Soc. **13**(2) (2017)
8. Zagal, J.P., Rick, J., Hsi, I.: Collaborative games: lessons learned from board games. Simul. Gaming **37**(1), 24–40 (2006)
9. Wendel, V., Gutjahr, M., Göbel, S., Steinmetz, R.: Designing collaborative multiplayer serious games. Educ. Inf. Technol. **18**(2), 287–308 (2013)
10. Costikyan, G.: Where stories end and games begin. Game Dev. **7**(9), 44–53 (2000)
11. Gymnasiou, C.B.: http://ebooks.edu.gr/ebooks/v/html/8547/2206/Chimeia_B-Gymnasiou_ html-empl/. Accessed 17 July 2021
12. RPG MAKER MV. https://www.rpgmakerweb.com/products/rpg-maker-mv. Accessed 17 July 2021
13. Hsieh, H.F., Shannon, S.E.: Three approaches to qualitative content analysis. Qual. Health Res. **15**(9), 1277–1288 (2005)
14. Gee, J.P.: What Video Games have to teach us about Learning and Literacy, 1st edn. Palgrave Macmillan, New York (2003)

Posters

Serious Game Rapid Online Co-design to Facilitate Change Within Education

Daisy Abbott[1]([✉]) [iD], Olga Chatzifoti[1] [iD], and Joanne Craven[2] [iD]

[1] The Glasgow School of Art, Glasgow, UK
d.abbott@gsa.ac.uk
[2] Edinburgh, UK

Abstract. Serious games have potential for facilitating change processes but require rigorous, interdisciplinary design to be effective. A novel, rapid online workflow was developed for co-design of games for change with school teachers. Major design challenges included: short timescale; appropriately scaffolding a complex process; remote online interactions; and interdisciplinary communication. The resulting workflow is highly visual, structured, and focused on swift knowledge exchange between pedagogy and game experts, drawing on relevant frameworks. Two workshops used the new method, producing eight co-designed serious games. Analysis suggests the workflow is effective for knowledge exchange for the rapid and rigorous co-design of serious games and has advantages for inclusivity and confidence in the co-design process.

Keywords: Serious games · Education · Online co-design · Game design

1 Introduction

Serious games are increasingly benefitting from co-design methods in their conception, design, and production. Co-design is a participatory method that involves all stakeholders and creates shared understanding between them as they participate in equally valuable yet diverse roles [1]. It is crucial to bridging disciplinary boundaries and improving the quality and effectiveness of serious games but there is little practical guidance on how exactly to achieve this goal. We present a new method for 'Serious Game Rapid Online Co-design' (SGROC) with school teachers, applied during the Agents of Change Toolkit (ACT) project [2] to produce eight serious games for change in schools. The workflow and serious games are freely available and represent a contribution to the field of serious games for educational contexts.

2 Background

Game-based learning has considerable potential for delivering both knowledge and behavioral outcomes, as is now widely recognized in the literature [3]. However, it

---

J. Craven—Independent Researcher.

© Springer Nature Switzerland AG 2021
F. de Rosa et al. (Eds.): GALA 2021, LNCS 13134, pp. 233–238, 2021.
https://doi.org/10.1007/978-3-030-92182-8_22

is also acknowledged that there are still significant challenges in developing games that are well situated in practice [4] and where game elements (mechanics, aesthetics, etc.) are appropriately linked with both learning behaviors and intended outcomes [5, 6], not least because of the highly interdisciplinary requirements of serious game design.

The Agents of Change Toolkit (ACT) facilitates teachers and schools to act as agents of change towards the UN Sustainable Development Goals (SDGs) [7] by leveraging serious games. Following recommendations from the literature, co-design with educators and school leaders was identified as the most fruitful approach [8, 9] and embedded throughout the project. Unfortunately, relatively little precise guidance exists to support the all-important linking of pedagogical foundations with game design in co-design methods, which risks ineffective serious games [10] and educators becoming over-whelmed by complexity [6]. Previous research by the authors explicitly addresses these challenges by marrying workflows suitable for game design novices [8, 11] with rigorous matching of learning and game mechanics [12]. However, in the context of COVID19 lockdowns, a need emerged for online co-design (OCD) activities. OCD is increasingly discussed in the literature with examples of general principles for OCD workshops [13, 14] but little related to educational game design. A rare exception presents a hybrid online/physical method for developing minigame prototypes over multiple sessions [15], noting the research gap in OCD for serious games.

3 Serious Game Rapid Online Co-design Method (SGROC)

In the context of the ACT project, the following needs were identified for co-design workshops with school teachers: online delivery; very low time commitment (2 h); familiar technologies; small collaboration groups; and a strong link between pedagogical outcomes, learning behaviors, and game design. In order to meet these needs and the wider goals of ACT, we adopted a 'lean' methodological approach, i.e. collaborating closely with intended users to produce a minimum viable prototype which could then be further developed. It was necessary to devise a method which combined OCD with rapid prototyping of serious games, with heavily scaffolded game design processes that co-designers could grasp and productively use in a very short time. This was achieved by expanding recommendations in the literature specific to OCD [13–15] and co-design with teachers [e.g. 1] and significantly developing the visual and structural guidance required to achieve such rapid results. In particular, the game design workflow supporting both novices and experts [8] was applied in this context and combined with the robust Learning Mechanic Game Mechanic framework [16] and gameplay loops [17] to achieve rigorous yet feasible prototypes. The Serious Game Rapid Online Co-Design (SGROC) workflow is summarized in Fig. 1.

Miro (miro.com) was selected as the most suitable whiteboard interaction platform, used alongside Virtual Classroom and Zoom videoconferencing. To sufficiently scaffold the co-design process [cf. 1] and provide individual attention, workshops were offered to small groups of six educators with three serious game experts facilitating the design of two prototype games each, acknowledged as an ambitious target. Recruitment used the project team's extensive network of educators, school leaders, and educational policymakers and events were shared publicly to increase access. Two workshops were run, each with a full complement of 6 participants (12 overall). The workshops were also attended by 2–3 members of the ACT project team.

In advance of the workshops, participants were asked to define a specific change they wanted to achieve in their school, relevant to one of the SDGs. Prior to the event, desired changes were grouped into complementary pairs and assigned to each game designer to create the most fruitful collaborations.

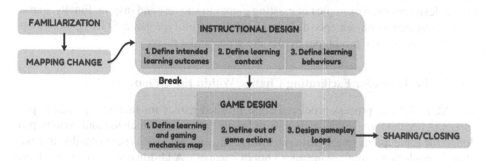

Fig. 1. Workshop protocol overview

As with any platform it was important to ensure that participants could concentrate on the content of the workshop rather than struggling with the controls [cf. 13]. To maximize engagement, the familiarization activity was intrinsically integrated with the workshop content; participants constructed a 'monster' representing their previously-defined change and its challenges, and annotated it using virtual sticky notes. To further orient the participants and save time, the whiteboard was meticulously set up for each group, with sticky notes and working areas color-coded and tagged with participants' names. All background and instructional elements were locked in place and clear labels provided for all icons and text that participants would be directly interacting with. This preparation was crucial in streamlining online interactions and keeping participants focused on content. All phases were illustrated with a worked example to provide inspiration, guidance, and continuity throughout the process.

The second short phase, Mapping Change, allowed the teachers to contextualize their own proposed change and align it with one or more of the SDGs.

The bulk of time was for rapid co-design, broken down into discrete tasks as shown in Fig. 1. The first phase, Instructional Design, built on the desired change and challenges from the familiarization phase to inform 1) the definition of brief Intended Learning Outcomes (ILOs); 2) clarify the learning context; and 3) experiment with a range of 'learning qualities' to allow the participants to get a sense of *how* the target audience would engage with the game or playful activity. Participants were offered a choice of learning verbs from Bloom's extended taxonomy [18] (as teachers were likely to already be familiar with this) and/or a Learning Qualities Framework developed specifically for this workshop (drawing on [8]) which supported participants in systematizing learning behaviors using a simple verb + adjective format. The verbs and/or qualities were then used to define a primary intended learning behavior for the game. This rigorously-defined learning behavior formed the basis of Game Design.

With the help of the game designers, participants used their instructional designs to identify and pair learning mechanics (LMs) and game mechanics (GMs) to construct an LM-GM map, following the procedure defined in [12, 16]. LMs were selected and annotated to explain the choice. Appropriate GMs were then linked to relevant LMs and annotated with how the GM would be used within the serious game. LM-GM maps were then used to brainstorm ideas for game prototypes which foregrounded the LM-GM pairings. Where time allowed, LM-GM pairs were formulated into gameplay loops [17]. Game designers used examples of existing games to suggest and inspire. Finally, participants produced a one-sentence description of their prototype game. SGROC workshops closed by sharing the prototypes across the group and a recap.

3.1   Eight Games for Facilitating Change Within Education

The ACT SGROC process produced eight finished games for facilitating change processes. After the workshops, games were briefly refined and finalized and content produced for game assets (e.g. question banks, cards, and boards). Where possible this was also via co-design with the educator (5 out of 8 games). Additional assets were produced where necessary (for example card sets, jigsaws, powerpoint) using original or Creative Commons art and crediting all creators. Each finished game document provides 1) a summary of the overall purpose; 2) any assets required; 3) how to play; 4) suggestions for different application areas which could also benefit from a similar LM-GM map and gameplay loop; 5) detail of the instructional design; and 6) gameplay loop annotated with LM-GM mappings [2]. The games are also contextualized in relation to the overall ACT project.

4   Discussion

On balance, the SGROC method provided advantages over face-to-face methods. Not requiring travel reduced the time commitment (particularly important for school teachers) and expanded our geographical reach. One participant had to drop out due to poor connectivity – this may have been exacerbated by the 'image heavy' familiarization exercise (which was then streamlined for the next event). Despite connectivity barriers, OCD is considered to be more inclusive for those with caring responsibilities or neurodiversity [19]. The care and attention given scaffolding the workflow was crucial to success, as was the choice of technologies appropriate to use from (often restricted) school premises. Acute time pressure provided a way to kick-start the complex process of serious game design, forcing swift collaborative decisions to produce a 'good enough' prototype. (The rapid games design approach for complex systems in the context of sustainability is discussed in [11].) Most of the games were further developed and/or tweaked after the workshop (varying between 1–4 h) to improve their gameplay and content. Furthermore, the highly scaffolded workflow was particularly useful when participants were working independently, increasing confidence and productivity. Participants provided very positive feedback at (and after) both workshops: e.g. "I just wanted to say a big thank you for a fascinating, gruelling but very productive and optimistic event". There was also evidence of considerable knowledge exchange within the interdisciplinary project team itself. Overall, the SGROC method achieved its design outcomes and contributes to OCD methods for serious games, as well as empowering educators as change agents. A formal evaluation of the SGROC workflow would provide deeper insights into user experience (across different roles) and goal attainment.

Unsurprisingly, as each arose from a specific desired change, the games are diverse: three highly structured games with associated assets, two loosely structured games, and three freeform playful and/or creative activities. Limited feedback on the games was gathered anonymously and thematically analyzed. Games were seen as useful, relevant, and understandable; suggested adaptations for (and adaptability of) games to individual contexts was considered very beneficial; games being contextualized within the change process was valuable; and the value of (and need for more) exemplification was noted. The Toolkit was launched in Sept 2021 and is being implemented within schools and teacher education degrees. A larger scale, systematic evaluation with users is needed to validate results and provide further insight (this is in progress).

5 Conclusion

The SGROC workflow provides a contribution with ongoing value to those undertaking rapid online games design with educators. Particular advantages of this method are: quick results; inclusivity; knowledge exchange; reduced demand on teacher time; genuine collaboration; and rigor. Main recommendations for successful use of the SGROC method are: use of blended spatiotemporal techniques to increase engagement, commitment, and rigor; meticulous preparation of online platforms; meaningful grouping of participants; meaningful familiarization activities; and a workflow structured to foreground each disciplinary expertise appropriately. This work was funded by the Scottish Universities Insight Institute. All of the games produced by the ACT project are freely available online [2] and the SGROC workshop template can be provided on request.

References

1. Dodero, G., Melonio, A., Gennari, R., Torello, S.: Gamified co-design with cooperative learning. In: Conference Human Factors Computing System – Proceedings, pp. 707–716 (2014). https://doi.org/10.1145/2559206.2578870
2. Pantić, N., Abbott, D.: Agents of Change. http://www.agentsofchangetoolkit.org/
3. Clark, D.B., Tanner-Smith, E.E., Killingsworth, S.S.: Digital games, design, and learning: a systematic review and meta-analysis. Rev. Educ. Res. **86**, 79–122 (2016). https://doi.org/10.3102/0034654315582065
4. Catalano, C.E., Luccini, A.M., Mortara, M.: Best practices for an effective design and evaluation of serious games. Int. J. Serious Games. **1**(1) (2014). https://doi.org/10.17083/ijsg.v1i1.8
5. Grey, S., Grey, D., Gordon, N., Purdy, J.: Using formal game design methods to embed learning outcomes into game mechanics and avoid emergent behaviour. Int. J. Game-Based Learn. **7**(3), 63–73 (2017)
6. Lameras, P., Arnab, S., Dunwell, I., Stewart, C., Clarke, S., Petridis, P.: Essential features of serious games design in higher education: linking learning attributes to game mechanics. Br. J. Educ. Technol. **48**(4), (2017). https://doi.org/10.1111/bjet.12467

7. United Nations Sustainable Development Goals. https://sdgs.un.org/goals
8. Abbott, D.: Intentional learning design for educational games : a workflow supporting novices and experts. In: Schmidt, M., Tawfik, A., Jahnke, I., Earnshaw, Y. (eds.) Learner and User Experience Research: An Introduction for the Field of Learning Design and Technology. EdTech Books (2020)
9. Marklund, B.B., Alklind Taylor, A.S.: Educational games in practice: the challenges involved in conducting a game-based curriculum. Electron. J. e-Learning. 14(2), 122–135 (2016)
10. Westera, W.: Why and how serious games can become far more effective: accommodating productive learning experiences, learner motivation and the monitoring of learning gains. Educ. Technol. Soc. 22, 59–69 (2019)
11. Lankford, B.A., Craven, J.: Rapid games designing; constructing a dynamic metaphor to explore complex systems and abstract concepts. Sustain. 12(17), (2020). https://doi.org/10.3390/su12177200
12. Lim, T., et al.: Strategies for effective digital games development and implementation. In: Baek, Y. and Whitton, N. (eds.) Cases on Digital Game-Based Learning: Methods, Models, and Strategies. pp. 168–198. IGI Global, Hershey, PA (2013)
13. Galabo, R., Nthubu, B., Cruickshank, L.: Redesigning a Workshop from Physical to Digital : Principles for Designing Distributed Co-design Approaches. Proc. Des. Vert. Horiz. Growth. (2020)
14. Davis, A., Wallace, N., Langley, J., Gwilt, I.: Low-contact co-design: considering more flexible spatiotemporal models for the co- design workshop. Strateg. Des. Res. J. 14, 124–137 (2021). https://doi.org/10.4013/sdrj.2021.141.11
15. Agbo, F.J., Oyelere, S.S., Suhonen, J., Laine, T.H.: Co-design of Mini Games for Learning Computational Thinking in an Online Environment. Springer, US (2021)
16. Arnab, S., et al.: Mapping learning and game mechanics for serious games analysis. Br. J. Educ. Technol. 46(2), 391–411 (2015). https://doi.org/10.1111/bjet.12113
17. Czauderna, A., Guardiola, E.: The gameplay loop methodology as a tool for educational game design. Electron. J. e-Learn. 17(3), 207–221 (2019). https://doi.org/10.34190/JEL.17.3.004
18. Anderson, L., Krathwohl, D.: A Taxonomy for Learning, Teaching, and Assessing: A Revision of Bloom's Taxonomy of Educational Objectives. Allyn & Bacon, Boston, MA (2001)
19. Batchelor, J.: Autistica play launches inclusive game jam. https://www.gamesindustry.biz/articles/2020-03-02-autistica-play-launches-inclusive-game-jam

The Hero's Lock Down: Differences in Learning Potential Between Linear and Non-linear Narratives in Serious Games

Fredrik Breien[1,2]([:envelope:]) [iD] and Christina Gkini[1,3] [iD]

[1] Centre for the Science of Learning and Technology, Bergen, Norway
[2] Department of Information Science and Media Studies, University of Bergen, Bergen, Norway
fredrik.breien@uib.no
[3] System Dynamics Group, Department of Geography, University of Bergen, Bergen, Norway
christina.gkini@uib.no

Abstract. Narratological models can be used to classify serious games as linear narratives, non-linear narratives, or non-narratives and enable an exploration of whether there are differences in evaluations of motivation, engagement and learning in narrative serious games that classify as either non-linear or linear. This paper uses the extended ludo narrative variable model (eLNVM) and its categories as identification criteria to uniquely classify serious games by their narrative structure. To investigate differences in self-reported effects on engagement, motivation, and learning, a dataset of 15 serious games has been classified. The results show differences in effectiveness with the non-linear narrative serious games evaluating better than the linear ones across the three effect types. This research provides recommendations related to what class of narrative to target in future serious games development and propose interesting grounds for future research to further detail the results presented.

Keywords: Narratological models · Digital game-based learning · Serious games classification · Serious games evaluation · Serious game design

1 Introduction

In serious games that include stories, some sort of narrative structure is always followed. The act of specifying storylines for serious games–events that occur from some beginning to some end–implicitly means that the storyline events and their content can be dissected in hindsight and categorized according to models found in narrative theory. Consequently, when analyzing serious games, it is possible to place their storylines inside narratological models, whether the designers are conscious of using these models or not. There are two main branches of narrative theory that can be employed to categorize stories in serious games. The first branch is classic narratology, which broadly consists of three-acts [1], five-acts [2], and monomythical models [3]. These classic narratology models (often used to describe narratives in books, movies, or theatrical plays), can be used to categorize the narrative component of all serious games that present sequential, non-optional, and predefined story elements to the observer. The second branch is

F. de Rosa et al. (Eds.): GALA 2021, LNCS 13134, pp. 239–244, 2021.
https://doi.org/10.1007/978-3-030-92182-8_23

ergodic narratology [4], defined as any narrative that is evolved by the observer's non-trivial actions. Using the extended Ludo Narrative Variable Model (eLNVM) [5], it is possible to categorize all serious games using ergodic narratological theory including both serious games that can already be categorized through classic narratology, and ones that cannot. This identifies two classes of serious game narratives 1) linear narratives that can be categorized using both the eLNVM and models from classic narratology, and 2) non-linear narratives that can only be categorized using the eLNVM.

Ludology, e.g., [6], is the science of describing digital games. Whether the tasks presented in digital games are cognitive (e.g., solving a puzzle), or motoric (e.g., making a timed maneuver), digital games can be defined as systems that require observer's non-trivial actions to solve challenges and reach objectives. Ergodic narratology is thus a form of ludology. The eLNVM has a particular category for serious games that have no narratives and is as such usable to categorize serious games that have no narratives just as well as ones that have them. This adds a third class of serious games, referred to as 3) non-narratives that can be categorized using the eLNVM, but not using classic narratological models, since these serious games are not stories. Non-narratives are not explored further in this research.

The objective of this research is to investigate the difference in reported effects on engagement, motivation, and learning from linear and non-linear serious games to derive recommendations for which of the two narrative classifications is preferable for designing serious games. In a previous research of effects from narratives in Digital Game-Based Learning (DGBL), 15 narrative serious games were categorized using the eLNVM [5]. This research further classifies these 15 serious games as either linear or non-linear narratives, and explores differences in self-reported effects on engagement, motivation, and learning between the two classifications. Recommendations on which narratological model should be used for designing future narrative serious games are derived.

2   Method

To explore if there are different effects found between the classes of linear and non-linear narrative serious games, a schema to unambiguously identify the serious games as one the two classes is developed based on the categories of the eLNVM (world, objects, agents, events). The schema is used for the classification of the 15 serious games. Subsequently, differences in reported effects between the groups of linear and non-linear narrative serious games are examined, before recommendations about what form of linearity best supports learning in serious games is presented.

3   Results

What separates linear from non-linear serious games is whether they can be categorized using classic narratological models. A serious game that can be categorized using both the eLNVM and classical narratological models can be classified as a linear narrative serious game, separating it from the non-linear narratives. To develop a schema on which linear and non-linear narrative serious games can unambiguously be separated from one another, this research explores the eLNVM to identify the combinations of its categories that describe serious games that can also be categorized using classic narratology. Differentiating a game that is a narrative from one that is not is determined by how it categorizes on the events ontology of the eLNVM. A game that categorizes as 'No kernels' is not a narrative. Any game that categorizes as any other type under the events ontology is classified as a narrative serious game, linear or non-linear.

In the eLNVM, the *agents* ontology concerns itself with the detail in which story characters are described. The *objects* ontology concerns itself with what the observers can use the objects for: from simply observing them, to inventing them. Since any story, classic or ergodic, can contain characters described from rich detail to the stereotypical and beyond, and since any story can allow for objects ranging from ones that characters cannot use to ones that they invent themselves, these dimensions are not suitable for distinguishing non-linear from linear narratives. Thus, the *world* and the *events* ontologies need to be used to identify the classification. Tables 1 and 2 show the categories of the world and events ontologies, and whether it can be categorized using classic narratological models.

Table 1. The world ontology

Category	Categorizable using classic narratology
Inaccessible	Yes
Single room	Uncertain[a]
Linear corridor	Yes
Multicursal labyrinth	No, is not sequential, and/or is optional
Hub shaped quest landscape	No, is not sequential, and/or is optional
Open landscape	No, is not sequential, and/or is optional, and/or is dynamic

[a]The single room category is ambiguous, since it can be structured as inaccessible, where the room is the story backdrop, or open landscape, where the world is confined in a room but where options still are free. Single room serious games must be classified individually.

Table 2. The events ontology

Category	Categorizable using classic narratology
Fully plotted	Yes
Linear fixed kernels, dynamic satellites	Yes[b]
Interchangeable fixed kernels, dynamic or fixed satellites	No, is not sequential, and/or is optional
Dynamic kernels	No, is not predefined
No kernels	No, is not a story

[b]Whereas the kernels dictate the important story elements in a narrative, the satellites concern themselves with details that are not necessary to classify the narrative. Linear fixed kernels adhere to what can be categorized using classic narratology; satellites can be disregarded since they do not need to be there at all.

As shown in Tables 1 and 2, any narrative serious game categorized under the eLNVM as either multicursal labyrinth, hub shaped quest landscape, or open landscape under the world ontology, as well as interchangeable fixed kernels, or dynamic kernels under the events ontology, breaches with the characteristics of classic narratology, and cannot thus be categorized using classic narratological models. Therefore, a serious game that categorizes as at least one of those, can be classified as a non-linear narrative serious game. Conversely, a serious game that categorizes as inaccessible, or linear corridor under the world ontology, and fully plotted, or linear fixed kernels under the events ontology can be categorized using classic narratological models and can therefore be classified as a linear narrative serious game. Finally, serious games categorized as single room worlds must first be re-categorized as either inaccessible or open landscape before they can be classified as either linear or non-linear. Table 3 summarises the identification criteria used to classify serious games' narratives.

Table 3. Identification criteria for serious game narrative classification

Identification criteria	Serious game type
World = (inaccessible OR linear corridor) AND Events = (fully plotted OR linear fixed kernels)	Linear
World = (multicursal labyrinth OR hub shaped quest landscape OR open landscape) OR Events = (interchangeable fixed kernels OR dynamic kernels)	Non-linear
World = (No Kernels)	Non-narrative
World = (Single room)	Determine inaccessible OR open landscape, then re-identify

To explore if there are different effects reported between classes of linear and non-linear narrative serious games, a dataset of 15 narrative serious games that have previously been categorized on the eLNVM and evaluated for effects on engagement, motivation, and learning [5] is utilized. The serious games are classified using their eLNVM categorizations and Table 3 as a classification schema. This reveals eight non-linear narrative serious games and seven linear ones.

For the linear narrative serious game class, from a total of 18 measures performed in evaluations, only eight show positive effects, and two of the effects reports as negative. Only two of the seven linear narrative serious games show positive effects on all measures, and only three of them reveal positive effects on learning, with one showing negative effects. In the non-linear narrative serious games group, 17 out of the total 18 measures performed in evaluations show positive effects, with only one measure for one serious game evaluating to a neutral effect. Seven of eight non-linear narrative serious games show positive effects on all performed measures, and seven of eight also show positive effects on learning. Table 4 presents positive measures as percentage of all reported measures, as well as the percentage of serious games in the dataset which report effects, for each class and in total.

Table 4. Summary of positive effects reported and percentage of measures between classes of narrative serious games.

	Engagement		Motivation		Learning		Total effects	
	Positive	Games measured	Positive	Games measured	Positive	Games measured	Positive	Games measured
Linear	60%	71%	33%	85.70%	42.90%	100%	44.40%	85.70%
Non-linear	100%	87.50%	100%	37.50%	87.50%	100%	94.40%	75%
Total	83.30%	80%	55.50%	60%	66.70%	100%	69.40%	80%

4 Discussion

This paper has identified that serious games are narratives of one of tree classes; 1) linear narrative, 2) non-linear narrative, and 3) non-narrative. 15 serious games have been classified as either linear or non-linear narratives and have been explored for their self-reported effects on engagement, motivation, and learning, indicating that the non-linear serious games perform better than the linear ones on all measures.

The dataset of narrative serious games evaluated for this research is limited, especially in relation to reported measures in effects on motivation and, to some extent, engagement. To solidify and extend this research and its findings, larger datasets of narrative serious games should be evaluated and classified by their narrative types. While the games evaluated in this research did not include any non-narrative serious games, it might be interesting to explore these as well to see their reported effects and be able to compare their result to the narrative groups. It would also be interesting to identify different sub-classes of non-linear narrative serious games. This could be used to further explore if serious games using non-sequential, optional, or dynamic events differ from each other in reported effects. Furthermore, given the less positive effects shown to incur from the linear narrative serious games, it would be interesting to compare those findings to similar findings from traditional linear narrative learning media, such as films and books to explore if serious games are more inhibited by linear storylines than other learning media.

Previous reviews of narratives in serious games show that they can have positive effects on engagement, motivation, and learning, but that they often do not (e.g., [7–9]). By classifying narrative models that are available in serious games, isolating them, and exploring their reported effects inside the individual classes, this research shows that separating linear narrative serious games from the dataset allows for a clear pattern of positive effects among the remaining non-linear narrative ones. Since a large number of serious games use linear narratives, it may be speculated that mixed results reported in previous research can be attributed to the mix of narrative classes being investigated, and that the evaluation of serious games could benefit from their prior narrative classification. This initiates a discussion on how narratives in DGBL should be modelled to reach the potential of the effects from them.

5 Conclusion

After comparing the classes of narrative serious games identified in this research, it can be concluded that using classic narratological models as basis for storylines might not be a good idea. The results indicate that opting for non-linear narratives is a better strategy to ensure positive effects on engagement, motivation, and learning in players of the serious game. This research has provided initial evidence that linear narrative serious games evaluate differently from non-linear ones, which may indicate that mixed effects reported in previous reviews of narratives in serious games may be attributed to the treatment of all narrative serious games as a single class. Distinguishing the classifications of narratives in serious games can help better understand how and under what conditions narratives have effects in serious games, and the eLNVM has proven a useful tool for this purpose. This research is an extension of ongoing research on the development of a design framework for serious games called eLuna.

References

1. Aristotle, Butcher, S.H.: Aristotle's Poetics, Hill and Wang, New York (1961)
2. Freytag, G., et al.: Freytag's Technique of the Drama: An exposition of Dramatic Composition and Art, S.C. Griggs & Company, Chicago (1895)
3. Campbell, J.: The Hero with a Thousand Faces. The Hero with a Thousand Faces, Pantheon Books, pp. xxiii, 416-xxiii, 416 (1949)
4. Aarseth, E.J.: Cybertext: Perspectives On Ergodic Literature. Johns Hopkins University Press, Baltimore, (1997)
5. Breien, F.S., Wasson, B.: Narrative categorization in digital game-based learning: engagement, motivation & learning. Br. J. Edu. Technol. **52**(1), 91–111 (2021)
6. Juul, J.: Half-Real: Video Games Between Real Rules and Fictional Worlds, The MIT Press, Cambridge (2005)
7. Connolly, T.M., et al.: A systematic literature review of empirical evidence on computer games and serious games. Comput. Educ. **59**(2), 661–686 (2012)
8. Clark, D.B., Tanner-Smith, E.E., Killingsworth, S.S.: Digital games, design, and learning: a systematic review and meta-analysis. Rev. Educ. Res. **86**(1), 79–122 (2016)
9. Novak, E.: A critical review of digital storyline-enhanced learning. Educ. Tech. Res. Dev. **63**(3), 431–453 (2015). https://doi.org/10.1007/s11423-015-9372-y

How to Design Personalized Challenges for Mobile Motivational Systems? Ask Your Players!

Scanagatta Mauro[(⊠)] and Marconi Annapaola

Fondazione Bruno Kessler, Via Sommarive 18, Povo, Italy
{mscanagatta,marconi}@fbk.eu

Abstract. Gamification techniques have proven to be effective in inducing positive changes in the user's behavior. However, their difficulty has to be carefully calibrated to avoid both frustration and boredom. We present a novel algorithm for automatic challenge generation, calibrated from players' opinions and evaluated in the context of a large-scale and long-running sustainability urban mobility game. The results suggest that our methodology was effective in increasing player participation and performance.

Keywords: Gamification · PCG · DDA · Challenge generation

1 Introduction

Gamification techniques have proven to be effective in inducing positive changes in the user's behavior [5,7,9,10]. However, a crucial aspect of these applications is the user's long-term participation. To be truly effective, the promoted behavioral change must be sustained over time.

The gamification technique of *Challenges*, which proposes a demanding but achievable goal and rewards its completion, have empirically proven effective to keep players' interest alive and to sustain their engagement over time [11]. However, the effort required for the periodic manual generation of those playable units by the game designers would be unfeasible. Instead, we tackle this problem through Procedural Content Generation (PCG) [8]. Furthermore, the automatic generation of challenges offers the opportunity to dynamically calibrate the *difficulty* of each goal to the player's performances, as it should increase as the player's skills increase [3].

To reach this objective, we decided to devise a novel algorithm for calibrating it on the players' opinions. We collected their answers to a dedicated *visual* questionnaire, asking them to give a numeric target for the challenge goal to issue to a player, basing their judgment on a graph of its past performances.

We evaluated the proposed approach in the context of a large-scale and long-running sustainable urban mobility campaign, supported by a gamified mobile

© Springer Nature Switzerland AG 2021
F. de Rosa et al. (Eds.): GALA 2021, LNCS 13134, pp. 245–251, 2021.
https://doi.org/10.1007/978-3-030-92182-8_24

App. We found statistically significant higher levels of player's participation, engagement, and performances.

The presented approach can be easily generalized, and can be directly applied to any other gamification application which bases user advancement on its performance.

2   Related Work

Recent studies aimed at understanding which factors play a role in whether gamified applications are successful [13]. These studies revealed that a key aspect is tailoring the game experience to the player's preferences and capabilities [1,7,15]. However, the field of adaptive gamification is still young and growing, especially for what concerns dynamic adaptation [6].

According to [12], an "ideal game should be able to adjust its difficulty dynamically governed by the player's performance". A solution is to exploit personalization techniques. Procedural Content Generation (PCG) [8] is a set of techniques designed to automate the construction of Game Design Elements (GDEs), such as game items, encounters, buildings, or even whole levels. This allows reducing repetition, which is usually perceived negatively.

Special attention must be given to the calibration of the difficulty of the game. "Given that both failure and success can become repetitive quickly, games must address the problem of meeting all players with the correct level of challenge" [14]. Rather than rewarding only with points and badges, there is the need to provide opportunities for the player to succeed in a game by overcoming challenges [2]. The difficulty calibration has the objective of keeping players engaged, following the concept of *flow*: the balance between challenge and competence, or between complexity and boredom [4].

A compelling solution is offered by Dynamic Difficulty Adjustment (DDA), defined as a method for automatically modifying a game's features, behaviors, and scenarios in real-time, depending on the player's skill so that the player does not feel bored when the game is very simple, or frustrated when it is very difficult [16].

3   Application Context

We implemented our approach in the context of Play&Go, a gamified application whose purpose is to induce a Voluntary Travel Behavior Change (VTBC) towards more sustainable mobility habits. The game aims to promote CO_2-free means of transportation and public transportation. This project was performed annually starting from 2015. In the last edition, it was conducted over 28 weeks, starting in October 2019 and ending in August 2020 (the COVID-19 pandemic forced a temporary interruption of the game lasting from March to June).

To incentive players, the app assigns points depending on the number of kilometers tracked and on the level of sustainability of the transportation mean (walking, bike, bus, and train).

To further incentivize players and to keep them engaged, personalized weekly *challenges* were recently introduced [11] in the game. The challenge's goal was set as the result of multiplying the performance observed during the last week with a fixed improvement factor of 1.3. This technique has been proven effective to keep players' interest alive and to sustain their engagement over time.

However, this approach was shown to become quickly unfeasible for new players, as the goal after few weeks inevitably grows outside the ability of the player to reach it. Furthermore, this approach showed low adaptability to changes in the performance of a regular player.

4   Difficulty Calibration Design

To devise a more advanced approach for automatic challenge generation, we first reflected on the opportunity of taking into account not only the player's performance on the last week, but also on the previous weeks. Thus taking into consideration also changes in the player's usual performance.

We decided to directly involve Play&Go players and elicit from them what an "appropriate" improvement should be asked. To this extent, we designed a questionnaire that would help us understand the range of improvement that we should expect from a player. We feared that eliciting an answer from a written description would have resulted in a high level of confusion, so we decided instead to provide the players a *visual* representation of the question. We choose to use graphs, which showed a time series of six values, representing the past weekly performance of a player in a performance indicator (a mean of transportation).

In total, we produced nine graphs. Their point values were taken from real data, and they were chosen to represent all types of possible performance progression. Each player received a questionnaire with a randomly shuffled graphs order.

We submitted the questionnaire directly to the players of the game, during the 2018–19 edition of the game. To incentivize them to complete it, a small number of in-game points were awarded for filling it. The questionnaire was presented only to players that had reached at least the first level - so we could ensure that the respondents were all aware of the game and its mechanics, and actively engaged in it. In total, 98 players submitted the questionnaire. Their age were within the range of 20 to 60, and the male/female ratio was 54%/46% (in line with the whole players' statistics).

We asked each player to give a numeric target for the *correct* challenge goal to issue to that particular player, taking into account only the six weeks window of its past performance. Players were also able to give a short description of their thought processes.

4.1   Calibration Design

The next step was to find a function able to approximate the opinions expressed in the collected responses. By its definition, a challenge requires an increment of the player's efforts. So we chose to model the challenge prediction as $C = P * I$, where C is the goal of the challenge, P is the prediction of the player's efforts, and I is the improvement. We choose to model it as a linear function to be of easy interpretation; as a future work other functions could be assessed.

We considered the following *extrapolation* functions: Linear, Polynomial, Conic, Moving Average, Weighted Moving Average. All methods were tested taking into consideration several previous points in the range [2,5] meaning basing the prediction on the player's performance of the past two weeks, three weeks, etc. up to five. This was motivated by observing the descriptions of the thought process of the respondents: more than 90% of them reported that their rationale for deciding the goal of the challenge took into account not only the last reported performance, but a set of them, going from the last two to the last six.

The functions were evaluated by comparing the difference of their outcome to the mean responses of the questionnaire, using the MAPE (mean absolute percentage error) as an error function, since the graphs pertained to different performance indicators with different ranges. In the end, the lowest MAPE (25.61) was found with the combination of WMA-5 as the prediction function (Weighted Moving Average over the last 5 recorded levels of performance), and $I = 1.3$, corresponding to an increase of 30% over the predicted player performance. Being the function that was closest to the average responses of the questionnaire, we chose it for automatically computing the goal of the procedurally generated challenges.

5   Evaluation

We employed the proposed approach during the last edition of the Play&Go game. The edition started on 26th October 2019. It was originally planned to end on 15th May 2020, corresponding to 28 weeks of total playtime. The game was put on hold on 10th March 2020 due to the COVID pandemic, at the 20th week. It was resumed on 20th June 2020, lasting for the final eight weeks and ending on 14th August 2020.

Our goal was to analyze the improvement brought by our novel approach for dynamic difficulty adjustment of the challenges' difficulty. To this end we modeled an A/B test, dividing the players into two groups (treatment and control). For each player, the evaluation started when she/he reached the first level (meaning the player showed a minimal amount of interest in the game), and the evaluation ended after six weeks from that moment.

We ensured that each player had exactly 50% of probability of being assigned to either group, but also that the two groups had the same size. In the end, we had 84 players assigned to the control group, and 83 assigned to the treatment one.

Each week, for each player still undergoing the evaluation (less than six weeks of active game), we computed the challenges using two different approaches.

For the *control* group we used the traditional approach: the goal was directly computed using the performance observed during the last week with a fixed improvement factor of 1.3. This correspond to the strategy based on expert opinion previously employed. For the *treatment* we used our novel approach. After six weeks of relative game, the evaluation ended and all players were switched to the novel approach.

COVID Impact: The evaluation was ended after 11 weeks from the start of the game, having observed that no new players were starting to play. Thus the COVID pandemic did not impact the evaluation, since the first Italian national lockdown occurred on the 20th week of absolute playtime.

5.1   Comparison

We first compare the mean difficulty of the challenges proposed - to rule out that any following result is due to the challenges generated by the novel approach to be simply easier or harder. We find that the difference in difficulty is not statistically significant (Unpaired t test, p-value = 0.645). We observed that the mean difficulty during the first week was higher, since the players were starting to play, but quickly converged to a stable value around 1.35.

We then compared the *choice rate* of the challenges, as the main objective of this work was to improve player's engagement in the game. When the player reached a fixed level they were proposed a set of challenges, and were able to choose their challenge for the next week. If the player didn't make a choice, the system would automatically choose one challenge for them. The *choice rate* measures the percentage of active players that did choose their challenge. We observed a higher choice ratio for the treatment group on the initial six evaluation weeks (Unpaired t test, p-value = 0.0132).

We then compared the *completion rate* of the challenges - that is the percentage of challenges that were successfully completed. During the first weeks, the completion rate overall degraded, probably due to the novelty of the game wearing off. Nevertheless, we observed a higher completion rate for the treatment group on the initial six evaluation weeks (Unpaired t test, p-value = 0.0256).

We then compared the player's *performances* for each indicator available in the game during the first 6 weeks. We observed a higher overall recorded performance for the treatment group in 4 out of 5 of them. The indicators were: the total number of kilometers recorded by walking (Unpaired t test, p-value = 0.0315), biking (Unpaired t test, p-value = 0.0295), bus (Unpaired t test, p-value = 0.0102) or the train, or the number of game points collected (Unpaired t test, p-value = 0.0413).

Interestingly, for *Train km* we did not observe a statistically higher performance for the treatment group. This is probably due to the fact the performance mostly depended on the daily commute between home and workplace, and there were little room for enhancing personal improvement.

5.2   Limitations and Future Work

We evaluated the novel approach in the initial part (6 weeks) of the relative player's experience. While we found a significant difference regarding players participation, engagement, and performances, a longer evaluation should be performed to validate these results for the whole players' game experience.

The main contribution of this work is that the presented approach can be easily generalized, and can be directly applied to any other gamified application which bases player advancement on its performance. Further evaluations in new contexts should be performed to validate the presented results.

Finally, the class of functions considered for approximating the intentions expressed in the collected responses were purposely kept very simple to be of easy interpretation. More complex functions could be considered to better capture the player's opinions.

6   Conclusion

We introduced a novel approach for the automatic generation of personalized challenges in a mobile gamified system, whose purpose is to promote sustainable mobility behaviors. The difficulty of each challenge is calibrated on each player's past performances. The algorithm was calibrated using the players' answers to a *visual* questionnaire, designed to understand the range of improvement that we should expect from a player. The evaluation results suggest that the novel approach was effective in inducing an improvement in players' participation, engagement, and performance within an urban mobility gamified application.

References

1. Aldenaini, N., Alqahtani, F., Orji, R., Srinivas, S.: Trends in persuasive technologies for physical activity and sedentary behavior: a systematic review. Front. Artif. Intell. 85 (2020)
2. Charles, D., Kerr, A., McNeill, M., McAlister, M., et al.: Player-centred game design: player modelling and adaptive digital games. In: Proceedings of the Digital Games Research Conference, vol. 285 (2005)
3. Csikszentmihalyi, M.: Finding flow: The Psychology of Engagement with Everyday Life. Basic Books, New York (1997)
4. Csikszentmihalyi, M.: Flow and the Foundations of Positive Psychology, Springer, Dordrecht (2014). https://doi.org/10.1007/978-94-017-9088-8
5. Gabrielli, S., Forbes, P., Jylha, A., et al.: Design challenges in motivating change for sustainable urban mobility. Comput. Hum. Behav. **41**, 416–423 (2014)
6. Hallifax, S., Serna, A., Marty, J.C., Lavoué, G., Lavoué, E.: Factors to consider for tailored gamification. In: Proceedings of the Annual Symposium on Computer-Human Interaction in Play, pp. 559–572 (2019)
7. Hamari, J., Koivisto, J., Sarsa, H.: Does gamification work? a literature review of empirical studies on gamification. In: 47th Hawaii International Conference on System Sciences (2014)

8. Hendrikx, M., Meijer, S., Van Der Velden, J., Iosup, A.: Procedural content generation for games: a survey. ACM Trans. Multimedia Comput. Commun, Appl. **9**, 1–22 (2013)
9. Holleis, P., Luther, M., Broll, G.E.: Tripzoom: a system to motivate sustainable urban mobility. In: 1st International Conference on Smart Systems, Devices and Technologies (2019)
10. Kazhamiakin, R., Marconi, A., Perillo, M., et al.: Using gamification to incentivize sustainable urban mobility. In: First International Smart Cities Conference (2015)
11. Khoshkangini, R., Valetto, G., Marconi, A., Pistore, M.: Automatic generation and recommendation of personalized challenges for gamification. In: User Modeling and User-Adapted Interaction, pp. 1–34 (2020)
12. Missura, O., Gärtner, T.: Player modeling for intelligent difficulty adjustment. In: Gama, J., Costa, V.S., Jorge, A.M., Brazdil, P.B. (eds.) DS 2009. LNCS (LNAI), vol. 5808, pp. 197–211. Springer, Heidelberg (2009). https://doi.org/10.1007/978-3-642-04747-3_17
13. Nacke, L.E., Deterding, S.: The maturing of gamification research. Comput. Hum. Behav. **71**, 450–454 (2017). https://doi.org/10.1016/j.chb.2016.11.062
14. Pagulayan, R.J., Keeker, K., Wixon, D., et al.: User-centered design in games. In: The Human-computer Interaction Handbook, CRC Press, Boca Raton (2002)
15. Seaborn, K., Fels, D.I.: Gamification in theory and action: a survey. Int. J. Hum.-Comput. Stud. **74**, 14–31 (2015)
16. Zohaib, M.: Dynamic difficulty adjustment (DDA) in computer games: a review. Advances in Human-Computer Interaction 2018 (2018)

Puzzle Battle 2.0: A Revisited Serious Game in VR During Pandemic's Period

Gianni Viardo Vercelli, Saverio Iacono, Mario Vallarino, and Daniele Zolezzi[✉]

Università degli Studi di Genova – DIBRIS, Genoa, Italy
{gianni.vercelli,saverio.iacono}@unige.it, {mario.vallarino,
daniele.zolezzi}@edu.unige.it

Abstract. Puzzle Battle 2.0 is a Serious Game in Virtual Reality created within the 3D Lab Factory. It is the second version of puzzle game created in 2017 to teach art history. The goal was to complete all the proposed paintings to collect them in a personal museum. The COVID-19 epidemic has generated an increase in the earnings of the videogame sector but also brought many experiences designed to be enjoyed in specific places to be unusable. This article proposes a redesign of the original project to make available even at a distance an experience that until now had only been used in a VR Corner.

Keywords: Virtual reality · Serious games · Cultural heritage

1 Introduction

1.1 Gaming World During COVID-19 Pandemy

The videogame was the mass media that benefited most from the global COVID-19 pandemic. The inability to leave our houses combined with the closure of other forms of entertainment such as cinemas and theaters, have pushed people to invest in the gaming industry to seek a home entertainment capable of eliminating boredom dictated by isolation.

Based on data provided by Statista.com, during the week between 16 and 22 March 2020, therefore at beginning of the lockdown phase in most countries, 4.3 million video games were sold worldwide for a total increase sale of 63% compared to the previous week [1]. The Virtual Reality (VR) sector has also benefited from the lockdown. The data provided by the market analysis company [2] predicted at the end of November 2020 that 6.4 million headsets would be sold by the end of the year and the overall gain related to VR experiences would have exceeded the 1.1 billion dollars mark [3].

The constant rise of the videogame as a medium able to teach and tell stories combined with the great sales that help his expansion have led us to reformulate some videogames experience that in the era of COVID-19 need to be modernized in order not to risk being unusable. The main example are the VR corners, Virtual Reality installations designed to be available only in certain places such as museums or exhibitions. If on one side the public is increasingly accustomed to the use of Virtual Reality games and Head Mounted Displays (HMD) are increasingly entering users' homes, on the other side many experiences have remained closed and unusable due to the lockdown.

F. de Rosa et al. (Eds.): GALA 2021, LNCS 13134, pp. 252–257, 2021.
https://doi.org/10.1007/978-3-030-92182-8_25

1.2 State of Art

Technology has made possible to create increasingly dynamic, photorealistic and ultra-detailed virtual worlds that increase the perception of total presence of users within Virtual Reality. Being placed in an environment that can be conditioned directly by our choices and the active involvement of our body leads us to feel part of what surrounds us, perceiving it as a credible alternative world. The use of HMDs, since the dawn of the sector, has been a key element for the definition of the concept of presence within the VR's environment that allows us to explain how it is possible to feel inside an environment on the comparison of experiences lived in the everyday world and in a world mediated and presented through technology [4].

The sharp drop in the prices of the hardware used in VR had made it possible to land this technology outside the military and academic world which were the initial main areas of development. Serious Games in Virtual Reality offer a different solution to learning and training. High-immersive VR experiences have been developed in teaching numerous subjects such as language, math, health, computer science etc. leading to concrete results thanks to the ease with which users are able to visually understand the concepts proposed, reducing the possibility of misunderstandings, and the general excitement that the public has towards a technology that is still perceived as new [5]. Serious Games overturn the traditional teaching approach in which the teacher is the cornerstone of teaching and the students are mere listeners. Users immersed in the game world are the fundamental element for which teaching is successful because without their in-game actions they would not be unlocked and given the necessary notions for teaching. For these reasons we can say that Serious Games are activities that place students at the center of the educational process.

The developers of Serious Games have used storytelling more and more frequently over the years to create meaningful interactive experiences that were able to thrill the gamers, leading him to continue his adventure in the virtual world. According to Lugmayr et al., we can talk of "serious storytelling" as a new potential media genre in which storytelling within Serious Games is used "outside the context of entertainment, where the narration progresses as a sequence of patterns impressive in quality, relates to a serious context, and is a matter of thoughtful process". The use of fiction has now been adopted in numerous different contexts such as psychology, health, marketing etc. to bestow teachings based on the axiom that "stories encode and decode knowledge" [6].

Virtual reality combined with digital storytelling is a powerful tool able to interest users of various ages in the activities and problems proposed by the experience. Our game experience was developed on the basis of the MDA (Mechanics, Dynamics, Aesthetics) model created by Robin Hunicke, Marc LeBlanc and Robert Zubek in 2004 [7].

2 Puzzle Battle 2.0

2.1 Original Game Design and Critical Issues

Puzzle Battle is a Serious Game in Virtual Reality created in 2017 to teach art's history and help the user recognize the works of some of the most famous artists in history [8].

The game was heavily focused on fast-paced gameplay that echoed the characteristics of classic puzzle games. The player found himself inside an arena and had to collect puzzle pieces that fell from the sky at different speeds depending on the level of difficulty. The goal of the game was to complete all the puzzles depicting the proposed paintings before your opponent did it. The pieces had different shapes and not all of them were correct: if the user tried to grad the wrong puzzle piece, it would shatter in his hands, making him waste time. The pieces that fell to the ground broke and became unusable.

The original project has critical issues due to the passage of time and the pandemic situation we are experiencing. The first problem nowadays is being able to try the game that until now had only been available in the offices of the 3D Lab Factory within Savona's Campus of University of Genoa. The experience has never been published online stores because it is strictly used as a research base in learning the artistic subject and in the study of Serious Game's design. Therefore, given the impossibility of moving around, no one can now actively try Puzzle Battle.

The second problem relates to game design and how the user was placed in contact with the teachings. Although the formula used has been appreciated by those who have tried the game, the Serious Game nature with which Puzzle Battle was born needs to be modernized. The main criticality is due to the fact that most of the notions that use could learn within the game were concentrated in the Gallery Mode and so only in optional form. The virtual museum's visit, however, was not to be understood as a desire to improve art's history knowledge, but to check player's progress and focus on which frameworks and objectives it was still necessary to work to 100% complete the game. Therefore, it is necessary to analyze the system with which the teachings are given so the user can acquire more knowledge even during the gameplay phase in Arcade Mode.

2.2   Methodology and Goals

The purpose of Puzzle Battle 2.0 is to improve the effectiveness of the didactic without affecting the relevant play section developed in the first version of the game. The goal remained to make students learn the art through a fun and frenetic puzzle game but giving greater value to the use of narrative to involve users and make the experience more memorable. The use of Virtual Reality predisposes the user to a high involvement in the game action making him more aware of what is happening. The player is in a state of flow in which every action is important for achieving the final victory and in which everyone's mind becomes a fertile ground for acquiring new knowledge [9, 10].

Focusing on adding a narrative section capable of blending gameplay with teaching is a tool that aims to exploit this latter aspect. The union of Serious Games with Puzzle Games created a sort of paradox. The narrative context within Serious Games is heavily used and plays a fundamental role combining the "serious" context with the purely playful one [11]. The Puzzle Games, on the other hand, are the genre of videogames that are based on gameplay alone, not considering storytelling or doing it very little. This dual nature within Puzzle Battle had seen gameplay prevail over history, generating an effective but superficial teaching method compared to initial expectations.

The exploitation of the painters' avatars was used merely within the next challenger screen and the game scenario, without any actual interaction between the player and the opponent. Puzzle Battle 2.0 therefore provides a Story Mode in which the player will be able to cross the various artistic eras and with their choices can influence the currents and the painters with whom they will come into contact. The possibility of changing the course of the careers of artists and his popularity based on their choices makes each action fundamental for the continuation of the story and helps to better understand the context in which is acting, also developing a critical sense of various aspects that characterized the cardinal principles of each artistic current. Direct interaction with information is more effective than the optional past one provided by the Gallery, which however will remain present precisely to allow achievers to be able to check their progress. The performance situated in various historical periods also provides that the scenarios in which the matches will take place will no longer in a standard steel cage but will be in thematic stages able to recall the historical moment in which they take place. The player will find himself in an area that recalls in the architecture, atmospheres and outfits the iconic places represented by the challenged artist. The scenarios will contain numerous citations to the works of the challenged artists, immersing the player in some iconic scenes represented by the painters and improving the represented image-artist association. The decision-making system highlights the importance of using characters who until now were simple challengers while now they are knowledge's sources. The relationship between the player and the artists is important for the development not only in the game but, in the playful world, also in the entire art's history. The gamer has the role of "hero of the art's history" in a context in which, however, there are no real nemeses. The puzzle challenges in Story Mode will see us pitted against the artists but will serve to help them make decisive choices to direct their careers. The entire adventure in the world of Puzzle Battle 2.0 will be accompanied by a robot buddy that will have the function of travel companion and mentor.

The choice to switch from a purely arcade game system to one focused on storytelling was made necessary based on the weakness expressed previously of the first version of Puzzle Battle. The use of narration has proven over the years to be a very effective element for imparting various kinds of teachings in Serious Games, such as social problems like bullying or cyberbullying [12].

The reachable target is strongly influenced by the way in which players will approach the adventure. The arcade based original release was based to a target that went from primary school children to adults thanks to a frenetic action and the use of simple and immediate mechanics. However, although the game still makes it possible to play in this way, this approach is not effective for learning. Based on how the themes are addressed through the narrative, Puzzle Battle 2.0 has as its main target high school students, university students or simple art lovers looking for an alternative way to learn new notions.

2.3   Gameplay and Game's Experience

The gameplay within the battles with artists is almost unchanged. The player will have to choose the correct puzzle pieces to complete the stages and defeat the opponents. The only variations are in the objects that the player can use to hinder the work of their opponents. In the first version there were five power ups like bombs, chain, etc. [8] Each opponent will receive a themed power up that can be unlocked following the victory that can be used in all modes. The unlocked power up will trace a characteristic aspect of the life or work of the newly defeated artist.

The teaching characterized by direct interaction proposes a new narrative approach in which the main concept is that the player does not want to destroy art but wants to rebuild it thanks to his own commitment. The humanistic teaching inherent in the experience is the will to create rather than destroy. This aspect can be found both in the pure gameplay present in the challenges with the artists in which the player reassembles the puzzles, but also within the entire storyline in which the user will have to travel from age to age to put the art's history in order. In the only moments in which the player will be able to break parts of the scenarios through the use of power ups, the destruction is seen for a good purpose as it serves to stop the opponent from making bad decisions. For example, the player will be able to help the artist to create the work as it is historically known, thus avoiding any temporal paradoxes for which the same painting has not obtained the success that everyone knows today or worse the artist has prematurely ended his career.

Puzzle Battle 2.0 will also feature a multiplayer mode online, collaboration with other users is a tool that motivates the player to learn through interpersonal interaction in the game world. The opportunity to discuss and help each other is an aspect that facilitates the memorability of the actions carried out and the topics covered [13]. The more the user will feel immersed in the virtual environment, the greater the educational benefits obtained from the collaboration with other players. Mixing the exploratory and collaborative parts must be calibrated with the proposed storytelling in such a way that the players constantly feel they are integral parts of the action, actors capable of changing the fate of art's history with their decisions. The importance of one's actions increases the sense of responsibility and presence of the players in the game world.

The improvements presented so far are seen with a view to evolving the Puzzle Battle project to make it available online. The prototype created to represent the future standalone version of Puzzle Battle 2.0 was developed with Unreal Engine 4, Epic Games graphics engine. The graphic and stylistic choices were influenced by the implementation problems dictated by the desire to make the experience available on several different HMDs.

3   Future Works

The evolution of the Puzzle Battle 2.0 project does not have the only purpose of publishing a game that can help students of various educational levels to approach and learn art's history. The demo created will be tested as soon as possible in territorial laboratories and living labs, appropriately sanitized, to evaluate not only the effectiveness of the proposed educational system, but also to obtain direct feedback from the different classes of different ages to whom the serious game will be proposed. Within these educational activities, data will be collected to obtain information on how the mechanics and the narrative system chosen can be perceived differently during the game experience from primary school children to university students.

The effectiveness of the proposed teachings will be tested through a quiz given to the players following the experience. The questions will be calibrated on the basis of their age and will flow into a future study focused on the use of storytelling in Serious Games.

Pre and post-game activity tests will be administered in order to evaluate the validity of the teaching material and the actual understanding by the students. The evaluation of the results obtained will modify the way in which the information will be given both within the virtual museum and in the story created to involve the players.

References

1. Statista.com.   https://www.statista.com/statistics/1109977/video-game-sales-covid/. Accessed 6 Apr 2021
2. Omdia.tech.informa.com.   https://omdia.tech.informa.com/OM005309/Consumer-VR-Headset-and-Content-Revenue-Forecast-202025. Accessed 6 Apr 2021
3. Omdia.tech.informa.com.   https://omdia.tech.informa.com/pr/2020-dec/six-and-a-half-million-consumer-vr-headsets-will-be-sold-in-2020. Accessed 6 Apr 2021
4. Steurer, J.: The Communication During the Years of VR. LEA Publishers, Philadelphia (1995)
5. Checa, D., Bustillo, A.: A review of immersive virtual reality serious games to enhance learning and training, Multimedia Tools Appl. **79**, pp. 5501–5527 (2019)
6. Lugmayr, A., Sutinen, E., Suhonen, J., Islas Sedano, C., Hlavacs, H., Montero, C.: Serious Storytelling – a First Definition and Review, Springer Science+Business Media New York (2016)
7. Hunicke, R., Leblanc, M., Zubek, R., MDA: A formal approach to game design and game research. In: Proceedings of the AAAI Workshop on Challenges in Game AI (2004)
8. Iacono, S., Vercelli, G., Zolezzi, D., Virtual reality arcade game in game-based learning for cultural heritage, virtual reality arcade game in game-based learning for cultural heritage. In: Proceedings of the 5th International Conference, AVR 2018, Otranto, Italy, 24–27 June 2018, Part II (2018)
9. Liu, M., Horton, L., Olmanson, J., Toprac, P.: A study of learning and motivation in a new media enriched environment for middle school science. Educ. Technol. Res. Devel. **59**(2), 249–265 (2011)
10. Nakamura, J., Csikszentmihalyi, M.: The concept of flow. In: Flow and the Foundations of Positive Psychology, pp. 239–263. Springer, Dordrecht (2014). https://doi.org/10.1007/978-94-017-9088-8_16
11. Kampa, A., Haake, S., Burelli, P.: Storytelling in serious games. In: Dörner, R., Göbel, S., Kickmeier-Rust, M., Masuch, M., Zweig, K. (eds.) Entertainment Computing and Serious Games. LNCS, vol. 9970, pp. 521–539. Springer, Cham (2016). https://doi.org/10.1007/978-3-319-46152-6_19
12. Calvo-Morata, A., Alonso-Fernandez, C., Freire, M., Martinez-Ortiz, I., Fernandez-Manjòn, B.: Serious games to prevent and detect bullying and cyberbullying: a systematic serious games and literature review. Comput. Educ. **157**, 103958 (2020)
13. Brown, C., Bhutra, G., Suhail, M., Xu, Q., Ragan, E.D.: Coordinating attention and cooperation in multi-user virtual reality narratives. In: 2017 IEEE Virtual Reality (VR). IEEE (2017)

Towards an Integration of the Multi-role Dimension in the Design of Learning Games: a Review of the Literature

Gaëlle Guigon[1,2]([✉])(iD), Mathieu Vermeulen[2]([✉])(iD), Mathieu Muratet[1,3]([✉])(iD),
and Thibault Carron[1]([✉])(iD)

[1] Sorbonne Université, CNRS, LIP6, 75005 Paris, France
`gaelle.guigon@imt-nord-europe.fr`,
`{mathieu.muratet,thibault.carron}@lip6.fr`
[2] IMT Nord Europe, Institut Mines-Télécom, Univ. Lille, Centre for Digital Systems,
59000 Lille, France
`mathieu.vermeulen@imt-nord-europe.fr`
[3] Sorbonne Université, CNRS, INS HEA, LIP6, 75005 Paris, France

Abstract. Serious Games (SG) have become popular and their efficiency
has been proven in numerous domains throughout the years. You can find
them for a plethora of subjects, in bountiful forms and consequently, to
answer various needs. They are particularly efficient to reproduce concrete
situations and to train on specific objectives. However, most of them are
only designed for one player. One explanation might be their design that
seems indeed more complex for multiplayer SG. This paper focuses on a
certain type of multiplayer SG: those based on multi-role. Thus, this paper
aims at drawing a state of the art of multi-role SG and their design, as a
first step to propose a design model of multi-role SG.

Keywords: Learning game · Multi-role · Multiplayer · Serious game ·
TEL design

1 Introduction

Years ago, serious games emerged, took shape and have been developed ever
since, taking various forms and fulfilling countless goals. Their definition can
be quite complex so here we are choosing the one stated by Michael and Chen
[20]: "games whose first purpose was not mere entertainment." As technology
facilitates their creation for designers, the number of SG is constantly growing
as well as their popularity in the world of education. A special approach of SG,
role playing, is particularly interesting as Cheng et al. [11] said: "Role playing
allows participants to attain knowledge in a different manner and improve their
approach to problem solving in a real-world context." It is thus necessary to
define a role, as Warrin et al. did [27]: "in a game, the set of objectives, behaviors,
rights, and duties assigned to a person or a group of persons is called a role. A
person may play several roles, or inversely, a role may involve several people."
We could also add the notion of competences, objects, and powers as roles'

© Springer Nature Switzerland AG 2021
F. de Rosa et al. (Eds.): GALA 2021, LNCS 13134, pp. 258–264, 2021.
https://doi.org/10.1007/978-3-030-92182-8_26

attributes. Here we are assuming that multi-role games are multi-users, Calandra et al. [10] precised that "Multi-user refers to the possibility, for different users in different places, to play the available roles all together and at the same time in a shared experience." So it is really important to consider this in the scenario, so that nobody stays inactive during the game. Everyone should have his/her proper objectives within the game and should not be completely dependent on the actions of other players. This complicates even more the conception of the game. We know it can be difficult to design SG in solo mode [16,18], and naturally the same assessment seems established concerning multiplayer games [21]. Therefore, we can suppose that multi-role games are even trickier to conceive. The research question is: how can we design training scenarios that allow several different roles to be implemented simultaneously? To that end, the present paper aims at drawing a state of the art of multi-role SG. To begin with, the method with which the present state of the art was set up will be introduced. Then, we will explain the categorization of the selected papers. That will allow us to analyse the results in order to exhibit some tracks to answer the research question.

2   Method

Selection and Source. The papers selected for this state of the art are dealing with multi-role serious games or their design. The goal was to find out if some papers concerning the design of multi-role SG already exist. This research was focused on the websites of those editors and academic research databases: ScienceDirect, IEEE, ACM, Scopus, Web of Science and Springer Link. The keywords used on their search engines were: "multi-role" (with and without hyphen) AND "game" and no restriction of date. Here are the results that led to the remaining papers in the first part of Table 1.

Science Direct: the access was given via institution and the papers selected are open access and full text access. Only one result was found with the keywords "multirole game" in the title, the abstract or the keywords. No result was found with the keywords "'multi-role' game". The quotation marks were necessary to avoid all the other words beginning with 'multi-'.

IEEE: (access via institution) Four results were found. Yet, even if the words "multi-role" and "games" were present in the abstract, two papers didn't deal with a game or its conception, so they were deleted from the selection.

Scopus: (access via institution) the search was based within the title, the abstract or the keywords. The search with open access only resulted in five papers. But as before, three papers had no link with multi-role games so they are not included in the analysis.

Web of Science: the search provided five results in open access (four of them were already found previously).

ACM: focused on the title, keywords and abstract. Only one result was available.

Springer Link: without the "preview only content" we found four results that were restricted to the articles containing the word "game" within the abstract. This filter resulted in two papers. Unfortunately, their content was not in relation with the subject of this survey so they were not selected either.

Classification Framework. In this survey, we are looking for papers presenting a model or a tool to create multi-role SG. The aim is to find a generic model or tool, if possible, easily understandable by non IT-professionals. Thus, the papers will be sorted in three categories: 1) the theme (to see if it is restricted to a sector or if it is generic), 2) the type (*e.g.* a game, a model or a tool) and 3) the public (to find if it is usable by anyone).

Table 1. Categorization of multi-role serious games

Paper	Theme	Type	Target
Agustin et al. [1]	Generic	Conceptual graph model	IT-professional
Baturin et al. [5]	Situational analysis	Situational modeling	General public
Breitner et Smith [8]	IT	Software	IT students
Calandra et al. [10]	Fire safety	Game	General public
Cheng et al. [11]	Water	Game	General public
Li et al. [15]	Doudizhu (Poker like)	Card-playing framework	CNN Specialists
Warin et al. [27]	Information system project	Game	Students
Argenton et al. [2]	Gliding	Game	General public
Arif et al. [3]	Transactions activities	Game	General public
Babu et al. [4]	Post disaster management	Game	General public
Bierre [6]	Game design	Game	Students
Burton [9]	Irrigation	Game	Professionals
Lee et al. [14]	Manufacturing industry consultancy	Game	Students
Schrier [22]	21st century skills	Game	Students
Schulz et al. [23]	Health and care	Game	Professionals
Sequeira et al. [24]	Environment	AI	General public
Stroe et al. [25]	Fire-safety	Game	Students

As this search led to few papers, it was extended to multiplayer SG in those same scientific research tools. Indeed, the results on the second part of Table 1 appeared with the keywords: "multiplayer" or "collaborative" or "competitive" or "cooperative" and "serious game" and deal also with multi-role games.

3   Analysis

First of all, based on this research, we can see that the term "multi-role" (with or without the hyphen) is not often used in SG. Furthermore, even within multiplayer games, they are scarce. Among the seven initial articles, we can see that only one is generic, but is only usable by IT-professionals. All the other papers are dealing with a specific theme and are not supposed to be adapted for another theme. Concerning the extended search, all the results are games (only one paper presents an AI for a game) but the entire selection is oriented to a particular theme and none is generic. It means that there is a genuine need to define a model, a generic tool or at least to be advised on the creation of multi-role SG. Among these papers, only a few explains how the games were designed, how the scenarios were thought through, at least not for non IT-professionals. Usually, the games were presented to explain their benefits and their special features but there is no mention of a specific game engine allowing them to create their game. Unity was mentioned in [10], authors affirm that the possibilities are infinite with this game engine, but it is not easy to handle for teachers, instructional designer or non professionals. Furthermore, the aim is not to create a video game, but to structure a game, to be guided during the scenario creation process and to define the paths, objectives and particularities of each role. We can note that multi-role games can be in a physical environment: they are not device-dependent, as several games prove it here [6, 9, 11, 15, 27].

The paper presented by Agustin [1] is the closest to what we are looking for: they propose "a conceptual graph model to represent the concept of gaming" and a "building block of the engine to run and control the game". Even if it seems flexible and quite generic, it appears to be only usable by IT-professionals.

4   Discussion

Existing Tools. As stated before, we found no paper tackling the generic design of multi-role SG. However, a few approaches are interesting and could meet this need. Apart from the results found, a few tools should be mentioned as they bring interesting aspects to answer our questioning: Marne [17] created a generic tool, *MoPPLiq*, to design game scenarios. *MoPPLiq* has not especially been created for multi-role games, but the method used to conceive a scenario could be adapted to meet this need because it is used to model pedagogical scenarios, with objectives to achieve and conditions to go to different steps. One strategy can be used to reach our goal: we can separate the roles within the same scenario. For instance, Marty [19] used a multiplayer game where the players have the same scenario, but are paced differently in order to avoid that all the students progress simultaneously in the game. Another strategy supporting the same scenario is to offer side quests to the players to regulate the flow [7].

Next, the tool *MAGES* [13], based on the models *SEGAM* [12] and DISC [26], could be adjusted for multi-role SG since it is made for multiplayer games. It covers the whole organization part, the pedagogical part and the structure of the game. It would be interesting to adapt it because it has already been made to be generic, so usable in any discipline. Thus, pedagogy can be adapted because the learning objectives can be approached at any moment of the scenario, if they are consistent with the previously defined prerequisites. The tool is structured like a form so it seems easy for non programmers to create a pedagogically coherent scenario. It is also planned to create a database to save several projects on it and to share them.

To Go Further. Another aspect to consider is management of resources in multi-role games. To encourage cooperation, everyone should not access the same elements at the same time. We could go further and define that only one or a few roles can use a specific resource. It would be convenient if the tool could handle it directly. The question of the persistence of items is also to take into account: do they disappear after a player took them? Definitely or temporarily? All these parameters should be adjustable according to the game objectives.

Thus, many criteria are in our sights concerning the design of a multi-role SG authoring tool (*e.g.* pedagogy, distribution of roles, interactions between players, scenarios, genericity etc.).

5   Conclusion

To conclude, this state of the art showed that, to our knowledge, there is no model or generic tool created to help designing multi-role SG and usable for non IT-professionals. However, gathering experiences and methods of the papers seen here can give clues to get there. So, creating a model and the reified tool could potentially be very helpful in the process of creating them - in particular for the promotion of cooperative SG which could fit perfectly for multi-role games. In future works, we plan to establish a model based on the relevant concepts seen in this article. This model will lead to the creation of a tool which will eventually enable its users to create games, taking into account the obstacles reviewed in this state of the art. They could be tested in a context of differential learning throughout an asymmetrical gameplay, for instance the reproduction of a scenario between a doctor and a patient or in the civil engineering field, being able to play each actor involved in BIM (Building Information Modeling) process.

References

1. Agustin, R.D., Suwardi, I.S., Purwarianti, A., Surendro, K.: Knowledge representation and inference engine model of SAPS gaming concept. Procedia Technol. **11**, 696–703 (2013)
2. Argenton, L., Muzio, M., Shek, E.J., Mantovani, F.: Multiplayer serious games and user experience: a comparison between paper-based and digital gaming experience. In: De Gloria, A. (ed.) GALA 2014. LNCS, vol. 9221, pp. 54–62. Springer, Cham (2015). https://doi.org/10.1007/978-3-319-22960-7_6

3. Arif, Y.M., Pradana, R.P., Nurhayati, H., Nugroho, S.M.S., Hariadi, M.: A blockchain-based multiplayer transaction for tourism serious game. In: 2020 International Conference on Computer Engineering, Network, and Intelligent Multimedia (CENIM), Surabaya, Indonesia, pp. 138–143, November 2020

4. Babu, S.K., McLain, M.L., Bijlani, K., Jayakrishnan, R., Bhavani, R.R.: Collaborative game based learning of post-disaster management: serious game on incident management frameworks for post disaster management. In: IEEE 8th International Conference on Technology for Education, Mumbai, India, pp. 80–87 (2016)

5. Baturin, Y., et al.: Situational analysis with analytical support in virtual environment for decision making process under high-risk and crisis conditions. In: 2008 International Conference on Cyberworlds, pp. 837–842, September 2008

6. Bierre, K.: Implementing a game design course as a multiplayer game. In: 2012 IEEE International Games Innovation Conference, Rochester, NY, USA, pp. 1–4, September 2012

7. Bodin, M., Marty, J.C., Carron, T.: Specifying collaborative tools in game-based learning environments: clues from the trenches. In: Int., A.P. (ed.) European Conference on Game Based Learning, Athènes, Greece, pp. 46–56 (2011)

8. Breitner, J., Smith, C.: Lock-step simulation is child's play (experience report). Proc. ACM Program. Lang. 1(ICFP), 3:1–3:15 (2017)

9. Burton, M.A.: The irrigation management game: a role playing exercise for training in irrigation management. Irrig. Drain. Syst. 7(4), 305–318 (1994)

10. Calandra, D., Pratticò, F., Migliorini, M., Verda, V., Lamberti, F.: A multi-role, multi-user, multi-technology virtual reality-based road tunnel fire simulator for training purposes. In: Proceedings of the 16th IJC on Computer Vision, Imaging and Computer Graphics Theory and Applications - GRAPP, pp. 96–105, September 2021

11. Cheng, P.H., Yeh, T.K., Chao, Y.K., Lin, J., Chang, C.Y.: Design ideas for an issue-situation-based board game involving multirole scenarios. Sustainability 12(5), 2139 (2020)

12. Guigon, G., Humeau, J., Vermeulen, M.: A model to design learning escape games: SEGAM. In: 10th International Conference on Computer Supported Education, Funchal, Madeira, Portugal, pp. 191–197. SCITEPRESS - Science and Technology Publications, March 2018

13. Guigon, G., Vermeulen, M., Humeau, J.: A creation tool for serious puzzle games. In: CSEDU 2019. Proceedings of the 11th International Conference on Computer Supported Education, Heraklion, Greece, vol. 2, pp. 556–561, May 2019

14. Lee, H., et al.: Cooperation begins: encouraging critical thinking skills through cooperative reciprocity using a mobile learning game. Comput. Educ. 97, 97–115 (2016)

15. Li, S., Li, S., Cao, H., Meng, K., Ding, M.: Study on the strategy of playing Doudizhu game based on multirole modeling. Complexity (2020)

16. Marfisi-Schottman, I., George, S., Tarpin-Bernard, F.: Tools and methods for efficiently designing serious games. In: European Conference on Games Based Learning, ECGBL, p. 226 (2010)

17. Marne, B., Carron, T., Labat, J.M., Marfisi-Schottman, I.: MoPPLiq: a model for pedagogical adaptation of serious game scenarios. In: 2013 IEEE 13th International Conference on Advanced Learning Technologies, Beijing, China, pp. 291–293, July 2013

18. Marne, B., Labat, J.M.: Model and authoring tool to help teachers adapt serious games to their educational contexts. Int. J. Learn. Technol. 9(2), 161–180 (2014)

19. Marty, J.C., Carron, T.: Observation of collaborative activities in a game-based learning platform. IEEE Trans. Learn. Technol. **4**(1), 98–110 (2011)
20. Michael, D.R., Chen, S.L.: Serious Games: Games That Educate, Train, and Inform. Muska & Lipman/Premier-Trade (2005)
21. Oliveri, M., Hauge, J.B., Bellotti, F., Berta, R., Gloria, A.D.: Designing an IoT-focused, multiplayer serious game for Industry 4.0 innovation. In: 2019 IEEE International Conference on Engineering, Technology and Innovation (ICE/ITMC), Valbonne Sophia-Antipolis, France, pp. 1–9, June 2019
22. Schrier, K.: Using augmented reality games to teach 21st century skills. In: ACM SIGGRAPH 2006 Educators program on - SIGGRAPH 2006 (2006)
23. Schulz, R., Smaradottir, B., Olsen, J.T., Prinz, A.: Scenario-based serious game to teach about healthcare. In: IEEE 7th International Conference on Serious Games and Applications for Health (SeGAH), Kyoto, Japan, pp. 1–8, August 2019. ISSN 2573–3060
24. Sequeira, P., Melo, F.S., Paiva, A.: "Let's save resources!": a dynamic, collaborative AI for a multiplayer environmental awareness game. In: IEEE Conference on Computational Intelligence and Games (CIG), Taiwan, pp. 399–406, August 2015
25. Stroe, I.P., Ciupe, A., Meza, S.N., Orza, B.: FireEscape: a gamified coordinative approach to multiplayer fire-safety training. In: 2019 IEEE Global Engineering Education Conference (EDUCON), pp. 1316–1323, April 2019
26. Vermeulen, M., Guigon, G., Mandran, N., Labat, J.M.: Teachers at the heart of the learning games design: the DISC model. In: 2017 IEEE 17th International Conference on Advanced Learning Technologies (ICALT), pp. 145–149, July 2017
27. Warin, B., Talbi, O., Kolski, C., Hoogstoel, F.: Multi-role project (MRP): a new project-based learning method for STEM. IEEE Trans. Educ. **59**(2), 137–146 (2016). Conference Name: IEEE Transactions on Education

Serious Games for Crowdsourced Design Innovation and Testing

E. P. Oates(⊠) ⓘD

Defence and Security, Cranfield University, Shrivenham, UK

Abstract. Equipment procured for defence and security organisations often require a human-computer interface. The current UK defence procurement process seeks design ideas from a small community of experts through synchronous meetings, attendance at human factors laboratories, and subjective assessment at the manufacturer's location. These traditional design methods, while termed 'user-centred', assume that the expert users are able to travel and meet, which was difficult to achieve even pre-covid pandemic. The use of Serious Games in the defence design context and the crowdsourced objective testing of the design options is novel and untried. This research offers a route for incremental asynchronous design and test activities. Using a crowdsourcing construct, designers, expert and less-skilled users share views and prototype human-computer interface design ideas as part of a Serious Game hosted in a web browser. This research is a worked example of how a Serious Game can support remote design with this paper reporting on crowdsourced objective testing of human-computer interfaces for defence and security equipment.

Keywords: Innovation · Crowdsourcing · Human factors

1 Introduction

Research into the use of serious games for design innovation has been reported by Oates [1, 2] and this paper provides further findings following completion of the research. Previous reports identified the benefits of crowdsourcing for innovation in human-computer interface design through the gathering of design ideas for elements, features and functions. The Serious Game, incorporating an emulation of the Merlin Mk2 helicopter tactical interface, with a maritime surface search task, within a pre-hostilities United Nations (UN) backed constabulary operations story line was made available on the defence intranet. It was advertised with competitions and small financial prizes. Feedback for design ideas were made by email, telephone and face-to-face meetings and then built into the game interface. Design ideas ranged from minor interface corrections, through design ideas seen on other defence platforms, to imagined or envisaged improvements. For example, waterfall displays commonly in use in under-water acoustic displays were proposed and transferred for use in the electronic warfare displays, illustrated in Fig. 1 below.

© Springer Nature Switzerland AG 2021
F. de Rosa et al. (Eds.): GALA 2021, LNCS 13134, pp. 265–270, 2021.
https://doi.org/10.1007/978-3-030-92182-8_27

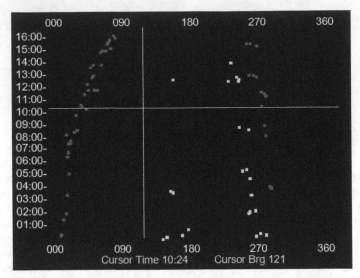

Fig. 1. Electronic warfare waterfall display showing detections of radar transmissions (y-axis time min:sec, x-axis true bearing deg, colour code NATO hostility designation)

The ability to locate the source of a radar transmission was considered useful. A position ellipse-forming function, which had been seen on another nation's defence equipment interface was proposed and included in the game interface, as shown in Fig. 2 below.

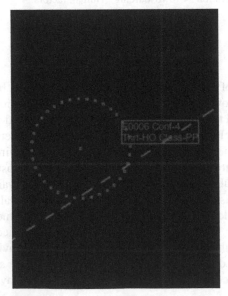

Fig. 2. Radar transmission source location function (position estimate shown as a dotted ellipse with latest detected bearing shown as a dashed line)

The research began with a web browser Serious Game being built with an emulation of the existing human-computer interface and a synthetic environment containing the military scenario. This game was then played by a wide variety of personnel on the UK defence intranet with no restrictions on the players' location, status or organizational affiliation. The crowdsourcing construct of this research followed Surowiecki's [4] conditions for safe reliance on the 'wisdom of crowds':

- **Diverse Opinions**. The members of the crowd do not all share the same view.
- **Independence**. The members of the crowd are not affected by 'group-think' or influenced by hierarchy.
- **Decentralisation**. The members of the crowd are from different specialities and areas of expertise so that they bring differing experiences and knowledge.
- **Aggregation Mechanism**. The output from the crowd is brought together constructively to meet the aims of the crowdsourcing.

The fourth stage of safe crowdsourcing: 'Aggregation Mechanism' was brought together by competitive use of the serious game. Log files recording interface selections from 1000 games played by 100 players were analysed to assess the difference between the Pre-Crowdsourced (emulation of the real equipment) human-computer interface, and the Post-Crowdsourced interface and to down-select the design elements that were objectively assessed as increasing 'efficiency' and 'effectiveness' in the completion of the military task assigned within the game.

2 Data Collection

After the trials reported in Oates [2], a further series of trials were conducted with players experienced in the real equipment being emulated and with inexperienced players. The results showed that those with experience of the real equipment did not consistently gain higher scores or faster game-play times than the inexperienced players and that some experienced players continued to use real equipment functions when more efficient options were available from new human-computer interface functions developed during the crowdsourcing phase.

The requirements for the final interface test were for players to have an interest in maritime search tasks but not to have experience of current warfare equipment, as previous experience could affect the way that the interface was used. The Britannia Royal Naval College at Dartmouth, UK was able to support this requirement with a new entry of approximately 25 Cadets each academic term. The entrant Cadets were divided into alternating termly groups between the Pre- and Post-Crowdsourced game interfaces. All Cadets were aware of their participation in a Ministry of Defence (MOD) sponsored trial, were volunteers, were assured that any results submitted were anonymous and would not affect their careers. The subjects were made aware of small financial prizes for the highest score at each game level competition with a further prize awarded at random picked from the log-files submitted. The trials were conducted under ethical and academic supervision of Cranfield University.

Testing began in 2018 and continued over four academic terms until 2019. All Cadets were scheduled for five 90-min periods. The first period allowed for orientation and familiarisation of the game interface and the search task. Five training scenarios were embedded in the game and were offered as the starting point for the game's use during this familiarisaton period. The remaining four periods were for competing in game levels 1 to 4, with each game level offering increased complexity of maritime search tasks within the UN constabulary operations story-line.

Data collection for a human-computer interface design task within current procurement processes based at a manufacturer's human-factors laboratory would also include an opportunity for questions to be asked of the user. The data collection format in this research could only include an on-line questionnaire completed after the game was played. This limited the level of detail in the data collection to the game log-files which recorded function selection counts and display durations, and the pre-set questionnaire. This limited set of data was balanced by the opportunity to gain objective data from many more users than could be included in conventional trials.

3 Analysis

The serious game collected data on the use of 35 game functions and displays as well as the time taken to play and complete tasks, and the points scored. The analysis looked for differences between the Original interface (Pre-Crowdsourced) and the Crowdsourced interface (Post-Crowdsourcing), and in this, very little difference was seen at the highest aggregation level. Further analysis using dendrogram plots looked for unordered groups of interface functions used leading to high scores, but again there was no clear evidence. A step-wise regression analysis was also used to look for single functions and paired functions leading to high scores but there was no statistically significant signal. The data was also analysed using binomial-logistic charts to see if the use of a function or display 'at least once' affected the scores or game-play times, but again there was no clear conclusion. To reduce data dimensions by variance, principal component analysis was used which highlighted some players' style of play but not a consistent winning approach.

The next stage of the analysis used the technique of 'clickstream' web site analysis described by Scholz [5]. Commercial web site analyses look at web page loading sequences, from product search through to purchase completion. The sequences of key or button selections are referred to as 'clickstreams' and in this research, the action of changing a marker confirming a ship's identity was the clickstream end point with the sequence of selections traced back from the score change event (event number 36 in Figs. 3 and 4) to find the button selections that lead up to this.

Crowdsourcing is offered as a method to discover 'wildcard' solutions Byren [6] which are successful solutions only discovered by a few players and shown in Fig. 4.

The clickstream analysis may have missed 'wildcard' solutions by burying their success under the results from the majority so, function and display selection counts and summed display durations within each game were divided by the game Score and game-play Time. Where high value outlier groups (n > 5) were found, they were considered as 'wildcard' functions and plotted in Fig. 4 above. This showed the importance of crowdsourced functions 34 and 35 but also showed that the pre-existing route through functions 30 and 33 was also of value to the players.

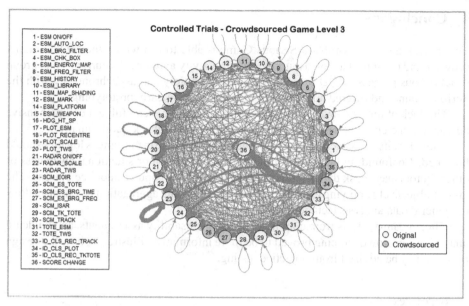

Fig. 3. Clickstream analysis of game level 3 with crowdsourced interface showing functions as vertices, used at least 20 times

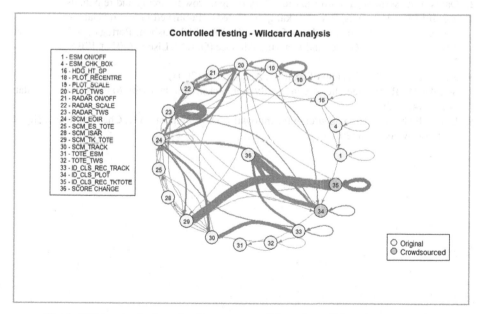

Fig. 4. Wildcard selections (outlier groups > 5) based on click count: score ratios

4   Conclusions

This research has shown that a Serious Game is able to run within the MOD intranet browser and to support a crowdsourcing design activity avoiding the current small group synchronous process. MOD personnel engaged remotely and asynchronously with the Serious Game and offered novel design ideas supporting early prototyping.

The lack of direct contact with the test players requires careful and comprehensive design and incremental development of the game test feedback questionnaire.

The difficulty in extracting a useful signal from the noise in the game's log files should be noted. Confounding factors from the players' cognition or situational awareness or other factors may mask the difference between human-computer interface options. The task of objectively applying tests within the crowdsourcing aggregation mechanism drew on general data analysis techniques.

Clickstream analysis from commercial web site usability assessments, and wildcard analysis from crowdsourcing proved to be more informative, illustrating how the design process may be advised from objective testing.

References

1. Oates, E.P.: Learning and designing with serious games: crowdsourcing for procurement. In: De Gloria, A., Veltkamp, R. (eds.) Presentation and Published Paper in "4th International Conference, GALA 2015, Rome, Italy, 9–11 December 2015, Revised Selected Papers". Games and Learning Alliance (GaLA), Rome (2015). ISBN 978-3-319-40216-1
2. Oates, E.P.: Serious games for participatory design, crowdsourcing and remote usability testing. In: Dias, J., Santos, P.A., Veltkamp, R.C. (eds.) Published Paper in "Games and Learning Alliance 6th International Conference, GALA 2017, Lisbon, Portugal, 5–7 December 2017, Proceedings". Games and Learning Alliance (GaLA), Lisbon (2017). ISBN 978-3-319-71940-5
3. Surowiecki, J.: The Wisdom of Crowds, Abacus, UK (2004)
4. Scholz, M.: R Package clickstream: analyzing clickstream data with Markov chains. J. Stat. Softw. **74**(4) (2016)
5. Byren, E.: Internal Crowdsourcing for Innovation Development, MSc. Chalmers University of Technology, Sweden (2013)

Development of a Game-Based Approach for Business Process Knowledge

Julian Bozem$^{(\boxtimes)}$, Johannes Beckert, and Alexander Dobhan

University of Applied Science Würzburg-Schweinfurt, Schweinfurt, Germany
erp.fwi@fhws.de

Abstract. Business process knowledge is essential for efficiently executing business processes. Game-based approaches with their advantages (e.g. emotional involvement) are a promising way for building and keeping business process knowledge within an organization. Therefore, the purpose of this article is to explore, how game-based approaches support the creation of business process knowledge. The article contains three major contributions: (1) a weighted overview of game design elements in literature, (2) an extension to existing process models for game development, (3) a prototype for board game for business process knowledge.

Keywords: Business process knowledge · Game-based approach · Game Development Process · Game-based learning design elements · Gamification elements

1 Introduction

Business process knowledge as an element of competence is a success factor in the digitization of business processes [1]. 'Business process knowledge [...] is knowledge about the motivation behind processes, reasons for their existence, knowledge about process structure and logic, the required resources for their execution, as well as its interfaces, process environment, capability, performance and documentation' [2]. A game-based approach for business process knowledge has countless advantages in this regard, most notably, the emotional involvement and motivated behaviors that individuals develop when playing a game [3–5]. Scientific approaches include the approaches of gamification, serious games, and game-based learning [3]. Despite the increasing popularity of board games [6], they have been neglected for teaching business process knowledge, favoring digital approaches instead. It is precisely this gap that this paper fills with a prototype for an analogous board game. The current state of research is of great importance for the development of the game. Therefore, this article focuses on the theory-driven development of a prototype. Firstly, we describe the results of a literature review on the use of methodological elements of gamification and game-based learning. Subsequently, it follows a description of a process model for game development, and finally, the prototype of the game will be covered.

© Springer Nature Switzerland AG 2021
F. de Rosa et al. (Eds.): GALA 2021, LNCS 13134, pp. 271–276, 2021.
https://doi.org/10.1007/978-3-030-92182-8_28

2   Literature Review and Game Elements Overview

To consider a broad spectrum of views, opinions, and perspectives, we conducted a structured literature review. The value added of this Structured Literature Review[1] compared to the existing literature reviews is the combination of the concepts of gamification (GAF) and game-based learning (GBL), as well as the weighting of the design elements according to the frequency of their consideration. The preceding table summarizes 23 studies that have dealt in detail with at least 1 of the 22 identified design elements.

Design element	Number of mentions		Literature	
	GBL	GAF	GBL	GAF
Feedback	6	12	[9], [11], [12], [13], [14], [21]	[6], [7], [15], [16], [22], [23], [24], [25], [26], [28], [29],
Progress	3	11	[9], [10], [21]	[6], [7], [15], [16], [17], [22], [25], [26], [28], [29], [30]
Collaboration	5	9	[9], [10], [11], [13], [21]	[7], [15], [22], [24], [25], [26], [27], [28], [29]
Social interaction	5	9	[9], [10], [11], [13], [21]	[7], [15], [22], [24], [25], [26], [27], [29], [30]
Rewards	5	9	[9], [10], [11], [13], [21]	[7], [15], [17], [22], [23], [24], [25], [29], [30]
Rules	4	9	[10], [11], [13], [21]	[6], [7], [15], [16], [22], [23], [24], [26], [29]
Goals	8	4	[8], [9], [10], [11], [12], [13], [14], [21]	[25], [26], [28], [30]
Challenge	7	4	[8], [9], [10], [11], [12], [13], [21]	[6], [25], [30], [31]
Points		7		[6], [15], [16], [17], [25], [28], [30]
Level		7		[15], [16], [17], [25], [26], [28], [30]
Badges		7		[15], [16], [17], [25], [26], [28], [30]
Simulated marketplace		7		[6], [7], [15], [22], [24], [28], [29]
Virtual Environment		7		[6], [7], [22], [24], [26], [29], [31]
Competition	4	2	[10], [11], [13], [21]	[28], [30]
Story	3	2	[9], [10], [21]	[15], [25]
Strategic thinking	5		[9], [10], [11], [12], [14]	
difficulty	5		[8], [9], [10], [11], [21]	
Leaderboards		5		[15], [16], [17], [25], [30]
Quest		4		[15], [16], [28], [31]
Exploration	3		[9], [11], [13]	
Achievements		1		[16]
Avatar		1		[15]

Fig. 1. Clustering of game-based learning and gamification design elements

When developing new design elements, a dynamic level of **difficulty** has to be determined [7, 8]. **Strategic thinking** describes the cognitive engagement with the subject matter in which the application is situated [9]. **Exploration** is the opportunity to interact with a game or simulation to find out something new [8, 10]. The design element **challenge** describes hurdles that a player must overcome [10, 11]. **Competition** refers to goals that serve as catalysts for actions, measures, and interactions with other game participants [11]. **Rewards (e.g. points)** describe a design element that positively reinforces players for defined achievements or reaching goals [8, 12]. **Goals** generate deeper meaning for players' actions [8, 13]. **Social interaction** describes interpersonal activity [14]. **Collaboration** is a subtype of Social Interaction and means the cooperation of multiple players to achieve a common goal [10]. A **story** defines a background for the gameplay [14]. **Feedback** describes the communication between the player and the game board [8]. **Rules** form the internal and formal game structure [14]. The design element **progress** describes the growth, increase, or enhancement for a goal defined by the game [14]. **Virtual Environment** is a design element that is exclusive to digital applications [4]. The **simulated marketplace** is an implementation of a progress or competition mechanism in the form of a simulation of an economic system [15]. An **avatar** allows users

---

[1] Search terms: gamification, game-based learning, learning game, and simulation game and their combination; search engine: scholar.google; forward and backward search in bibliographies of the studies found.

of a gamification application to personalize their profile [16]. **Leaderboards** provide a way to compare the results of users or teams [15, 17]. **Badges, achievements,** and **points** are rewards players receive for reaching a specific goal or milestone [16]. A **level** is a milestone that illustrates the achievement of intermediate goals [15]. The **Quest** motivates users to pursue a specific goal [15]. Figure 1 shows that in these 23 studies the design elements feedback, progress, collaboration, social interaction, and rewards are the most popular design elements. The value added of this Literature Review compared to the existing ones is the weighted overview of the individual design elements created as a broad foundation for the development of the game.

3 Game Design Process

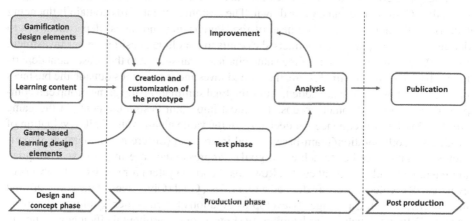

Fig. 2. The Game Design Process for developing a game-based approach to knowledge transfer

To realize the strengths of gamification and game-based learning we introduce a new process model integrating both concepts. The process model is based on the most popular existing process models [18, 19]. Furthermore, the practical concepts of Blitz Game Studios and Juego Studios have influenced the model below. Unlike existing models the new process model (Fig. 2) explicitly considers elements of gamification and game-based learning. For the game below, we made sure to consider especially the most popular design elements of Fig. 1. The learning content was derived from the content of widely known textbooks. Further, the learning content is combined with the most frequently mentioned design elements of the literature review. The production phase of the Game Design Process consists of an iterative cycle. In the testing phase, 'refinement testing' and 'accessibility testing' are performed [19]. The Game Development Process is implemented in this work and includes the relevant sub-process steps of the production phase.

4   Game Idea, Gameplay and Rules

Basically, the goal of the four players in the game presented in this paragraph is to achieve as many scores as possible. The scores depend on the value added in the value chain of Carp AG and the answers of Quiz cards. The players intend to achieve a successful year for the chairmen of the business units - Purchasing and Sales, Research and Development, Production, and Service. The players pursue the common goal of generating the best possible process output at the end of their one-year term of office as department heads. Each product that passes through the value creation process increases the process output. With the premise of generating as much process output as possible, customer requirements and other event cards affect the players' decision-making. The game's target group are students and professionals who are beginners in the context of business processes.

The game consists of five phases for each of the six rounds in total. In the beginning, the 'Customer' event card is drawn. The customer event cards contain influencing factors on the departments. The head of the 'Purchasing and Sales' department has to decide how many purchase contracts she wants to conclude considering her investment funds. After that, all products of the value chain are transferred to the subsequent department. To determine the final score, the earned investment resources outside the business process and those within are added. After the final summation, the game group can compare themselves with other groups. The most important design elements in the game are: Feedback (Consequences of decisions in the value chain (value balls), valuation of products), Collaboration/Team-based social interaction (different collaborating departments working together to achieve a goal), Progress (Increase in game-specific goal, increasing difficulty in event cards), Rewards (Scoring system for results and answers of event cards), Rules (Precisely defined game rules), Goal (Objectives of the company and their departments), Challenges (Developing solutions for customer requirements (event cards)), Different levels/rewards/difficulty (Levels for departmental efficiency, difficulty of event cards (Quiz and Memory), Strategic thinking (developing solutions for various requirements), Ranking list (superordinate ranking list based on the collaboratively earned scores final).

Numerous studies have already shown the superiority of GBL and GF over traditional knowledge transfer e.g. in the area of user acceptance as well as the learning success [12, 32–34]. Similar results can be expected from an evaluation of this board game. Nevertheless, it is essential to use this board game in the next steps and to compare the learning success with traditional methods in the area of business process knowledge.

5   Conclusion

This article intended to develop a game-based approach for teaching business process knowledge. Based on a literature review, we identified design elements of a game. In addition, the frequency of their consideration in literature was used for evaluation. After that, we developed a game for teaching business process knowledge. The Development Process followed a new process model with three phases that consider elements of the various models in the literature. As a result, a board game with various design elements is created. In future, experiments are to be conducted, if playing the game fosters the business process knowledge of participants. There is also a need for a final analysis of user acceptance and the validation of the learning content. Finally, for the digital age, an app connection is also conceivable.

References

1. Zouaghi, I., Abderrazak, L.: Aligning key success factors to ERP implementation strategy: learning from a case study. Int. J. Bus. Inf. Syst. **22**(1), 100–115 (2016)
2. Hrastnik, J., Cardoso, J. S., Kappe, F.: The business process knowledge framework. In: ICEIS, vol. 3, pp. 517–520 (2006)
3. Koivisto, J., Juho, H.: The rise of motivational information systems: a review of gamification research. Int. J. Inf. Manage. **45**, 191–210 (2019)
4. Bhuiyan, T., Wong, W.P., Imran, M.: Measuring learning motivation of students in supply chain management games setting: a case study of Innov8. 0 game. Probl. Persp. Manage. **13**(4), 92–101 (2015)
5. Seethamraju, R.: Enhancing student learning of enterprise integration and business process orientation through an ERP business simulation game. J. Inf. Syst. Educ. **22**(1), 19 (2011)
6. Arizton: Global board games market value from 2017 to 2023 (in billion U.S. dollars). Statista. Statista Inc. (2018). Accessed 01 July 2021. https://www.statista.com/statistics/829285/glo bal-board-games-market-value/
7. Embi, Z.C.: The implementation of framework for edutainment: educational games customization tool. In: 2008 International Symposium on Information Technology, pp. 1–5. IEEE (2008)
8. Kiili, K.: Digital game-based learning: towards an experiential gaming model. Internet High. Educ. **8**(1), 13–24 (2005)
9. Chew, B.: An efficient framework for game-based learning activity. In: 2017 IEEE 6th International Conference on Teaching, Assessment, and Learning for Engineering (TALE), pp. 147–150. IEEE (2017)
10. Anyanwu, E.G.: Anatomy adventure: a board game for enhancing understanding of anatomy. Anat. Sci. Educ. **7**(2), 153–160 (2014)
11. Barendregt, W., Bekker, M.: Towards a framework for design guidelines for young children's computer games. In: Rauterberg, M. (ed.) ICEC 2004. LNCS, vol. 3166, pp. 365–376. Springer, Heidelberg (2004). https://doi.org/10.1007/978-3-540-28643-1_47
12. Adams, B.L.: Using game-based learning to raise the ethical awareness of accounting students. Bus. Educ. Innov. J. **2**(2), 86–93 (2010)
13. Said, N.S.: An engaging multimedia design model. In: Proceedings of the 2004 Conference on Interaction Design and Children: Building a Community, pp. 169–172 (2004)
14. Khine, M.S. (ed.): Learning to Play: Exploring the Future of Education with Video Games, vol. 53. Peter Lang, New York (2011)
15. Nah, F.F.H., Eschenbrenner, B., Claybaugh, C.C., Koob, P.B.: Gamification of enterprise systems. Systems **7**(1), 13 (2019)
16. Alcivar, I., Andres, G.A.: Design and evaluation of a gamified system for ERP training. Comput. Hum. Behav. **58**, 109–118 (2016)
17. Morschheuser, B., Hrach, C., Alt, R., Lefanczyk, C.: Gamifizierung mit BPMN. HMD Praxis der Wirtschaftsinformatik **52**(6), 840–850 (2015). https://doi.org/10.1365/s40702-015-0188-3
18. Hendrix, K., Yang, G., Mortel, D.V.D., Tijs, T., Markopoulos, P.: Designing a head-up game for children. People Comput. XXII Cult. Create. Interac. **22**, 45–53 (2008)

19. Ramadan, R., Widyani, Y.: Game development life cycle guidelines. In: 2013 International Conference on Advanced Computer Science and Information Systems (ICACSIS), pp. 95–100. IEEE (2013)
20. Garris, R., Robert, A., James, E.D.: Games, motivation, and learning: a research and practice model. Simul. Gam. **33**(4), 441–467 (2002)
21. De Freitas, S., Martin, O.: How can exploratory learning with games and simulations within the curriculum be most effectively evaluated? Comput. Educ. **46**(3), 249–264 (2006)
22. Cronan, T.P., Douglas, D.E.: A student ERP simulation game: a longitudinal study. J. Comput. Inf. Syst. **53**(1), 3–13 (2012)
23. El-Telbany, O., Ahmed, E.: Gamification of enterprise systems: a lifecycle approach. Proc. Comput. Sci. **121**, 106–114 (2017)
24. Foster, S., Hopkins, J.: ERP simulation game: establishng engagement, collaboration and learning. In: PACIS, p. 62 (2011)
25. Hamari, J., Koivisto, J., Sarsa, H.: Does gamification work?- a literature review of empirical studies on gamification. In: 2014 47th Hawaii International Conference on System Sciences, pp. 3025–3034. IEEE (2014)
26. Herzig, P., Strahringer, S., Ameling, M.: Gamification of ERP systems-exploring gamification effects on user acceptance constructs. In: Multikonferenz Wirtschaftsinformatik, pp. 793–804. GITO, Braunschweig (2012)
27. Kuem, J., Wu, J., Kwak, D. H., Deng, S., Srite, M.: Socio cognitive and affective processing in the context of team-based gamified ERP training: reflective and impulsive model. In: Proceedings of the Midwest Association for Information Systems Annual Conference, Wisconsin (2016)
28. Kutun, B., Schmidt, W.: BPMN-Rad: Brettspiel zur Modellierung von Geschäftsprozessen mittels BPMN. In: Workshops der INFORMATIK 2018-Architekturen, Prozesse, Sicherheit und Nachhaltigkeit, Köllen Druck + Verlag GmbH (2018)
29. Léger, P. M., Robert, J., Babin, G., Lyle, D., Cronan, P.: ERP simulation game: a distribution game to teach the value of integrated systems. In: Developments in Business Simulation and Experiential Learning: Proceedings of the Annual ABSEL Conference (2010)
30. Schmidt-Kraepelin, M., Lins, S., Thiebes, S., Sunyaev, A.: Gamification of Enterprise Systems: A Synthesis of Mechanics, Dynamics, and Risks (2019)
31. Schwade, F., Petra, S.: The ERP challenge: an integrated e-learning platform for the teaching of practical ERP skills in universities. Proc. Comput. Sci. **100**, 147–155 (2016)
32. Wiggins, B.E.: An overview and study on the use of games, simulations, and gamification in higher education. Int. J. Game-Based Learn. (IJGBL) **6**(1), 18–29 (2016)
33. Dicheva, D., Dichev, C., Agre, G., Angelova, G.: Gamification in education: a systematic mapping study. J. Educ. Technol. Soc. **18**(3), 75–88 (2015)
34. Taspinar, B., Schmidt, W., Schuhbauer, H.: Gamification in education: a board game approach to knowledge acquisition. Proc. Comput. Sci. **99**, 101–116 (2016)

Realism of Simulation Models in Serious Gaming

Urban Water Management in Cities: Skylines

Darwin Droll and Heinrich Söbke[✉] [ID]

Bauhaus-Institute for Infrastructure Solutions (B.Is), Bauhaus-Universität Weimar,
Goetheplatz 7/8, 99423 Weimar, Germany
`heinrich.soebke@uni-weimar.de`

Abstract. For games used in educational contexts, realism, i.e., the degree of congruence between the simulation models used in the games and the real-world systems represented, is an important characteristic for achieving learning goals well. However, in the past, the realism of especially entertainment games has often been identified as insufficient. Thus, this study is investigating the degree of realism provided by the popular city builder game Cities: Skylines. To this purpose, the simulation model of Cities: Skylines is analyzed regarding the support of the domain urban water management (UWM). Thereby, different degrees of realism in UWM-related game components are revealed. All in all, there are still considerable deficits regarding the degree of realism in the CS simulation model. However, modding as a means of achieving more realistic simulation models is more widely supported than in the past.

Keywords: Authenticism · Cities: Skylines · Game-based learning · Validity · Simulation game

1 Introduction

The domain urban water management (UWM) addresses the engineered design of water infrastructure. Among key engineering design tools are simulations [1]. Simulation refers to the time-dependent imitation of a real-world system [2]. The underlying simulation model is a purpose-oriented abstraction of the real-world system to be simulated, i.e., only those aspects of the system that are relevant to the purpose are modeled. **Serious Games.** Simulations are also applied effectively in educational contexts of engineering domains [3], for example to enable learners to experiment exploratively with simulation models and thus to understand the systems simulated, hence the learning content. Some simulations in educational contexts take the form of digital games. Fundamental part of digital games are simulation models. The games aim to motivate learners and thus increase the learners' engagement with the games and consequently indirectly with the learning content [4]. For example, in the domain UWM exist many educational simulation games, also referred to as serious games [5–8]. **Realism.** The domain-specific content of games is considered very relevant for learning [9]: domain-specific content

F. de Rosa et al. (Eds.): GALA 2021, LNCS 13134, pp. 277–282, 2021.
https://doi.org/10.1007/978-3-030-92182-8_29

should contribute to the authenticity of the learning environment [10], and consists, among other things, of the terminology and simulation models used. Furthermore, the domain-specific content of serious games is supposed to be as close to reality as possible [11, 12]. In this regard, simulation models are considered to have a driving role in serious games [13, 14]. Tashiro and Dunlap [15] regard realism as one of the key dimensions of learning outcomes in educational games, along with engagement. A term used similarly to authenticity of domain-specific content is *validity* [13]. In serious games with the purpose of learning, one may also refer to learning goal orientation, i.e., the aspects of the systems modelled that are necessary to achieve the learning goals are considered specifically in the simulation models. Accordingly, realism might be defined as the degree of congruence between the simulation models used in the games and the real-world systems to be represented. Thus, in this study, the term realism is used to describe the quality of games whose domain-specific content in the form of simulation models and terminology is oriented as closely as possible to the relevant aspects of the modeled system being addressed in the game. **Entertainment Games as Serious Games.** In addition to serious games created explicitly for learning purposes, the use of entertainment games in educational contexts is also common, such as *Civilization* [16] or *Roller Coster Tycoon* [17]. Among the advantages of using entertainment games as serious games is the non-existent development effort [18]. At the same time, entertainment games are optimized for being enjoyable, i.e., entertainment games are characterized by high attractiveness. However, even in the case of entertainment games that are used for learning, the game domain-specific content—to a large extent the simulation models—needs to be oriented to learning goals, i.e., the games show a high degree of realism in the previously defined sense. However, in general, simulation models of entertainment games in educational contexts are attributed inaccuracies [19]. The entertainment game studied here, Cities: Skylines, also appears to lack technical accuracy for the domain urban planning [20]. Such inaccuracies of simulation models might need to be considered in the design of learning scenarios, for example, for addressing learning outcomes outside of the game [21]. Thus, the value of entertainment games is also often seen in additional effects, e.g., as a trigger for learning processes with further media [22]. For example, Bawa et al. [23] exploit the motivation nurtured from MMOGs for learning with media beyond the MMOG, such as wikis. **The Case of SimCity.** The impetus for the study outlined in this article arose from the observation that entertainment games are not necessarily designed with learning goals in mind. More precisely, entertainment games often do not offer the degree of realism necessary to support specific learning goals. This may also be the case with entertainment games that appear to be very realistic at first glance. The case that illustrates these statements is SimCity [24] in relation to the learning objectives of the domain UWM [25]. In consequence, exemplarily from the perspective of the domain UWM, thus, the research question arises to what extent the progress in game development in recent years, visible among others in the currently most popular city builder game Cities: Skylines (CS) [26], has led to a higher degree of realism, which is expressed for example by more detailed simulation models that might support a wider range of learning goals than before. This research question yet recognizes that by carefully aligning learning goals and learning scenario using an entertainment game, some domain-specific learning goals may be achievable, and that beyond domain-specific learning objectives, additional higher-order learning goals (e.g., metacognitive learning goals) may be reachable. However, the research questions targets the extent, to which domain-specific learning objectives may be achieved without significant alignment effort. The remainder of the paper is organized as follows: in the next section the methodology applied is outlined, CS and the analysis of its simulation model are presented. Section 3 discusses the results and summarizes the findings. In an extended version of the article, additional information, including further references, a comparison with a dedicated serious game and a survey among serious gaming-interested CS players, is available [27].

2 Simulation Model

Since its launch in 2015, CS has been one of the most popular city builder games, which is reputed having a high degree of realism and has also been used in real urban planning contexts, e.g., in transportation planning for the city of Stockholm [28]. CS exhibits a high degree of realism especially in the domain transportation [29]. Actual georeferenced data have also been displayed in CS [30]. Overall, therefore, as a recent game with detailed simulation models, CS appeared to be a candidate for investigating the degree of realism of UWM-specific simulation models in an entertainment city builder game, especially since CS is considered a de facto successor to SimCity. For an evaluation of the current degree of realism of simulation games in UWM, the simulation model of the CS was analyzed regarding the support of the domain UWM. The model analysis was performed by two UWM experts, both spending about 20 h of specific playing time. The experts first independently assessed the games for UWM components, such as water treatment plants (WTPs), identified parameters of the components selected, and analyzed whether and how they were presumed to be incorporated into the simulation model. In cases where the experts' assessments did not correspond, the experts elaborated in discussions unified assessments. Since CS is a city builder game, players build cities from components and thus influence the simulation model. CS was examined for components relevant to UWM based on the authors' gaming experiences and on developer-provided documentation [31], source code or other formal models were not available. The following enumeration describes the components identified and introduces discrepancies to reality using the keyword *Reality Check*.

Pipes. Water pipes supply water and discharge wastewater. *Reality Check:* Drinking water pipes and wastewater pipes are always positioned simultaneously and therefore on the same route, which is independent of further construction, such as roads. Parameters such as flow rates, pressure or pipe gradients do not exist. **Water Tower.** The water tower acts as a groundwater pump, providing a constant flow of 60,000 m^3/week. If water tower is constructed in an industrial area, polluted water is pumped. *Reality Check:* There is no connection with precipitation water, groundwater is assumed to be an infinite reservoir. **Water Pumping Station.** A water pumping station conveys with constant flow of 120,000 m^3/week, is placed at a water body and connected to the water network. *Reality Check:* The capacity of the water body is rather overestimated. **Water Drain Pipe.** The water drain pipe is initially the only means of discharging wastewater, it is connected to a water body and discharges untreated wastewater with a flow of 120,000 m³/week into the water body. The pollution is visualized after a short time by brown coloration of the water body in the flow direction below the wastewater pipe. The water pumping station therefore is to be built in flow direction above the water drain pipe, otherwise polluted water will be pumped. *Reality Check*: Water drain pipes are not very common in the western industrialized countries simulated in CS. **Water Treatment Plant.** The water treatment plant is unlocked after progressing in the game and cleans a wastewater flow of 16,000 m³/week at 85%. *Reality Check*: No distinction is made between purification process steps, further, the 85% purification performance is given in general and not on specific contaminants. **Rain.** CS features rain. *Reality Check:* Rain has no influence on water management components such as water bodies or groundwater.

CS Extensions. A prominent feature of CS is its support for modding. The software is open for programmatic program changes and is further developed by the developer ("extension packs") as well as by third parties ("mods"). Both, certain extension packs and several mods complement CS from the perspective of UWM. The following are examples: **Heating Pipes.** The heating pipes are part of the expansion pack *Cities: Snowfall*, which adds heating pipes to the water network and interlinks energy management and UWM. **Stabilization Basin.** The stabilization basin is an alternative to the water treatment plant. The stabilization basin percolates the water and therefore has a low capacity only. **Ground Water Pump.** The pump operates independently of a water body and differs from the water tower not functionally, but in appearance and parameters. **Modular Sewage Treatment Facility.** Very close to real water treatment plants are the buildings of this mod, which represent all the main steps of the purification process and is modeled after a real water treatment plant in Denmark. *Reality Check*: Again, no specific contaminants in the water are distinguished.

Basically, mods and expansion packs support the continuous expansion of the CS simulation model, so that currently also significantly more types of water treatment plants are available. In this respect, progress can be seen compared to SimCity. However, the expansions refer to the components themselves, but the descriptive parameters of the components remain unchanged and are the same for all components, such as cost, upkeep, noise pollution, water, electricity consumption and size. This limitation renders developing domain-specific extensions harder.

3   Discussion and Conclusion

More than a decade ago, it has been reported that the simulation model of the entertainment game SimCity is optimized for entertainment purposes rather than providing urban water management (UWM)-specific knowledge. Hereby, potential learning goals supported by SimCity in learning contexts are limited. Thus, the aim of this study was to conduct a current review of realism in entertainment games regarding the domain UWM by an analysis of the simulation model of the popular entertainment game Cities: Skylines (CS). A primary limitation of the study is that it is based only on CS and thus is not representative. Nevertheless, it is to be assumed—and this is aligned with the literature referenced in the introduction—that in most other entertainment games the degree of realism is similarly simplistic. Likewise, there is the restriction that the analysis of CS refers to the initial version without extension packs. However, even a subsequent ad-hoc analysis of the extension packs released to date did not reveal any qualitative discrepancies from the results. Compared to SimCity, CS does not show any significant progress in the level of detail of the simulation model from an UWM perspective. However, due to the game engine used [32], CS offers the possibility to comprehensively access the simulation model via modding. Therefore, building a simulation model with higher degrees of realism seems to be costly, but in general conceivable. Further, it has to be mentioned that the degree of realism necessary depends on the learning goals. Although we have no indication that these findings are limited to CS and the domain of UWM, the generalizability of the findings to other domains remains to be confirmed through further research.

References

1. AbouRizk, S.: Role of simulation in construction engineering and management. J. Constr. Eng. Manag. **136**, 1140–1153 (2010)
2. Banks, J.: Principles of simulation. In: Banks, J. (ed.) Handbook of Simulation Principles, Methodology, Advances, Applications and Practice, pp. 3–30. Wiley (1998)
3. Magana, A.J., de Jong, T.: Modeling and simulation practices in engineering education. Comput. Appl. Eng. Educ. **26**, 731–738 (2018)
4. Deshpande, A.A., Huang, S.H.: Simulation games in engineering education: a state-of-the-art review. Comput. Appl. Eng. Educ. **19**(3), 399–410 (2009)
5. Savic, D., Morley, M., Khoury, M.: Serious gaming for water systems planning and management. Water **8**, 456 (2016)
6. Zhou, Q., Mayer, I.S.: Models, simulations and games for water management: a comparative Q-method study in The Netherlands and China. Water **10**(1), 10 (2017)
7. Aubert, A.H., Bauer, R., Lienert, J.: A review of water-related serious games to specify use in environmental Multi-Criteria Decision Analysis. Environ. Model. Softw. **105**, 64–78 (2018)
8. Arnold, U., Söhke, H., Reichelt, M.: SimCity in infrastructure management education. Educ. Sci. **9**, 209 (2019)
9. Galván-Pérez, L., Ouariachi, T., Pozo-Llorente, T.M., Gutiérrez-Pérez, J.: Outstanding videogames on water: a quality assessment review based on evidence of narrative, gameplay and educational criteria. Water **10**(10), 1404 (2018)
10. Lee, Y.Y.R., Samad, H., Miang Goh, Y.: Perceived importance of authentic learning factors in designing construction safety simulation game-based assignment: random forest approach. J. Constr. Eng. Manag. **146**, 04020002 (2020)
11. Roungas, B., Bekius, F., Meijer, S.: The game between game theory and gaming simulations: design choices. Simul. Gaming **50**, 180–201 (2019)
12. Harteveld, C., Guimarães, R., Mayer, I., Bidarra, R.: Balancing pedagogy, game and reality components within a unique serious game for training levee inspection. In: Hui, K.-C., et al. (eds.) Edutainment 2007. LNCS, vol. 4469, pp. 128–139. Springer, Heidelberg (2007). https://doi.org/10.1007/978-3-540-73011-8_15
13. Van der Wal, M.M., de Kraker, J., Kroeze, C., Kirschner, P.A., Valkering, P.: Can computer models be used for social learning? A serious game in water management. Environ. Model. Softw. **75**, 119–132 (2016)
14. Craven, J., Angarita, H., Corzo Perez, G.A., Vasquez, D.: Development and testing of a river basin management simulation game for integrated management of the Magdalena-Cauca river basin. Environ. Model. Softw. **90**, 78–88 (2017)

15. Tashiro, J.S., Dunlap, D.: The impact of realism on learning engagement in educational games. In: Proceedings of the 2007 Conference on Future Play, Future Play 2007, pp. 113–120 (2007)

16. Squire, K.R.: Replaying History: Learning World History Through Playing Civilization III (2003)

17. Foster, A.N.: The process of learning in a simulation strategy game: disciplinary knowledge construction. J. Educ. Comput. Res. **45**, 1–27 (2011)

18. Söbke, H., Bröker, T., Kornadt, O.: Using the master copy - adding educational content to commercial video games. In: de Carvalho, C.V., et al. (eds.) Proceedings of the 7th European Conference on Games-Based Learning, vol. 2, pp. 521–530. ACPIL, Reading (2013)

19. Lieberman, D.A.: What can we learn from playing interactive games. In: Vorderer, P., Bryant, J. (eds.) Playing Video Games: Motives, Responses, and Consequences, pp. 379–397. Lawrence Erlbaum Associates, Mahwah (2006)

20. Khan, T.A., Zhao, X.: Perceptions of students for a gamification approach: cities skylines as a pedagogical tool in urban planning education. In: Dennehy, D., Griva, A., Pouloudi, N., Dwivedi, Y.K., Pappas, I., Mäntymäki, M. (eds.) I3E 2021. LNCS, vol. 12896, pp. 763–773. Springer, Cham (2021). https://doi.org/10.1007/978-3-030-85447-8_64

21. Breuer, J., Bente, G.: Why so serious? On the relation of serious games and learning. J. Comput. Game Cult. **4**, 7–24 (2010)

22. Squire, K., Jenkins, H.: Harnessing the power of games in education. Insight **3**, 5–33 (2003)

23. Bawa, P., Lee Watson, S., Watson, W.: Motivation is a game: massively multiplayer online games as agents of motivation in higher education. Comput. Educ. **123**, 174–194 (2018)

24. Wright, W.: SimCity. www.simcity.com

25. D'Artista, B.R., Hellweger, F.L.: Urban hydrology in a computer game? Environ. Model. Softw. **22**, 1679–1684 (2007)

26. Collossal Order: Cities: Skylines (2015)

27. Droll, D., Söbke, H.: Realism of simulation models in serious gaming: two case studies from urban water management higher education. http://arxiv.org/abs/2109.10572

28. Nutt, C.: Did you know stockholm used cities: skylines for urban planning? https://www.gamasutra.com/view/news/267926/Did_you_know_Stockholm_used_Cities_Skylines_for_urban_planning.php

29. Thompson, T.: How traffic works in cities: skylines. https://www.gamasutra.com/blogs/TommyThompson/20200827/368667/How_Traffic_Works_in_Cities_Skylines.php

30. Pinos, J., Vozenilek, V., Pavlis, O.: Automatic geodata processing methods for real-world city visualizations in cities: skylines. ISPRS Int. J. Geo-Inf. **9**, 17 (2020)

31. Paradox Wikis: Water and sewage. https://skylines.paradoxwikis.com/Water_and_sewage

32. Unity: Colossal Order's Cities: Skylines brings excellence back to the city building genre. https://unity3d.com/showcase/case-stories/cities-skylines

Covid-19 Survivor: Design and Evaluation of a Game to Improve Students' Experience During Social Isolation

Marianthi Grizioti[1]([envelope]) [iD], Wilk Oliveira[2,3] [iD], and Varvara Garneli[4] [iD]

[1] Educational Technology Lab, University of Athens, Athens, Greece
`mgriziot@eds.uoa.gr`
[2] University of São Paulo, São Paulo, Brazil
`wilk.oliveira@usp.br`
[3] Tampere University, Tampere, Finland
[4] Audiovisual Art Department, Ionian University, Corfu, Greece
`vgarneli@ionio.gr`

Abstract. In socio-economic crises, such as the recent Covid-19 pandemic, it is crucial to enhance children's understanding of the new situation and their choices to protect their physical and mental health. In this paper, we discuss the design of a serious choice-driven simulation game, called "Covid-19 Survivor", as a means to empower students' awareness of pandemic risks and consequences through decision making and system analysis. The online game simulates the daily routine of a school student through a system of available choices and consequences to five game fields. We qualitatively evaluated the game in a classroom setting with twenty-six 13 years old students and one IT teacher. The preliminary results demonstrate its potential to influence students' perceptions and knowledge about the pandemic as well as to enhance their decision-making and systems thinking skills.

Keywords: Educational games · Simulation games · Covid-19 · Students' behavior · Qualitative study

1 Introduction

Children and adolescents were highly affected by the changes that Covid-19 pandemic brought to our lives [1]. In cases of social isolation and country lockdown, young people must deal with changes in their daily routines, school dynamics, and social relations, which can directly impact their phycology and mental health [2]. As relevant research has shown they often fail to understand the rationale behind these rapid changes, leading to more stress, worry, or fear. In such situations, it is crucial for the education system to support the empowerment of higher order thinking skills in young students, such as systems thinking, probabilistic thinking, and decision making, that would enable them to make informed decisions in complex situations, reflect on their impact and respond to local and global challenges [3]. However, as education researchers and scientists have

© Springer Nature Switzerland AG 2021
F. de Rosa et al. (Eds.): GALA 2021, LNCS 13134, pp. 283–288, 2021.
https://doi.org/10.1007/978-3-030-92182-8_30

claimed, traditional domain-specific instructional pedagogical approaches and tools may be insufficient for supporting skill development and understanding of complex socio-scientific issues, *i.e.* issues with both societal and scientific aspects [4, 5]. Attempting to address this challenge, we propose using a digital simulation game about life during Covid-19 to enhance students' ability to make informed decisions, protecting their physical and mental.

Thus, in this paper we present the design of the "Covid-19 Survivor" game (http://etl. ppp.uoa.gr/choico/?covid19survivor), developed and tested by academics in collaboration with a middle-school teacher, and the preliminary results of a short pilot study with junior high-school students. The game belongs to the genre of choice-driven simulation games [6]. It consists of two game map-like areas (City and Home) in which the player makes choices of action (*e.g.* go to the park) affecting a set of game parameters related to the player's condition (*e.g.* Health, Fun). The designers aim to provide students with a fun way to discover and reflect on the possible risks in their daily routine and realize the importance of balancing physical health, communication, and personal interests during such difficult times. In May 2021, we conducted a pilot study with 26 junior high-school students aiming to investigate a) whether and how students' awareness of Covid-19 and can be enhanced by playing the game and b) what decision-making strategies students develop while playing the game.

2   Theoretical Background

Serious games have long been used in formal and informal education to support knowledge and skill development [4, 7]. Playing a game involves, apart from fun and entertainment elements, the aspect of problem-posing and problem-solving [8]. According to Gee [7], players are engaged in a four stages cycle while playing a serious game: "Probe - Hypothesize - Reprobe - Rethink". Through this mental process, the player forms a hypothesis about a possible pattern, tests it, and reflects on their actions based on the provided feedback. This reflective practice is central to how people deal with and respond to complex situations of the real world. Similarly, Garris, Ahlers, Driskell [9] describe the gaming experience as a repeated cycle involving the three steps of "user judgments, user behavior and system feedback", which also requires the development and application of problem-solving practices such as decision-making, critical thinking, and strategy. This process can be identified more intensively in simulation games since they are based on decision-making and system balancing. These games, *e.g.* "the Sims" series, simulate a complex system of connected variables, relations, and rules which are changing dynamically according to the actions of the player upon the simulation, creating a non-linear game flow [8, 9]. The players have to make informed and thoughtful decisions considering the current game state and the different available choices.

The use of serious games or simulation games in educational settings traditionally focuses on core curricula subjects through content-specific problems [7, 8]. Recently, though, there has been an effort to develop and utilize games to enhance children's understanding of open-ended complex issues that have societal and scientific aspects [10]. Nevertheless, there is still a lack of studies focusing on the pedagogical value of simulation games for increasing student awareness and knowledge related to socio-economic crises like Covid-19.

3   The "Covid-19 Survivor" Game

The "Covid-19 Survivor" is a serious game developed by an academic team collaborating with a secondary school IT teacher with the online game design platform ChoiCo (Choices with Consequences). ChoiCo is an open-source environment developed by the NKUA Educational Technology Lab that allows the creation, play and modification of choice-driven simulation games that deal with systemic socio-scientific issues [6]. The game represents the daily life of a middle-school student during the lockdown period. It has a set of 5 fields, *i.e.* "Covid Risk", "Money", "Physical", "Fun", and "Social", which start with specific values and change during the gameplay according to the player's choices. The game interface consists of two interactive maps, "City" and "Home", each including a set of pinpoints (e.g. "Supermarket", "Park", "Birthday Party") representing the available choices in that area. By clicking on a pin, the "point information" board informs the player about the possible consequences of this choice on the game fields. If the player selects a choice, it will affect the game fields respectively (Fig. 1). The aim is to survive for as long as possible, balancing these fields and preventing them from crossing specific upper or lower limits hidden to the player. Thus, the best player is the one who will make the most choices without losing. The game ends if "Money" becomes less than 0, the "Covid Risk" greater than 90 or if "Physical", "Fun", or "Social" less than 5.

Fig. 1. The player has selected the choice "Birthday Party" which affected the 5 game fields

The gameplay is based on decision-making, prediction, and balance. Every choice has both positive and negative consequences to the game fields, so there is no "ideal" choice to make, but this depends on the current state of the game fields. The consequences values for the field "Covid Risk" were designed according to the official reports of WHO and the National Public Health Organization (NPHO) of Greece. Since risk can have variations, the precise number is picked up randomly between a specific values range. The values for the four other fields are based on literature review and input by a teacher concerning children's preferences for fun and socializing. The game keeps a history log with the player's choices and game field values which can be downloaded as a PDF file. The ChoiCo environment also offers a "Design Mode" where end-users can modify main game elements with high-level computational tools, allowing users with no technical experience, such as teachers, educators or students, to intervene with the game data and create their personalized version.

4 Pilot Evaluation

The pilot study was implemented with 26 junior high-school students (13 females and 13 males) with average age 13 years old and aimed to evaluate whether and how the game enhances their awareness of daily choices during Covid-19 social isolation. Before the study, the participants had experienced a strict national lockdown for four months. The research followed was in alignment with institutional rules and ethics. Before the implementation, the participants answered an online pre-questionnaire with questions about their gaming background and Covid-19 awareness. According to the pre-questionnaires, most participants (73%) enjoyed playing digital games and considered themselves regular players (2–3 times/week). The implementation took place in the school's computer laboratory with the participation of the IT teacher. For 45 min, students played the game online several times downloading the game logs. They were prompted to discuss their choices while playing, allowing the teacher to ask them questions and keep observation notes. After the study, the researchers had a semi-structured interview with the IT teacher to discuss his observation notes.

4.1 Data Analysis Process

We qualitatively analyzed the collected data. *i.e.,* teacher's observations, interview, and the game log files, performing an inductive content analysis [11]. First, the descriptive data were anonymized, and the interesting phrases were coded. Then the coded results were further analyzed by 2 researchers separately to develop a coding schema each. Finally, the schemas were compared, evaluated and integrated to a final one with hyper-categories of codes. The collected game log files for each student were analyzed and coded in two axes: a) regarding student choices in each gameplay, aiming to identify their views or misconceptions and b) in cases students had played the game 3 times or more, we looked for possible patterns or changes in their choices between the gameplays, aiming to identify how their perception and attitude towards covid evolved through the game.

5 Preliminary Results and Discussion

The inductive content analysis of the qualitative data revealed some coding patterns regarding student perceptions, views, attitudes, and knowledge on how to act on the Covid-19 pandemic. From the initial analysis, four coding hyper-categories emerged: Personal/Social Views, Safety Understanding, Risk-Taking, and Strategy (Table 1).

According to the game logs analysis, most students lost the game due to the low value of the "Physical" (35%) game field, which means they neglected to make fitness-positive choices. The second most common reason to lose the game was high levels of "Covid Risk" (22%). This was detected especially by children who made choices according

Table 1. Coding categories that emerged from the data analysis

Coding hyper-category	Examples
Personal/social views	"I do not understand… why it is not a good choice to stay at home, using my PC for learning and gaming reasons?", "But I do not want to go out, I am fine at home"
Safety understanding	"If I see a person who has covid, I must stay at home and test myself". In-game logs: Make "low risk" choices several times
Risk-taking	"Maybe it was worth taking the risk of increasing covid_risk because I have to increase Fun"
Strategy	In the game logs: Make a repeated pattern of choices that balance the values e.g. Home→Workout→Exit home→Local store

to their daily routine before the pandemic, *e.g.* play football or go to a birthday party, without considering the possible risks for Covid-19. To keep Covid Risk low most students avoided fitness choices. This was also highlighted by the teacher who claimed that some students at first were hesitant or negative towards more social or fitness-related choices and made statements such as "*I prefer to stay at home, I can speak with my friends through the internet*" or "*I do not want to go out running or walking*". All students achieved a higher score after playing the game several times, with a maximum score of 22 choices. Considering the sequence of the choices, in students' first attempts we did not detect any specific patterns. On the contrary, the subsequent game logs revealed that students formed and repeated patterns of choices, especially the players who achieved a high score (code "Strategy" Table 1). Finally, according to the teacher, some students changed their initial views considering social, fitness and entertainment choices. As they claimed: "*Maybe, I can go out with my friends to swim and play by the sea, if I am careful*", "*I think I should stay home for some time and then go out to take some air and then home again*". Moreover, the game raised some critical topics for discussion that students had not considered before, such as "*where is it safer to go shopping during the pandemic?*" or "*how can I save money?*".

6 Concluding Remarks

In this paper, we presented the design, implementation, and evaluation of a choice-driven simulation game called "Covid-19 Survivor", which concerns a socio-scientific problem that significantly influences student lives [1, 2]. Since this was a pilot study with a reduced sample size and a short duration, the results cannot be generalized. Nevertheless, it provides insights into how simulation games like Covid-19 could enhance informed decision-making on crises that change children's daily routines, such as a pandemic. Initial results demonstrate that students gradually developed strategies such as pattern recognition, prediction of the consequences and the risk of their actions, and analysis of the interconnections and the rules of a system. Finally, the game raised important issues for discussion considering safe/unsafe choices and the importance of balancing their choices, *e.g.,* not neglect physical exercise. Future work will involve further data analysis and a new study with a larger sample of students who will also modify parts of the game in ChoiCo's design mode, such as available choices, consequence values, and ending conditions allowing us to compare their experiences and perceptions of the pandemic.

References

1. de Figueiredo, C.S., et al.: COVID-19 pandemic impact on children and adolescents' mental health: biological, environmental, and social factors. Prog. Neuro-Psychopharmacol. Biol. Psychiatry **106**, 110171 (2021)
2. Phelps, C., Sperry, L.L.: Children and the COVID-19 pandemic. Psychol. Trauma Theory Res. Pract. Policy **12**(S1), S73 (2020)
3. United Nations: 2018 Sustainable Development Goals (2020)
4. Kafai, Y.B., Burke, Q.: Connected Gaming: What Making Video Games Can Teach Us About Learning and Literacy. MIT Press, Cambridge (2016)
5. Jonassen, D.H.: Toward a design theory of problem solving. Educ. Technol. Res. Dev. **48**(4), 63–85 (2000). https://doi.org/10.1007/BF02300500
6. Kynigos, C., Grizioti, M.: Modifying games with ChoiCo: integrated affordances and engineered bugs for computational thinking. Br. J. Edu. Technol. **51**(6), 2252–2267 (2020)
7. Gee, J.P.: What Video Games Have to Teach Us About Learning and Literacy, 1st edn. Palgrave Macmillan, New York (2003)
8. Qian, M., Clark, K.R.: Game-based learning and 21st century skills: a review of recent research. Comput. Hum. Behav. **63**, 50–58 (2016)
9. Garris, R., Ahlers, R., Driskell, J.: Games, motivation and learning: a research and practice model. Simul. Gaming **33**(4), 441–467 (2002)
10. Grizioti, M., Kynigos, C.: Children as players, modders, and creators of simulation games: a design for making sense of complex real-world problems. In: Proceedings of the 20th ACM Conference on Interaction Design and Children. ACM (2021)
11. Maguire, M., Bevan, N.: User requirements analysis. In: Hammond, J., Gross, T., Wesson, J. (eds.) Usability, pp. 133–148. Springer, Boston (2002). https://doi.org/10.1007/978-0-387-35610-5_9

An Authoring Tool to Engage Younger Audiences in the Development of Nature Preservation Games: The G4N Toolkit to Game Design

Pedro Beça[✉] ⓘ, Mónica Aresta ⓘ, Rita Santos ⓘ, and Ana Isabel Veloso ⓘ

Department of Communication and Art, University of Aveiro, Aveiro, Portugal
{pedrobeca,m.aresta,rita.santos,aiv}@ua.pt

Abstract. Although research indicates that integrating students as active agents in the development of games encourages awareness and learning by doing and can be seen as a basis for the development of critical thinking skills, it also stresses that there are some obstacles in involving students to explore educational contents through digital game design. This paper introduces the Gamers4Nature toolkit to Game Design and its use by upper-secondary (N = 53) and undergraduate (N = 114) students along several game design sessions addressing an environmental preservation theme. As result of these sessions, 66 prototypes of digital games were produced. The toolkit was used through questionnaires applied by the end of the game design sessions. Results indicate that the Toolkit was a very useful resource in scaffolding the narrative construction process and that its resources are adequate to be used by for both upper-secondary and undergraduate students, and that it can be seen as a valuable resource to support educators and trainers in educational and serious game design activities.

Keywords: Game design toolkit · Methodology · Authoring tool · Environmental awareness · Serious games · Digital games

1 Introduction

Integrating students as active agents in the development of games enhances and encourages awareness and learning by doing, promotes collaboration and the exchange of ideas, and can be seen as a basis for the development of critical thinking skills [1, 2]. Nevertheless, research also stresses that there are some obstacles in involving students to explore educational contents through digital game design [3, 4]. Aware of the difficulties faced by teachers and students when engaging in design game-creation-based learning approaches, the Gamers4Nature project developed a Toolkit to Game Design, to be used by individuals with and without experience and previous knowledge in the game design field to develop digital games able to foster positive behaviour changes towards the environment. The Toolkit was used by upper-secondary and undergraduate students (N = 167) throughout several game narrative design sessions. This paper presents the results of these sessions to evaluate its potential as a tool able to support educators and trainers in the design of activities aiming to engage students in the creation of their own digital

The original version of this chapter was revised: this chapter was previously published non-open access. The correction to this chapter is available at
https://doi.org/10.1007/978-3-030-92182-8_32

F. de Rosa et al. (Eds.): GALA 2021, LNCS 13134, pp. 289–294, 2021.
https://doi.org/10.1007/978-3-030-92182-8_31

games for learning. Following this introduction, Sect. 2 presents an overview of the use of games in the educational field and presents toolkits developed to support game creation activities. Section 3 introduces the Gamers4Nature Toolkit to Game Design validation process and its main results. The paper ends with considerations and potential paths for future research (Sect. 4).

2 Creating Games for Environmental Education

As research on the use of games designed to foster awareness for nature's conservation indicates an increase on biodiversity-related knowledge and student's motivation [5], and an improvement on understanding of the practical challenges of environmental sustainability [2, 6], a somewhat complementary approach based on challenging students to create their own games for learning indicates outcomes related with an enhancement on awareness and learning by doing, a promotion of collaboration and development of critical thinking skills [2, 4], and the development of digital literacy skills [7, 8]. Nevertheless, this new approach of games in education also stresses that designing a game able to provide motivated engagement can be a challenging task: low or undeveloped programming skills and low interest in the educational subject [4], a focus on storytelling and character development and a disregard to content integration and gameplay mechanics [9, 10] are pointed out as some obstacles on involving students in exploring educational contents through game design.

2.1 Authoring Tools to Support the Game Creation Process

Challenging students to design games for learning requires teachers an additional effort, as there is the need to provide students the tools and techniques that can help them complete a task whose outcome will be both pedagogical and playful in nature. Toolkits, because of its problem-solving features and support materials and resources, are considered as powerful tools able to transmit valuable insights about the production of interactive artefacts, allowing faster prototyping and supporting creative design [11]. Often developed and adopted in the Human-Computer Interaction field, toolkits are used as tools to support and influence interactive systems' design and implementation [12], emerging as a useful resource to be used in: the conceptual and methodological definition of games (e.g. [13, 14]); game ideation and/or brainstorming activities (e.g. [15, 16]); game narrative creation activities (e.g. [17–19]); and game implementation activities (e.g. [13, 20]) either by game design experts or by users with no relevant experience in the game design field.

3 Use of the Gamers4Nature Toolkit to Game Design

3.1 Background

The Gamers4Nature (G4N) project aims to develop and operationalize a set of strategies that encourage younger audiences (i.e. upper-secondary and undergraduate students) in game creation activities, while promoting knowledge about environmental preservation and biodiversity conservation. One of these strategies is the promotion of Game Creation Sessions addressing an environmental related theme, with participants being challenged to create the prototype of a nature-related game. It was the project's premise that, in order to create the game, participants would have to access and explore information on the problem and thus enhancing greater knowledge on the addressed subject. In order to support the game creation process, the G4N project developed a Toolkit to Game Design to be used by individuals with and without experience and previous knowledge in the game design field. The Toolkit (Fig. 1) comprises several resources designed to support and encourage the participation of young public in the development of mobile games, while giving them curated information about specific environmental themes. It is composed of a game construction cards set with 12 cards each one addressing a different game element (e.g. players, objectives, rules, story); a rapid game design document, presenting a path to explore the cards; sets of 20 thematic cards addressing environmental awareness themes (e.g. microplastic pollution, endangered species, invasive species); and a set of 27 cards presenting guidelines to be followed when developing mobile games interfaces.

Fig. 1. G4N toolkit to game design

All resources were developed following a User-Centered Design approach, with experts in the game design field and potential users (i.e. undergraduate and upper-secondary students with and without experience in the game design field) being involved in the design and validation process.

3.2 Method

The G4N Toolkit to game design was used by upper-secondary students (n = 53) and undergraduate students (n = 114) with and without experience in creating games, throughout different game narrative design sessions: 2 one-day sessions; 2 two-days sessions; 2 long-term (one month) sessions and one 72 h online Game Jam. Although all students already had basic programming skills, none had specific knowledge about game design. Sessions took place from December 2019 to January 2021, and as result of these sessions 66 digital games prototypes were produced.

3.3   Results: Environmental Awareness Games

As result of the game design sessions 66 prototypes of playable digital games were produced, with several programing languages and applications being used for the game implementation: MIT App Inventor and Scratch were used by upper-secondary students, while undergraduate students used web-based games and javascript. Games' analysis revealed that the environmental awareness theme was incorporated in the game narrative, not only in characters but also along the game's story, goals and outcomes. Several games also included quizzes with questions addressing the environmental related theme. Games were analyzed by the project's research team, with several dimensions being addressed: game narrative, compliance with the theme, gameplay, graphic consistency, relation between game and game narrative. All games addressed the environmental theme either through characters or through the game story, and specific information about the theme (e.g. how microplastics are produced) was given through dialogues between characters and short quizzes or game cutouts scenes (e.g. "do you know that microplastics can be released from your clothes through washing?").

3.4   Toolkit's Contribution in Supporting the Game Development Process

Aiming to access the toolkit's contribute along the game narrative construction process, a short questionnaire was applied to all participants (N = 167) by the end of the several game design sessions. Asked to give their opinion about the Toolkit's contribution for the game narrative construction process, 80% of the participants considered that the toolkit helped to organizing ideas, 75% that it eased the narrative construction process and 73% that it helped to understand how to build a game. Only 19% considered that using the toolkit to support the game narrative process limited creativity. When asked to give their opinion about the G4N toolkit's different resources, 78% considered that texts presented in the cards and in the rapid game design document were clear, and 74% considered that the questions provided on the front of the cards helped to understand the concepts. Nevertheless, 23% considered that too much information was presented in the Toolkit's resources, and 15% considered that in order to understand the cards, previous knowledge was needed. Finally, and in what concerns participant's overall opinion about the toolkit, 75% of the participants considered that the toolkit was useful in the process of designing a game, 72% considered that its format was easy to use and 71% considered that it provided a good experience when designing the game.

4   Conclusions and Future Work

This paper describes the use of the G4N Toolkit to Game Design by 167 students in several game design sessions, where they were challenged to design and implement digital (serious) games related addressing an environmental theme using the Toolkit. The analysis of the 66 produced games evidences the compliance with the nature-related theme and the inclusion of specific scientific information about the addressed theme. It also indicates that there was a concern to not only comply with the theme but also to provide a good game experience for future players, as gameplay mechanics were carefully integrated in the game and there was the concern to create an engaging game narrative. As for the G4N Toolkit's capability to support the game creation process, results indicate that it can be considered as a useful and valuable resource to support the narrative construction process, either by upper-secondary and undergraduate students. Overall, participants considered that the Toolkit was useful in the process of designing a game, that its format was easy to use, and that it provided a good experience when designing the game. The use of the toolkit continues to be boosted by the research team. Besides the game design sessions with upper-secondary and undergraduate students, the toolkit is also being used by secondary school teachers who are attending a training course developed in the framework of an Erasmus + project. Future additional game design sessions will be held with upper-secondary and undergraduate students, in order to strength its validation or to or discover points hitherto unconsidered. New sets of thematic cards are also being produced.

Acknowledgments. This work is part of the Gamers4Nature project Gamers4Nature (POCI-01-0145-FEDER-031047) that has the financial support of FCT - Foundation for Science and Technology (Portugal)/MCTES – Ministry of Science, Technology and Higher Education and FEDER under the PT2020 agreement.

References

1. De Grove, F., Bourgonjon, J., Van Looy, J.: Digital games in education? A contextual approach to teachers' adoption intention of digital games for learning purposes. Comput. Hum. Behav. **28**(6), 2023–2033 (2012)
2. Giannakos, M.N., Jaccheri, L.: From players to makers: an empirical examination of factors that affect creative game development. Int. J. Child-Comput. Interact. **18**, 27–36 (2018)
3. Laine, T.H., Lindberg, R.S.: Designing engaging games for education: a systematic literature review on game motivators and design principles. IEEE Trans. Learn. Technol. **13**(4), 804–821 (2020)
4. Falcão, T.P., Peres, F.N., de Morais, D.C., Oliveira, G.: Participatory methodologies to promote student engagement in the development of educational digital games. Comput. Educ. **116**, 161–175 (2018)
5. Tan, C.K.W., Lee, J.W., Hii, A., Loo, Y.Y., Campos-Arceiz, A., Macdonald, D.W.: The effect of using games in teaching conservation. Peer J. **6**, e4509 (2018)
6. Smith, K., Shen, Y., Shull, J., Dean, T., Michaeli, J.: A toolkit for presenting advanced mathematics in serious games. In: SoutheastCon 2016 (2016)
7. Huizenga, Dam, G., Voogt, J., Admiraal, W.: Teacher perceptions of the value of game-based learning in secondary education. Comput. Educ. **110**, 105–115 (2017)
8. Papavlasopoulou, S., Giannakos, M., Jaccheri, L.: Exploring children's learning experience in constructionism-based coding activities through design-based research. Comput. Hum. Behav. **99**, 415–427 (2019)
9. Howland, K., Good, J.: Learning to communicate computationally with flip: a bi-modal programming language for game creation. Comput. Educ. **80**, 224–240 (2015)
10. Ke, F.: An implementation of design-based learning through creating educational computer games: a case study on mathematics learning during design and computing. Comput. Educ. **73**, 26–39 (2014)

11. Wobbrock, A., Wilson, A., Li, Y.: Gestures without libraries, toolkits or training: a $1 rec-
    ognizer for user interface prototypes. In: 20th Annual ACM Symposium on User Interface
    Software and Technology (2007)
12. Ledo, D., Houben, S., Vermeulen, J., Marquardt, N., Oehlberg, L., Greenberg, S.: Evaluation
    strategies for HCI toolkit research. In: Proceedings of the 2018 CHI Conference on Human
    Factors in Computing Systems - CHI 18 (2018)
13. Mascarenhas, S., et al.: A virtual agent toolkit for serious games developers. In: 2018 IEEE
    Conference on Computational Intelligence and Games (CIG), pp. 1–7 (2018)
14. An authoring toolkit for creating digital learning board games for cognitive and social skills
    development. In: 2017 IEEE Global Engineering Education Conference (EDUCON), Athens,
    Greece (2017)
15. Belman, J., Nissenbaum, H., Flanagan, M., Diamond, J.: Grow-a-game: a tool for values
    conscious design and analysis of digital games. In: Proceedings of DiGRA 2011 Conference:
    Think Design Play, vol. 3, pp. 14–17 (2011)
16. Tahir, R., Wang, A.: Transforming a theoretical framework to design cards: LEAGUE ideation
    toolkit for game-based learning design. Sustainability **12**(8487), 1–25 (2020)
17. Beça, P., Ortet, C., Aresta, M., Santos, R., Veloso, A.I., Ribeiro, S.: Supporting the construction
    of game narratives using a toolkit to game design. In: Videojogos 2020 (12th International
    Conference on Videogame Sciences and Arts), Bragança (2020)
18. Nadolski, R.J., et al.: EMERGO: a methodology and toolkit for developing serious games in
    higher education. Simul. Gaming **39**, 338–352 (2007)
19. Beça, P., et al.: Developing a toolkit to game design - the Gamers4Nature project: from concept
    to artefact. In: 15th Conference on the Foundations of Digital Games (FDG), Malta (2020)
20. Bonillo, C., Marco, J., Cerezo, E.: Developing pervasive games in interactive spaces: the
    JUGUEMOS toolkit. Multimedia Tools Appl. **78**(22), 32261–32305 (2019). https://doi.org/
    10.1007/s11042-019-07983-6

Correction to: An Authoring Tool to Engage Younger Audiences in the Development of Nature Preservation Games: The G4N Toolkit to Game Design

Pedro Beça⬛, Mónica Aresta⬛, Rita Santos⬛,
and Ana Isabel Veloso⬛

Correction to:
Chapter "An Authoring Tool to Engage Younger Audiences in the Development of Nature Preservation Games: The G4N Toolkit to Game Design" in: F. de Rosa et al. (Eds.): *Games and Learning Alliance*, LNCS 13134, https://doi.org/10.1007/978-3-030-92182-8_31

Chapter "An Authoring Tool to Engage Younger Audiences in the Development of Nature Preservation Games: The G4N Toolkit to Game Design" was previously published non-open access. It has now been changed to open access under a CC BY 4.0 license and the copyright holder updated to 'The Author(s)'. The book has also been updated with this change.

The updated version of this chapter can be found at
https://doi.org/10.1007/978-3-030-92182-8_31

© The Author(s) 2022
F. de Rosa et al. (Eds.): GALA 2021, LNCS 13134, p. C1, 2022.
https://doi.org/10.1007/978-3-030-92182-8_32

Author Index

Printed in the United States
by Baker & Taylor Publisher Services